Freedom's Main Line

Civil Rights and the Struggle for Black Equality
in the Twentieth Century

Series Editors
Steven F. Lawson, Rutgers University
Cynthia Griggs Fleming, University of Tennessee

Freedom's Main Line

The Journey of Reconciliation and the Freedom Rides

DEREK CHARLES CATSAM

THE UNIVERSITY PRESS OF KENTUCKY

Scholarly publisher for the Commonwealth, serving Bellarmine University,
Berea College, Centre College of Kentucky, Eastern Kentucky University, The
Filson Historical Society, Georgetown College, Kentucky Historical Society,
Kentucky State University, Morehead State University, Murray State University,
Northern Kentucky University, Transylvania University, University of Kentucky,
University of Louisville,
and Western Kentucky University.

Editorial and Sales Offices: The University Press of Kentucky
663 South Limestone Street, Lexington, Kentucky 40508–4008
www.kentuckypress.com

13 12 11 10 09   5 4 3 2 1

Library of Congress Cataloging-in-Publication Data

Catsam, Derek.
  Freedom's main line : the journey of reconciliation and the freedom rides /
Derek Charles Catsam.
      p. cm. — (Civil rights and the struggle for Black equality in the twentieth
century)
  Includes bibliographical references and index.
  ISBN 978-0-8131-2511-4 (hardcover : alk. paper)
  1. Freedom Rides, 1961. 2. African Americans—Civil rights—
Southern States—History—20th century 3. African Americans—
Segregation—Southern States—History—20th century. 4. Civil rights
demonstrations—Southern States—History—20th century. 5. Segregation
in transportation—Southern States—History—20th century. 6. Southern
States—Race relations—History—20th century. I. Title.
  E185.61.C295 2008
  323.1196'0730904—dc22   2008041540

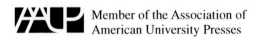 Member of the Association of
American University Presses

To Ana. I love you.

Contents

Acknowledgments

Like any lengthy project, this one owes a great deal to a number of people who helped bring it to fruition. For most of these, a simple word of thanks seems insufficient, to say the least. Nonetheless, a public acknowledgment of what is ultimately a very personal debt is warranted. I delayed writing these acknowledgments until the last possible moment, facing the wrath of my editors at Kentucky, because I was almost paralyzed by the fear of leaving someone out. The standard caveat for projects such as this is that all mistakes contained herein are my own, and of course that holds here as well—with an exception or two. I will point these out in due course.

First, I would like to thank the institutions that provided me with research support for this project. These include Ohio University's Contemporary History Institute and Department of History, which provided several grants for research in the early years of this project. Ohio University's Baker Peace Fund gave me a year of funding through a Baker Peace Fellowship in 2001–2002. I received grants and other support from the North Caroliniana Society's Archie K. Davis Fellowship in 2000–2001; from the Supreme Court Historical Society in 2001; from Houston's Black History Workshop in 2003; from the Virginia Historical Society's Mellon Research Fellowship in 2003; from the University of South Carolina's Institute for Southern Studies, which made me a research fellow, in 2003–2004 (and again in 2008–2009 for a new project); and from Tulane University's Deep South Regional Humanities Center, which also made me a research fellow, in 2003. The American Political Science Association's Centennial Center for Political Science and Public Affairs allowed me to be a visiting scholar in January 2004. I was also able to work out some ideas on regional change and Southern identity as a participant in the National Endowment for the Humanities Summer Institute, "Appalachia Up Close," at Ferrum College in 2004.

Two major long-term residential fellowships allowed me to write, revise, and reflect on the project as it developed. I cannot possibly repay the debts I owe to the Virginia Foundation for the Humanities, which provided me with collegial surroundings and an unparalleled work environment for the first half of 2004. David Bearinger, Andrew Chancey, Roberta Culbertson, Nancy Damon, Pablo Davis, Judy Moody, Jeannie Palin, and VFH President Rob Vaughn helped facilitate my stay and make it fruitful. Ann White Spencer went above and beyond the call of duty at all times. Eben Smith served as a gracious host and landlord. Bill Freehling embraced my work instantly and continues to provide the sort of gracious model for scholarship to which all in the profession aspire. The other fellows during my tenure, J. Blyton, Gordon Blyton, Tico Braun, and Larissa Smith, provided the sort of intellectual community that any scholar welcomes.

Similarly, I was able to spend a few months as a visiting fellow at the Rothermere American Institute at the University of Oxford in 2005. Andrea Brighton, Paul Giles, Laura Lauer, and Ruth Parr all helped to facilitate my stay, as did the staff at Holywell Manor. It was in Oxford that I met Roger Johnson and the rest of our loose and bawdy collective known as the Armitage Shanks. That alone made the time across the pond worth it, despite their tragic mispronunciations and mangling of the language.

Both of these experiences were transformative, providing intellectual nourishment and also fellowship in the truest sense of the word. If you are now, or have ever been, affiliated with either of these world-class institutions, thank you. You helped change my career for the better.

I received generous support from Minnesota State University, Mankato, when I taught there, including summer funding from a teacher-scholar research grant and support from the College of Social Sciences. Above all, my current home institution, the University of Texas of the Permian Basin, has been exceedingly generous in its support, providing me with two Faculty Development Fund for Academic Excellence grants, as well as funding from the College of Arts and Sciences. The university's LaMancha Society granted me its Golden Windmill Award for excellence in research in 2006, which came with a generous research grant.

If sources of funding are the first and most necessary source of gratitude, they nevertheless come in behind the numerous archivists who make any project worth doing. Without the tireless work of a number of individuals at a range of institutions, this project would quite simply never have gotten off the ground. I would thus like to extend my sincerest thanks to those people who gave so much of their own time and expertise to allow me to build mine, saving unimaginable amounts of time spent following dead ends and furthering my love of scholarship and time spent in the trenches of dusty papers and files. Since I do not want to slight individuals, I will simply thank all of those who made my work at the archives and libraries listed in my bibliography such a bountiful pleasure.

At Ohio University, many people made life easier (most of the time) or provided guidance, advice, ideas, conversation, or a social outlet. Norm Goda, Michael Grow, Joan Hoff, Steve Miner, Hal Molinieu, Chester Pach, and Bruce Steiner were the administrators in the Contemporary History Institute and/or the Department of History when I was at Ohio. Katherine Jellison and Lewis Randolph read every chapter of a much earlier version of this book and helped make it better. Charles Alexander always showed me how to do things the right way. Kara Dunfee makes the Contemporary History Institute work. Robert Davis, Rick Dodgson, Ray Haberski, Bill Kamil, Ren Lessard, Kim Little, Kevin O'Connor, Marc Selverstone, Jeff Woods, and J. D. Wyneken made life better. Jeffrey Herf, first at Ohio University and then the University of Maryland, has been a constant source of advice, support, mentorship, and golf.

During my brief detour at Minnesota State University, Mankato, Melodie Andrews and Don Strasser provided light when there was darkness in the vast expanses of southern Minnesota. I owe them much for that. Not everyone there was so generous of spirit.

At the University of Texas of the Permian Basin, I have been blessed with an abundance of good friends, colleagues, and administrators. Jaime Aguila, sadly for all of us, moved on to even hotter climes in Arizona with Holly, Ben, and Eliana, but I would not be in Texas were it not for this family, nor would I have met Ana, so I owe them a pretty big thank you. Roland Spickermann is a supportive department chair, colleague, and friend. Jay Tillapaugh has been not only a wise senior colleague but a supporter of my ongoing research. Lanita Akins has been like a surrogate mom and guardian angel. Diana Hinton has encouraged my productivity. Chad Vanderford has shared his own interest in Southern history. Outside of the department, Don Allen, Sophia Andres, and Jim Olson embody all that senior faculty members should be. Jason Lagapa and Todd Richardson have redeemed my faith in the English professoriate. Kyle Beran, Randy Lee, Gary McCullough, Steve Nelson, Dave Poindexter, and Robert Worley have taught me several lessons about all work and no play. Zero Eldridge and Doug Hale have shown me what faculty leadership means. Chris Stanley, my former department chair; Craig Emmert, the associate dean of the College of Arts and Sciences; Bill Fannin, the university's vice president for academic affairs and provost; David Watts, its president; and especially Lois Hale, the dean of the College of Arts and

Sciences (and her assistant Daniella Santiago) have supported my work in ways big and small from the day I arrived in Odessa. Tramaine Anderson, Chris Buck, Matt Garcia, Chris Giles, Andrew Hopskotch, Jeremy Lane, Sara Ornelas, and Mauricio Quintela have provided invaluable research help. Sylvia Rede, the senior administrative assistant in humanities and fine arts, makes everything work; we'd all fall apart almost instantly without her.

Steve Tootle is a friend, sounding board, spirited foe in political debate (wrong on nearly everything, but charmingly so), indie-rock companion, and lunch not-date. Tom and Terrie Bruscino and their three gorgeous children have helped keep me sane (when not enabling my insanity). Tom is, allegedly, my partner in anger and sometime doppelganger. (And, going against convention, any errors of judgment or fact contained herein are probably these individuals' faults.)

Friends far and wide have provided support, comfort, shelter, and perspective on where work fits into the larger whole. This list includes, but is surely not limited to, Brendan O'Sullivan, Drew Erdmann, Matt and Heather Dickens, Katie Boyle and Katherine Fischkoff, Rob Simler, David Pottie, Josh Pepin, Michael Stark, Fuzzy Wiggins, Marilyn Catsam, Marcus Catsam, John Inge, Richard Holmes, and the D.C. gang, especially Don and Melissa Graves, Ken and Michelle Richardson, Ned and Vanessa Johnson (and all of the D.C. children: Uncle Derek will be back in town soon enough), Josh and Jessica, and Peter and Veronica.

My family has been a constant source of support even when I suspect they did not know what exactly I was doing. To my mom and dad, thank you for your encouragement, support, and love. I love you both. There is little more to say, because nothing will ever suffice for what I owe you. Gram and Papa, I wish you were here to read this, but Papa's probably too busy yelling toward St. Peter's gate to those standing outside: "Come on in. You're standing outdoors." I miss you both every day.

So many fellow historians outside of my immediate professional circles have provided me with insights and other support that this is where I truly fear dropping the ball. Brooks Blevins, Joan Browning, Dan Carter, Pete Crow, Jane Dailey, Kate Dossett, Rand Dotson, Dan Dupre, Charles Eagles, Glenn Eskew, James Hershman, Tera Hunter, Michael Klarman, Nelson Lankford, Paul Leavengood, George Lewis, Alex Lichtenstein, Ralph Luker, Paul Maylam, Sonia Michel, Julie Cary Nerad, Andrew Offenburger, Dick Pious, Sylvia Rodrigue, Chris Saunders, Amilcar Shabazz, Larissa Smith, Steve Tuck, Peter Wallenstein, and Dan Woods provided me with commentary, advice, support, ideas, and sometimes criticism; all have been most welcome.

Ray Arsenault encouraged this project above and beyond the call of duty. Not only is he a fellow Red Sox fan and a great guy, but he also shared ideas and information with me even though we both were working on books about the Freedom Rides. His is great. You should own it. Bill Leuchtenburg, another Red Sox fan, read this project and provided tremendous insight, trenchant criticism, and an editorial touch that is both overwhelming and inspiring. Every scholar should be lucky enough to have him take an interest in his or her work. Tony Badger has long encouraged my work and invited me to give a talk in 2005 before the Gilder-Lehrman Institute on the Civil Rights Movement, which he leads at Cambridge.

I have been fortunate to have a number of mentors and teachers and editors who have shaped me in ways that I cannot adequately convey. My first true model of what a historian should be was Charles Dew at Williams College. He is a first-rate scholar and teacher and an even better human being. I consider him my first and one of my most important mentors.

I first met David Goldfield when I was a new graduate student at UNC-Charlotte and he was my advisor. Ever since he has been a mentor and friend, role model and guide. Early on I hoped that David would be willing to look at the occasional chapter and give me some direction. Instead, he has been as enthusiastic a supporter of this project as anyone—an insightful editor with a steady hand who shared much of his knowledge of Southern history and culture with me and served as a wonderful source of support.

The staff at the University Press of Kentucky has been essential in making this book a reality. Steve Wrinn, who embraced this project from the outset, has gone above and beyond to make it as good as my limitations as a writer and scholar allow. Steven Lawson and Cynthia Griggs Fleming, the editors of the series "Civil Rights and the Struggle for Black Equality in the Twentieth Century," embraced my work enthusiastically and made my transition to Kentucky seamless. Carol Sickman-Garner proved a wonder as a copyeditor, saving me from innumerable embarrassments, as did Lin Wirkus, who oversaw the copyediting process. Mack McCormick has been essential in making the book look great and pushing the publicity process. Ann Dean Watkins and Candace Cheney served as coordinators and ringmasters for my pesky phone calls and emails. My guess is that they are as happy to see this book go to press as I am. Finally, the anonymous readers at the press gave me fantastic feedback and improved the book immeasurably, and if I stubbornly resisted any of their advice, it is to my own peril. Bob Pratt at the University of Georgia has been especially supportive on this front.

Alonzo Hamby, my Ph.D. adviser at Ohio University, provided model support from the outset, pushing when necessary and letting me alone to succeed or fail otherwise, as I preferred. He valued my work from the beginning, and his vast knowledge of history and historiography meant that he could always find ways to steer me toward something more productive, more insightful, more significant. There is no higher praise than to hear Dr. Hamby say, "I think you might be onto something." In the last few years, I've heard this more and more, which is as much as anything a reflection on the important role he has played in my scholarly and professional development. I cannot possibly thank him enough for all he has done for me and meant to me. He is my professor. He is my mentor. And I hope I can say that he is my friend.

There is one group I should thank collectively. The Freedom Riders put their lives on the line for a cause that was greater than themselves, greater than all of us. In a time when we must reconceptualize the meaning of freedom and its demands of sacrifice, those who fought for civil rights should mean more and more. I have been lucky enough to meet a number of these great women and men, to have them speak with me about their experiences, and to watch them interact with one another. I thank them for their openness and courage and convictions and actions—truly a brave and wonderful thing.

Finally, and most important, I need to thank Ana Luisa Martinez-Catsam. I moved to Texas for a job. I stay because of her. We met on the first day of new faculty orientation and have been together ever since. And as a bonus, I have inherited a wonderful family, including Lupe, Ari, Leslie, James, and Mary; Yolanda, the most loving mother-in-law imaginable; and the kids, including Ana's godchildren Kayla, Lauren, and Matthew, our goddaughter Dani, and our godson J.J. (but to us always "George"). Ana is my friend, cheerleader, confidante, colleague, and carpool partner. She is my love, she is my light. And it is to her that this book is dedicated.

Prologue

From Bigger Thomas to Henry Thomas

Bigger Thomas and Public Transportation

In his 1941 essay "How Bigger Was Born," Richard Wright wrote about the various "Bigger Thomases" he had come to know in his life and who served as the models for his character in *Native Son*. Bigger, crushed by fear that stemmed from his plight as a black man in America and the rage that manifested itself as a result of that fear, inadvertently kills his new employer's daughter and tries to cover the evidence by stuffing her body in the furnace of her family's home. Inevitably, Bigger's role in the crime is discovered, and he has to go on the run. He is eventually caught and sentenced to death, but not until after a long court scene in which Thomas's lawyer blames Bigger's deeds as much on society as on Bigger, who is thus depicted as a victim of a society that impelled him to his crimes.

Wright encountered one of these "Bigger Thomases" on the Jim Crow streetcars of the Deep South. Unlike those who passively acquiesced to the mandates of Jim Crow, with its sections for blacks and sections for whites, this "Bigger" "always rode the Jim Crow streetcars without paying and sat wherever he pleased." Wright recalled one day when the conductor challenged "Bigger," telling him, "Come on nigger. Move over where you belong. Can't you read?" "Bigger"'s response was, "Nah, I can't read."

> The conductor flared up: "Get out of that seat!" Bigger took out his knife, opened it, held it nonchalantly in his hand, and replied: "Make me." The conductor turned red, blinked, clenched his fists and walked away, stammering: "The goddamn scum of the earth."[1]

When the conductor turned away, a group of Negroes overheard the angry white men gathered at the front, wondering how to address this clear affront to not only law and tradition but also white authority. One of the

1

men murmured, "That's that Bigger Thomas nigger and you'd better leave 'im alone." Upon hearing this, "The Negroes experienced an intense flash of pride and the streetcar moved on its journey without incident."[2]

There was perhaps no public indignity for blacks as great as that posed by Jim Crow transportation. It is easy to forget that the Supreme Court's decision in *Plessy v. Ferguson* established "separate but equal" as doctrine as the result of a case involving not education, but interstate transportation. Segregation on the whole was a monstrosity and an affront, but in the midst of segregation, blacks managed to develop a whole range of vibrant institutions. While segregated education would prove to be the central focus for driving out Jim Crow, black schools and universities were often sources of racial pride. Jim Crow at lunch counters often resulted in the emergence of black business establishments. White insurers and bankers refused to provide policies or loans, so black insurance companies and banks stepped into the breach. Black churches were, then as now, a source of pride, spirituality, and organization. Jim Crow was always onerous, to be sure; all the same, the black community was not a mere collection of supplicants kowtowing to white authority. But there were always the buses to remind them of their station. And the streetcars. And the trains. For it was one thing to develop an insurance agency or a real estate company or a sandwich shop or even a university that could produce a professional class. It was another thing to challenge Jim Crow transportation. At the local and municipal levels, local whites controlled the highways and byways, the contracts and laws governing public transportation. Further, all-black interstate railroads or bus companies were a practical impossibility for a range of reasons.

Jim Crow would become particularly pervasive in transportation, both intra- and interstate, and in facilities serving travelers, such as bus stations, rail terminals, and all facilities such as restaurants located therein. The first Jim Crow train car for blacks had made its way into law in Mississippi by 1888, and soon after the rest of the South and some border states followed apace.[3] Of course, Jim Crow practices predated Jim Crow legislation, so even before the passage of laws, segregation was de rigueur across Dixie and in most border states.[4] By the beginning of the twentieth century, Jim Crow was codified in law, sanctioned by the courts, and enforced by the ubiquitous threat of physical violence even more than legal reprisal.

In his monumental 1944 study of American race relations, *An American Dilemma,* Gunnar Myrdal discussed transportation and segregation, as he did almost every other area of American life affected by race, which is to say almost every area of American life. Myrdal explains how legal segregation impelled bus and railway companies to segregate passengers, effectively passing the cost of state-mandated segregation on to the companies, many of which "are more solicitous about Negro customers than local governments are about Negro citizens."[5] The companies may have been better than the municipalities, but nonetheless, to cut down on costs while at the same time adhering to the wholly separate facilities mandated in the many statutes, Myrdal noted, it was "notorious that the companies—with a few exceptions—save money by giving Negroes inferior service for equal charge."[6] The problems many companies faced were exacerbated by the fact that many blacks chose not to frequent segregated facilities when they had other transportation options. Well into the 1940s, and in most cases beyond, Jim Crow prevailed in all of the states of the old Confederacy, plus Oklahoma. Delaware had optional Jim Crow provisions. Missouri courts had accepted that private companies could choose to segregate their conveyances and facilities.[7] Myrdal points out that "it is a common observation that the Jim Crow car is resented more bitterly among Negroes than most other forms of segregation."[8] On top of all of this, most streetcar conductors in the South in the late nineteenth and early twentieth centuries had virtual police powers. Some even carried firearms, largely if not solely to preserve racial order.[9]

So if you were black and worked far from home in Montgomery or lived in Chicago but had family in Jackson, your options were restricted. And if you did not have a car of your own, they were circumscribed further. So you rode the bus, moving to the back, standing when told, waiting for the next bus when necessary. You took your meals in your own car (on those rare instances when a sleeper car was available to you), waited to eat until you got to your destination, switched from the front to the back of the bus when crossing into Dixie, avoided the bus stations or crossed the threshold into the "Colored Only" side, and bit your tongue.

Of course, a few did not bite their tongues. Over the years many individuals tested the limits of Jim Crow on various modes of transport, intrastate and interstate. Sometimes organized protests would occur. But usually these faded before achieving anything substantial, and the status quo prevailed. Bigger Thomas would push the limits, but whites had a way of dealing with the Bigger Thomases of the South.

Wright had no knowledge of what happened to that Bigger Thomas, but he had a pretty good idea of what his fate may have been. The "Bigger Thomases were the only Negroes I know of who consistently violated the

Jim Crow laws of the South and got away with it, at least for a brief sweet while." Eventually, the whites reasserted dominance. The Bigger Thomases paid "a terrible price. They were shot, hanged, maimed, lynched, and generally hounded until they were either dead or their spirits broken."[10]

Later in "How Bigger Was Born," Wright made a prediction. While he was "not saying that I heard any talk of revolution in the South when I was a kid there . . . I did hear the lispings, the whispers, the mutters which some day, under one stimulus or another, will surely grow up into open revolt unless the conditions which produce Bigger Thomases are changed."[11]

While Bigger Thomas is a fictional character, the Bigger Thomases whom Wright had known and seen were very real, and the invocation of Bigger Thomas here does not establish a straw man. The indignities of Jim Crow created acquiescence, but they also created fury. Segregation fueled some self-sufficiency, but it also led to resistance. It resulted in humiliation but sometimes provided the impetus for pride. When Joe Louis defeated Max Baer in 1935 to put himself in a position to win the heavyweight championship, the New York Post music critic Samuel Chotzinoff revealed the ways in which resistance and pride might manifest themselves in unexpected ways. Louis represented "sweet recompense for a degrading past and a hopeless future." Perhaps Louis's successes might make it "easier to bear the usual number of lynchings in the year. If you are riding by compulsion in a Jim Crow car it is something to know that Joe Louis is ready and willing to take all comers."[12] For those millions who celebrated Louis's victory, Louis represented another way—perhaps not Bigger Thomas's way, not revolution, but also not quiescence. The idea of Louis physically defeating a white man opened up a world of possibilities that were glorious to black Americans and frightening to whites.

Eventually, there was a revolution in the South. But it was not the revolution Richard Wright envisioned—open racial warfare fomented by Bigger Thomases who could not and would not any longer deal with the indignities of Jim Crow. Instead the revolution in the South was primarily the result of a post–World War II generation of activists, white and especially black, embracing a nonviolent form of direct action civil rights protest. Bloodshed there would be, but it would not come from the fists and knives and rifles of Bigger Thomases whose rage translated into action. Instead that violence marked the death throes of white supremacy, the inchoate, vicious, sputtering rage of a privileged class losing its hold on power even while it asserted that power in the most menacing way it knew how.

The new era brought about a revolution not in the person of Bigger Thomas, but instead in the form of Hank Thomas. Hank Thomas was a Howard University senior in 1961. He had grown up in poverty conditions in rural Georgia and St. Augustine, Florida, where he was a schoolboy football star. For some time, Thomas had been a civil rights activist functioning in the concentric circles extending from Howard's campus in Washington, D.C. He had engaged in civil rights actions in the District, in suburban Maryland, and in northern Virginia. In April 1961 he heard about something called "Freedom Ride, 1961" that was going to take integrated buses into the South to test adherence to the Supreme Court's recent decision in *Boynton v. Virginia* and continue the ongoing wave of civil rights action sweeping the South. Thomas knew he had to go on this Freedom Ride. The rules required him to be twenty-one years old, and he was only nineteen, but he figured he could pass, so he forged his mother's name and sent out the application to the Congress of Racial Equality (CORE), which was organizing the challenge. He was accepted along with just over a dozen other participants. They met in Washington, D.C., where the Ride would begin after nonviolence workshops. Hank Thomas, not Bigger Thomas, would thus pose the ultimate challenge to Jim Crow transportation and to the facilities that served interstate passengers. It would indeed be a revolution, but not the one Wright had so fatalistically imagined just two decades before.

Introduction

How the Freedom Rides Were Born (And What They Mean)

The Journey of Reconciliation and the Freedom Rides

The Freedom Rides proved to be the culmination of one of the most important series of events in the Civil Rights Movement. The movement to desegregate interstate transportation is significant for a range of reasons. First, and most important, the Journey of Reconciliation and the Freedom Rides quite literally took the Civil Rights Movement national, transforming it from a phenomenon of isolated events creating crises from place to place—here Little Rock, there Montgomery's bus boycott, somewhere else protests against a lynching. Freedom Riders, whether known as such formally or not, went from one place to another, connecting communities, pulling the discrete pods of resistance together. The Rides thus caused a continuous civil rights crisis that reached from Washington, D.C., to New Orleans. As good as many Southern politicians were at suckling at the teat of federal largesse, they were equally adept at proclaiming almost all issues related to the crisis in the South matters for the states to handle. The Freedom Rides drew attention to the bankrupt claims of these Southern politicians and others and garnered tremendous support for civil rights.

Although the focal point of this book is the 1961 Freedom Rides, the events of the late spring and summer of 1961 did not appear out of nowhere, simply springing from the fertile imaginations of the leadership of the Congress of Racial Equality. The antecedents of the Freedom Rides are vital to understanding the Civil Rights Movement, and key among these is the 1947 Journey of Reconciliation. Further, the struggle to desegregate interstate transportation played out not only on the highways and byways, in the bus stations and train terminals of the South. It also played out in courtrooms, on editorial pages, and sometimes even on prison chain gangs. One of the most significant developments in the historiography of the Civil Rights Movement has been breaking free of the false chronological barriers that depict the movement as emerging from the Supreme Court's May

1954 decision in *Brown v. Board of Education*. *Freedom's Main Line*, as part of that trend, traces the long development of the fight against Jim Crow in interstate transportation. But it also reveals the ways in which long-term continuity nonetheless relied on short-term tactical and contingency-based improvisation, not only among activists but among players on all sides, from local police to the president of the United States.

The best studies of the Civil Rights Movement also give the lie to some of the false walls historians create within the profession, inviting people to label themselves "political" or "social" or "legal" or "women's" or "cultural" historians or any of a myriad of other subdisciplines that attempt to limit the field. These labels make history seem more manageable, but they also impose false limitations on the study of how real people live real lives. Historians of civil rights necessarily look at the law and social movements and politics—local, state, and national—and culture and gender and international relations and intellectual life. *Freedom's Main Line* attempts such a holistic approach because the only way to convey a sense of the world that the Freedom Riders inhabited is to try to understand that world as it operated. This is thus not a work of social history or of political history. It is simply a work of history.[1]

The Freedom Rides of 1961 came about as a logical extension of the student sit-in movement, which began in February 1960 and marked a culmination of several years of activism. A logical extension of a civil rights struggle that had been ongoing since at least World War II, the Rides served as both the outgrowth and the confluence of the work of national organizations such as the Congress of Racial Equality (CORE) and the Student Nonviolent Coordinating Committee (SNCC), furthering the movement's development by bringing together its many disparate strands. The Freedom Rides thus provide an ideal opportunity for examining local movements, especially as many of these grassroots struggles fit into the context of larger national trends. Simultaneously, the Freedom Rides reveal fissures among existing civil rights organizations, including what at times seemed to be a significant generation gap in the movement. As the Freedom Rides progressed, they attracted adherents along the way, so that by late May 1961 CORE and SNCC had successfully drawn in the National Association for the Advancement of Colored People (NAACP), the Southern Christian Leadership Conference (SCLC), and myriad local organizations, but not without significant contentiousness along the way. The actions of similarly mobilized white opposition groups culminated in violence that drew national and international attention.

This attention in turn led to the involvement of the Kennedy administration. The new president entered office with little experience or interest in civil rights, though his rhetorical opposition to Jim Crow and support of equal opportunity gave many within the black community hope. The Freedom Rides forced the callow president to act in ways he did not expect and did not wish. But he did act. At times he did so effectively. At other times he sold out civil rights activists, moral principle, and bedrock constitutional foundations to avoid crises. This marked the true beginning of both Robert Kennedy's and John Kennedy's learning curve on civil rights, thus representing an important moment in political history.

The violence in Alabama in May 1961 also grabbed the attention of ordinary Americans, bringing civil rights into people's homes and forcing many to confront the inequities that black Americans faced on a daily basis in the South. Civil rights thus reached a level of dialogue that it had rarely enjoyed in the United States. Further, it drew international media attention to America's civil rights problems, unwelcome in the context of the Cold War, in which the United States claimed moral and political superiority based largely on its supposed respect for fundamental human rights. The Freedom Rides threatened to reveal the hypocrisy of such assertions, and Cold War tensions thus provide a vital backdrop to the events of 1961, informing almost every decision the Kennedy administration made in addressing the crisis. In addition, white supremacists often cynically used the Cold War as an excuse to accuse civil rights activists of being communists or dupes, playing to fears held even by nonsegregationists.

At the same time it would be simplistic to see the Cold War (and the oftentimes overheated responses to it) as an impediment that served to halt an earlier movement dedicated to comprehensive economic justice and, by midcentury, anticolonialism, leaving in its wake a movement that had narrowed its scope by pursuing short-term, legalistic objectives. The struggle for civil rights was daunting enough—white supremacy so deeply entrenched, local conditions so vital—that a simple debate over "radical" versus "practical" aims was rarely particularly significant for those operating on the ground to achieve freedoms long denied. Even without the Cold War and its concomitant anticommunism, it is quite likely that the Freedom Rides (or the sit-ins, or the Selma-to-Montgomery March, or what have you) would have been necessary.

If the Civil Rights Movement truly became national with the Freedom Rides, however, the Rides also demonstrate the importance of local and state politics. The violence that the Freedom Riders encountered reveals the role of law enforcement agents, local politicians, and especially state politicians in either ensuring safety or fomenting violence. This is a key historical lesson because time and again—during the school integration crises in Little Rock and New Orleans, during the riots surrounding James Meredith's entry into Ole Miss or Autherine Lucy's into Alabama, during George Wallace's Stand in the Schoolhouse Door—the reactions of Southern political actors largely set the stage for how individuals and groups responded to integration. The Freedom Riders and their story highlight the fact that different states had different political cultures and that leadership could either stoke or extinguish the flames of violent white supremacy that were so easily kindled throughout Dixie. North Carolina was different from South Carolina was different from Alabama. In other words, local and state conditions mattered, and they varied from place to place and time to time. These lines were certainly not fixed, but neither were they fictive. The Freedom Rides thus provide a good avenue to begin expanding our understanding of these differences, of how and where these lines were drawn, and how they manifested themselves in the black and white communities, in the state houses and ultimately at the bus stations. These various circumstances and contexts—local, state, and national—are at the heart of this book.

The Freedom Rides also had substantial long-term legacies. They initiated a federal engagement with civil rights, however tepid at first, that led directly to the Kennedy administration pushing the Interstate Commerce Commission to act to eradicate Jim Crow on interstate facilities, culminating in Kennedy's Civil Rights Bill, which Lyndon Johnson strengthened and pushed through Congress. After the Freedom Rides, civil rights never left the public stage. But more than this, the very term "Freedom Rider" became shorthand across the South for "civil rights activist." Coming from black (and many white) mouths, it might be a term of honor, pride, or respect. From the sneering lips of hostile whites, it was a term of derision, loathing, and fear. Either way, for the next few years, civil rights activists were "Freedom Riders," whether they were working for the black vote or marching in Birmingham.

An odd example of this: A few years after the Freedom Rides, during the summer of the passage of the Civil Rights Act and the acme of the Civil Rights Movement, Ken Kesey's motley band of proto-hippie Merry Pranksters rode into New Orleans in their multihued bus, *Further*. One of the white Southern witnesses watching the odd agglomeration pour from the bus was heard to say, "What, are they Freedom Riders?"[2] The term had stuck, whatever its deviation from its initial reference to a band of heroic whites and blacks testing the limits of Jim Crow transportation in the spring and summer of 1961. That same day, June 22, 1964, a New Orleans newspaper ran a headline that Ken Kesey, at the time, knew nothing about: "Freedom Riders Missing in Mississippi."[3] Mickey Schwerner, Andy Goodman, and James Chaney were not really Freedom Riders. But then again, by 1964, who was to say?[4]

Chapter 1

"We Challenged Jim Crow"

*The Journey of Reconciliation and the Emergence of
Direct Action Civil Rights Protest in the 1940s*

On April 13, 1947, police arrested four men for breaking Jim Crow laws
requiring the segregation of passengers on a bus in Chapel Hill, North
Carolina. The men were traveling with a group representing the Fellowship of Reconciliation (FOR), a pacifist human rights organization, and the
Congress of Racial Equality (CORE), a civil rights organization dedicated
to gaining black rights through nonviolent protest action. The group was
engaged in a "Journey of Reconciliation" to test the application of the
Supreme Court's 1946 decision in *Morgan v. Virginia* outlawing Jim Crow
seating for interstate passengers.

The Journey originated in Washington, D.C., and carried through Virginia, North Carolina, Tennessee, Kentucky, and back through Virginia before returning to Washington. There were sixteen male participants on that
early Freedom Ride, eight black, eight white. Passengers on the Journey
of Reconciliation sat dispersed throughout the conveyances in contraven-
tion of Jim Crow statutes that required black and white passengers to sit
separate from one another, with blacks in back and whites in front, and that
also required black passengers to give up their seats to whites when there
were more riders than seats. On trains, Jim Crow policy usually required
black and white passengers to ride in separate cars and to use separate dining and wash facilities. In twenty-six tests of bus and train policies, police
arrested participants on six occasions; they arrested a total of twelve men
in the course of the trip. Each arrest occurred while passengers rode on
buses, not on trains, and each time the offending passenger reacted non-
violently and courteously, invoking his rights under the *Morgan* decision
without being either aggressive in his assertion or abrasive in his manner.

The Journey of Reconciliation marked a significant moment in direct action protest against Jim Crow in the South. Although at initial glance its long-term effects might appear negligible, the Journey and its aftermath in fact revealed both the limits of and the prospects for long-range assaults on Jim Crow in transportation, as in other areas. It further revealed that nonviolent action could be effective in challenging Jim Crow even in the face of threatened and actual violent response. It served to educate observers of the tests, as well as audiences that the participants addressed in mass meetings over the course of the Journey. Finally, it provided a model for the Freedom Rides of 1961.

The pervasive system of Jim Crow in the South derived its legitimacy from the *Plessy* decision. There was no more noisome symbol or manifestation of the perniciousness of Jim Crow than on public conveyances, particularly public buses, which provided the backbone of black mobility in cities and towns all across the South. Thus, segregated transport provides an especially apt venue for investigating the challenges to Jim Crow that began in the 1940s and culminated in the many Freedom Rides of 1961 and beyond.

It is clear, at least in the case of the desegregation of interstate buses, that a movement was under way well before 1954—still the traditional starting date of many civil rights accounts—and that direct action campaigns did not begin in Montgomery under the leadership of Martin Luther King Jr.[1] Furthermore, the various and disparate campaigns of the 1940s paved the way for a generation of younger activists to challenge an unjust system in the 1950s and 1960s. CORE, FOR, and many other organizations and individuals established a foundation that would provide the basis for a more aggressive version of nonviolence that would blossom in Greensboro and Nashville in 1960 and spread across the South in the years that followed.

"We Hold the Virginia Statute in Controversy Invalid": *Morgan v. Virginia*

Irene Morgan, a twenty-seven-year-old defense plant worker, was still feeling weak when she stepped onto a Greyhound bus bound for Baltimore via Washington, D.C., in Gloucester County, Virginia, on July 16, 1944.[2] Recovering from a recent miscarriage and anxious to see her husband, a stevedore on Baltimore's Inner Harbor, Morgan boarded the crowded bus in the sweltering Virginia heat. She stood for several miles, sat on the lap of a friendly young black female passenger for a handful more, and finally took a seat three rows from the back of the bus but in front of white passengers in Saluda, Virginia. The bus driver insisted that she yield her seat, as the local and state Jim Crow laws mandated segregated seating on public conveyances. After she refused, kicking, clawing, and shouting as she was forcibly removed, Morgan was arrested, tried, and convicted of violating section 4097dd of the Virginia Code, which stated that "all persons who fail while on any motor vehicle carrier, to take and occupy the seat or seats or other space assigned to them by the driver, operator or other person in charge of such vehicle . . . shall be deemed guilty of a misdemeanor, and upon conviction thereof shall be fined not less than five dollars nor more than twenty five dollars for each offense."[3] Morgan was fined ten dollars. She appealed, but the appellate court of Virginia upheld the conviction and fine.

In October 1945 the Supreme Court heard the arguments of the NAACP lawyers who had taken on the case, including Spottswood Robinson, Oliver Hill, Martin A. Martin, the state legal committee of Virginia's NAACP, and the national organization's Thurgood Marshall and William H. Hastie. They argued that the Virginia statute requiring segregation on interstate carriers (and others like it) placed an undue burden on interstate commerce and thus violated the Commerce Clause of the Constitution. Their argument emphasized the 1878 case *Hall v. DeCuir*, in which the Court voided a Louisiana law prohibiting segregation in interstate transportation, specifically on steamboats that traveled with passengers up the Mississippi River, because such a statute placed an undue burden on interstate commerce.[4] It is unclear whether the irony of invoking a case in which the justices had ruled unconstitutional a law banning segregation in order to attack Jim Crow seating practices was lost on the NAACP lawyers or the Court. In both cases the Court solved the case before them on the grounds of the Commerce Clause, with remarkably similar interpretations that led to diametrically different tangible results. Because each decision rested on arguments about the undue burden placed on commerce, not on segregation per se, such a seeming contradiction became entirely possible, the outcomes indeed bearing a remarkable, if ironic, consistency.[5]

On June 3, 1946, the Court announced its decision. In a 7-1 ruling the Court reversed the appellate court and struck down the Virginia statute and by extension all similar laws mandating Jim Crow practices on interstate conveyances. Justice Stanley Forman Reed of Kentucky wrote the majority opinion for the Court. Justice Harold Burton of Ohio was the lone dissenter. Justices Wiley Rutledge, Hugo Black, and Felix Frankfurter wrote concurring opinions. Justice Robert Jackson was presiding over the Nuremberg Trials and thus did not participate.

Reed accepted the invocation of *Hall v. DeCuir* and quoted Chief Justice Morrison Waite's 1878 opinion at some length in a footnote, including the most famous line from that opinion, in which Waite asserted that "commerce cannot flourish in the midst of such embarrassments" as the law in question posed—that is, the violation of the Commerce Clause. At the center of the Court's ruling in *Hall* was the argument that "if each state was at liberty to regulate the conduct of carriers while within its jurisdiction, the confusion likely to follow could not but be productive of great inconvenience and unnecessary hardship."[6] One wonders what Waite would have thought of his opinion being used in the service of eradicating Jim Crow laws, the exact phenomenon that his 1878 decision upheld.

Reed focused his opinion on two fundamental issues: first, whether the Virginia statute was "repugnant to Clause 3, Section 8, Article I" of the Constitution, the Commerce Clause, and second, whether or not the Tenth Amendment gives the state "the power to require an interstate motor passenger to occupy a seat restricted for the use of his race." Reed then pointed out that it was only necessary to address the first question, since "if the statute unlawfully burdens interstate commerce, the reserved powers of the state will not validate it."[7] If the statute violated the Commerce Clause, the question of states' rights as extended under the Tenth Amendment was rendered moot. States do not have the right to violate the Constitution.

It was clear to Reed that the statute was repugnant to the Commerce Clause. Prior to presenting the precedent set in *Hall*, he argued: "The interferences to interstate commerce which arise from state regulation of racial association on interstate vehicles has [*sic*] long been recognized. Such regulation hampers freedom of choice in selecting accommodations."[8] The Court thus concluded: "Seating arrangements for the different races in interstate motor travel require a single, uniform rule to promote and protect national travel. Consequently, we hold the Virginia statute in controversy invalid."[9] And with that, the justices reversed the decision of the lower courts.

Burton was adamant in his dissent. He asserted that the Court's decision supplanted the role of Congress to establish uniformity in federal transportation if such laws were necessary for interstate commerce. He argued that the question at hand was "neither the desirability of the statute nor the constitutionality of racial segregation as such." Instead, the Court was basing its decision on the belief that "the burden imposed by the statute upon the nation's interest in interstate commerce so greatly outweighs the contribution made by the statute to the State's interest in its public welfare as to make it unconstitutional."[10] Justice Burton clearly did not believe this judgment to be sound. He argued that the decision would effectively invalidate laws requiring segregation on interstate carriers.

Burton believed that the appellants had failed to show "facts and findings essential to demonstrate the existence of" a "serious and major burden upon the national interest in interstate commerce as to outweigh whatever state or local benefits are attributable to the statute and which would be lost by its invalidation."[11] Burton concluded that it was "a fundamental concept of our constitution that where conditions are diverse the solution of problems arising out of them" may well have to be addressed diversely by localities or states.[12]

Justice Frankfurter began his concurrence by stating that "my brother Burton has stated with great force reasons for not invalidating the Virginia statute." Nonetheless, the principle of stare decisis was most important to him, so he argued that "for me *Hall v. DeCuir* . . . is controlling. Since it was decided nearly seventy years ago, that case on several occasions has been approvingly cited and has never been questioned." For this reason he concurred with Reed's majority decision.[13]

Justice Black's concurrence came with more reservations than did Frankfurter's, but ultimately, the pressure of precedent swayed him. Although he believed that "Congress can regulate commerce and . . . the courts cannot," he also understood that "in recent years this Court over my protest has held that the Commerce Clause justifies this Court in nullifying state legislation which this Court concludes imposes an 'undue burden' on interstate commerce." Although he clearly opposed such a stance, "So long as the Court remains committed to the 'undue burden on commerce formula' I must make decisions under it," especially given the fact that the burden imposed by the Virginia law was to him of a far more serious nature than in other cases the Court had recently faced. Black thus acquiesced in the majority decision.[14]

These lukewarm responses aside, the Court had firmly and clearly struck down Virginia's laws mandating segregated seating on interstate conveyances. The announcement of the *Morgan* decision did not earn public condemnation. Indeed, despite the momentous nature of the decision, it received scant attention, no more or less than almost any other Supreme

Court decision. It would be almost a year before the ramifications of the *Morgan* decision would become evident.[15]

"My Friend, I Believe That Is an Unjust Law": Early Challenges to Jim Crow Busing, 1942–1946

Even before the Journey of Reconciliation, some brave pioneers had attempted to test the limits of Jim Crow transport with challenges to bus and train seating rules. Bayard Rustin, the black pacifist leader, cosecretary of race relations for the Fellowship of Reconciliation, and ardent advocate of nonviolent resistance to Jim Crow, had challenged Jim Crow on a bus in Louisville in 1942, well before Irene Morgan's case wound its way through the court system. Rustin had been traveling from Louisville to Nashville when he decided to confront the inequities of the system directly. He purchased his ticket and proceeded to the second seat behind the bus driver, who challenged Rustin immediately, telling him he was supposed to go to the back. When Rustin asked why that was the case, the driver responded, "Because that's the law. Niggers ride in the back." Rustin replied, "My friend, I believe that is an unjust law. If I were to sit in back I would be condoning injustice." The bus driver went into the bus station but returned a few moments later and took the regular bus route for which he was scheduled. At each subsequent stop, however, he confronted Rustin, who remained resolute.[16]

About thirteen miles from Nashville, a police car and two police motorcycles stopped the bus and confronted Rustin, who once again stated his belief in the basic unjustness of the law he was breaking. The police responded by beating Rustin, first about the head and shoulders. When he fell to the floor, they kicked him and then dragged him from the bus, continuing to kick and punch the prostrate pacifist. Finally, when he was able, he stood up, held his hands parallel to the ground, and said, "There is no need to beat me. I am not resisting you." By this point several of the white passengers had gotten off the bus to see what was transpiring. At one point a smallish man grabbed the arm of a club-wielding police officer who was about to rain another blow on Rustin and shouted, "Don't do that." When the officer turned to bash Rustin's protector, Rustin stepped in and told the man that he did not want the man to fight for him. "I do not wish to fight, I am protected well," he told his protector. An elderly, well-dressed white man then went up to Rustin, telling him that he would make sure that Rustin received proper justice.[17]

Rustin continued to show both calm and pride on the way to the police station, in a situation that must have been terrifying, given the reputation of Southern justice on issues of race in the 1940s. During his time in custody, one of the police officers concurred with the account Rustin had given the assistant district attorney regarding what happened before and after his arrest. Eventually, the authorities released Rustin. This experience left him more committed than ever to nonviolence as the only approach to fighting Jim Crow.[18]

Rustin's early attempt to challenge Jim Crow busing was revelatory, validating his approach to solving racial problems. His experience on the bus and at the Nashville police station further confirmed for him the possibilities of nonviolent protest. When he and George Houser later organized the 1947 Journey of Reconciliation, this incident and many others provided a guideline for action. Whether future adherents of the strategy of nonviolence adopted it because of a strong moral commitment or merely as a tactical approach, Rustin's guidance in using Gandhian nonviolent resistance would prove vital in the future of the civil rights struggle. Rustin would apply such teachings and tactics not only when organizing the Journey of Reconciliation but also as a mentor to Martin Luther King Jr. in the Montgomery bus boycott and as a leader in the direct action campaigns that accelerated across the South in 1960. The culmination of his work would be the 1963 March on Washington, which Rustin was central in organizing.[19] Confronting Jim Crow transportation was important to Rustin's development as a civil rights activist.

In the immediate aftermath of the *Morgan* decision, yet another individual attempted to challenge segregation on an interstate bus. In July 1946, one month after the Court's ruling came down, black World War II veteran Wilson A. Head decided to test the ruling by taking a Greyhound bus from Atlanta to Washington, D.C., sitting wherever he chose. Over the course of his journey, he met with harassment from white bus drivers, contempt from fellow travelers, and intimidation from police. Head was made to fear for his life in Chapel Hill, when police pointed guns at his head in the police station. Despite these intimidations and threats, Head made his way safely to Washington. Although he was aware of the capital city's "Southern flavor," Head was nonetheless relieved to cross the Potomac into Washington from Virginia.[20]

While Head's lone protest had few direct effects, it still carries symbolic significance. Head showed that it would take courage, restraint, persistence, and some luck to challenge Jim Crow transportation.[21] But his experience also revealed that such a challenge could be undertaken. Civil rights struggles could happen at the grassroots and individual levels, as well as through more established, hierarchical organizations such as the NAACP, which tended to oppose direct action programs, preferring to challenge segregation in the courts.

Finally, Head's solo test revealed yet another aspect of the nascent civil rights struggle: while Court proclamations were important and necessary, alone they were insufficient. The NAACP's strategy would only bear fruit when the rulings had the force of law behind them. The *Morgan* decision would only have meaning when blacks could sit where they liked when they liked on buses and trains and airplanes without fear of harassment, arrest, beatings, and intimidation. Such challenges would require organization, volunteers, and the development of a new movement ethos with new leaders to supplement the NAACP's ongoing legal strategies.

One such organization was the Congress of Racial Equality, which had first formed in 1942. CORE was just beginning to establish itself as a new and important force in civil rights in 1947, when it decided to jointly sponsor a "Journey of Reconciliation" with the New York–based Fellowship of Reconciliation. Bayard Rustin was one of the prime movers in getting the Journey off the ground.[22]

"I Think You Are Doing a Brave and Wonderful Thing": The Journey of Reconciliation, 1947

Houser and Rustin, who began planning the trip in late 1946, selected April 9, 1947, as the starting date for the Journey. Although the trip was intended to test existing laws and their enforcement in the face of the *Morgan* decision, ultimately its purpose was greater. Many years after the trip, George Houser outlined some of the considerations that made the idea of the Journey so appealing. Segregation on transportation in the South was an important issue, one that had to be tackled; such a campaign would draw attention, and it would have behind it the force of law.[23] Once CORE and FOR jointly decided to sponsor the trip, they developed a more schematic threefold purpose for the project. First, they would "gather data in a planned and scientific fashion on what is happening when Negroes and whites travel together without heed to patterns of segregation in states where Jim Crow laws prevail." The second purpose was "to develop techniques for dealing creatively with possible conflict situations that will arise when segregation patterns are ignored on buses and trains." And third, they wished "to do an educational job by passing on the experiences and data obtained from the trip."[24]

Rustin, who used this opportunity to bring some of his considerable organizing skills to the fore, would later write that the participants also "wished to learn the reaction of bus drivers, passengers, and police to those who non-violently and persistently challenge Jim Crow in interstate travel."[25] Reverend Homer Jack, another of the participants, reflected years later: "The Journey was not meant to be just another testing of existing laws. It was primarily to ascertain whether an unpopular court decision could be enforced using the spirit of aggressive goodwill or, more accurately, nonviolent direct action."[26]

As for the educational component, at each stop the activists would give talks in churches to members of the black, and occasionally white, community. They would explain what they were doing and why, outlining the *Morgan* case and giving an account of their experiences.[27] Scenes of arrest or confrontation would further provide an opportunity to educate observers, bus drivers, and even police and judges through conversations and communication.[28] All of these motives display a well-thought-out and ambitious program for a larger civil rights struggle that could extend beyond the trip itself to serve as a model for future attacks on Jim Crow.

Several months before the Journey, Bayard Rustin and George Houser traversed the route, adhering to Jim Crow restrictions, in order to canvass the itinerary, line up lawyers, raise funds, contact local leaders, and organize meetings. In either late March or early April 1947, the sixteen participants met at a co-op house in Washington, D.C., for an intensive two-day training institute on nonviolent approaches to confronting Jim Crow.[29] All of the participants were men. Initially, Houser and Rustin had assumed that members of both sexes would participate in the Journey.[30] However, Houser later explained that mixing both the races and the sexes "would possibly exacerbate an already volatile situation," and instead they planned for a later Journey involving only women, a decision that the few women involved in the planning met with dismay.[31] The distaff Journey never occurred. Two other men accompanied the activists as observers for portions of the trip: Lem Graves of the *Pittsburgh Courier* and Ollie Stewart of the *Baltimore Afro-American.*

This first meeting in Washington served as a precursor to similar programs that movement leaders initiated as direct action protests became the preferred method of dealing with segregation in the South. The Interracial Workshop in Washington, which engaged in nonviolent training seminars from the 1940s on, and the Highlander Folk School and Training Center, which would train masses of black and white college students in the 1960s, are two other examples. In the Washington workshop, Rustin, Houser, and others explained the course of action that the participants would take. They also provided training, advice, and admonishments to help the group prepare for the inevitable hostilities they would face from bus drivers, police, passengers, and observers. The group engaged in a lot of role-playing over the course of the weekend, although the participants were well aware that no amount of role-playing could simulate what they were about to confront. With sixteen participants, and a balance of blacks and whites, they had enough people to mount challenges to Jim Crow on the buses of both Greyhound and Trailways, the two major carriers at that time. Rustin and Houser prepared a sheet of instructions for their companions, many of whom would be engaging in their first nonviolent actions. The guidelines were clear:

1. If you are a Negro, sit in a front seat. If you are white, sit in a rear seat.
2. If the driver asks you to move, tell him *calmly and courteously:* "As an interstate passenger I have a right to sit anywhere in this bus. This is the law as laid down by the United States Supreme Court."
3. If the driver summons the police and repeats his order in their presence, tell them exactly what you said when he first asked you to move.
4. If the police tell you to "come along," without putting you under arrest, tell them you will not go until you are put under arrest. Police have often used the tactic of frightening a person into getting off the bus without making an arrest, keeping him until the bus has left and then just leaving him standing by the empty roadside. In such a case this person has no redress.
5. If the police put you under arrest, go with them peacefully. At the police station, phone the nearest center of the NAACP, or one of their lawyers. They will assist you.
6. If you have money with you, you can get out on bail immediately. It will probably be either $25 or $50. If you don't have bail, antidiscrimination organizations will help raise it for you.
7. *If you happen to be arrested the delay in your journey will only be a few hours. The value of your action in breaking down Jim Crow will be too great to be measured.*[32]

Although some of the guidelines shifted—often, for example, blacks and whites would sit together throughout the bus, rather than observing a simple stratification of blacks in front and whites in back—these basic standards remained consistent throughout the Journey and served as a broad framework for future nonviolent actions. On every leg of the journey, some participants were to adhere to Jim Crow conventions so that they could post bail for any participants who might be arrested.[33]

Rustin and Houser had made arrangements for NAACP lawyers to represent the riders in the event of the inevitable arrests. However, the NAACP's national office was not especially supportive of the Journey, regardless of its nonviolent approach. Some of its more visible figures opposed the ride, revealing the schisms in the black community between newer groups and the more established organization, as well as fissures along the fault lines of age and class. These tensions would periodically emerge not only over the course of the Journey but also in the two decades to follow. Such disagreements also reveal philosophical struggles within the movement about significant questions of tactics, goals, and approaches.

Among the more vocal critics of the Journey was none other than Thurgood Marshall of the NAACP's Legal Defense Fund, one of the lawyers who had shepherded Irene Morgan's appeal through to the Supreme Court the previous year. In a speech entitled "The Next Twenty Years toward Freedom for the Negro in America," given before a New Orleans audience on November 22, 1946, Marshall revealed the extent of both the NAACP's nonconfrontational approach and the schism between his organization and groups such as CORE and FOR, clearly aiming many of his remarks at them. Criticizing "well-meaning radical groups in New York," he argued that a "disobedience movement on the part of Negroes and their white allies, if employed in the South, would result in wholesale slaughter with no good achieved." He also expressed his skepticism about the prospects for a nonviolent campaign akin to Gandhi's in India succeeding in the South.[34]

Marshall's remarks made the *New York Times* and elicited a response from Rustin, who wrote an article for the *Louisiana Weekly* in which he argued that Marshall was "either ill-informed on the principles and techniques of nonviolence or ignorant of the processes of social change":

Unjust social laws and patterns do not change because supreme courts deliver just decisions. One needs merely to observe the continued practice of Jim Crow in interstate travel, six months after the Supreme Court's decision, to see the necessity of resistance. Social progress comes from struggle; all freedom demands a price. . . . At times freedom will demand that its followers go into situations where even death is to be faced. . . . Resistance on the buses would, for example, mean humiliation, mistreatment by police, arrest, and some physical violence inflicted on the participants. . . . This is why Negroes and whites who participate in direct action must pledge themselves to nonviolence in word and deed. For in this way alone can the inevitable violence be reduced to a minimum.[35]

The Journey did receive the support of a number of leading African American figures, such as the eminent black educator and activist Mary McLeod Bethune, who wrote to Houser, "This is a sane and natural approach and a good project," and Howard Thurman, the prominent religious leader and teacher, who wrote, "I endorse the proposal very heartily and am certain that it will provide a much-needed rallying point for those people in the South who are personally and collectively dedicated to good will." The project also received support from A. Philip Randolph and Bishop F. W. Alstork of the AME Zion Church. Bayard Rustin would later recall that Roy Wilkins also had a "fairly positive response."[36]

On the morning of April 9, 1947, the sixteen men boarded two buses, one Trailways and one Greyhound, to begin the Journey.[37] As planned, interracial groups of two or three sat in both the front and the back of the buses. They did not encounter any difficulties on the first leg of their trip, from Washington, D.C., to Richmond, nor were there any problems as they began their trip from Richmond to Petersburg, Virginia, the next day. There had been so many challenges to Jim Crow on the buses in Richmond up to that point that the police had ceased making arrests. Indeed, Houser believed that their challenge "spurred others to violate the accepted segregated pattern." For example, "a white couple took seats beside two blacks on the back seat. . . . Rustin gave his seat, third from the front, to an elderly black woman and then sat by a white lad directly behind the driver. Nothing was said."[38]

Although the riders did not encounter any direct hostility from authorities, they did get a glimpse of some of the ambivalence felt in the black community on the bus from Richmond to Petersburg. A black man in the rear of the bus spoke with the Fellowship of Reconciliation's George Houser and Igal Roodenko, a white activist from New York who had spent time in a Denver prison as a result of his conscientious objection to World War II, and said, "A Negro might be able to get away with riding up front here, but some bus drivers are crazy, and the farther South you go, the crazier they get." Meanwhile, James Peck was sitting in the back of the bus reading the *New York Times* when two black women jokingly said, "He wouldn't know what it was all about if he was asked to move." The women laughed.[39]

The jocular mood swiftly changed when the riders boarded the buses departing Petersburg for Raleigh, North Carolina, on April 11. That morning, after sitting in a prohibited section of a Trailways bus, black rider Conrad Lynn became the first from the group to be arrested. Lynn, a New York attorney, had tried to explain to the bus driver that the *Morgan* decision allowed him to ride where he pleased. The bus driver was courteous but insistent, asserting that he worked for the bus company and not the Supreme Court, and thus he followed company rules regarding segregation. He said, loudly enough for other passengers to hear him, "Personally I don't care where you sit, but I have my orders." He then asked Lynn if he was going to move. As trained, Lynn said that he would not. Without any verbal abuse or threats, the bus driver summoned the police, and an hour and a half later, they had a warrant for his arrest on the grounds that he had engaged in disorderly conduct by disobeying a bus driver's reasonable order to move to the rear of the bus in compliance with company rules. The bus driver apologized for having to arrest Lynn, and one of the police officers remarked, about equality for Negroes, "I guess I'm just not Christian enough."[40]

The most vocal opposition to the protesters again came from black observers. A corpulent black porter whom the locals called "Shorty" expressed his displeasure with Lynn: "What's the matter with him? He's crazy. Where does he think he is? We know how to deal with him. We ought to drag him off."[41] Lynn would later recall that most of the passengers felt inconvenienced by the delay, "but only a few complained. They seemed to sense that a much larger issue was at stake." At the same time, a crowd had gathered outside the bus, and some in the crowd "threatened to beat me up, and worse." Opponents of the challenge the riders presented included a group of students from a nearby black school, Virginia Union College, who empathized with the feelings of the porter who had been so distressed by Lynn's defiance. Lynn believed that the students "were unwilling to admit that they had suffered discrimination in public transportation," and so they "pretended that discrimination did not exist for them."[42]

This theme of denial and resentment would recur in the Civil Rights Movement, as activists continually encountered inertia within the black community that was almost as pervasive as the white resistance against which they struggled. Oftentimes black anxiety stemmed from a legitimate fear that outsiders came in, disrupted race relations, and then departed, leaving local blacks to face the wrath and recriminations of an enraged white community that lumped the alien protesters with even the most acquiescent of local blacks. But where activists occasionally stirred up resentments and fears, they also often inspired the emergence and growth of locally based protests. Thus, the overt expressions of hostility from blacks toward protesters should not necessarily be perceived as representative of the feelings of the black community as a whole. Just as civil rights organizations disagreed with regard to goals and tactics at the national level, similar tensions tugged at black communities across the South in the postwar era.

Lynn was released on twenty-five dollars bail, and the Journey continued through to Durham, North Carolina, where more trouble would occur. Before arriving in Durham, the bus driver warned the offending patrons to move and even stopped in several towns both immediately before and after the state border, insistently asking them to move, going so far as to stop the bus and try to summon police, to no avail. In Oxford, North Carolina, the bus driver called the police, but they would not make an arrest. In the midst of a forty-five-minute delay in Oxford, the driver allowed an aged black schoolteacher to board the bus to try to convince the activists to cease and desist. He entreated the men: "Please move. Don't do this. You'll reach your destination either in front or in back. What difference does it make?" When it became clear that no arrest was forthcoming, the teacher, sweating and nervous under a starched collar, pleaded with Peck not to use his name in his account of the events: "It will hurt me in the community. I'll never do that again."[43]

This incident as much as any other reveals the ambivalence within segments of the black community. On the one hand, the teacher feared the repercussions from the intransigence of the itinerant protesters. On the other hand, when he realized that no arrests were imminent, he grew equally worried that he would be perceived as an Uncle Tom. Each option had distasteful consequences.

On a crowded Trailways bus traveling from Raleigh to Durham on April 12, the riders continued with their mission. The driver did not press the matter until two white college-aged men got on the bus. At that point the driver told Lynn and Wally Nelson, a black freelance lecturer and CORE activist from Cincinnati, to move from their seat in the next-to-last row of the bus. They refused, and the bus driver said they would deal with the insubordination in Durham. A white passenger offered to help the driver solve the problem, presumably through physical means, but the driver said, "No, we don't want to handle it that way."[44] The crowding had been alleviated by the time the bus arrived in Durham, and the driver did not pursue the issue any further.

Later that day, however, on a Trailways bus preparing to depart Durham for Chapel Hill, more trouble occurred, this time resulting in the arrest of three of the passengers: Andrew Johnson, a student from Cincinnati; James Peck; and Bayard Rustin. In an account of the Journey, Peck described Durham as a typical town in the Jim Crow South: "One glance at the Durham bus station was enough to illustrate the separate and unequal treatment which Negroes receive in the South." He went on to describe the Jim Crow facilities not only in the bus station but throughout the city: "This inequality was observable throughout the downtown Negro section of town," which was "decrepit, squalid, cheerless—in sharp contrast to the modern, bustling, white downtown section."[45] Despite the apparent inequities, Durham proved similar to many of the other towns through which the Journey passed. The riders met with resistance from an entrenched black bourgeoisie who "opposed action which threatens their privileged status." Despite this opposition from a few elite or frightened blacks, the depth of support for the Journey—a countervailing trend to the resistance of the privileged few—came through clearly when a few black persons tried to prevent the mass meeting that the NAACP had planned for a church that night. The meeting went on as scheduled, the church packed with a mass of supporters. This recurrent theme of a divided black community reveals the depth of the schism among blacks, which tended to undermine direct action campaigns against segregated conditions.[46]

Eventually, Durham officials would drop all charges after an NAACP lawyer arrived to defend the three men, and the Journey lawyers countered with a suit charging the Durham police with false arrest. The bus driver indicated that he and other Trailways drivers had been aware of the group of interracial riders testing the Jim Crow statutes. He told the police: "We know all about this. Greyhound is letting them ride. But we are not."[47] It appears true that Greyhound officials had decided not to challenge the integrated groups. Of the six incidents of arrest over the two weeks, each occurred on a Trailways bus, none on Greyhound. The participants did not realize this until late in the trip.[48] Significantly, there appear to have been far fewer difficulties in Greyhound's acquiescence to the Supreme Court dictates than in Trailway's defense of Jim Crow.[49] Most problems arose when officials of either the bus company or the police, acting at their behest, confronted the riders. Problems did not arise as a result of the complaints of fellow passengers. In some ways, this provides a microcosm of the futility of massive resistance, a strategy that would manifest itself across the South in the 1950s. Ultimately, civil rights protesters would emerge vindicated, but at tremendous physical, mental, and economic costs to both sides in the cases where massive resistance held sway. In essence, Trailways chose to fight on, while Greyhound recognized the inevitability of change and adjusted its policies accordingly.

"Coming Down Here to Stir Up the Niggers": Chapel Hill

The next day saw the only violence that occurred over the course of the Journey. As Lem Graves of the *Pittsburgh Courier* wrote in his lead article describing the event: "This sleepy little Piedmont village, regarded far and wide as the citadel of democracy in the South, seat of the University of North Carolina, became a scene of sudden mob violence here late Sunday afternoon as taxicab drivers and young hoodlums assaulted an interracial group of young lecturers in the Chapel Hill bus station."[50] Chapel Hill had long been at the center of liberal thought on racial and other matters in the South. Its president, Frank Porter Graham, had a national reputation for liberalism and in 1946 had been appointed to the President's Committee on Civil Rights. Yet the only violence on the Journey took place in the midst of this epicenter of Southern tolerance, where Wilson Head had experienced his harrowing encounter with police just a few months earlier.[51] On a beautiful April Sunday afternoon in Chapel Hill, a number of taxi drivers began to gather to witness the arrests of the protesters. The first two arrestees were Cincinnati student Andrew Johnson and Joseph Felmet, a white Asheville native and representative of the Southern Workers Defense League. They had taken a seat in the front of the Trailways bus and remained there after the driver, Ned O. Leonard, had asked them to move. After a period of stalemate, the bus driver had crossed the street to the nearby police station. Soon after the arrests of Johnson and Felmet, Bayard Rustin and Igal Roodenko moved from their seats in the back of the bus to take their spots. They, too, were arrested and brought to the police station.

When James Peck, the white editor of the Workers Defense League *News Bulletin* and an avowed pacifist, left the bus to post bail for his four colleagues, one of the taxi drivers, a large man with "steel grey eyes," smashed him in the head with his fist, accusing Peck of "coming down here to stir up the niggers."[52] Peck did not retaliate, which seemed to confuse his assailant. Peck then posted bond for his arrested colleagues.[53] He would later write that their "action on the bus was but one of a series of events" challenging Jim Crow in Chapel Hill. "It just happened to be our action which exploded the growing hatred of the poor whites, who tenaciously hold on to their only privilege in our society—that of being recognized as superior to the Negroes." As he watched the mob from a distance after the assault, Peck could not help but think about how out of thirty-one men indicted two months earlier for lynching a black man in Greenville, South Carolina, twenty-eight were cab drivers.[54]

Igal Roodenko, soon after the confrontation, recounted some of the events that transpired inside the bus as he and Rustin moved up to take the seats vacated when Johnson and Felmet were arrested. Upon the initial arrest, the bus driver had tried to gather anyone who could back up what he had done, presumably so that he would have witnesses if the cases came to trial. But instead of overwhelming support, the driver encountered some hostility. A Northern woman said, "You don't want my name and address: I'm a damn Yankee and I think this is an outrage." Roodenko later wrote that "she was quite excited and said a little more, like 'I thought this was the United States,' and things like that." Roodenko discovered that she was from Brooklyn, and she was enthusiastic about his and Rustin's decision to continue the protest action by taking the seats of their departed comrades. Meanwhile, the only other black riders on the bus, two young women, refused to give their names. Another young white woman was curious about the actions of the two men. She told Roodenko that she was a Southerner (from Asheville, like Felmet) and that she thought that Jim Crow was wrong, "but she felt we were pushing things a little too fast." The two men used this as an opportunity to teach. Rustin asked her what the moral difference was between a premeditated action and a spontaneous one. Another girl sitting in front of them, according to Roodenko, "suddenly said—and with considerable emphasis—'None whatsoever.'"[55] It seems clear that part of the plan was to help Southerners reach conclusions about the moral righteousness of the civil rights cause for themselves.

A few days later, Roodenko wrote, "No other passengers participated verbally in this open forum, but it was obvious that they were in it, for they listened not only with their ears, but also with their eyes: they felt they were in it, for when a person is overhearing a conversation of which he is not a part he generally looks elsewhere."[56] Finally, the girl who had spoken up so emphatically told Roodenko, "I think you are doing a brave and wonderful thing." She gave him her name and address so that they could contact her if they needed her support if the case went to trial.[57] The Chapel Hill case revealed both the best and the worst faces of white Southerners. This young woman's reaction to the arrests and to the Journey as a whole was not isolated, as not only the Brooklyn woman's outrage but also the apparent acceptance of the other passengers indicates. But at the same time, the gathering of the taxi drivers revealed the ugly and menacing side of racism in full blossom.

The white thugs did not disperse after Peck disappeared into the police station to post bail. If anything, they gained in strength of numbers and intensity. Ray Sylvester, a University of North Carolina student active in interracial activities, said he had been called out of a nearby restaurant and warned to "look out," as hostilities were about to occur.[58]

The taxi drivers were still in the vicinity when the police released the four men on bail into the custody of Charles M. Jones, the minister of the Presbyterian Church located across from the University of North Carolina campus. Jones had a reputation as being "liberal minded" and "on the cutting edge of racial and social issues." He had been active in labor organizing and had received heavy criticism for permitting an interracial Congress of Industrial Organizations meeting at his church. Thus, to many whites in the community, his willingness to host the interracial group of agitators while they stayed in Chapel Hill was a final sign of eccentricity, iconoclasm, or betrayal. Many branded him a "nigger lover."[59]

When the four group members left the police station, two taxicabs full of men followed them to Jones's house. One observer had been heard to say, "They'll never get a bus out of here tonight," and the pursuit seemed to justify such a pessimistic outlook. The cab drivers and their associates grabbed rocks and sticks outside of Jones's house. Then, for reasons unknown, one of the taxi drivers stood before the crowd and convinced them to disperse. A few moments later, Jones received the first of what would prove to be many threatening phone calls and letters. On the other end of the phone, an anonymous caller said, "Get those damn niggers out of town or we'll burn your house down. We'll be around to see that they go."[60] This threat, coupled with the events that had transpired throughout the day, convinced Jones that it would be best to get the riders out of town and on to their next destination. Chapel Hill police chief W. T. Sloan told newspaper reporters that Jones had received several threatening phone calls.[61]

Jones made some calls to students at the university and was able to convince a few to muster up cars to drive the group to their next intended destination, as the last buses for Greensboro had already left town. Jones then called the police and asked for a protective convoy. They refused until Jones threatened civil action should any harm befall the activists. At that point the police dispatched one car with "the nicest man on the police force," in the estimation of Jones's wife, Dorcas. The students and officer accompanied the riders out of the county and toward Greensboro. Jones also removed his wife and two children to safety for the short term.[62] After the riders safely departed town, a visitor to Chapel Hill, Hilton Seals, was pelted with stones as he helped Reverend Jones home.[63]

At about the time that the Journey was meeting its fiercest resistance in North Carolina, the *Greensboro Daily News* entered the fray with an editorial that illustrated the ambivalent attitudes of many in the state, neither endorsing nor wholly condemning the Journey:

> If interracial collaborators are determined to test the Jim Crow regulations in intra-state traffic, there is nothing to do about it save let them go ahead. . . . Of course there is the natural resentment that men of both races should come from other states and use buses at Chapel Hill and Durham for carrying out their experiment. . . . Anyhow, let's not help grow a fresh crop of martyrs. The seating arrangements are part of our state traffic regulations; but if they run counter to federal law all of us know which will prevail.[64]

This editorial captures the mood of many North Carolinians in 1947. The editorial writers labeled the Journey an intrastate challenge, but in Washington the riders had made a point of buying their tickets together in a full sequence so that the stated destination was always in another state. Thus, the trip was always interstate and fell under the auspices of the *Morgan* decision. A tone of resignation—awareness that the federal government would prevail in any conflict—pervades the piece, a sentiment that varied from state to state. Through much of the South, massive resistance to integration would become the standard tactic for confronting federal demands for desegregation. In North Carolina, however, massive resistance did not generally fit the approach of the state's business, professional, and political leadership, who believed token compliance and gradual concessions to civil rights demands or the federal government preferable to direct confrontation.[65]

A few days later, after the Journey had departed town, several hundred students, professors, religious leaders, and other members of the Chapel Hill community gathered to attempt to determine just what had gone wrong in the previous few days. At the university's Memorial Hall, a number of eyewitnesses, including Reverend Jones, spoke about the crisis. Another speaker was Martin A. Walker of High Point, a bystander who had been talking with a black woman on the scene in Chapel Hill. Three taxi drivers approached Walker, a disabled veteran of World War II and a former Golden Gloves boxing champion, and attacked him. Walker was, at the time of his beating, a student at the university. Police arrested the three assailants.[66]

Chapel Hill marked the emotional pinnacle of the Journey of Reconciliation, but there were still ten days remaining on the trip. The riders received their warmest greeting at a meeting in Greensboro at the Shiloh Baptist Church.[67] Despite respites such as the one in Greensboro, as George Houser later noted, "The sense of tension which accompanied each violation of the Jim Crow pattern never diminished."[68] Homer Jack, the white executive secretary of the Chicago Council Against Racial and Religious Discrimination, who joined the trip a week after the participants had left Washington, wrote: "It was a group of men exhibiting the somewhat taut morale of ten arrests that I encountered. . . . All members of the party were dead tired, not only from the constant tenseness, but also from participating in many meetings and conferences at every stop."[69]

Even though little happened on the trip from Chapel Hill to Asheville, the route through small towns and mountainous areas fueled the anxieties of the riders and created a tense mood.[70] On a Greyhound bound from Greensboro to Winston-Salem, a South Carolinian sat next to Ernest Bromley, a white Methodist minister and North Carolina native. The white man, seeing Conrad Lynn sitting at the front of the bus, told Bromley, "In my state, . . . [he] would be killed." The man was nonetheless calm as Bromley explained the *Morgan* decision to him.[71]

On the hilly trek from Winston-Salem to Asheville, a Greyhound driver tried to remove Wally Nelson, who was sitting with Bromley in the second seat from the front. Nelson explained to the driver the nature of their challenge; the *Morgan* decision; and how, despite the fact that the bus was on an intrastate trip, their tickets were interstate, and thus the Supreme Court ruling applied. At one point, a soldier boarded the bus and asked why the driver had not forced Nelson to move. The bus driver responded that there was a Supreme Court decision, and there was nothing he could do about it. He said, "If you want to do something about this, don't blame this man [Nelson]; kill those bastards up in Washington." The soldier in turn explained the reason for the driver's inaction to a large man traveling with his family who vocally expressed his discontent about the seating on the bus. The man responded, "I wish I was the bus driver." As the bus approached Asheville, it was crowded to the point where two women had to stand. When they asked why the black man sitting in front had not been moved, the driver once again explained that the Supreme Court decision tied his hands.[72] This example once again shows the ameliorative effect that a driver with his company's backing could have in forestalling white responses that amounted to more than grumbling and how, though people might not have liked the decision, most concluded that they could and would live with it.

On a Trailways bus leaving Asheville, the bus driver took an approach opposite to that of his Greyhound counterpart. While the bus was still in the station, Jim Peck and Dennis Banks, a Chicago musician, sat in the second seat from the front. The bus driver, D. L. Strange, asked Banks to move. He refused. The driver called the police and in their presence repeated his command. When Banks still refused to move, police arrested him. Peck then insisted that the police arrest him too, as he had been traveling with Banks. Peck was also charged with violating the state's "ABC" liquor laws because he was carrying a bottle of liquor with a broken seal in his suitcase. Both men also carried "considerable literature" on national and state laws and judicial rulings regarding race, as well as "literature tending to show that federal employees have the right to strike against the government."[73] Why the newspaper felt it necessary to point out this last fact is unclear, except perhaps to taint the men with radicalism. It also reveals the activists' involvement in a range of political, racial, and labor causes.

Peck's and Bank's cases came up for trial on April 18. The NAACP lawyer who defended them, Curtis Todd of Winston-Salem, was the first black lawyer to represent defendants in the Asheville court, as Asheville had no black lawyers. It was in this courtroom that James Peck saw what he would later call the "most fantastic extreme of segregation in my experience": Jim Crow Bibles, "one for black witnesses and a separate (but presumably equal) one for whites."[74] He later discovered that this seeming absurdity was common throughout the South.

The police witnesses "testified so accurately that it was not necessary to call defense witnesses," as they agreed that the protesters had not in any way acted in a disorderly fashion. The Journey participants were stunned to discover that neither the police judge, Sam Cathey, nor Will Hampton, the solicitor, had ever even heard of the *Morgan* decision, so they had to borrow Todd's copy. The judge, who was blind and widely believed to be corrupt, gave Peck and Bank the maximum sentence, a thirty-day term on a road gang, but released the men on two hundred dollars bond, pending appeal.[75] If the goal of the Journey was at least in part to test understanding of the *Morgan* decision, Asheville events proved that much of the South still had a long way to go.

Meanwhile, the trip continued. In Knoxville, Tennessee, Homer Jack and Nathan Wright, a black church social worker from Cincinnati, took seats at the front of a Greyhound bound for Nashville. Jack recounted his thoughts on that first overnight ride between Knoxville and Nashville: "The southern night, to northerners at least, is full of vigilante justice and the lynch rope. . . . We wondered whether, despite the current long-distance telephone strike, the bus company—or one of its militant employees—would phone ahead for a road block and vigilantes to greet us in one of the Tennessee mountain towns. Neither of us [Jack or Wright] slept a moment that night."[76] En route to Nashville, a redheaded soldier asked the bus driver to remove the two men from their seats. When the driver confronted them, Jack and Wright refused to move, and although the driver disappeared for fifteen minutes or so, when he returned he continued the trip. Two black men sitting at the back of the bus spoke loudly to one another while the bus driver was gone. One said, "They are going to get the police and they will probably hit him." The other commented, "When in Rome I believe in doing as the Romans do."[77] In Nashville another bus driver on a different bus bound for Louisville told Wright, "If we were in Alabama, we would throw you out the window."[78] Of course, part of the reason the Journey only covered the Upper South was because the participants understood that Deep South states such as Alabama still posed too much of a danger for anyone who dared to challenge Jim Crow.

In the waning days of the trip, when participants converged on Washington, there were two more arrests. One occurred when Wallace Nelson refused to move to the back of the bus in Amherst, near Lynchburg, Virginia.[79] The bus driver told Wallace and Houser, with whom Wallace was sitting, to move to the back. Houser argued that if he were to ride in the back, they would still be violating Jim Crow, at which point the driver amended his order, telling the men that they had to sit separately in the back. The driver apologized profusely to Houser when he got off to post bail for Nelson. A similar situation occurred when Dennis Banks refused to move to the back of the bus in Charlottesville. He was arrested even though Peck and Worth Randle, a Cincinnati biologist, were both violating the rules as well. It was quickly evident that separate but equal was a farce and that the real concern was keeping blacks from riding in traditionally white seating areas. There was considerably less interest in whites sitting where they pleased. On a full bus, blacks were even expected to cede their seats in the back for white riders in many parts of the South.

In the immediate aftermath of the Journey, it was unclear just what the trip had accomplished. Jim Crow still prevailed throughout the South in most facets of daily life, and transportation, even on interstate conveyances, was no different. Blacks across the region did not follow the lead of the Journey of Reconciliation and sit wherever they chose, even in the Upper South or on the bus routes that the Fellowship had putatively integrated. In his biography of Bayard Rustin, Jervis Anderson asserts that the Journey "achieved no significant breakthroughs" and that instead "the Journey's achievement was mostly psychological or symbolic, signifying the possibility of future nonviolent mass action in the South."[80] While this is undoubtedly true, Anderson underestimates the importance of the Journey, which became a direct model for more overt and well-publicized actions in the future. Rustin, Houser, Peck, and many of the others would provide inspiration, advice, support, and leadership in later efforts.

Accepting an award in New York on April 11, 1948, Rustin said that he and his comrades had undertaken the Journey "not only to devise techniques for eliminating Jim Crow in travel but also as a training ground for similar peaceful projects for employment and in the armed services."[81] The Journey stands as evidence of an already active Civil Rights Movement, more than merely a precursor of what would happen in the wake of *Brown.* The Journey in fact represents a small part of a general post–World War II upsurge in popular protest and direct action.[82] The culmination of this upsurge would be the events of the 1960s, but not until the courts had addressed the status of segregation laws on the highways, byways, and railroads of the United States.

The Chapel Hill Court Case

It took nearly two years for all of the Journey of Reconciliation legal cases to reach closure. Five of the six incidents, involving eight arrests, were dispatched reasonably quickly as officials either dismissed the charges or the accused gained acquittal. Chapel Hill, however, was more problematic. In that instance, the authorities chose to pursue the cases. Perhaps by co-incidence, when they went before the grand jury, the city court of Chapel Hill sat a black man on a jury for the first time in half a century.[83] This did not, however, help the four accused men.

In the first trial, in June 1947, Rustin and Roodenko were both found guilty, but the judge did not mete out equal punishment. While he fined Rustin only enough to cover court costs, he sentenced Roodenko to thirty days on a state highway road gang. When he announced his decision, the judge declared that he had intentionally given the white participant the heavier fine. On June 24, when Andrew Johnson and Joe Felmet went to trial and were found guilty, the judge responded similarly, fining Johnson twenty-five dollars, while giving Felmet, a native white Southerner from Asheville, a far stiffer penalty. Initially, he tried to give Felmet six months on a road gang, but he reduced the sentence accordingly when informed that the maximum penalty was thirty days. At first the four men had been charged and indicted for disorderly conduct and interfering with arrest, but this was changed to violating Jim Crow law, based on the argument that the men had planned three stopovers in North Carolina and thus were intrastate, not interstate passengers. This interpretation would later prove important when CORE, FOR, and the NAACP weighed whether to take the case to the U.S. Supreme Court, as passengers' status and their trip's relation to the Commerce Clause were crucial.[84]

Throughout the rest of 1947 and 1948, the appeals process continued. Even prior to the resolution of all of the cases from the Journey of Rec-onciliation, other transportation companies that carried passengers across state lines decided to fall into line with the principles of the *Morgan* deci-sion. In May 1948, the Pennsylvania Railroad announced that black rid-ers would be able to travel south on any car they requested and would no longer be forced to travel in a Jim Crow car. The general passenger agent for the railroad made the initial announcement of the decision to George Houser of the Fellowship and Margot Dukler of CORE in the presence of the railroad's attorney on May 27. This decision came about after the Inter-racial Workshop, another organization dedicated to nonviolent resistance to segregation, conducted a campaign in which it handed out leaflets to passersby outside of Penn Station in New York, an origination point for several southbound Pennsylvania Railways trains.[85] Once again direct ac-tion protest had played a role in changing Jim Crow policy.

Unfortunately for Rustin, Roodenko, Johnson, and Felmet, the officials in Chapel Hill were not so willing to relent. On March 17, 1948, Orange County Superior Court judge Chester W. Norris upheld the convictions on appeal and in two cases stiffened the penalties, handing out thirty-day sentences on the Highway Patrol work gang to all four men rather than just to the whites.[86] Even as Rustin and Houser prepared to celebrate being among twenty Americans awarded the Thomas Jefferson Award of the Council Against Discrimination in America, they faced an uphill battle in their court challenge.[87]

By that time, financial concerns were beginning to creep into the considerations of the organizations involved with the court challenges. CORE and FOR did not have a legal defense fund akin to that of the NAACP, which at the national level was still unwilling to commit itself to supporting direct action protests. It remained focused on continuing and possible future court challenges instead. This conflict was exacerbated by disputes over the fees and payment timetable that the lawyers for the Chapel Hill men had established. As a result of these conflicts and ongoing fiscal concerns, George Houser announced that the Fellowship of Reconciliation had established a special committee that would take control of decision making in the Chapel Hill case. This committee would make financial decisions, negotiate with lawyers, and organize fund-raising. It would also be responsible for deciding whether to pursue a challenge to the U.S. Supreme Court should they lose before the North Carolina Supreme Court.[88]

On December 14, 1948, the state supreme court heard arguments in the case. Chief Justice Walter P. Stacy told the two black attorneys who argued for the defendants that the Orange County jury had decided that the four were intrastate passengers, and "I think we are bound by that."[89] Clearly this did not bode well, and it came as no surprise when, in early January, the state supreme court affirmed the superior court's judgment and penalty. The court rejected all claims of error on the part of the lower courts, most notably on the assertion of the intrastate nature of the activists' trip.[90]

The Fellowship and its committee had to weigh their options. They could appeal to the U.S. Supreme Court. They could try to convince the governor, R. Gregg Cherry, to overturn the decision of the state supreme court. They could ignore the order, forfeit bond, and await the state's unlikely decision on whether to extradite. Or else they could have the four men report to serve their sentences.

Each approach had positive and negative aspects. The Supreme Court option, if it turned out in their favor, would be the best route, but given the lower courts' findings, the burden of proof effectively rested on the convicted travelers. This case was not an ideal one to attempt to reinforce and continue the Court's recent inclination to chip away at Jim Crow. A defeat might be a setback for the larger goals of the movement. Going to the governor was a long shot, and most participants agreed that they did not want the sentences commuted or lenience given. If the governor were involved, the four would have to receive absolution; otherwise the end result would be that in the eyes of the state they were still guilty—which is exactly what the Fellowship and CORE denied. Ignoring the conviction was the least preferable option, as it would cause them to lose the moral high ground. This high ground could be maintained if the four went to serve their sentences, and prison might provide an opportunity to practice the tenets of nonviolent resistance and education in a new form, as well as provide a model for the movement's future activists.

As 1949 commenced, the committee and other interested observers debated what to do. Rustin remained active. In January 1949, in India, he was the guest of Devadas Gandhi, the son of Mahatma Gandhi, Rustin's inspiration in nonviolent protest. He received a warm welcome as he made his way through the country, speaking to audiences about American race relations and Gandhian nonviolence. Newspapers in India devoted articles and columns to his speeches and to the Fellowship of Reconciliation. He told his listeners about the ongoing situation in the United States and especially about his case in Chapel Hill and the impending thirty days of hard labor. According to the *Chicago Tribune*, "Anecdotes of this kind do little to increase American prestige among Indians already incensed over treatment of fellow Indians by white South Africans."[91]

The Fellowship committee quickly decided not to pursue a Supreme Court challenge, largely on the grounds that it was "doubtful that the issues of whether the passengers were inter-state or not are as clearly cut as would make us certain of the consequence before the U.S. Court." Those who disagreed with this decision pointed out that the *Morgan* case had met with unfavorable judgments at every level below the Supreme Court as well. The committee members left the door ajar for the NAACP to take on the challenge, but they were dubious as to the prospects of this happening.[92] A few weeks later Robert L. Carter, assistant special counsel for the NAACP Legal Defense Fund, wrote to George Houser, confirming that the NAACP would not take the case to the Supreme Court. Carter's group had shown the case to three members of the NAACP's legal staff, who argued that "the record" of the case in question was "not full enough for us to make a good showing in the United States Supreme Court," and in fact "it may cause us more harm than good to raise this question . . . with the incomplete record we now have."[93] However, Carter continued: "There is a case pending in the courts in Virginia which presents the same issue which we would present to the Supreme Court in this case, but it has a much more complete and better record. That is an additional reason for [the belief] that we should not pursue this matter further. In that opinion [Thurgood] Marshall concurs. . . . I think it is advisable for us to wait on the better case rather than risk losing this in the Supreme Court because of the incomplete record."[94]

The Virginia case that Carter referred to was that of Norvell Lee, a Howard University student and a member of the 1948 U.S. Olympic Boxing Team, who had been arrested after refusing to sit Jim Crow in a train going from Covington, Virginia, to Washington, D.C.[95] Lee's would in fact prove to be a more suitable test case, and in 1950 the Virginia Supreme Court overturned his conviction.[96] It seems likely that the temper of the Court after World War II was such that, imperfect though the case was, the justices may have overturned the convictions of the Chapel Hill men. It is equally clear, however, that the NAACP Legal Defense Fund's consistent push for the most favorable cases was prudent in light of what was at stake. Lee's case marks a validation of the *Morgan* decision, at least in Virginia, to be sure, but it is no more important in aiding understanding of the 1940s postwar Civil Rights Movement than the Chapel Hill case is.

In a meeting soon after the NAACP decision, the committee members and the FOR executive council met to determine the appropriate course of action. The first option, and the preferred one, was to pursue a retrial in the superior court on the grounds that not all of the evidence had been put into the record in the original trial.[97] This went nowhere. The superior court had no reason or motivation to reexamine a case that had been validated in the chambers of the state supreme court. If relief were to come from the state of North Carolina, it would have to come from the newly inaugurated governor, W. Kerr Scott. This option seemed to offer some promise. Soon after entering office, Kerr had announced that North Carolina had to address the "Negro question." "I'm going to follow through," he promised, "to see that the minority race has a fair opportunity and gets the training" that would enable it to be integrated into the state's burgeoning economy. He continued: "I'm firmly convinced that we've got to go ahead and meet the issue of the minority race."[98] Clearly, one reason why North Carolina was later able to avoid most of the nightmares of massive resistance that bedeviled many other Southern states was the leadership of relatively liberal individuals such as Scott. Nonetheless, the possibility of having the sentences overturned never materialized, and thus as the court-imposed deadline for filing appeals approached, the options of Rustin, Roodenko, Felmet, and Johnson grew ever more circumscribed. The solicitor of the Tenth Judicial District had given the four until March 21, 1949, to appear to begin serving their sentences.

Twenty-Two Days on a Chain Gang

As an organization, FOR decided that the four men would serve their time on the prison road gang, onerous though the prospect seemed. Andrew Johnson, however, had been showing reticence for some time about the prospect of serving time on the road gang. He was a senior at the University of Cincinnati looking forward to attending the university's law school in the fall, and he was afraid of the consequences attendant on leaving school to serve prison time. Aware of Johnson's concerns, and hoping to persuade the student of the righteousness of their cause, Conrad Lynn wrote Johnson on Valentine's Day 1949. He first hinted that by offering to serve their terms, the four men would be calling North Carolina's bluff. "It is highly doubtful," Lynn wrote, that the state "could afford the national publicity of the four of you returning, one from India, another from the Mid West, one from their own state, and another from New York to serve time because they believed that Negroes should have the same rights in inter state traveling as whites." He also told Johnson that they held out hope that the governor would provide a pardon. Irrespective of these hopes, however, it was "essential to our case that the four be ready to serve their time." Lynn then more directly tried to address some of Johnson's fears and anxieties about the impact of his actions and the implications for his future: "I need not remind you that as a prelaw student, a question of honor is involved for you. The State of Ohio would hardly frown upon a candidate for admission to the Bar who had served thirty days for the cause represented by your case, but the State of Ohio might very well be somewhat dubious about a man who had jumped bail. I know, Andy, that you will make the right decision."[99] George Houser, too, wrote Johnson, who took some time in responding. When he did, he did not provide the answers many clearly had desired.

Johnson explained his academic circumstances and how close he was to graduating, noting that the Journey had already put him in a situation where he would have to attend summer school in order to move on to law school in the fall. He asserted that he had spoken to several lawyer friends, including Madison Perkins, an assistant attorney general for the state of Ohio, and they believed that even if he were extradited, "this particular offense would have very little affect on my future career, especially due to the nature of the offense." He also believed that Perkins "will have some influence with Governor Lausche, who was returned to office by the Negro voters of Ohio." Whether or not this last assertion was true, it reveals the growing belief of many blacks that their vote had become a major factor in postwar politics in the North.

Johnson pointed out that he had asked to pay the twenty-five-dollar fine he had been assessed after his initial conviction, and so, although it "disturbs me somewhat not to be able to go through with my case . . . my conscience is satisfied that I gave fair warning of what might happen." Finally, he argued, "In addition to the facts mentioned above, I am both mentally and physically unprepared to serve thirty days on the road gang."[100] This last assertion is certainly understandable given that Johnson was a black Northerner, nearly a college graduate, and an aspiring law student, and that he was facing thirty days of hard labor on a Southern road gang for challenging segregation. Finally, on the issue of the bail he was about to jump, he promised to do all that he could to reimburse the Fellowship of Reconciliation the one hundred dollars it had posted.

On March 20, Bayard Rustin and Igal Roodenko held a press conference at New York's Penn Station to announce that they were heading south to begin their sentence the next day. The FOR press release stated that Felmet and Johnson would also surrender to authorities, although Johnson had already reiterated, in his letter and in conversations with others, that he would not do so.[101] Immediately, CORE leadership made arrangements for Rustin and the others to make speeches at a New York CORE meeting upon their release in late April.[102] CORE and the Fellowship realized the importance of publicizing their actions and making visible the victims of the Jim Crow system. If the three men were going to serve their time, civil rights leaders knew the symbolic power of channeling their victimization into a public relations bonanza.[103]

The experience on the road crew was unpleasant, arduous, and degrading for all three men. Rustin left the most complete record of the three, as he wrote an article detailing his experiences for the *New York Post* that also appeared in the *Baltimore Afro-American,* "Twenty-Two Days on a Chain

Gang," which FOR later published as a pamphlet.[104] Letters both from and to the men also supplement Rustin's account, as do letters from CORE in which Houser garnered support for the prisoners.[105] The work was physically exhausting. The conditions were difficult, as the guards treated the men, especially Rustin, very harshly while they were in custody. The food was barely sufficient. They got one set of clean clothes per week. Physical abuse and other forms of corporal and psychological punishment were daily occurrences. Some of the blacks thought that Rustin was "a fool." A letter from Rustin's sister indicates that some of the men on the gangs were sexually assaulted, or as she phrased it, "He said that because of deprivation there is a great amount of sexual malpractice and the men are apt to gang up on someone who seems a little more sensitive than most."[106]

Rustin did his best to make as many friends as he could. He also continued his nonviolent teachings, practices, and philosophy as much as possible in captivity, while remaining true to his fundamental belief in racial equality and humanity. He refused to wear a cap so that he could avoid the indignity of having to doff it to a guard or other authority figure. Although he had some rough times dealing with guards, given his status as someone who had challenged Jim Crow, Rustin indicates that he felt he earned the grudging respect of some in the prison power structure through his integrity, courtesy, and probity. Rustin also grew to question the very nature of the prison system as it was applied in the South. All of these aspects of his experience were lessons that would benefit future prisoners in the movement, who would replicate, expand upon, and learn from them in the years to come.

The Movement Enters the 1950s: The Journey and Its Meaning

What, then, was the legacy of the Journey of Reconciliation? It did not end segregation in interstate transport. Jim Crow buses and trains continued to cross state borders, while overwhelmingly maintaining Jim Crow seating. Furthermore, facilities in bus and rail stations catering to interstate passengers such as cafes and restaurants, washrooms and drinking fountains, continued to bear the emblems of Jim Crow. "Whites Only" and "Blacks Only" signs rigidly marked the caste system that prevailed in the old Confederacy and in the border states surrounding it. Nonetheless, after the midway mark of the trip, Ollie Stewart of the *Baltimore Afro-American* could write, "I think the 'Journey of Reconciliation' knocked several props from the already tottering Jim-Crow structure."[107] In a slightly less ambitious tone, George Houser, looking back on the Journey of Reconciliation in 1992, argued that he could make "limited but important claims" for its success.[108] Looking back across the years, Houser wrote, "As I think back on my many experiences and projects . . . this is one of the highlights. I am glad we did it. It was a creative project, a bit ahead of its time, and, if I do say so, it took some guts."[109]

Houser believed that the Journey might have acted as an "entering wedge" in the South in the area of interstate transportation.[110] The same might be said for much of the civil rights activity in the 1940s. While none of the individual and collective protests in the era before the *Brown* decision led, on their own, to wholesale change, they did help to make subsequent challenges more viable. The trip garnered a good deal of attention in newspapers, magazines, and other journals of the day. A dramatization of the trip was even turned into a radio play on New York station WMCA's program *New World A'Coming,* in November 1947.[111] But how did this attention translate in the long run?

Houser argued in 1992: "Perhaps the Journey was a project ahead of its time to achieve maximum results. The backup machinery was not there to make it more than it was—a planned and often audacious attack on Jim Crow before the civil rights movement was full blown."[112] He went on to assert that the project had yielded some concrete and important accomplishments. It had received extensive publicity for a civil rights challenge in the South prior to the mid-1950s. Newspapers across the country ran articles about the Journey. Southern newspapers editorialized about it, writers sometimes wringing their hands over what the frontal challenge meant to Southern institutions. National magazines also published editorials. The *New Republic* proclaimed it "a remarkable journey."[113] African American newspapers particularly hailed the Journey, not just for what it accomplished but also for what it might portend. It was at least as important for readers of the *Washington Bee,* the *Chicago Defender,* the *Pittsburgh Courier,* and the *Baltimore Afro-American* to read about and be inspired by the Journey of Reconciliation as it was for readers of the *New York Times* and the *New Republic.*

The ride was also important in that it served as what Houser would call "an educational vehicle." For both the observers on buses and in bus stations and for those attending mass meetings in the towns where the riders stopped, the Journey served to force people to confront Jim Crow as well as the Supreme Court's *Morgan* decision. For black people the meetings "helped to strengthen the resolve of the hundreds of people . . . we addressed along the way either to question their own compliance with Jim Crow laws, or to look with sympathy on those who refuse to obey unjust laws."[114] At the end of many of these meetings, James Peck later recalled, "Men and women came up to congratulate us with tears in their eyes," and at meetings with students, both blacks and whites "pledged to carry on by traveling in an unsegregated manner when they go home to another state."[115] This education therefore helped people to learn about the tactics of nonviolent protest and revealed that nonviolent action could produce positive results. As Houser asserted, "Nonviolence can by no means guarantee defusing crowd action. However, in our case it helped that passengers, police and drivers were not aroused to encourage mob action."[116] These would be lessons well learned for the coming wave of activists who would challenge Jim Crow, including those who saw the Journey of Reconciliation as a model for the Freedom Rides.

Perhaps above all, the Journey served to inspire and shape the Freedom Rides. The Congress of Racial Equality, after cosponsoring the Journey of Reconciliation, used it as a model in 1961, when it sponsored the Freedom Rides.[117] Several participants and planners have pointed out the undeniable connection between the Rides and the Journey. Houser avers that the most important aspect of the Journey was that "it served as a model for the Freedom Rides of 1961 which opened up a new chapter in CORE history."[118] Houser and other CORE members believed that a project would be organized well before 1961.[119] James Peck, the only person who participated in both the Journey and the Freedom Rides, wrote about the Journey in the first chapter of his 1962 book, *Freedom Ride,* arguing that the Journey was a direct precursor to the events of 1961.[120] Peck would continue to explicitly draw this connection in interviews.[121] Bayard Rustin, too, confirmed the Journey's influence on the Freedom Rides: "In retrospect I would say we were the precursors. The things we did in the '40s were the same things that ushered in the civil rights revolution. Our Journey of Reconciliation preceded the Freedom Rides by fourteen years."[122] James Farmer of CORE provides even more direct evidence linking the two events. In his memoir of his time in the movement, *Lay Bare the Heart,* Farmer reveals that in 1961, "Gordon Carey proposed a second Journey of Reconciliation patterned after the first one conducted in 1947. . . . Unlike the 1947 Journey . . . the target would be segregated bus terminal facilities as well as segregated seating on the buses. Also unlike the previous project, he suggested that we go into the Deep South. . . . But it should not be called a Journey of Reconciliation. Such a name would be out of touch with the scrappy nonviolent movement that had emerged. The cry, I said, was not for 'reconciliation' but for '*freedom.*'"[123]

As the 1940s prepared to give way to the 1950s, a Civil Rights Movement had been under way for at least the better part of a decade. As the Journey of Reconciliation shows, this Civil Rights Movement consisted of a number of different organizations and individuals with occasionally differing agendas, tactical approaches, and short-term goals. Such differences would be a defining characteristic of the civil rights struggle throughout its existence. The 1940s laid the groundwork in the courts, on the streets, and in the buses through direct action campaigns intended to attack Jim Crow at its roots, in the communities where it was most pervasive. The system of Jim Crow transport was a significant, visible, entrenched, and ubiquitous symbol and manifestation of the system, and as such it provided an opportune laboratory for social action. The Fellowship of Reconciliation, CORE, and the NAACP, along with dozens of other organizations and hundreds of other individuals who mounted challenges to Jim Crow, represent more than merely a diffuse and episodic phenomenon in search of a movement. They influenced a generation of activists in their own day and in the generation to come.[124] They were, in fact, part of an ongoing Civil Rights Movement in America. At least on the issue of segregation in the realm of interstate transport, however, there was still work to be done on the ground and in the courts. Jim Crow rode on as the 1950s arrived.

Chapter 2

Erasing the Badge of Inferiority

Segregated Interstate Transport on the Ground and
in the Courts, 1941–1960

The years after *Morgan* were characterized by the interplay between activist challenges to Jim Crow and court decisions at the local, state, and
national levels. In the years before *Brown v. Board,* courts heard a number
of important cases, the roots of which can be traced back even before Irene
Morgan's 1946 arrest.[1] Courts need litigants in order to have cases, but
oftentimes litigants get lost in the celebration of court decisions. Before
the Freedom Rides, the courts had to sort out some of the questions raised
in *Morgan,* subsequent cases usually raising yet more questions. Despite
being an architect of the Journey of Reconciliation, George Houser has
maintained that "at the time of our 1947 project, we did not pay a lot of
attention to court opinions, other than the Irene Morgan decision." The
Journey was a "direct action program with a Court decision to back us up.
Conrad Lynn was [a] lawyer and we talked about the Commerce Clause,
but did not put much emphasis on an analysis."[2] Whatever the situation in
1947, the role of the courts would take on tremendous significance for a
great number of people in the 1950s.

"An Engine of History": Norvell Lee, Elmer Henderson, and the Courts

After the Journey of Reconciliation, Jim Crow transport receded from the
national consciousness, if it had ever been there in the first place. This does
not mean, however, that the issue of fighting Jim Crow—on buses and in
terminals, in restaurants and restrooms—ever lost its place in the minds
of activists. When the Fellowship of Reconciliation and CORE chose not

to challenge the sentences of the four Chapel Hill activists, they did so because they were afraid that theirs was not the perfect case to present before a court. While morally and legally the arrestees were in the right, the architects of the challenge knew that tactically they could not afford to present a case that would not solidify the *Morgan* decision. The time Rustin, Felmet, and Roodenko spent on the chain gang was worth avoiding the risk of losing at the appellate level and setting their cause back instead of moving it forward.

The dictates of *Plessy* had eroded in the arena of interstate transportation since at least the late 1930s. *Mitchell v. United States,* for example, presented the case of a black passenger holding a first-class ticket in 1937 who had been denied a Pullman seat even though it was unoccupied and available to white patrons. The railroad had set aside a specific number of Pullman cars for blacks, and once that number was filled, even blacks possessing the proper tickets had to accept second-class accommodations.[3]

The appellant, Arthur Mitchell, a black congressman from Chicago, had been refused his place on the Pullman car in Arkansas, on the Chicago, Rock Island & Pacific Railway. In 1941, when his case reached the Supreme Court, Franklin D. Roosevelt's solicitor general, Francis Biddle, sided with Mitchell against the Interstate Commerce Commission (ICC), even though the solicitor general's office would normally support the agency. The court ruled in Mitchell's favor in a unanimous majority, Chief Justice Charles Evans Hughes announcing its decision on April 28, 1941.[4] The Court declared, "If facilities are provided, substantial equality of treatment of persons traveling under like conditions cannot be refused." The Court thus overturned the lower court's decree and remanded it for further deliberations.[5] The Court did not, however, base its decision on constitutional grounds, but rather on the fact that Mitchell had paid for a first-class fare but had been forced to ride in a second-class car.[6] It would take the *Morgan* decision and subsequent cases to force a wedge into the constitutionality of Jim Crow in interstate transportation.

One of the cases that FOR and CORE hoped might reinforce *Morgan* was that of Norvell Lee. Lee's greatest fame stemmed not from his fight against Jim Crow, but from his fisticuffs in the squared circle. Lee, a U.S. Army veteran and a Howard University alumnus, had fought for Howard's varsity boxing squad after only a few sparring rounds in the military. In 1948 he was an alternate for the U.S. Olympic boxing team as a heavyweight, and in 1952 he won an Olympic gold medal in the light-heavyweight division. By that time he also had three Golden Gloves and two Amateur Athletic Union titles. He fought on the U.S. Pan-American Games teams in 1951 and 1955, the latter year winning a silver medal in his final performance for the United States. He would later chair the Washington, D.C., boxing commission and serve as chief judge on the executive committee of the World Boxing Association. These exploits would earn him induction into both the Howard University Athletics Hall of Fame and the Washington, D.C., Boxing Hall of Fame.[7] However, on September 14, 1948, near Clifton Forge, Virginia, local train and police authorities did not see a boxing champion standing before them, but a black man who refused to acquiesce to Jim Crow.

Lee, who lived in Eagle Rock, Virginia, was arrested on a charge of failing to take a seat assigned to him on a Chesapeake and Ohio Train near Clifton Forge, in Allegheny County. On September 13, the day before his arrest, Lee had purchased a ticket from Clifton Forge to Covington, sat in the white section of the train, and refused to move when asked, riding in the white section from Clifton Forge to the end of his journey. The next day, Lee purchased a ticket from Covington to Clifton Forge and again took a seat in the front section of a whites-only car in which there were both black and white passengers. The conductor ordered Lee to change his seat. Lee refused to do so. When the conductor called the sheriff, Lee got off the train and asked for and was granted a refund on his ticket to Clifton Forge. He then asked for a new ticket, this one covering the journey from Covington to Washington, D.C., in its entirety. When he boarded the train again, this time with an interstate ticket, the sheriff arrested Lee for violating section 3983 of the Virginia State Code, similar to section 4097dd, which the U.S. Supreme Court had invalidated in the *Morgan* decision. The trial judge found Lee guilty and fined him five dollars plus court costs. Lee appealed the decision to the Circuit Court of Allegheny County, pleaded not guilty, and waived his right to a jury trial. Allegheny County Court judge Earl L. Abbott found Lee guilty and fined him twenty-five dollars.[8]

Was Lee's challenge intentional? Did he plan to challenge Jim Crow? We do not know. If he did, he seems to have acted on his own. But one can surmise that a Howard-educated army veteran who had been an alternate for the U.S. boxing team was well aware of exactly what he was doing. That he knew to purchase an interstate ticket when initially challenged by authorities lends further credence to the speculation that he understood the *Morgan* decision and was perhaps even aware of the Journey of Reconciliation. That Lee carried his protest through to the Virginia Supreme Court is further evidence that his determination and pugnacity did not necessarily stop at the turnbuckles. In any case, by the time the case reached the high court of Virginia, Lee knew the ramifications of his challenge, and in that court he achieved his desired outcome.

On September 7, 1949, a week short of a year after the arrest, Justice C. Vernon Spratley presented the opinion of the Virginia Supreme Court of Appeals, reversing the lower court's judgment and dismissing the case against Lee. The question at hand was "whether the appellant, while traveling as an interstate passenger, on a railroad engaged in interstate commerce, 'did unlawfully fail to take a seat assigned to him *pursuant to the segregation law of the State of Virginia.*' The validity of the segregation law is directly brought into question."[9] The court believed that the law was clearly invalid. Spratley pointed out the similarity of the code under which Lee had been convicted to that which Irene Morgan had challenged. The court also held that it was irrelevant whether or not the actual train upon which Lee rode was only traveling within Virginia's borders (he would have to change trains in order to get to Washington), as the purpose of his trip was interstate travel. The court invoked *Morgan* specifically before reaching its conclusion:

> The federal courts in recent years have uniformly held invalid state statutes requiring segregation of the races in interstate commerce as contrary to the commerce clause of the United States Constitution, and have upheld statutes requiring equality of treatment of white and colored passengers in interstate commerce as constitutional and in accord with national policy. . . . We can see no valid distinction between segregation in buses and railroad coaches. Virginia Code, section 3983 is obviously subject to the same objections which caused the Supreme Court to invalidate Code, section 4097dd. There is no reasonable legal distinction between the two section(s). If one is invalid as to the segregation of the white and colored races in interstate commerce, the other is necessarily invalid to the same extent.[10]

And with that, the court reversed the lower court decision. Lee had won his case.

The decision drew a great deal of attention in civil rights circles. In an October 12, 1949, letter to George Houser, Martin A. Martin of Richmond's Hill, Martin & Robinson Law Firm assessed the significance of the case. It was the opinion of the firm, Martin wrote, that the Lee decision would prove to "have wider implications in interracial travel than any case decided by" the Virginia Supreme Court, other than *Morgan* and one other. The other case in question involved Lottie E. Taylor, who had recently been arrested and charged with violating a disorderly conduct statute, which the court had then ruled could not apply on interstate travel. One of the most important elements of Lee's case for the Virginia lawyers was the fact that the Virginia high court, "contrary to the decision of the Supreme Court of North Carolina," had decided that a person holding an interstate ticket could not be convicted for violating state segregation laws even if the particular conveyance upon which he rode was traveling intrastate. Martin quoted Stratley's decision, which determined that "it is the character of the journey, not the character of the train which determines his status."[11]

Houser and others believed that the *Lee* decision might have ramifications across the South, "since a precedent is now set."[12] Even into the mid-1950s, the *Lee* case was on the minds of Houser and others. In a May 5, 1950, letter ("typed on a moving train without benefit of an eraser") to Sue E. Watts of Jacksonville, Florida, who had written FOR regarding the current state of the laws on interstate transport, Houser still seemed upbeat about the decision.[13]

Watts, a white woman, had written asking about an incident in which she was traveling with a black friend on the weekend before Easter 1951. Traveling from Jacksonville, Florida, to Asheville, North Carolina, they were forbidden to ride in the same coach together. She wrote, "We *thought* that it was illegal to segregate on interstate travel." She hoped Houser could clarify.[14] Houser agreed that the *Morgan* decision appeared to outlaw segregation on interstate buses. However, he acknowledged that state courts still upheld different standards and that he already anticipated the need for more action, as questions remained as to just what the Supreme Court's decision would mean in the long run. One worry he had was that court decisions to that point had only addressed state actions: "Therefore it might be legal for the company itself to say that segregation was their ruling. They would have to enforce it without state aid and without police power." Houser's prescription should come as no surprise: he believed that "the only way a clear decision on" these questions of gaps in the meaning (or practice) of the law could be attained was "for an increasing number of Negroes and whites to refuse to abide by segregation on interstate travel." He felt that "at the very least . . . white people and Negroes should raise the question in the minds of company officials by asking questions about seating arrangements." He did point out that with regard to Pullman passage at least, "the law is very clear."[15]

Houser was well-aware that direct action challenge to the realities of segregation in interstate transport was an ongoing process, with groups such as CORE and even the occasionally reluctant NAACP at the forefront. And in some cases the courts had to intervene and thus continue to clarify the meaning of the law. A U.S. Court of Appeals decision in Cincinnati in late 1949 had addressed the question of bus-company segregation policy. Basing its decision on *Morgan,* the court ruled that the Southern Bus Lines requirement that Elizabeth Whiteside change her seat as soon as her bus crossed from Ohio into Kentucky was "a breach of the uniformity which, under the *Morgan* case, is a test of the burden placed upon interstate commerce." The NAACP had brought the case after Whiteside's forcible ejection from a bus traveling from St. Louis to Paducah, Kentucky, in May 1946.[16]

However, cases such as Whiteside's and Lee's would prove secondary in comparison with a case that the U.S. Supreme Court heard in October 1949. Elmer W. Henderson was not an Olympic boxer, and he did not take an especially dramatic stance against Jim Crow. His challenge stemmed from an incident on a Southern Railway train traveling from Washington, D.C., to Atlanta back in 1942, far before Irene Morgan's challenge, back in the era when Wilson Head and Bayard Rustin had made their seemingly quixotic solo challenges to segregated transportation. However, the case that would eventually become *Henderson v. United States et al.* proved vitally important on the journey to end Jim Crow on trains, planes, and buses.[17]

Henderson, a Baltimore native, possessed a bachelor's degree from Morgan College and a master's in sociology from the University of Chicago. He was a field representative for the Fair Employment Practices Committee (FEPC), serving as the head of Region VI, based in Chicago.[18] He was traveling to Birmingham to help prepare local FEPC hearings when he left his first-class Pullman car to head to the dining car for dinner on Sunday, May 17, 1942.[19] It was approximately 5:30 when the first dinner call was sounded as the train traveled through Virginia.[20] In the dining car, the practice was to keep two tables at the end reserved for black patrons, unless there was an overflow of white diners, which was the case on this particular day. Curtains separated the conditionally black tables from the rest, and when there were black diners, those curtains were drawn shut. They remained open if white patrons used them. When Henderson arrived for dinner, the car was full to the point that there were white patrons at one but not both of these tables. The dining-car steward would not seat Henderson in the extra seat next to the white diners but instead offered to serve him in his Pullman car at no additional charge. Henderson declined, and the steward offered to send for him when the seats were unoccupied. However, no word arrived, even though Henderson returned to the dining car twice before it was detached at nine o'clock that night.[21]

Incensed, Henderson took action upon his return to Washington. He contacted a black lawyer, Belford V. Lawson Jr., a native of Roanoke who had attended the University of Michigan and Yale Law School. Lawson was well-known in the capital's black community and in 1938 had won an important Supreme Court decision prohibiting federal courts from enjoining peaceful picketing against employers who engaged in discriminatory hiring practices.[22] Upon hearing of Henderson's situation, Lawson took the matter to the executive council of Alpha Phi Alpha, the oldest black fraternity in the nation, for which Lawson had served as general counsel since 1937, asking for their support. His fraternity brothers agreed that Henderson's was a worthwhile case, and with their pledge of organizational support, Lawson filed a complaint with the Interstate Commerce Commission on October 10, 1942, charging that the Southern Railway had violated the nondiscrimination clause of the Interstate Commerce Act.[23] The relevant section of that act made it unlawful for a railroad engaged in interstate commerce "to subject any particular person . . . to any undue or unreasonable prejudice or disadvantage in any respect whatsoever."[24]

The case took some time to wind its way through the court system. A division of the ICC found that Henderson had been subject to "undue and unreasonable prejudice" but that such prejudice had been the result of bad judgment on the behalf of an employee, not of railroad policy, and so the ICC did not enter an order as to future practices. A three-judge panel of the U.S. District Court for Maryland found that the railroad's general practice violated the nondiscrimination clause of the Interstate Commerce Act.[25] In February 1946, the district court remanded the case for further proceedings. Acting quickly, the Southern Railway Company announced that effective March 1, 1946, there would be new rules in effect. The rules would provide for the reservation of ten tables with four seats each for white passengers and one table with four seats for black passengers. In both cases, the tables would be "exclusively and unconditionally" set aside for the patrons of the respective races. Between the lone black table and the others would stand the curtain, to be drawn at mealtimes.[26] The full commission of the ICC looked at the new regulations, believed them to be in accordance with the Interstate Commerce Act, and thus felt that no new order was necessary.

With this ICC decision not to act further, Henderson's legal team returned to the U.S. District Court of Maryland and the same three judges from whom they had found relief earlier, asking that the ICC's order be set aside and that a cease-and-desist order be issued to the Southern Railway. With one dissent, the judges refused to grant the order. The case went to the Supreme Court on direct appeal.[27] On April 3, 1950, the Court heard arguments. In this case brought against the ICC, an agent of the United States, by a Roosevelt-era government employee, the U.S. government, specifically the Truman administration's Justice Department, filed a brief and presented oral arguments for Henderson. The Truman administration had begun its policy of filing amicus briefs in the 1948 case *Shelley v. Kramer,* one of the Court's four restrictive covenants cases.[28]

Writing in the *New York Times* more than a half century after the court heard arguments in *Henderson v. United States,* Anthony Lewis argued that the government's entering the case on Henderson's behalf made the case "an engine of history." The Antitrust Division of the Justice Department had defended the ICC up until the case reached the Supreme Court, but the solicitor general's office took an interest in *Henderson,* and a lawyer of "extraordinary skill and vision" became involved. Philip Elman was a longtime assistant to the solicitor general, who in 1949 was Philip Perlman. Elman urged Perlman to "tell the Supreme Court that the dining car segregation was indefensible—to confess error, as lawyers say."[29] Perlman agreed, and the government took an active role on Henderson's behalf in October 1949, when the Court received the documentation for the case. Elman wrote a sixty-six-page brief in which he asserted that segregation "is universally understood as imposing . . . a badge of inferiority" on blacks. The curtain on the Southern dining cars therefore served as a "naked and unadorned" symbol of "the caste system which segregation manifests and fosters."[30] The brief thus urged the Court to find that the segregated dining setup, however its appearance may have been shifted, violated the Interstate Commerce Act.[31]

Lewis is undoubtedly correct in his assertion that the government's intercession on Henderson's behalf was at minimum an act of symbolic power, the federal government actively stepping in on behalf of those on the wrong end of segregation's divide. Unlike its predecessors and several of its successors, the Truman administration showed a notable, and at times noble, commitment to civil rights—advocating desegregating interstate transportation, for example. While Truman may not have always been able to live up in action to his administration's symbolic and rhetorical civil rights stances, he still took such stances at a time when doing so was utterly unexpected and courted political disaster. To pinpoint the government's intervention in *Henderson* as the point at which the "engine of change" was revved, however, is to misunderstand much of the case and the history surrounding it. Symbolically, perhaps, the government's involvement allows for a good story. In point of fact, however, the Court's ruling stemmed far more from both its own recent history and the circumstances of the case before it.

The Court announced its 8-0 decision, Justice Tom Campbell Clark having taken no part in hearing the case, on June 5, 1950. Justice Harold Hitz Burton, who wrote the opinion for the majority, had been born and raised in Massachusetts and educated at Bowdoin College and Harvard Law School. He rose to the Supreme Court as Truman's first appointee in 1945, after a highly successful career in Ohio law and politics that included serving as mayor of Cleveland and as a U.S. senator. The parallels between *Mitchell* and *Henderson* were "inescapable" for Burton and his brethren. The issue at stake, as in *Mitchell,* was "whether the railroad's current rules and practices cause passengers to be subject to undue or unreasonable prejudice or disadvantage in violation of" Section 3 (1) of the Interstate Commerce Act. They believed that those rules did:

> Where a dining car is available to passengers holding tickets entitling them to use it, each such passenger is equally entitled to its facilities in accordance with reasonable regulations. The denial of dining service to any such passenger by the rules before us subjects him to a prohibited disadvantage. Under the rules, only four Negro passengers may be served at one time and then only at the table reserved for Negroes. Other Negroes who present themselves are compelled to await a vacancy at that table, although there may be many vacancies elsewhere in the diner. The railroad thus refuses to extend to those passengers the use of its existing and unoccupied facilities. The rules impose a like deprivation upon white passengers whenever more than 40 of them seek to be served at the same time and the table reserved for Negroes is vacant. . . . We need not multiply instances in which these rules sanction unreasonable discriminations. The curtains, partitions and signs emphasize the

artificiality of a difference in treatment which serves only to call attention to a racial classification of passengers holding identical tickets and using the same public dining facility.[32]

While the government presented a passionate brief before the Court, so too did many others, not least Lawson and his legal team. Rather than focusing solely on the particular case of discrimination before the Court, Lawson explicitly called for the Court to overturn *Plessy*. The end result of *Henderson* in a sense did exactly that, declaring Jim Crow on interstate transport conveyances null and void. *Henderson* marked an important moment in the gradual chipping away of *Plessy*, which included a number of prominent cases that Burton cited in the majority opinion, including *Missouri ex. Rel Gaines v. Canada* (1938); *Mitchell* (1941); *Morgan* (1946); and *McLaurin v. Oklahoma State Regents*, a 9-0 decision that the Court announced on the same day as *Henderson*. Although it was not cited in *Henderson*, the Court announced its decision in *Sweatt v. Painter* on the same day, again by unanimous majority. June 5, 1950, thus marked a major day in the legal history of American civil rights.[33] But if the 1950s began momentously, it would soon be clear that court pronouncements were a necessary but not sufficient condition for the attainment of full civil rights in the area of transportation and just about everywhere else.

The Era of *Brown:* Challenge and Response

In light of the recent wave of unanimous decisions supporting civil rights and eroding *Plessy* to a nub, sympathetic observers were justified in thinking that the Court's decision in *Brown v. Board of Education* would both turn out in their favor and prove to be a turning point in American race relations. They were correct on both counts, though perhaps not in the way that they anticipated.[34]

In his classic work on massive resistance, Numan Bartley argues the importance of *Brown* in accelerating white intransigence toward civil rights. At minimum, the decision "focused race politics in the South." Initially, the response from Dixie "encompassed a broad spectrum of opinion, but much of the political power structure rallied to the defense of the southern past."[35]

In the year between the 1954 decision and the 1955 implementation, the South witnessed a range of responses: "Border states used the interlude to make constructive preparations for compliance; the Deep South

entrenched itself yet further."[36] Virginia first developed the most coher-
ent policy of massive resistance to the specific question of school desegregation. However, throughout the South, especially in Mississippi and
Alabama, Citizens' Councils sprang up and spread like kudzu. Politicians
fulminated, newspapermen wrung their print-stained hands, and slowly
many Southerners mobilized against what they expected to be an impending onslaught of integrationist dictates coming from the Court, the federal
government, the NAACP, and waves of activists. The fact that many of those
demanding change were outsiders—and, in the imagination of politicians
across the South, communists—only exacerbated oppositionist sentiment.

Activists across the country agreed, and in the wake of *Henderson* they
hoped to gain the support of the Interstate Commerce Commission. The
ICC began to hear of more and more violations of the Supreme Court's
mandates. James Peck had already taken action to force the hand of the
Greyhound bus company, becoming a shareholder in the Greyhound Corporation in order to place a proposal on the 1950 shareholder meeting's
agenda: "A Recommendation that Management Consider the Adviseabil-
ity of Abolishing the Segregated Seating System in the South." In 1950,
the Securities and Exchange Commission (SEC) had declared Peck's to be
a proper subject for action, but Greyhound maintained that the SEC decision came too late to place the item on the meeting's agenda.[37]

Peck submitted his proposal again in 1951. Upon reconsideration, the
SEC reversed itself, upholding Greyhound's refusal to place the item on
its 1951 meeting agenda. In a letter to Merrill Buffington, the secretary
of Greyhound, Harry Keller, the assistant director of the SEC's Division
of Corporation Finance, wrote, "Normally, stockholders in our opinion
should not be denied the right of making suggestions and recommenda-
tions for consideration by the management of a company and of having
their fellow stockholders vote on such matters." After further consideration, however, the SEC backed away from this basic premise: "We realize
that some proposals may be improper . . . particularly if they are in fact
urged for propaganda purposes or to require the management in effect to
take consensus of stockholders in respect to what is essentially a general
political, social or economic problem."[38]

Given his individual history of putting his body on the line for civil
rights, this formulation, reducing his aim to "propaganda purposes," severely understates Peck's commitment to racial justice. Furthermore,
whether it was a general "political, social or economic problem," segregation was a problem that the Supreme Court had strongly declared unconsti-

tutional on interstate conveyances. Peck clearly believed that addressing a constitutional matter would be in the interest of the company and of some concern to its shareholders. He pressed forward. After the SEC's decision, Peck obtained an opinion from Nathan Kagan, an attorney who specialized in stockholder issues. Kagan believed that the SEC was in error and that Peck's proposal was a proper subject for action. Conrad Lynn filed suit on Peck's behalf. Greyhound itself had some powerful representation, in the form of Sullivan & Cromwell, a firm that represented, among others, John Foster Dulles.[39]

Peck did not gain the relief he sought. In early 1952, Conrad Lynn presented a petition to the court of appeals on Peck's behalf. Prior to this, Peck had attempted to secure a preliminary injunction preventing Greyhound from holding its shareholders meeting unless Peck's item was included on the agenda. The court, however, ruled that Peck had not exhausted the administrative remedies suggested by the SEC.[40] After going through those options, Lynn brought the case before the Second Circuit Court of Appeals, his petition outlining the case, explaining why the SEC was in error, and generally making an impassioned plea for remedy.[41] The court refused to grant his request.

Not easily daunted, Peck moved from the courts back to the grassroots, where he felt most comfortable. Despite his inability to convince a court to intervene on his behalf, Peck organized a group of sympathetic stockholders, who had presumably purchased their stock primarily for the purpose of challenging the company's segregationist policies. Peck again dusted off his statement and adjusted it for the fact that he now had thirteen stockholders owning 282 shares.[42] With some fifty thousand stockholders who together held ten million shares, Greyhound was likely not especially worried.[43] Nonetheless, if the company refused to allow the proposal to be heard at the May 20, 1952, meeting at Greyhound corporate headquarters in Wilmington, Delaware, Peck's group would make a procedural attempt to get their plea heard. Since the question was not on the printed agenda, they raised it under Point 3, the final point of the meeting, which was "to transact such other business as may properly come before the meeting."[44] Their proposal fell on deaf ears, and Greyhound buses continued to allow local practices to prevail throughout most of the South.

By the end of 1952, the *Pittsburgh Courier* expressed fears that "because of indifference, ignorance, and insubordination," the Court's ban of Jim Crow seating was under siege. The *Courier* sent a reporter to conduct tests throughout the Upper South. He found that segregation prevailed.[45]

In May 1953, a young woman from Asheville, North Carolina, engaged in her own test of Southern buses when she traveled from Georgia to Alabama. Talladega College senior Mary Weaver emerged unscathed. In the May 16, 1953, *Courier,* Weaver published an account of her experience, which had first appeared in the *Talladega Student,* her college newspaper.

She had begun her trip in Atlanta, sitting down in the back half of a near-empty bus. However, after the bus began to fill up, a number of white people sat behind her. The bus driver tried to get her to move. Weaver refused. The bus driver explained that he could not have white people sitting behind her. She responded by telling the driver, "If you force me to move I must ask your name because I am going from Georgia to Alabama and so long as I'm going from one state to another, I'm supposed to be able to sit anywhere I please." She was frightened when the driver instructed her to "wait a minute" while he left the bus. The driver soon returned, said nothing, and sat down and began to drive. By this point she could hear the whispers. There were still seats available—one next to her, one next to a black soldier, and some at the very rear of the bus, all places that would be considered off-limits to most whites versed in regional tradition and practice—but Weaver wondered what would happen if more whites got on the bus.[46]

Her answer came twenty-seven miles from Heflin, Alabama. An elderly white man got on the bus, surveyed the situation, and chose to stand, at which point a young white soldier offered his seat and stood in the older man's stead. By that point, Weaver wrote, "the stares in my direction were so pointed that I decided it was time for me to go to sleep." She barely got settled in when the white soldier tapped her on the shoulder and asked her if she would move next to the black soldier. She instead told the white soldier that she did not mind if he sat in the vacant seat next to her. He responded pointedly, "Well you may not mind, but I do." Her response was equally emphatic: "Well, I'd rather not move."[47]

Another white passenger, to whom Weaver acidly referred to as "one of our country's defenders," chimed in by asking, "Who are you, some privileged character?" Her response was that she had the right to sit where she pleased on interstate buses. The man responded with a less than veiled threat: "If you are going as far as Birmingham we'll see about that." Weaver's only response was "O.K.!" She then fell asleep. Perhaps the remark about Birmingham had its desired effect. Or maybe while Weaver slumbered—remarkable in and of itself, under the circumstances—there was further coercion, but when Weaver awoke, the black soldier was sitting in the back, the white soldier having taken his place. In Anniston she had to change buses. There were no further incidents.[48] Anniston would not remain quiescent forever, and Birmingham would fulfill its promise as a place unfriendly to those who tested Jim Crow's resolve on interstate buses. But on that day, Mary Weaver won a small victory.

Clearly, Weaver was familiar with the various court rulings bolstering her right to travel as she pleased. A bright student at Talladega (she would go on to attend the University of Chicago Law School), Weaver was probably more aware of the state of the law than most Southerners, white or black, before the *Brown* decision crashed into the consciousness of almost every Southerner. Nonetheless, her largely forgotten bus ride marks a brave challenge in a region where to confront the status quo was to risk more than some time in jail and a fine. Her experience drew substantial attention in certain circles. Two days after the appearance of her story in the *Courier*, George Houser wrote her a letter in which he congratulated her for her "courage in standing up before the threats" that she described. He believed that "there were a few people on the bus who also secretly sided with you although they were probably afraid to speak up." He told Weaver how her experience reminded him of the 1947 Journey of Reconciliation. If she was not aware of the Journey when she took her stand, she became immersed in its history when Houser sent her a copy of "We Challenged Jim Crow." Clearly, the Journey was still on the minds of this core group of activists, who had never lost interest in the transportation issue. Using his letter as a recruitment pitch, Houser told Weaver about a summer workshop in Washington that year and asked if she knew of some students who would participate.[49]

Houser, Peck, and many other activists had clearly continued to push for an end to segregation on interstate conveyances. They helped with many of the court challenges, worked hard to keep transportation on the front burner of a number of organizations, and would keep working on the issue through to the Freedom Rides.

Houser was not the only correspondent to send congratulations to Weaver. In June 1953 the *Courier* excerpted a number of the supportive letters she had received from all over the country. Mrs. Thomasina W. Norford of Washington, D.C., wrote, "Well good for you! May this be the beginning of much activity by you along these lines until it will not be necessary. I admire your courage." Jauquin McCain of Patterson, New Jersey, told her that a number of individuals just like her had "engaged in similar challenges." Alonzo J. Perry, a freshman at Philadelphia's Lincoln University, itself a place known for producing leaders, in particular a number of Africans who were active in the African struggle against colonialism, wrote to say how much Weaver inspired him: "If we fail to bear our own burdens we shall find ourselves lost in a world of unstable equilibrium." The early and mid-1950s was a time when many in the black community were not sure how to react to the possibility of challenging segregation. On the question of interstate segregation, two more major events would take place largely in the courts before the terrain would be fertile enough for a more visible challenge to Jim Crow transport.

The Road to Boynton: The ICC and the Courts Lay Down the Law

Leaders at CORE, FOR, and the NAACP's Legal Defense Fund (LDF) exchanged a series of letters throughout 1954, as the ICC prepared to hear two cases that activists hoped would settle the question of where the federal government stood on Jim Crow on the roadways. In March 1954 Robert Carter, LDF assistant counsel, wrote to George Houser, telling him about the cases winding their way through the ICC system. The LDF had filed suit in hopes of getting the ICC to bar "segregation of Negroes in railroad coaches in interstate commerce, in waiting rooms, and restaurants." Carter and his associates believed that "the station and waiting room is a part of interstate commerce and, therefore is governed by the Interstate Commerce Act." He then entreated Houser not to take on any other cases—that is, to let the existing caseload work its way through the system before any other challenges to Jim Crow complicated the matter: "If we succeed in the ICC action, it will settle the proposition, certainly as far as the interstate carriers and the station waiting rooms etc. are concerned."[50]

In October Carter wrote to Billie Ames of the Congress of Racial Equality. Carter had heard that CORE was actively planning a challenge to Jim Crow on trains. In greater detail, he explained that the LDF had provided legal support for the Journey of Reconciliation, but he opined, "Insofar as trains and waiting rooms are concerned, there would seem to be little need for such a trip at the present time," given the challenges before the ICC. He was optimistic that the ICC would support the LDF requests and that the mandate would soon extend to bus facilities, including stations and waiting areas.[51]

While the NAACP believed it was important to let the current cases make their way to the proper tribunals before complicating matters with further tests, CORE, meanwhile, was anxious to test the facilities on the ground. However, in this case, CORE acceded to the desires of the NAACP and its teams of lawyers. Four days after Carter wrote to Ames, she replied: CORE too was optimistic about the prospects of a favorable decision from the ICC, and she noted that an amicus brief from the Justice Department would only help their cause. Given the circumstances, CORE agreed that it was unnecessary to conduct a trip at that time. However, she did disagree with Carter on one point: "[That] our purpose has been accomplished as soon as the Commission hands down a favorable decision. . . . A favorable decision . . . is not going to mean that white people are immediately going to start sitting in the back and the colored people in the front or that integrated eating will take place in depot restaurants. It may be years before this comes about."[52]

The Court's *Brown* decision had not ended the practice of segregation in the schools. *Henderson, Mitchell,* and *Morgan* had not ended discrimination either. Ames and the rest of the CORE staff were correct: while a favorable ruling before the ICC was vital, CORE would still have to engage in action to test the rulings and eventually make them valid. Ames knew this, and she informed Carter that CORE would eventually conduct a trip: "By riding interracially and refusing to comply with requests to move, we would dramatize and publicize the decision." Ames was in no position to be too firm with the NAACP, as she told Carter that her organization would require NAACP help in two important areas—arranging speaking engagements en route and providing legal support. The proposed ride would likely take place in either February or July 1955, assuming that the ICC ruled favorably around the first of the year.[53]

The Interstate Commerce Commission did rule in favor of disbanding Jim Crow in two cases that came down later than CORE or the NAACP had anticipated. On November 7, 1955, the ICC presented its rulings in *Keys v. Carolina Coach Co.* and *NAACP v. St. Louis–San Francisco Railway Co.*[54] Part of the reason for the delay was that the ICC wanted to pronounce judgment on both cases simultaneously. As had been the situation with *Brown, Keys* and *NAACP* both involved a number of challenges that were consolidated into one comprehensive case. The ICC was clear that *Brown v. Board* had a direct bearing on these cases. Using by now familiar arguments and language, the ICC finally and irrevocably struck down Jim Crow on trains, on buses, and in station waiting rooms, declaring Jim Crow regulations to be in violation of the antidiscrimination section of the

Interstate Commerce Act. The ICC did not, however, prohibit discrimination in privately owned and operated facilities in bus terminals or train stations. That would be a question for another day. The order would go into effect on January 10, 1956.

The implementation date was an important one, and it almost certainly helps to explain why there was no second Journey of Reconciliation in 1956 or 1957. For by early 1956, black residents of Montgomery, Alabama, were engaged in their own struggle against Jim Crow seating, albeit on local buses. It would have made little sense in the midst of the national drama of the Montgomery bus boycott to mount a challenge to Jim Crow, testing compliance with the ICC decision but perhaps muddying the national attention to Montgomery.

After Montgomery, there remained one final court challenge before the time would truly be right for the sort of test CORE had been envisioning since before *Brown*. While the ICC had ruled on segregation at bus and train facilities, the Supreme Court had not yet weighed in. It would do so in 1960, in the case of *Boynton v. Virginia*.

Setting the Stage: *Boynton v. Virginia*

In December 1958, Bruce Boynton, a Howard University law student, was traveling from Washington, D.C., to Selma, Alabama, for Christmas break. Boynton had always been precocious. He had graduated from high school when he was fourteen and received his degree from Fisk University when he was only eighteen, and on that chilly December night on the bus back to Alabama, he was a twenty-one-year-old in his last year of law school. He came from a family that had long been active in fighting for equal justice. Boynton's parents, Sam and Amelia, were, in the words of historian Frye Gaillard, "the most courageous civil rights activists in Selma."[55]

When his Trailways bus stopped at the crowded terminal in Richmond at about 10:40 at night, he went inside to try to get a sandwich and a cup of tea at the black lunch counter. That counter was too congested, however, so Boynton went to the white restaurant, where he sat at the counter to order his small meal. He simply wanted a bite to eat during a forty-minute layover on what would prove to be a long trip. The white waitress refused to serve Boynton, but he insisted on his right to be served as an interstate traveler. The waitress called her assistant manager, who told Boynton to leave the white portion of the restaurant. He could be served in the "colored" section. Police arrived and arrested the young law student, and the

Police Justice's Court of Richmond found him guilty and imposed a fine of ten dollars on the charge that he "unlawfully did remain on the premises of the Bus Terminal Restaurant of Richmond, Inc. after having been forbidden to do so."[56]

Initially, Martin A. Martin, the LDF cooperating lawyer in Richmond, took the case for Boynton. Martin would argue through the appellate courts that Boynton had been convicted in violation of the Commerce Clause, the Interstate Commerce Act, and the equal protection clauses of the Fourteenth Amendment. Martin made no effort to discern who owned the restaurant itself, which would prove to be an important question when the case reached the Supreme Court.[57]

Boynton lost his appeals before both the Hustings Court of Richmond and the Virginia Supreme Court, which held without opinion that Boynton's conviction "was plainly right." The U.S. Supreme Court granted certiorari "because of the serious federal questions raised concerning discrimination based on color."[58] The state of Virginia had initially failed to respond to the LDF brief on behalf of Boynton. This was an appeal based upon a state law, and so the U.S. Supreme Court could not rely upon any evidence that the Virginia Supreme Court had not considered. Traditionally, when a state does not respond to a brief, the Court directs its clerk to ask the state's lawyers to do so. Justice Frankfurter suggested that the clerk of the court ask the state lawyers to "deal with the intercorporate relationship" between the restaurant and Trailways. In this manner, the Supreme Court could tackle *Boynton* in the narrow way it preferred.[59]

By the spring of 1960, the LDF, from a strategic standpoint, had linked the Boynton case with a series of others related to the burgeoning sit-in movement that students had initiated across the South. In March 1960 Thurgood Marshall called a lawyer's conference at Howard University to map out a legal strategy for the sit-in cases and *Boynton*.[60] Bruce Boynton almost scuttled the situation by insisting that he was capable of defending himself, but he was persuaded to dump that idea, and everyone eventually agreed that Thurgood Marshall would argue the case before the Supreme Court. *Boynton* would be the last case Marshall argued for the Legal Defense Fund.[61]

The petition for certiorari that Marshall and the LDF presented asked that the court consider the case based on two questions: first, whether Boynton's conviction was invalid based on the Commerce Clause; and second, whether it violated the Due Process and Equal Protection clauses of the Fourteenth Amendment.[62] However, based largely on Frankfurter's initiative, and with the eventual help of the Justice Department, the Court drew a link between the restaurant and Trailways.[63] And so Justice Hugo Black's opinion revealed that the Court had incorporated a third question:

> Ordinarily we limit our review to the questions presented in an application for certiorari. We think there are persuasive reasons, however, why this case should be decided, if it can, on the Interstate Commerce Act contention raised in the Virginia courts. Discrimination because of color is the core of the two broad constitutional questions presented to us by petitioner, just as it is the core of the Interstate Commerce Act question presented to the Virginia courts. Under these circumstances we think it appropriate not to reach the constitutional questions but to proceed at once to the statutory issue.[64]

Black went on to assert that the decisions in *Mitchell* and *Henderson*, though they dealt explicitly with train facilities, gave the court "no reason to doubt that the reason underlying" those decisions "would compel the same decision as to the unlawfulness of discrimination in transportation services against interstate passengers in terminals and terminal restaurants owned or operated or controlled by interstate carriers."[65] In Boynton's case, the interstate carrier, Trailways, did not own, operate, or directly control the restaurant. However:

> If the bus carrier has volunteered to make terminal and restaurant facilities and services available to its interstate passengers as a regular part of their transportation, and the terminal and restaurant have acquiesced and cooperated in this undertaking, the terminal and restaurant must perform these services without discriminations prohibited by the [Interstate Commerce] Act. In the performance of these services under such conditions the terminal and restaurant stand in the place of the bus company in the performance of its transportation obligations.[66]

The contract between the bus company and the restaurant showed that the primary purpose of the restaurant was to provide service for Trailways passengers, many of whom were engaged in interstate transportation and thus protected by the Interstate Commerce Act. Black noted that "interstate passengers have to eat, and the very terms of the lease of the built-in restaurant space in this terminal constitute recognition of the essential need of interstate passengers to be able to get food conveniently on their journey and an undertaking by the restaurant to fulfill that need." In contrast to the claims of Virginia's lawyers, who had asserted that Boynton's refusal to move put him "unlawfully" on the premises, Boynton had a "federal right to remain in the white portion of the restaurant. He was there under 'authority of law'—the Interstate Commerce Act—and it was error for the Supreme Court of Virginia to affirm his conviction."[67]

Black went on to clarify that this decision did not mean that "every time a bus stops at a wholly independent roadside restaurant," the Interstate Commerce Act was in effect. Instead, reflecting the narrow approach it had chosen, the Court had decided "only this case, on its facts, where circumstances show that the terminal and restaurant operate as an integral part of the bus carrier's transportation service for interstate passengers."[68]

Unlike some previous cases, this one did not meet with unanimity. Missourian Charles Evans Whittaker wrote a dissent, with which Texan Tom Campbell Clark joined. Both thought that the granting of certiorari was dubious and that the Court had not proved the connection between the restaurant and the bus company. Nonetheless, the Court's 7-2 decision broke down one of the final barriers that activists had been waiting for the Court to address. The time was ripe to test what the Court had decided. George Houser, Billie Ames, and the rest of the CORE staff were more than willing to step into the breach.

Chapter 3

"The Last Supper"

Preparing for the Freedom Rides

With the announcement of the *Boynton* decision, the foundation for the re-newed challenge to Jim Crow on the highways that CORE had envisioned since the Journey of Reconciliation ended was in place. Many Americans remained unaware of these court proceedings. Most knew about *Brown* and were aware of the civil rights struggle going on in the South. But even as the Freedom Rides progressed, *Time* magazine saw the need to clarify some questions for its readers. Engaging "three questions of law," *Time* revealed the clear legal justification behind the Riders' challenge.[1] That the law was clear, of course, did not mean that it was enforced across the South, and testing enforcement was a major component of the Freedom Ride that began in May 1961. Not only did the Riders want to see whether Southern authorities adhered to *Boynton* and the rest of the body of deci-sions in their favor (they were dubious about such a prospect), but they also wanted to determine whether the new administration of John F. Ken-nedy would enforce the law, ensuring that the Supreme Court's decisions carried weight.

"Human Dignity Is the Most Important Thing in My Life": Planning Freedom Ride '61

On February 1, 1961, James Farmer became the national director of the Congress of Racial Equality. Farmer had been born in Marshall, Texas, in 1920. He attended impoverished segregated schools where he excelled despite the lack of any real challenges. At the age of fourteen, he enrolled at historically black Wiley College in Marshall. Farmer's father taught phi-losophy at Wiley, where he was the only faculty member who held a Ph.D.

After majoring in chemistry, Farmer moved on to Howard (following his father, who took a position at the School of Religion), where his graduate work focused on the relationship between religion and race. After he graduated from Howard, Farmer began his civil rights career in earnest as a founding member of CORE in 1942.[2]

Farmer's 1961 ascension was the final stage in a restructuring of CORE that had begun on December 4, 1960. James Robinson, CORE's former executive secretary, now became its membership director. Marvin Rich maintained his position as community relations director, and Gordon Carey remained the field director. All three white men would report directly to Farmer. The field secretaries working under Carey were the same in the new organization: James McCain, Thomas Gaither, Genevieve Hughes, and Joseph Perkins. Hughes, the only white field secretary, was also the only woman in the organizational hierarchy before or after the restructuring.[3] CORE reconfigured largely to gain the benefits of Farmer's visibility as a national spokesperson and perhaps in part because of an implicit understanding among CORE's leadership that the organization ought to have a black director. According to August Meier and Elliott Rudwick, "Securing Farmer was part of a broad effort to make CORE better known and give it a more important role in the civil rights movement."[4]

Even before the change in leadership, Gordon Carey and Thomas Gaither had discussed the possibility of another trip along the lines of the Journey of Reconciliation. On a bus traveling between their Southern field offices and New York, the two men had been stranded for twelve hours at a bus station on the New Jersey Turnpike. The only reading material they had between them was a copy of Louis Fischer's biography of Mohandas Gandhi. As they discussed the *Boynton* decision and read about Gandhi's March to the Sea, they developed the idea of analogous action in the South, which soon evolved into the notion of another bus trip along the lines of the Journey.[5] With Farmer's promotion, as well as institutional memories of the Journey and numerous aborted discussions, work toward a new multistate challenge accelerated. In February 1961, Carey raised the idea in a CORE council meeting in Lexington, Kentucky. The topic was buried amid an array of ephemera, however, and the CORE hierarchy did not make any concrete decisions. One participant recalled, "To all of us, it seemed like another appropriate application of the direct action approach."[6]

Unlike the Journey of Reconciliation, this proposed ride would challenge segregated bus terminal facilities as well as segregation on the buses themselves. Another difference was that this trip would cross into the Deep

South. Farmer "thought it a capital idea, a superb answer to the question 'What next?'"[7] He would later recall that in his first days as national director of CORE, he found letters on his desk from blacks in states such as Mississippi, Alabama, Georgia, and Louisiana "who complained that when they tried to sit on the front seats of the buses or to use the bus terminal facilities, they were beaten, or jailed, or thrown out, or all three."[8] As noted earlier, he did not believe that the new action should be called a Journey of Reconciliation, but a "Freedom Ride."[9]

With the new action appropriately named, Rich, Carey, McCain, and Farmer began to make plans. Jim Robinson did not take part in this organizing with any zeal; CORE's restructuring disappointed him because he had been demoted. Farmer sympathized with Robinson and understood why he did not embrace the new program, but he also knew that CORE had to adapt to new realities. CORE had changed, and the Freedom Ride would represent its biggest challenge yet.[10]

On February 1, 1961, Farmer announced CORE's plans before a small audience, but his words were little noted. In early March, CORE issued a letter announcing "Freedom Ride 1961": "a dramatic move to complete the integration of bus service and accommodations in the Deep South."[11] The planned trip would begin in Washington sometime around May 1 and end in New Orleans on May 17, the seventh anniversary of the *Brown* decision. Its goals were comprehensive: "The Freedom Ride will dramatize the recent Supreme Court decision banning segregation of interstate passengers in lunchroom facilities operated as an integral part of a bus terminal. We will challenge every form of segregation met by the bus passenger. In this highly dramatic nonviolent action project we plan to inspire local nonviolent action against all forms of the segregated policy. Along the way we will make numerous overnite stops and speak before interested college and civic groups."[12]

CORE wanted "to make bus desegregation a reality instead of merely an approved legal doctrine." "By demonstrating that a group can ride buses in a desegregated manner even in the Deep South," it hoped to encourage "other people to do likewise."[13] CORE would organize a training session in Washington, D.C., prior to the group's departure. All participants had to be committed to nonviolence. CORE's press release underlined a warning to potential participants: they "must be willing to accept threats, violence and jail sentences."[14] The proposed itinerary would cover Washington, D.C.; Richmond, Petersburg, and Lynchburg, Virginia; Greensboro and Charlotte, North Carolina; Rock Hill and Sumter, South Carolina; Augusta and Atlanta, Georgia; Birmingham and Montgomery, Alabama; Jackson, Mississippi; and New Orleans, Louisiana. CORE would cover expenses except for incidentals. The number of participants, who would travel by Greyhound and Trailways buses, would be "very limited."[15]

A later press release indicated that the Freedom Ride had drawn its inspiration from the Journey of Reconciliation. The 1961 effort, however, would differ from its predecessor in three important ways. First, it would "penetrate . . . into the Deep South." Second, it would challenge segregation not only aboard buses but also in eating facilities, terminals, waiting rooms, rest stops, and so forth. And third, participants who were arrested would remain in jail rather than accept bail or the payment of fines. Replacement teams might be prepared to pick up where arrestees left off.[16]

Within a few days of the issuance of the initial letters and press release about the Freedom Ride, Gordon Carey began sending letters to individuals in the cities on the itinerary, asking them for their support, welcoming applicants to participate in the Ride, offering the Riders for speaking engagements, planning rallies, and so forth.[17] By mid-March preparations for the Ride were in full swing.

The process of recruiting participants had to move quickly. Once CORE had sent its letter to civil rights organizations, churches, schools, and sympathetic individuals throughout the country, it followed up with a simple application form.[18] The application briefly explained the nature of the trip and the importance of accepting "violence without retaliation" and asked for basic information, including the civil rights groups to which an applicant belonged and his or her experiences with nonviolent action.[19] CORE's Marvin Rich also sent a letter to Harold Keith, the managing editor of the *Pittsburgh Courier*. He reminded Keith that on the 1947 Journey, the *Courier* had sent reporter Ollie Stewart along as a correspondent and welcomed another reporter to accompany the 1961 journey.[20]

Applications poured in from across the country, many from established civil rights workers. Jim Peck sent in an application from New York City. In lieu of two references, Peck, a familiar figure to CORE's leadership, wrote "known."[21] Peck had participated in the Journey of Reconciliation in 1947, but evidently he thought that his work was not done in 1961. Even James Farmer filled out an application.[22]

Farmer and Peck were the first two applicants for the Ride.[23] Many others followed. Perhaps the most thorough and heartfelt application came from John Lewis, a student at Nashville's American Baptist Theological Seminary (ABT). Lewis had established himself as one of the standard bearers of the Nashville protest movement.[24] The Nashville movement had not drawn the headlines that the Greensboro Four had garnered in February 1960, but it had been equally important in developing the new decade's new phase of civil rights activism. In his application, Lewis matter-of-factly asserted that he had been arrested five times since February 1960 and that he was a "student leader" in the Nashville Student Leadership Council. He was to graduate from the seminary in June, but he believed that the Freedom Ride represented "much more of [a] challenge to what I believe than a degree." As important as an education was to him, "at this time, human dignity is the most important thing in my life." Indeed, his decision to participate in the Freedom Ride represented "the most important decision in my life, to decide to give up all if necessary, that justice and freedom might come to the Deep South."[25]

On April 25, 1961, CORE sent out acceptances to successful applicants. Freedom Ride 1961 would begin at Fellowship House, on L Street NW in Washington, D.C., on May 1, 1961. The first meeting was to be held that evening at seven o'clock. James Farmer would be the project leader. Participants were expected to dress "neatly at all times." For men this meant a business suit or sport jacket with a tie; women would wear skirts or dresses; all participants needed dress clothes for meetings. Nonetheless, given the circumstances of travel, participants were to pack lightly. Those selected needed to acknowledge their participation immediately, as "one or two persons dropping out at the last minute could seriously hamper this project."[26]

Just as it had done with George Houser in 1947, CORE sent field secretary Tom Gaither along the path of the Freedom Ride itinerary in order to investigate the route and make sure the proper arrangements were in place for such an extensive undertaking. Gaither spent the last week or so in April traversing the planned route, working closely with field director Gordon Carey.[27] Gaither secured housing, organized mass meetings, confirmed local contacts, double-checked bus itineraries, and generally ensured that CORE had done everything within its power to ensure that the trip ran smoothly from the organizational perspective.[28]

From CORE headquarters, James Farmer attempted to draw the attention of national figures. Embracing what he called a "Gandhian principle of being open and aboveboard," Farmer wrote a letter, sending copies to several important people, including President John Kennedy; Attorney General Robert Kennedy; the presidents of Trailways and Greyhound; the chair of the Interstate Commerce Commission, Kenneth Tuttle; and the chair of the Civil Rights Commission.[29] Farmer also talked to Martin Luther King Jr. about the Rides, but King believed them to be a CORE endeavor. Further, King was well acquainted with the sort of internecine struggles that often characterized the Civil Rights Movement even at that early date, so he did not involve his organization, the Southern Christian Leadership Conference, except to indicate support. As King told members of his staff, "CORE started the Freedom Ride and should get the credit. We will play a supportive role."[30]

Farmer's letter began simply: "We expect you will be interested in our Freedom Ride, 1961. It is designed to forward the completion of integrated bus service and accommodations in the Deep South." He explained the itinerary and nature of the trip and then proclaimed: "Freedom Ride is an appeal to the best in all Americans. We travel peaceably to persuade them that Jim Crow betrays democracy. It degrades democracy at home."[31] And in a clear reference to the Cold War tensions so central to Kennedy's administration, Farmer reminded the president and other recipients of the letter that Jim Crow "debases democracy abroad. We feel that there is no way to overstate the danger that denial of democratic and constitutional rights brings to our beloved country."[32]

When asked years later whether the Justice Department tried to step in and halt the planned Ride, Farmer indicated how seriously the Kennedy administration took CORE: "We got no reply. We got no reply from Justice. Bobby Kennedy, no reply. We got no reply from the FBI. We got no reply from the White House, from President Kennedy. We got no reply from Greyhound or Trailways. *We got no replies.*" Years later, Farmer could laugh at the lack of response to his earnest letter.[33] In a 1968 interview, John Seigenthaler, an administrative assistant to Robert Kennedy, remembered the advance notice from CORE. He maintained that the letter, which was passed along to the Civil Rights Division of the Justice Department, "was more a press release than anything."[34] Simeon Booker, a black reporter from *Jet* magazine who was going to accompany the group as a journalist, went to see the attorney general to tell him that there might be trouble on the trip. According to Seigenthaler, "Bob [Kennedy] said 'O.K., call me if there is. If you can't get me call Burke [Marshall] or John [Seigenthaler]. I wish I could go with you.' They treated it rather lightly; nobody thinking this could be much trouble."[35] Burke Marshall also recalled seeing CORE's mailing: "They had sent us their schedule; but they didn't even come in before they started. So, I knew about it, but not in a very dramatic way, until they got in trouble."[36]

Though they paid it little heed, John and Robert Kennedy did receive the CORE memo. CORE also sent along a list of the Ride's itinerary and participants.[37] Even before the memorandum reached the White House, however, the administration was trying to maneuver behind the scenes to deal with discrimination in transportation in at least two areas. Back in March, Burke Marshall had circulated a memo suggesting that the administration look into more effective federal action in Alabama, particularly with regard to discrimination in airports that had been built in part or whole with Federal Aviation Administration grants. Further, however, a particularly vexing and embarrassing issue had emerged. Recent months had seen increasing numbers of reports of the imposition of Jim Crow on foreign diplomatic representatives, particularly from Africa, who had received shoddy treatment or no service at all when traveling to and from Washington in the nearby states of Maryland and Virginia.[38] This added not only an international component but also a Cold War imperative to the issue of segregation on interstate transport. Increasingly, the Cold War had come to affect national politicians' view of civil rights. Similarly, the emergence of an aggressive Civil Rights Movement had itself led to a "Southern Red Scare" in which civil rights and communism became intertwined in the minds of many white Southerners.[39]

In the meantime, CORE continued to prepare for the arrival of the Freedom Ride participants in Washington. Fellowship House, where the group was to meet, was an old Victorian row house that Quakers used as a meeting facility and dormitory for a number of pacifist organizations.[40] Even in the days leading up to this first meeting, the roster for the Ride was in flux, with CORE unsure of exactly who would be participating.[41] Nonetheless, by May 1 thirteen individuals had arrived in Washington, D.C., to prepare for an event that would change the course of the Civil Rights Movement.

"No Graduation Present Could Have Been Sweeter Than This": The Original Freedom Riders

The participants came from a range of backgrounds and brought a variety of experiences with them to Fellowship House. The application process had been intended to develop a list of committed participants with not only the proper credentials as activists but also the sort of character that would inure CORE from later recriminations. Farmer, Carey, and the rest of the CORE staff knew that once the Freedom Ride garnered attention, its detractors would be on the lookout for flaws such as communist affiliation, criminal records (other than arrests for previous activism, which CORE saw as marks of honor), and personal improprieties.[42]

James Farmer, who had conceptualized and organized the Ride since his emergence as CORE's national leader, would now be one of the Riders. He had not participated in the Journey of Reconciliation, but he would join the Freedom Ride. He relished the opportunity.

The white participants were on the whole older than their black counterparts, and most of them were affiliated with peace organizations. Albert Bigelow was a rugged Harvard-trained architect from Cos Cob, Connecticut, who was in his forties. Although he had captained three combat ships for the navy during World War II, he embraced pacifism in the years after the war; in 1958 he had caused a minor sensation when he was arrested for captaining his small craft, the *Golden Rule,* into a nuclear testing zone in the South Pacific as an act of protest against atomic weapons.[43]

James Peck was the only holdover from the Journey of Reconciliation. He was a contemporary of Bigelow, but his embrace of pacifism had come earlier. Peck, the heir to a clothing company fortune, had been jailed for his stance as a conscientious objector during World War II, as well as for other human rights activities. His racial commitments were long-standing. As far back as 1933, he had shocked his Harvard classmates by arriving at the freshman dance with a black date. A longtime CORE stalwart, he had served the group in many capacities, including as the editor of *CORElator,* the organization's newsletter.[44]

The husband-and-wife team Walter and Frances Bergman were the oldest Riders: Walter was sixty-one, Frances fifty-seven. Both had long been committed to direct action projects. They claimed membership in CORE, the American Civil Liberties Union, the Committee for a Sane Nuclear Policy, and in Frances's case the Women's International League for Peace and Freedom. Both were retired school administrators in Detroit and were sympathetic to socialist causes. Walter Bergman had also been an education professor at Wayne State University and at the University of Michigan, and he had been involved in United Nations education projects in Germany.[45]

Genevieve Hughes and Edward Blankenheim, the final white Riders, were members of CORE. Hughes, a recently hired field secretary previously employed by Dun & Bradstreet, had been active in the New York CORE office. Blankenheim was a carpenter from Arizona. He also belonged to the NAACP and Students for Equality, which was affiliated with the Tucson branch of CORE.

Many of the black participants came from the new generation of students and young activists. For them, the threat of going to jail or accepting violence had become commonplace; they would not be cowed. They had challenged the status quo across the Deep South and were prepared to continue to do so. CORE's Freedom Ride provided a chance for them to continue work they believed they had already begun. Few were active in pacifist movements, though all accepted nonviolence as the most effective way to fight segregation in the South. They were a diverse lot who brought with them a range of experiences. Jimmy McDonald, a folksinger and entertainer, was a member of New York City's CORE chapter who also had participated in a number of national CORE projects. Joe Perkins, a CORE staff member from Kentucky, had participated in numerous direct action activities as a member of CORE in Ann Arbor, Michigan, and had served ten days in jail after his involvement in a sit-in in Miami. Elton Cox was a young minister from Pilgrim Congregational Church in High Point, North Carolina. He had served as a youth secretary for the NAACP and belonged to both the NAACP and the pacifist American Friends Service Committee.

The three youngest members of the group were John Lewis, Charles Person, and Henry "Hank" Thomas. A senior at Howard University, Thomas was a big, strong young man who had grown up in poverty without a father in rural Georgia and St. Augustine, Florida. He had been a star athlete in high school and would surely have been a college football star had he not suffered a severe illness in his senior year. He never felt entirely comfortable in the rarefied air of Howard, instead immersing himself in local civil rights campaigns. He had heard of the Freedom Ride through his roommate, John Moody, who was active in the D.C. Area Nonviolent Action Group and the Philadelphia NAACP. Moody himself, who had engaged in civil rights protests in northern Virginia, the District, and Maryland, was slated to go on the Freedom Ride, but he fell ill and could not join the group. Only nineteen, though his physical stature made him appear older, Thomas forged his mother's name on the Freedom Ride permission slip and took Moody's place.[46]

Charles Person was the youngest Freedom Rider at eighteen years old. He and CORE had kept his participation quiet, not publishing his name in any pre-Ride publicity, though the *Washington Post* did refer to an "eighteen year old Negro student from Morehouse College" the day after the Rides departed.[47] Reflecting upon his desire to keep his name out of print for as long as possible, Person wrote more than four decades later: "My mother and father and siblings lived and worked in the Atlanta area. If the Klan or other unscrupulous person could have made the association my father could have been fired or it may have invited a cross burning in our neighborhood."[48]

Lewis, the student body president of the American Baptist Theological Seminary, who had penned the heartfelt application, was one of the leaders of the Nashville student movement, which had drawn headlines for its challenges to Jim Crow. By early 1960 and the emergence of the student sit-in movement across the South, he had discovered that his true passion was racial justice. He already had been arrested five times for his participation in sit-ins.

When Lewis received his acceptance letter, itinerary, and one-way bus ticket to Washington, D.C., he felt that "no graduation present could have been sweeter than this."[49] He had just finished his degree at ABT and was unsure what to do next. He had entertained the idea of attending graduate school and had applied to the American Friends Service Committee to help build homes in Africa or India. But when he read about the Freedom Ride in SNCC's *Student Voice,* he knew what he most wanted to do. Lewis and his activist friend Bernard Lafayette had hoped to test bus-station segregation in Birmingham during his last year at ABT, and Lewis had written to Fred Shuttlesworth, a longtime minister and civil rights activist in perhaps the most aggressively segregationist city in America, telling him of the plan. Though the minister had long been committed to challenging Jim Crow, he informed Lewis that their plan was not a good idea: "Not only would it be too dangerous, he said, but the situation in Birmingham was already volatile enough without giving the authorities a group of 'outsiders' to target and blame for the racial climate that seemed to be getting stormier in that city every day."[50]

The Freedom Ride thus gave Lewis an opportunity to engage in the exact kind of action he craved along with other like-minded citizens, black and white, from across the country. Lewis's experience began inauspiciously: he missed his bus in Nashville and had to ask his friend and Nashville movement colleague, James Bevel, to drive him to catch up with it. Bernard Lafayette had also wanted to be a Freedom Rider, but because he was not yet twenty-one, he needed parental permission that was not forthcoming. His father in Tampa, Florida, telling his only son, "Boy, you are asking me to sign your death warrant," had refused to grant permission.[51] It was not without a little envy and pride, then, that Lafayette rode along as Bevel drove Lewis to join the Ride. They overtook the bus in Murfreesboro, and Lewis got on and rode overnight to Washington, D.C. Upon his arrival, Lewis looked around and saw the U.S. Capitol not far from the Greyhound station and the top of the Washington Monument. This was all new for him: "I had been in big cities before. But this was more than big. This was the seat of the nation's government, the place where laws were made, the center of all that the country stood for. That, combined with the purpose for which I had come, made the moment overwhelming, truly magical."[52]

Putatively, Washington was indeed the center of all that the country stood for. But the black denizens of the nation's capital had a different perspective: Washington was also a Jim Crow city. Segregation was not mandated in any laws, but it was palpable and real. The overwhelming majority of Washington's restaurants, bars, cafes, and lunch counters were segregated. With the exception of some government cafeterias, the YWCA cafeteria at Seventeenth and K Streets NW, and the facilities at Union Station, downtown Washington's eating and restroom facilities were off-limits to blacks.[53]

Since at least the 1930s, African American organizations had mobilized against segregation in the nation's capital. Founded in 1933, for example, the New Negro Alliance was a Washington-based organization that sought to use direct action protests such as pickets and economic boycotts to promote civil rights.[54] In 1941, A. Philip Randolph, head of the Brotherhood of Sleeping Car Porters and one of the most important black leaders in the twentieth century, made his famous call for a "March on Washington" to protest segregation and discrimination in all aspects of American society, but with particular emphasis on jobs and the military.[55] Randolph was able to extract concessions from President Roosevelt, including establishment of the President's Committee on Fair Employment Practices. Randolph would continue to lead a "March on Washington Movement" for the next several years, though the threatened march never transpired. Washington's Interracial Workshop also worked to advance racial equality in the 1940s. Indeed, in July 1947, in the wake of the Journey of Reconciliation, several Workshop members gathered in the District and composed a song, "You Don't Have to Ride Jim Crow."[56] Among the composers was the polymath Bayard Rustin, who among other things was renowned for his musicianship. The song would be one of many sung over the course of the Freedom Ride challenge. In 1943 and 1944, numerous students challenged segregation in restaurants and cafes near Howard University.[57] Howard students would continue to be vital in pushing for civil rights gains in the capital for the next two decades and beyond. In short, then, despite Lewis's assessment as he arrived in Washington, it was still a Jim Crow city. But for that weekend, at least, Lewis drew inspiration from its grandeur, its status as the beacon of freedom, and its representation of the ideals for which the country stood.

"What Would You Do if I Slapped You on That Cheek?": Nonviolence and the Freedom Riders

As they planned the Freedom Ride, Farmer, Carey, and the others anticipated violence, and they understood that violence might be a necessary catalyst to change. The Riders knew this when they applied, and it was reinforced for them in Washington. Bayard Rustin had earlier theorized about the need for nonviolent protest to meet with a violent response: "Protest becomes effective to the extent that it elicits brutality and oppression from the power structure."[58]

Farmer knew all along that the Freedom Ride would probably result in bloodshed, especially after he read the field reports that Thomas Gaither and Gordon Carey put together before the trip.[59] Farmer later recalled: "We were told that the racists, the segregationists, would go to any extent to hold the line on segregation in interstate travel. So when we began the ride I think all of us were prepared for as much violence as could be thrown at us. We were prepared for the possibility of death."[60] The anticipated violence was not merely collateral damage that would inevitably accrue as the Ride made its way through the South. In the course of the challenge, CORE organizers believed, violence would serve a larger purpose. Farmer and the others "felt that we could . . . count upon the racists of the South to create a crisis, so that the federal government would be compelled to enforce federal law. That was the rationale for the Freedom Ride."[61]

Gordon Carey was among the many CORE members who understood that the new direct action approach to civil rights was by its very nature confrontational. He rejected patience, arguing in an interview with *U.S. News and World Report,* "It seems to us that the civil rights movement will not get anywhere by merely being patient." But by using nonviolent action, he hoped that the transition to an integrated society would come as peacefully as possible, even if the movement met with violent resistance: "The Negro community in the South is not willing to wait next year for the rights which they should have had 10 or 20 years ago, and, unless the fight is pushed through non-violence, we fear that the forces of violence will really take over."[62]

Nonviolence had become a major buzzword among observers of the black Civil Rights Movement ever since Rosa Parks refused to give up her seat on a bus in Montgomery back in 1955. However, the roots of nonviolence both in America and internationally extended well before Parks's challenge served as the catalyst for the Montgomery bus boycott. Many activists could trace their intellectual and philosophical engagement with nonviolence to the Indian leader Mohandas Gandhi. In his work both in South Africa at the turn of the century and later in India, where he became known as the "Mahatma," or "Great Soul," Gandhi had developed an approach to challenging injustice at the hands of a powerful state that came to be known among the English as "passive resistance." In actuality, Gandhi and his followers embraced a more comprehensive and holistic approach to resistance, *satyagraha,* which can be translated as "hold fast to the truth." It can also be thought of as "Truth-Force," "the force of love," or simply "nonviolence."[63] Gandhi first launched his movement in the Natal and Transvaal provinces of South Africa, where he tried to confront racial injustice, particularly the discrimination that Indians faced on a daily basis. All individuals had to search within themselves to ensure that they had the strength both to pledge and to carry out the sacrifices that *satyagraha* required. Their pledge took the form of a sacred oath, taken only when they had had considered the full implications of their actions.[64]

As Gandhi's struggles garnered international attention and support, civil rights leaders in the United States began to look to Gandhi for inspiration. Gandhi had challenged what many leaders saw as two of the worst forms of oppression, racism and imperialism, and he had shown himself to be the sort of revolutionary who could inspire people to great deeds in the face of overwhelming opposition.

By the time of the Freedom Ride, almost every major civil rights group in the United States embraced "Gandhian nonviolence" as the best way to challenge segregation.[65] Most explicitly advocated nonviolent direct action campaigns. Since 1942, CORE had done so, as had its predecessor and sister organization, the Fellowship of Reconciliation. The Southern Christian Leadership Conference argued that "nonviolence is a way of life as old and permanent as Jesus of Nazareth, as new and growing as Mohandas K. Gandhi and Martin Luther King, Jr." For SCLC and others who adhered to nonviolence, it was "not pacifism or cowardice. It is an active way of living: it resists. It resists that which is opposed to LOVE.

Love, here, means not personal affection, but universal understanding and redemptive good will."[66]

James Peck had embraced nonviolence since the early 1940s, when he went to prison rather than fight in World War II. In a 1970 interview, Peck explained that "first," he believed in nonviolence because of "my own study, and then I saw how it worked in practice." He recounted how he had seen nonviolence work when he and some fellow inmates held a strike protesting segregation in the mess hall of the federal prison in Danbury, Connecticut. After joining CORE, "I saw again and again how effectively it worked in ending segregation in restaurants, barber shops, swimming pools, and all sorts of public places."[67]

The next generation of civil rights activists entered the movement committed to nonviolence as well. At its inaugural April 15, 1960, meeting at Shaw University in Raleigh, North Carolina, the Student Nonviolent Coordinating Committee issued a statement, based largely on the teachings of Reverend James Lawson, that "affirm[ed] the philosophical or religious ideal of nonviolence as the foundation of our purpose, the presupposition of our faith, and the manner of our action."[68]

Lawson, a seminal figure in the American nonviolent civil rights struggle, was an ordained minister who had served time in jail rather than fight in Korea. He had traveled as a missionary to India, where he learned of Gandhi's tactics and philosophies. He applied this knowledge and experience as a leader of the Nashville protest movement in 1960—the movement in which John Lewis had first been exposed to direct action protest. Lawson also served as an advisor to SNCC and was vital to the authorship of its statement of purpose. As a result of his agitation, Vanderbilt University expelled Lawson from its divinity school in 1960. Faculty members at the school admired Lawson's commitment to civil rights, and many worked to either have him reinstated or find him an institution he could attend, but before they could do so, Lawson transferred to Boston University, where Martin Luther King Jr. had received his Ph.D. In 1960 Lawson received a bachelor's degree in sacred theology. Lawson advocated nonviolence not only as a tactic, but as a philosophy: "As a technique, every nonviolent strategy is determined and shaped by the essential faith, Love, and the Cross, the gracious work of God both in the past and now. Thus expediency is always ruled out. The pure technique loses out to the faith in action, to the resistance in love which retains a quality of creativity throughout the social process. Means and ends become one and the same thing."[69]

If mainstream civil rights groups and leaders such as King and Lawson preached nonviolence, however, others understood nonviolence best as a tactical approach. If for many in the movement nonviolence was a modus vivendi, for others it was more a modus operandi. Even CORE, fully committed to nonviolent resistance to oppression, believed nonviolence to be more an approach than a way of life. James Farmer remarked: "We dreamed of a mass movement, and we did not think then that a revolution could be conducted by pacifists. For CORE, nonviolence was never more than a tactic. When a person participated in a CORE project he was required to be nonviolent." Farmer then went on to invoke the spiritual father of nonviolence and *satyagraha:* "But I agreed with Gandhi." Farmer explained: "'I would rather have a man resist injustice with violence than fail to resist out of cowardice.' Nonviolence did not have to be the personal philosophy of a CORE member, and he could be quite violent in other circumstances if he chose."[70]

Many within CORE, however, did embrace pacifism as a way of life. For much of his career, Farmer did. But over the course of his involvement in the movement, Farmer's perspective changed. Although at the time of the Freedom Rides, Farmer was committed to nonviolence, by the late 1960s he no longer accepted "nonviolence as a total philosophy or as a way of life," even for himself. In 1968 he said, "I . . . can conceive of wars in which I would fight—I would want to fight. For example if a war developed in South Africa between the blacks and the oppressive minority which controls them . . . I would consider that a justifiable war and would participate in it."[71]

It was easy to embrace nonviolence in the heady early days of the mass movement. As one veteran civil rights activist, Richard Haley, once noted, "Nonviolence was popular like baseball and motherhood."[72] However, even before Farmer had begun to waver, some black activists rejected the nonviolent approach. In 1959 the NAACP suspended Robert F. Williams, the controversial activist in Monroe, North Carolina, as head of the local office after he espoused violent resistance to racial oppression.[73] On the eve of the Freedom Riders' gathering in Washington, Williams went so far as to ask the United States to support war on the South. Williams sent out a telegram from the NAACP's Monroe office that Cuba's foreign minister, Paul Roa, read at the United Nations. At the same time, the message was read over a radio station in New York City. This telegram explicitly linked America's willingness to support Cuban revolutionaries with a request that Roa support a revolution among blacks in the South: "Now that the United States has proclaimed military support for people willing to rebel against oppression, oppressed colored people in the South urgently request tanks, artillery, bombs, money, use of American airfields and white mercenaries to crush the racist tyrants who have betrayed the American Revolution and Civil War. We also request prayers for this noble undertaking."[74] One imagines that the Reverends King and Lawson did not join in Williams's request for prayers for this particular undertaking. In any case, President Kennedy did not respond as Williams had hoped. As the Freedom Ride approached, the U.S. government was not prepared to wage war on the South, especially given how many Southerners played key roles in Congress and elsewhere in Washington. And most civil rights activists continued with nonviolent protest. In the same issue in which it published Williams's request, the *Baltimore Afro-American* revealed that more than forty restaurants in Maryland, Virginia, Kentucky, and North Carolina had desegregated after sit-down strikes.[75]

All of the Freedom Riders wholeheartedly accepted nonviolence as a tactic. Some were less comfortable with it than others, however. The New York folksinger and activist Jimmy McDonald in particular bristled at being called "nonviolent." In a 1969 interview, McDonald asserted, "I have never been a nonviolent [person] in my life." Like Farmer, McDonald "saw nonviolence . . . as a tactic rather than a philosophy." He told a story that summed up his relationship with nonviolent activism: "I was passing out leaflets in Times Square in front of Woolworth's when two white cats came up . . . and said suppose I take that flyer and slap you in the face with it, will you turn the other cheek? I said yes, and his friend said, what would you do if I slapped you on that cheek? And I said I'll put all my tens and a halfs right up your ass. Now I thought that was the way I had to react as a man, you know, not realizing that this did not sit well with the CORE downtown, but that is essentially the way I felt."[76]

While James Farmer understood nonviolence as only a tactic, he and the other CORE leaders knew that responding to violence with violence would prove disastrous for their cause. Jimmy McDonald and others might have doubted nonviolence as a way of life, but for the purposes of the trip they had to embrace it as a tactic. To ensure that this would be the case, CORE set up the Fellowship House workshop that began on May 1, 1961.

"The Last Supper": The Meeting in Washington and Departing on the Freedom Ride

The Freedom Rides are often associated with the student sit-in movement that exploded in the wake of the Greensboro A&T students' challenge to segregation in that city's Woolworth store on the first day of February 1960. The Rides and sit-ins share a number of commonalities. Both consisted at least partially of students engaged in direct action challenges to segregation. In each case the desired goals were clear. In the case of the sit-ins, participants wanted to desegregate lunch counters that, while privately owned, served the public and accepted black custom. The Freedom Riders' goal was to desegregate the conveyances and facilities that served interstate passengers. Both the sit-in movement and the Freedom Rides relied on nonviolent protest and embraced nonviolence as at least a sacrosanct tactic. In both cases many participants believed in nonviolence as a guiding philosophy.

There were also differences between the student protesters and the Freedom Riders, although obviously the former contributed participants to the latter. Sit-ins were by their very nature local affairs. Students in Greensboro sat in to try to force the local Woolworth's to integrate. Students in Atlanta used the tactic to integrate Kress's and other stores. The nature of the sit-in movement made it an aggregation of local movements that drew inspiration and guidance from one another but were fundamentally locally driven. The Freedom Rides, on the other hand, were by definition interstate. The Rides were not a local phenomenon, but a challenge to a regional policy and practice of segregation. Furthermore, the legal differences between the two were significant. As the civil rights lawyer Constance Baker Motley notes: "The law was on the side of the Freedom Riders. Their rights had been clearly established [in the legal challenges that culminated in *Boynton*]. . . . Consequently, the Freedom Riders were rebelling against recalcitrant state governments which . . . were still enforcing their own state segregation laws, the most common feature of massive resistance."[77]

Whatever its moral merits, the student sit-in movement had not yet been sanctioned by federal courts. These students challenged recalcitrant local governments that still held legal authority. Essentially, they engaged in civil disobedience of a kind that extended at least as far back as Thoreau. The Freedom Riders, on the other hand, were testing the efficacy of recent court decisions and the will of the federal government to ensure that these decisions had substance. These are subtle but important differences.

The Freedom Riders arrived in Washington ready to engage in workshops on nonviolence and strategy sessions to prepare them for what they would face as they traveled into the crucible of the Deep South. CORE's Marvin Rich was one of the chief architects of these training sessions.[78]

The program began with Farmer, who conducted an orientation session providing an overview of what the Freedom Riders planned to do, how they were going to do it, and the potential outcomes. A lawyer then gave a presentation on the legal aspects of the trip, explaining both the legal situation that had brought them to their current state and how the Riders would deal with arrests and other difficulties when they came. A social scientist told the group a little bit about folkways, laws, and attitudes in the Deep South.[79] For some, such as movement veterans John Lewis and Hank Thomas, this orientation covered familiar ground. Nonetheless, for some of the participants, the Freedom Ride would be the first significant time they had spent in the South, and Farmer and the rest of the CORE staff wanted to cover as much terrain as possible. Almost all of the members had attended similar workshops before, but Farmer believed that the Freedom Ride would present different challenges than any of them had faced picketing in the North or sitting-in in Southern cities.[80] After each session, the group engaged in intense discussion. Farmer recalled that "the discussions were neither academic nor undisciplined rapping; each person after all, was going to put his or her life on the line. The air was filled with electricity, not frivolity."[81]

The group also engaged in role-playing scenarios, some members pretending to be Freedom Riders integrating lunch counters or the fronts of buses. Others played the role of people in an angry white mob. Some took on the role of bus driver, police officer, or another individual who might play a part in potential confrontations. In these sessions, "realism was imperative so that we could learn how to reduce the probability of serious and permanent damage in the real-life situation facing us."[82] To this end, the simulations often took on a bizarre aura of reality. Those playing white thugs took their roles seriously, and when they took out their fictional frustrations, their actions could be genuinely realistic. Clearly, civil rights activists, even those putatively committed to nonviolence, carried within them the potential for outrage, mob action, violence, and frenzy. After each role-playing exercise, the group met for discussions about what had happened. Participants then switched roles and reenacted the same scenario. After the training sessions had concluded, Farmer "felt that everyone in the group was prepared for anything that might happen, including the ultimate."[83]

For John Lewis, who had spent so much time in Jim Lawson's rigorous workshops, the days in Washington "went by like a blur."[84] Because of his Nashville background, some of the training seemed a bit simplistic, "lacking in discipline and rigor."[85] But during this time, Lewis was able to begin to get to know some of his fellow Riders and to appreciate what they were about to go through together.[86]

Jimmy McDonald was skeptical of whether Farmer and the others really knew what to expect, as they had led the group to believe. "I suspect that the people who [were] leading the workshops thought that they knew what to expect but they didn't really," McDonald would later recall. He still believed that the experience was important because it did give people some idea of what they would face.[87]

The most critical account of the workshops came from Walter Bergman, who wrote a rather scathing indictment of the planning of the Rides in June, on his way back to Chicago. He believed that the training should have lasted longer than two days and thought that the discipline "should have been tighter," underscoring this by asserting that "all meetings were 30 to 60 minutes late." He also argued that participants should have been selected only after the workshops in Washington and that any potential alternates should have also received training. Bergman, a long-standing veteran of an array of nonviolent endeavors, was not impressed by CORE's Washington workshops.[88]

On May 3, the last night of the training sessions, Farmer took everyone out to a Chinese restaurant downtown. Toward the end of the meal, as the group drank coffee and ate dessert, Farmer spoke to them. Although he had a reputation as an electrifying speaker, his talk to the group was low-key. "There were no theatrics, no melodrama; the situation itself was too fraught with emotion for embellishment," Farmer would later recount. He knew that in their few days together the group had "become like a family," and he told them that "no one was obligated to go on this trip, except possibly me. There was still time for any person to decide not to go." When Farmer finished speaking, Reverend Cox suggested that they bow their heads in prayer. Farmer believed a moment of silence might be more appropriate since there were agnostics and atheists in the group. There was a five-minute silence. Some sipped coffee. Others prayed. Farmer announced that no one had to make a decision right then—anyone who changed his or her mind could come to him later.[89]

This was John Lewis's first meal at a Chinese restaurant. In fact, other than to demand the right to be served, he had never been in such a nice restaurant at all. Unlike his protest experiences, "this was different." And despite what awaited Lewis and his fellow passengers, "the atmosphere was pleasant and relaxed. The food was delicious, unlike anything I'd ever eaten before. The conversation and the company were delightful. I was, for the first time in my life, actually dining out."[90] Lewis was astounded by the silver bowls and platters and by the whole setting. They sat at a huge circular table. Chinese waiters scurried about bringing abundant amounts of food.[91]

The atmosphere may have been pleasant and relaxed, the company and conversation delightful, but the participants well knew what might follow. Invoking both religious imagery and gallows humor, someone in the group joked that they should enjoy themselves and eat well, because this might be their "Last Supper." In future years many of the participants, especially Lewis, would invoke this "Last Supper" metaphor to describe their last night in Washington.[92] The group did not know what would come, but they were prepared for anything. Several made out wills that last night just in case they did not return home alive. Lewis was not among them. He had arrived in Washington carrying all that he possessed: "There was no need for me to make out a will. I had nothing to leave anyone."[93]

On Thursday, May 4, the group congregated downtown, where the Greyhound and Trailways bus terminals sat across from one another. They bought their tickets and checked their bags without incident. They met with little fanfare. There were a few reporters and some curious observers, but on the whole, an event that would garner international attention commenced quietly. Farmer told observers that the Ride was intended "to focus public attention on segregation patterns in the South 'that are degrading and destructive of human dignity.'"[94] The Freedom Riders boarded the buses bound for points south.

In addition to the thirteen participants and the regular passengers on the buses, which had not been specially chartered, two other men and one woman boarded on that bright, clear spring day. CORE had invited journalists to accompany the Riders in a press release. Four accepted. One was Simeon Booker of the Johnson Publishing Company, which published both *Jet* and *Ebony* magazines, the premiere black magazines in the United States. James Farmer called Booker "a brilliant and courageous young black journalist."[95] Booker was the newsman who had tried, to no avail, to draw Bobby Kennedy's attention to the journey just weeks earlier.[96] Ted Gaffney was a young photographer and stringer for Johnson Publications. Charlotte Devree, a white writer from New York City, was committed to nonviolence and has often been mistaken for a Freedom Rider because of her full immersion in the journey.

The fourth journalist who volunteered to walk into the maelstrom was

Moses Newson, city editor for the *Baltimore Afro-American,* one of the most respected black newspapers in America, but he would not be able to join the group until they arrived in North Carolina. Newson had previously covered the Emmett Till case and the Little Rock School integration crisis.[97] He would witness history firsthand yet again.

The group split nearly evenly, according to plan, some riding on Greyhound, the others on Trailways. John Lewis's seatmate was the war veteran and pacifist Albert Bigelow. Lewis took the window seat; Bigelow sat on the aisle.[98] Jimmy McDonald remembered that the buses were somewhat crowded, as there were a number of other ticketed travelers occupying seats. Nonetheless, the group began the trip sitting in an integrated fashion scattered throughout the buses, just as they had planned. When vivacious Genevieve Hughes, the CORE staffer, arrived at the station and boarded the bus, McDonald recalled that some people "thought she was an actress—a Hollywood actress," both because of the way she looked and because some of the few photographers who were there from media outlets took her picture.[99]

Genevieve Hughes was no mere starlet, but she was about to step onto history's stage. This would prove to be the most important role that she or any of her colleagues could play. The buses pulled out from their respective stations. Freedom Ride 1961 was under way.

Chapter 4

"Hallelujah, I'm a Travelin'!"

Freedom Riding through the Old Dominion

"The Trickle Has Become a Flood"

A number of transportation-related events in early May garnered as much national attention as the departure of the Freedom Riders from Washington, even in civil rights circles. Prior to the Freedom Ride, federal judge William A. Bottle fined a bus company and one of its drivers one hundred dollars each for forcing interstate passenger Marguerite L. Edwards to the rear of a bus as it traveled through Georgia on September 7, 1960. That same week managers of the Continental and Greyhound bus lines in Memphis announced that they were discontinuing their policies of racial segregation. Similar pronouncements emerged regarding the Terminal Company in Birmingham and the Greyhound terminal in New Orleans. It was a busy week for transportation in Memphis. Even as the bus companies in the city that served as the gateway to the Deep South ended Jim Crow restrictions, a prominent black Memphian asked the U.S. Supreme Court to agree to hear a case involving discrimination in the city's airport.[1]

Company practices made up only one layer of Jim Crow in buses and terminals. These policy announcements did not mean that integration prevailed in, say, Birmingham's bus terminals, any more than court decisions had such an effect. For example, when the Atlanta Board of Aldermen struck down Jim Crow laws for local taxis, this might have seemed like good news. But the aldermen left a telling caveat: drivers were left free to offer or refuse service to anyone they wanted.[2] Mores stood fast even where the law yielded.

That same week the State Department launched a campaign to try to alleviate what was fast becoming an embarrassment in Cold War diplomatic circles: rampant discrimination against African and Asian diplomats in the South, as well as in Maryland and other border states.[3] A number of incidents had taken place across the region—problematic in an era when Africa and Asia were at the center of intense Cold War gamesmanship that asked nations to choose either the side of freedom and democracy, supposedly represented by the United States, or the side of oppression and communism, embodied by the Soviets and Chinese. Every time a diplomat from Africa was refused service at a roadside restaurant or told that he was not welcome at a hotel, the American case against communism seemed all the weaker. In a period when "unaligned" or "third world" nations needed to determine their political and economic courses and when nations across Africa were beginning to achieve independence, these embarrassments were especially dangerous.[4]

President Kennedy had recently acknowledged as much, asking Southern governors for help in assuring a "friendly and dignified reception" for foreign diplomatic representatives who passed through their states. Virginia's governor, J. Lindsay Almond, a staunch Kennedy ally and the chief executive of a frontline state in this public relations struggle, given Virginia's proximity to the nation's capital, nonetheless hedged in his response to the president's entreaties. Almond declared that Virginians were generally "in sympathy" with Kennedy's views and that the state would "make every reasonable effort to help achieve the ends" that he sought. The *Washington Post* opined that Almond's statements to that point "reflect[ed] credit on the quality of Governor Almond's leadership." Unfortunately, the *Post* went on to add, Almond coupled his stance "with an unfortunate suggestion that visiting diplomats avoid 'misunderstandings' by identifying themselves as official representatives of their respective governments." This moved the editors to ask, "Would this really be likely to lessen their mortification or to enhance their respect for the practice of democracy in the United States?"[5]

CORE, meanwhile, maintained its focus on the Freedom Rides as a way of increasing the organization's visibility, membership, finances, and efficacy. Although he was not happy with his recent demotion, membership director James Robinson wrote to several black newspapers to solicit donations and support for CORE endeavors. In the wake of the student sit-in movement and the first Freedom Ride, Robinson declared that "after almost 20 years of work, CORE is at last succeeding in popularizing the aggressive sacrifices without which discrimination would continue in America for many decades to come. Over all these 20 years, we have had a trickle of victories. This past year, the trickle has become a flood." Despite this deluge, however, Robinson wanted those reading his letter to understand that "the goal of integration and a brotherly America is still beyond our grasp." The group had many actions planned, including the Freedom Rides, which Robinson characterized as "the most dramatic" of the group's endeavors, just then getting under way. Almost everything was in place: "We have the methods which can win. We have the victories which can enlist many new participants for the struggles still to come. But we do not have the money to sustain and advance the CORE program."[6] With the Freedom Rides forging through the Virginia countryside, the group was confronting something of a period of calm, but CORE would need all of the support, financial and otherwise, it could get.

The Political Museum Piece: Civil Rights and Massive Resistance in Virginia

John Lewis took his place next to his seatmate, Albert Bigelow, on a Greyhound, and soon the buses holding Freedom Riders rumbled out of their terminals in Washington. Beneath his seat Lewis placed his carry-on bag, which contained the Bible, a book about Gandhi, and another by Thomas Merton. Because the group never knew when members might face arrest, CORE had recommended that the Riders keep their toothbrushes with them, as they would probably not be able to access their suitcases. Lewis adhered to this advice. He enjoyed the vistas of Washington as the bus left the station and wound its way through the city, with its grand monuments to human freedom, crossing the Potomac River and moving into northern Virginia.[7]

Northern Virginia is in many ways an extension of the District of Columbia as much as it is the northernmost outpost of the South. At various times in its history, parts of this section of the Old Dominion have been incorporated into the District of Columbia. The Pentagon, Arlington National Cemetery, and the headquarters of numerous military and government bureaucracies are based in Arlington, Alexandria, McClean, Quantico, and the other cities that make up Washington's innermost suburbs. Farther south or southwest, however, Virginia becomes more traditionally Southern. The accents, the attitudes, and the cuisine all take a turn toward Dixie as one moves away from Washington and its urban accoutrements and its focus on national politics. This was beginning to be the case even in 1961. In the words of one contemporary observer, "Northern Virginia [is] rapidly migrating northward in attitude and appearances."[8]

Virginia has a variegated past when it comes to civil rights.[9] On the one hand, the state was the midwife of white massive resistance. On the other hand, it prided itself on a tone of genteel moderation in politics and in race relations. Nonetheless, many of the vital court cases leading up to the Freedom Rides—*Morgan, Henderson, Boynton*—stemmed from violations of Virginia law and had wound their way through Virginia's legal system. While Virginia embraced segregation and would not tolerate much variance from Jim Crow practices, challenging legal or social segregation in most parts of this state was not like mounting similar challenges in the Deep South, where the outcome was as likely to be violent retribution as vigorous prosecution.[10]

Jim Crow streetcars had been an issue for civil rights activists in Virginia cities since the emergence of such cars as a viable mode of public transport.[11] Virginia held out until the end of the nineteenth century before establishing legislation segregating railroad cars.[12] After passage of a series of statutes from 1901 to 1906—the 1906 law culminating in the requirement of Jim Crow streetcars throughout Virginia—Alexandria, Fairfax County, Richmond, Newport News, Lynchburg, Portsmouth, and Danville all experienced black protest campaigns aimed at eradicating race-based seating rules.[13] This phenomenon was not exclusive to Virginia, as blacks in every state in the former Confederacy engaged in similar actions.[14] In 1906 the unsuccessful Warner-Foraker amendment to the Hepburn railway-rate regulation bill had attempted to ensure that where separate facilities did prevail on interstate conveyances, they at least remained fully equal in quality.[15]

By the time of the Freedom Rides, Virginia had further developed its curious approach to civil rights and white supremacy. Part of the peculiar nature of Virginia's race relations stemmed from the state's politics, which V. O. Key famously summed up as a "museum piece" in his classic study *Southern Politics in State and Nation.* Key claimed that "of all the American states," Virginia could "lay claim to the most thorough control by an oligarchy. Political control has been closely held by a small group of leaders who . . . have subverted democratic institutions and deprived most Virginians of a voice in their government."[16]

In the postwar era this oligarchy came in the form of the "Byrd Organization," its kingpin and namesake Harry Flood Byrd Sr., the state's senior U.S. senator, who ruled Virginia's Democratic Party in much the same way that machine mayors ruled some of the nation's largest cities.[17] In a de facto one-party state (which was itself in a de facto one-party region), Byrd controlled the mechanisms of patronage, power, and purse strings.

While Byrd had been considered a progressive governor by Southern standards, as he was able to enact tax reform, streamline bureaucracy, and push through an antilynching law, as a senator he was conservative: he believed in minimal federal involvement, and he was a fiscal watchdog who believed above all in the "pay as you go" approach to expenditures. And of course, he was a segregationist. This was a perfectly sensible balance to Southerners who had come of age before and during the New Deal ascendancy.[18] In the words of Numan Bartley, "White supremacy in the senator's scheme of values was part of a broad and profoundly neobourbon ideology." This ideology "revered economy in government, fiscal 'responsibility' and a balanced budget, states' rights and Virginia traditions, a static society and aristocratic prerogative."[19] While Byrd was not a New Dealer, he did utilize the strategic power of his senatorial position and the power of other Southerners to gain control for himself and for the Southern wing of his party. Byrd and those like him had a tenuous relationship with Roosevelt and his programs. They believed that the New Deal encroached too far on what should have been the domain of the states. They also worried that New Deal liberalism might threaten white supremacy back home. But given the power that their status within the party granted them, Byrd and his cohort were not going to abandon the party unless Roosevelt and later Truman too aggressively pursued civil rights.[20]

By May 1954, however, the Supreme Court decision outlawing segregation in public schools and by extension other public services had become too much for Byrd to take.[21] In Bartley's words, "The *Brown* decision cut into the core of Byrd's values. The schemes of radical reformers had been endorsed by the nation's highest tribunal."[22] It was at this point that Byrd coined the phrase "massive resistance" to characterize the way Southerners must respond to the encroachments of perceived radicals in the federal government. The *Richmond News-Leader*'s influential editor James Jackson Kilpatrick called for "interposition," the doctrine that held that the state could step between state rule and federal decree. And thus Virginia, not the states of the Deep South, began a campaign of white resistance to civil rights that would characterize the next decade and more of the struggle for racial equality in the region.[23]

Resistance could take many forms. Radicals and moderates may have agreed that maintaining segregation in Virginia's schools and elsewhere was important, but the means by which they would attempt to accomplish their goals were still very much up in the air. Virginia was not immune to the sort of radical groundswell that struck Mississippi, Alabama, and other points south. In the 1920s, a small group of white supremacists had begun a racial-integrity movement that manifested itself in the "Anglo-Saxon Clubs of America."[24] The group successfully brought before the state legislature an act "requiring the separation of white and colored persons at . . . public assemblages" in 1926, and then-governor Harry Byrd allowed it to become law without his signature.[25] These clubs were in many ways the progenitors of Virginia's equivalent to the Citizens' Councils—the Virginia Defenders of State Sovereignty and Individual Liberties, which became the most prominent of the organizations that dedicated themselves to the fight against integration in the months after *Brown.* Virginia's groups were not much like their ilk elsewhere. More than one historian has noted that "the Defenders were as different from the stereotyped white citizens' councils of the Deep South as Harry Flood Byrd was from the late Theodore . . . Bilbo."[26]

Still, despite the differences between Byrd and Bilbo, the Jackson Citizens' Councils and the Richmond Defenders of State Sovereignty, or for that matter the *Jackson Daily News* and the *Richmond News-Leader,* a simple fact remains. Byrd, the Defenders, and James Kilpatrick were all at the forefront of a movement that would both inspire and embolden racists farther south, where the supposedly genteel museum piece of the oligarchy gave way to a more virulent but not wholly dissimilar form of radical massive resistance in the Mississippi Delta. The differences would prove to be matters of degree, not of kind.

The ascension of Lindsay Almond to the Virginia governorship represented a break with the Byrd Organization. Or rather, it represented the emergence of an individual who had risen through the Byrd Organization with, in the words of one historian, "a streak of independence," as well as a "first-rate mind and a shrewd appreciation of what was politically possible in a state dedicated to the preservation of all vestiges of segregation."[27] Almond had inherited the policy of "massive resistance," but he also realized that resistance would ultimately prove futile. Although he had long been a critic of *Brown v. Board* and believed federal intervention in civil rights to be repugnant, in January 1959, mindful that the state's policies were going to destroy its educational system, Almond established a commission to develop plans to integrate public schools in the state.[28] This cost him the support of Harry F. Byrd and his many backers.[29]

Even before Almond won the governorship, Virginia had its white moderates and liberals.[30] Sarah Patton Boyle was a prominent activist and voice of racial tolerance.[31] Armistead Lloyd Boothe, a Virginia politician and a member of the state's House of Delegates from Alexandria, while proclaiming his support for segregation, attempted to stand up to those forces who advocated marshalling the state's forces for full-scale resistance.[32] In 1955, concerned Virginians formed the Virginia Council on Human Relations in order to counteract the forces of massive resistance and resurgent racism in the state.[33] When the school desegregation crisis hit Virginia, white citizens formed the Virginia Committee for Public Schools in order to combat the school closings.[34]

Above all, however, and ahead of white moderates, black citizens of the state rallied in the face of massive resistance. In the words of Virginia senator Henry Marsh, "Virginia's resistance to Brown created a counter-resistance among African Americans that laid a foundation for political success in Virginia later on."[35]

In the end, however, Virginia's moderates lost out to the more extreme elements in the state's Black Belt on the "Southside" and among many of its politicians, who were no less opportunistic than their Deep South cohort, whatever patina of respectability they maintained on the surface. The end result in Virginia was the closing of Prince Edward County's schools during 1958 and 1959. Massive resistance in Virginia collapsed more quickly than it did farther down in Dixie, but it had established a style of politics that would dominate parts of the South for more than a decade.

"Hallelujah Ain't It Fine": Riding through Virginia

The Freedom Riders left Washington and passed into the northern Virginia suburbs. Compared to most of the region, northern Virginia was progressive when it came to race relations. Fairfax County had one of the nation's most active NAACP branches. It was the first chapter in the country formed outside of a city, and it was the branch most responsible for Lottie Taylor's case being successfully heard in federal court. Taylor, in 1946, had been evicted from a bus traveling from Washington through Fairfax County for violating Jim Crow ordinances. The court's finding in her favor served as a foundation for court decisions in similar cases.[36]

The Freedom Riders passed not far from National Airport, which had opened in 1941. For years its concessionaire segregated black patrons, making them eat in a separate basement cafeteria. In November 1948, Charles Houston and the NAACP Legal Defense Fund had brought Air Terminal Services to court to end these segregated practices.[37] The end result was an NAACP victory in *Nash v. Air Terminal Services,* the judges ruling that airports could not operate on a segregated basis.[38]

Throughout the cities of Alexandria, Arlington, and Falls Church, the three northern Virginia cities closest to the capital, protests had led to relatively painless integration in an array of public accommodations. On February 2, 1959, four black students had integrated Arlington's Stratford Junior High School with no violence and relatively little fanfare.[39] Integration in the northern suburbs helped sound a death knell for massive white resistance to school integration farther south. In local and state elections, too, segregationists had lost ground in northern Virginia, and token but real integration of schools accompanied the desegregation of lunch counters in Alexandria and other cities.[40] In June 1960, spurred on by the wave of protests that had begun in Greensboro in February, members of Washington's Non-Violent Action Group (NAG) had engaged in sit-ins to protest segregated facilities. After some successes in Arlington (following several arrests and other confrontations), the NAG had expanded its protests to Alexandria, Fairfax, and Falls Church and into Maryland.[41] By the time the Freedom Riders passed through these first few towns outside Washington, the groundwork for integration had been laid.

The first stop on May 4 was in Fredericksburg, fifty miles south of Washington. The mood had been positive when the trip commenced. As they would throughout the ordeal of the Freedom Rides, the group sang spirituals and freedom songs, including one written specifically for their trip, "Hallelujah I'm a Travelin'," following in the tradition of the song that Bayard Rustin had introduced in 1947, "You Don't Have to Ride Jim Crow." Its words were in the style of the Negro spirituals that had become anthems for the movement, verses alternating with the chorus:

> Stand up and rejoice, a great day is here
> We're riding for freedom and the victory is near.
>
> *Chorus:*
> Hallelujah, I'm a travelin', hallelujah ain't it fine
> Hallelujah, I'm a travelin', down freedom's main line.
>
> In 1954 our Supreme Court said,
> "Look a here Mr. Jim Crow, it's time you were dead."[42]

The group improvised verses as they went along. They sang many other songs as well, and the fellowship of music would carry them through tough times in the days and weeks to come.

While the historian David Goldfield might be overstating the case when he avers that "the welcome mat had . . . been set out in the Old Dominion and in North Carolina," he is right that the Freedom Riders encountered little resistance on their first stop.[43] In Fredericksburg, Genevieve Hughes, the young woman earlier misidentified as a starlet, was the first to get off the bus and go into the station. According to Jimmy McDonald, Hughes was that day's chosen leader, the one who would go in and get a feel for the facilities and ascertain whether or not there might be difficulties. Since part of the trip's goal was to stir up a certain amount of trouble, the leader most often simply served as the person who would keep his or her hands clean of any hassles in case CORE officials had to be contacted.[44] The leader would also be sure to stay behind to cover a range of duties, such as taking care of the bags of any arrested persons and keeping in contact with the CORE New York office. He or she would then catch up with the rest of the group if they had gone ahead with the trip.[45]

McDonald recalled that Bert Bigelow and John Lewis were the first to enter the bus facilities in Fredericksburg.[46] Inside the terminal, "white" and "colored" signs stood sentry over the restrooms, but when James Peck and Charles Person crossed these racial barriers, nothing happened.[47] Similarly, when Peck, Person, and other members of the group went to the stand-up lunch counter and placed an order, they received service without incident.[48] As John Lewis recalled, one of the Riders mused, "Looks like they knew they were coming and baked us a cake."[49]

The next stop was in Richmond, Virginia's state capital and a city more Southern in flavor than Fredericksburg or Washington. Richmond also had a tradition of black protests against segregation.[50] The city had avoided some of the worst racial abuses that had swept most of the South in the last decade of the nineteenth century. It was not until 1900 that Virginia passed its first law requiring segregation on railroad cars, and that law passed by a one-vote majority. Until that point, blacks "sat where [they] pleased and among the white passengers on perhaps a majority of the state's railroads."[51] In 1904 blacks in Richmond had staged a widespread boycott against Jim Crow streetcars that may well have been the "first mass-based, organized, protest movement by blacks in the twentieth century."[52] It ultimately failed, and with it failed the hopes for integrated streetcars, trains, and buses in Richmond and throughout the state. But much like the Journey of Reconciliation, the boycott had lingering effects that would prove significant: the Richmond campaign "served as a 'rallying cry' for future protests that would eventually remove de jure segregation."[53]

Richmond in many ways was similar to most cities in the Upper South in the post–World War II era. Segregation was the accepted practice in Virginia's capital, and most of the time blacks accepted Jim Crow as an inevitable intrusion on daily life. Periodically, a black person would challenge the logic and practice of segregation, but to little avail. Whatever the Irene Morgan case may have decided in law, interstate transportation remained segregated. Alfreda Madison had discovered this in 1947 when she took the train on a round-trip ticket from Washington, D.C., to Norfolk. When she changed trains in Richmond, she sat in a semi-deluxe coach. The conductor of the new train told her to go to another car where there were black passengers. She refused. It was not until the train reached Suffolk that two men purporting to be police officers menaced and intimidated Madison until she moved to the Jim Crow car. Madison contacted the NAACP office in Norfolk as well as Martin A. Martin, the Richmond lawyer.[54] But without the names of the two men who claimed to be police officers or the name of the conductor, she was unable to receive relief for her humiliations.

As elsewhere in the South, Richmond had begun to experience change in the 1940s and 1950s.[55] The Richmond Public Library voluntarily desegregated in 1947. The city began to hire black firefighters and police officers in 1950 and 1953 respectively. In 1957 Richmond desegregated its buses, surely in reaction to the Montgomery bus boycott and subsequent court decisions. Still, this action reveals that the city of Richmond was not about to engage in full-fledged massive resistance, whatever the state's political leadership promoted.[56] Furthermore, what resistance there was would be matched with an equally rigorous push from blacks who wanted to end Jim Crow.

The most visible such push emerged after the February 1960 sit-ins in Greensboro. Students from Virginia Union College began a sit-in at Thalhimer's, one of the major department stores in the city. The sit-ins at the tea room and lunch counters at Thalhimer's began on February 22, 1960, and spread to a number of other businesses, students from other schools in the region joining in, including several from the white Union Theological Seminary, who joined their black peers in March.[57] The protests would finally come to an end in August 1961 with the successful integration of the businesses.[58] During the Thalhimer's protests, working-class residents of the East End carried out a boycott of the Springer Drug Company chain store in their neighborhood. Although conducted with different tactics and to less fanfare than the Thalhimer's protests, the East End Neighborhood Association's protests achieved a successful resolution of its conflict seven months before the student actions.[59]

Meanwhile, somewhat removed from the public eye, Virginia's governor, J. Lindsay Almond, was faced with a potentially embarrassing diplomatic problem. As noted earlier, the Kennedy administration had alerted Almond to the increasing U.S. presence of African diplomats and embassy personnel, hoping to avert the potential embarrassment of diplomats being refused service in the state. Kennedy brought to Almond's attention the fact that "unfortunately there have been incidents which have brought complaints to the Department of State and received adverse attention in the world's press." Almond was conciliatory, but he pointed out to the president that "the operation of private businesses . . . is under the control of the owners and proprietors." He believed that perhaps such diplomatic personnel should take care to make previous arrangements and to identify themselves as foreign representatives beforehand.[60] Such Cold War imperatives would continue both to haunt the Kennedy administration and to provide much of its rationale for addressing civil rights questions.[61]

This was the status of civil rights activity in Richmond on May 4, 1961, when the Freedom Riders passed through the city. While Bruce Boynton, the Howard University student whose case had set the stage for the Freedom Riders, had been arrested at the Trailways bus terminal in Richmond, the Freedom Riders would not encounter such difficulty.[62]

The group arrived in Richmond at three o'clock in the afternoon. In the bus station they found two cafeterias. According to Frances Bergman, one was "obviously for white[s]—larger, brighter, and better equipped." The other had "beaten up stools and 2 or 3 booths" and was intended for the use of black patrons. There were no signs posted, however, and the test groups entered with whites going to the black side and blacks to the white side. Both teams received service. As Frances Bergman wrote a few days later, "There was surprise and much curiosity but no incidents"—except that someone told one of the cameramen traveling with the group not to take pictures in a private establishment.[63] John Lewis recalled that nothing happened "but a few cold stares."[64] Police at the station did not interfere.[65] Authorities may not have harassed the Riders in Richmond, but the group had the distinct feeling that they were being watched, in part because news of their arrival had preceded them by word of mouth, so locals expected them. Many of the Riders welcomed the watchful eye, feeling that it would be useful to be under scrutiny "in enemy territory."[66]

Despite the removal of "white" and "colored" signs and the relative lack of difficulty the group faced, Jim Peck found what he saw in Richmond "disheartening." Even without the signs, blacks still adhered to segregated and inferior facilities: "Segregation still prevailed as it had aboard the buses in 1947. Our Freedom Riders were about the only persons to wait, wash, and eat unsegregated in these terminals." In Richmond, "Negroes were sticking to the formerly separate and grossly unequal colored waiting rooms and restaurants" in both the Greyhound and the Trailways terminals.[67]

The group left the terminals and as a group went to Virginia Union College to talk with students. It was apparent that news of their journey had spread, and Frances Bergman noted, "It is amazing . . . how many people have been involved with direct action."[68] These sorts of meetings characterized the support the group would encounter throughout their journey, buoying the Riders during times of strain.

Late that afternoon, the group left for Petersburg, a town just a few miles south of Richmond. There they would spend their first night on the trip. When they debarked in Petersburg, the bus station passed their test with no difficulties.[69] Soon after their arrival, they met local minister Wyatt Tee Walker, who had given up his ministerial post to take over as the executive director of the Southern Christian Leadership Conference.[70] Walker was a tall, slim, sharply dressed, flamboyant New Jersey native in his early thirties. He had joined the Communist Party in high school and had been an activist for many years. He was not very sympathetic with the student wing of the movement, even though he had undertaken a few ostentatious protests himself. The most outrageous of these probably came in 1958, when he walked into the Petersburg Public Library, which was off-limits to blacks, and tried to check out a book. Library officials called the police and had him arrested. Observers, including some reporters, found some irony in the volume that the fair-skinned black man had tried to borrow: a biography of Robert E. Lee.[71]

That night the group stood before a mass meeting at Walker's former church, where they were met with vigorous applause. John Lewis recalls that Albert Bigelow spoke for the group that night. They spent the night as guests in local homes.[72] These meetings were a vital part of the journey. James Farmer and the CORE staff had coordinated with Roy Wilkins and the NAACP to ensure that at every stop along the way, a network was in place to support, encourage, and protect the Riders and provide them with both physical and spiritual nourishment. The black communities across the South that the Freedom Ride visited were well-aware of this challenge to Jim Crow, before most of the rest of the world had any idea. The Riders were heroes to these people, and they used their pulpit to encourage locals to organize, to act against oppression and indignity. In Petersburg, an active citizens' organization engaged in an array of activities, and Frances Bergman noted that perhaps "some of them" were "things we could try."[73]

While most Americans fixated on Alan Shepard's becoming the first American in space aboard the *Freedom 7* spacecraft on May 5, the Freedom Ride continued virtually unnoticed. From Petersburg, on May 6, the buses headed westward, away from the interstate and into "Southside" Virginia, the state's Black Belt region. The first stop the next day was in Farmville, in the heart of Prince Edward County, which had been at the epicenter of Virginia's massive resistance when local whites closed the county's schools rather than allow black children and white children to attend them together. In the Farmville bus station, the "For Colored" and "For Whites" signs had recently been painted over, but their message was still visible through the fresh, thin layer of whitewash like a haunting specter from a past not yet fully gone. The group was served at the snack bar and used the restrooms without trouble.[74] As Taylor Branch has wryly observed, "The powers of Prince Edward County refused to extend their 'massive resistance' to interstate transportation."[75]

By nightfall the group had arrived in Lynchburg, where student sit-ins had spread by December 1960, continuing through spring 1961 to little avail, as segregation still reigned in most public facilities. Though there were no signs segregating patrons by color in the Lynchburg terminal, a divider in the middle of the counter wholly separated persons on one side from those the other.[76] That night the group received their "warmest reception by far" in the early stages of the trip. Local groups claimed that the Freedom Riders passing through had "given them a shot in the arm." So many people wanted to hear the Riders talk that eight of them stayed in Lynchburg to speak at eight different churches. Frances Bergman, who claimed not to be a "speaker-to-the-multitudes type," nonetheless was among those who stayed behind. She "found that I could do it because I believe so strongly in what we are doing as a group."[77]

"The Department of Justice Will Act": Robert F. Kennedy's Speech in Georgia

While the Freedom Riders were impressing the locals in Lynchburg, Bobby Kennedy made an impression of his own among supporters of civil rights.

Speaking before an audience of some sixteen hundred at the University of Georgia Law School's Law Day, the attorney general made the first statements of support for civil rights to come from the administration since it had taken office in January. The Georgia speech was Kennedy's first since taking over at the Justice Department.[78] After five weeks of preparation and at least seven drafts with a "Southern Brain Trust" of advisors, the speech was ready.[79] Kennedy delivered it with trembling hands.[80]

One of the listeners in the audience was Charlayne Hunter, a vivacious young woman who, along with Hamilton Holmes, had integrated the university just months before, in January.[81] Hunter, a journalism student, was there to cover the speech for the *Atlanta Daily World*, a black newspaper. Meanwhile, aware of what Kennedy might say in his speech, a number of Georgia's most prominent politicians were notable in their absence. These included Governor Ernest Vandiver, a consistent critic of the Kennedy administration who had been vocal in his opposition to Kennedy's legal effort to reopen the Prince Edward County schools. Vandiver had sent more than one hundred state patrolmen to the Georgia campus to quell rioting during the integration crisis that had brought Holmes and Hamilton to campus.[82] He chose to attend the Kentucky Derby rather than Law Day in Athens.[83] The most prominent Georgia politicians among those gathered to hear Kennedy speak were Athens mayor Ralph Snow and Julian Cox, a state senator.

Before Kennedy's arrival, a handful of protesters stood outside of the hall where the attorney general would speak. Police arrested five fundamentalist ministers wielding signs proclaiming, "The Bible teaches separation." The previous night, vandals had painted "Yankee go home" on a sidewalk, but that admonishment was washed away before Kennedy arrived on campus.[84] This was the extent of massive resistance in Georgia on that day.

As the Freedom Riders forged on in the early days of what would prove to be the Kennedy administration's first major challenge on civil rights, Bobby Kennedy got down to business before the Law Day crowd. After giving the expected praise to Georgia and its citizens, who, he acknowledged, had given John Kennedy the biggest percentage majority of any state, Kennedy got into the heart of his address. He spoke about the importance of respect for the law, lest society collapse. Along those lines, he raised three major areas of difficulty that the Justice Department faced. He quickly did away with the first two of these pressing issues—organized crime and illegal price fixing by businesses—to address "the one that affects us all most directly—civil rights."[85]

Kennedy pointedly connected the struggle for civil rights with the struggle against communism in the Cold War. He further invoked the integration of the university and singled out Hunter for her role: "In the world-wide struggle the graduation . . . of Charlayne Hunter and Hamilton Holmes will without question aid and assist the fight against Communist political infiltration and guerrilla warfare. . . . When parents [send] their children to school this fall in Atlanta, peaceably and in accordance with the rule of law, barefoot Burmese and Congolese will see before their eyes Americans living by rule of law."[86]

As the Freedom Riders tested the realities of adherence to the law on the ground, Kennedy spoke of events in Virginia. After pointing out that he lived in the state and had attended law school at the University of Virginia, Kennedy defended his actions with regard to the Prince Edward County school cases. He was adamant that "we are maintaining the order of the courts. . . . Our position is quite clear. We are upholding the law. Our action does not threaten local control." Furthermore, in words that should have provided comfort to the Freedom Riders, Kennedy asserted that "in this case, in all cases, I say to you today that if the orders of the court are circumvented, the Department of Justice will act."[87]

Kennedy praised Georgians for dealing with the university integration crisis, saying, "When your moment of truth came, the voices crying 'force' were overridden by the voices pleading for reason." He asserted his support for the *Brown* decision, maintaining that no matter what individuals believed about it, it was the law. He argued that guaranteeing the franchise to all Americans of voting age was integral to dealing with civil rights, an emphasis that would get him into some trouble a few days down the road. He chastised Northerners for their hypocrisy on the race question.[88]

Kennedy closed with a flourish. He reiterated his devotion to the rule of law. He expressed a hope that all sides could achieve "amicable, voluntary solutions without going to court." He hoped to avoid violence and attain voluntary compliance with decrees. When there was a problem, the government asked "responsible officials to take steps themselves to correct the situation." In cases where this had not happened, "we have had to take legal action."[89]

It was vital that America avoid crises such as what had happened at Little Rock or in the New Orleans school integration debacle:

It is not only that such incidents do incalculable harm to the children involved and to the relations among people. It is not only that such convulsions seriously undermine respect for law and order and cause serious economic and moral damage. Such incidents hurt our country in the eyes of the world. . . . For on this generation of Americans falls the full burden of proving to the world that we really mean it when we say all men are created free and are equal before the law. . . . To the South, perhaps more than any section of the country, has been given the opportunity and the challenge and the responsibility of demonstrating America at its greatest—at its full potential of liberty under law.[90]

But these words of hope and opportunity and Cold War concern came with a stern warning. Kennedy posed and answered a rhetorical question: "You may ask: Will we enforce the civil rights statutes? The answer is: Yes, we will." He went on to say, "We will not threaten, we will try to help. We will not persecute, we will prosecute. We will not make or interpret the laws. We will enforce them vigorously without regional bias or political slant."[91] He closed by reiterating the importance of respect for law, which he illustrated with a quotation from Henry Grady, the Georgia author of the New South Creed, invoking both national loyalty and a commitment to liberty above all else. Kennedy sat down, and after a brief pause the audience broke into applause for some thirty seconds.[92] The young attorney general's first speech had made an impression.

Even before the Law Day speech, the civil rights community, including the black press, was cautiously optimistic about the new administration. In an editorial cartoon in its May 6 edition, the *Baltimore Afro-American* depicted two large crows straddling the East and West Wings of the White House. The first, "Jim," listened as "Crow" squawked across the White House roof to him: "This guy acts like he means business! We'll have to build our nest farther south!"[93] Portentiously, however, on Tuesday, May 9, White House press secretary Pierre Salinger announced that President Kennedy was backing away from civil rights planks that he had supported in the party platform in November. Governor Ernest Vandiver announced that Kennedy had promised never to use force to back civil rights gains in Georgia. Civil rights leaders such as Roy Wilkins publicly questioned the president's commitment to civil rights even as *Afro-American* readers were being led to believe that the new president was on their side.[94]

In the days to come, the Kennedys would have ample opportunity to show that they meant business, to test their commitment to the rule of law, to reveal their desire to abide by statutes and court decisions, and to indicate their willingness to stand up to those who would resist unlawfully and violently. As the Freedom Riders traveled hopefully through Virginia, the attorney general's talk might have given them comfort in the face of the unknown. It remained to be seen how well deeds would match words.

Southside: The First Challenge

The last stop in Virginia came in Danville, a town just across from the North Carolina border. Danville had served as the last capital of the Confederacy in the waning days of the Civil War in April 1865. In 1943 the *Pittsburgh Courier* had reported in a front-page banner headline that a "Comely Ohio War Worker," Melba Rosalyn Wilson, had been arrested and forced to spend a night in jail for violating Jim Crow statutes on a bus in Danville, where she was visiting her gravely ill father.[95] Danville would also be the site of the only civil rights protests in Virginia that turned violent, when protesters took to Danville's streets from May through July 1963. Events in the city reached their nadir on "Bloody Monday," June 10, 1963, when police and deputized garbage workers brutalized fifty or so protesters who were trying to march from Bibleway Church to the city jail to hold a prayer vigil.[96]

Not far from Danville is Martinsville, a small textile town that had been the scene of perhaps the most racially charged legal case in the state's history. In 1951 seven black men were sentenced to death for the brutal rape of a white woman.[97] Many saw the events surrounding the rape as akin to the infamous Scottsboro case of more than a generation before, but the differences in the Martinsville instance were significant.[98] Although the men were undoubtedly guilty, the seven executions over two days revealed a great deal about racial justice in the region and the lengths to which whites would go to maintain white supremacy. The story of the Martinsville Seven illuminates how Virginia led the rest of the country in developing a policy of massive resistance. The implicit bargain between the racist whites of Southside Virginia and their politicians was that the state would defend white supremacy so that there would be no need for the emergence of the sort of Klan activity that characterized the Deep South.[99] This bargain also might serve to explain why the Freedom Riders encountered no violence as they wound their way through Virginia.[100]

The Freedom Riders encountered their first resistance in the Southside stronghold of Danville when they arrived on Sunday, May 7. Because one group had remained in Lynchburg to talk to groups in churches, the two buses of Riders passed through Danville's terminal at different times. When the first group entered the terminal, Ed Blankenheim sat for ten minutes at a counter designated for "colored" patrons. He never received service and departed when his bus was ready to leave the station.[101] The black Riders were able to use the white facilities with no difficulties.[102] Perhaps the bus terminal officials believed that only preventing blacks from using white facilities would put them in disfavor with the law. Maybe they ostracized the white Riders out of a sense of disgust that whites had taken up roles as agitators against the white South. Whatever the reason, the Danville authorities attempted to turn Jim Crow on its head.

At first they were effective in doing so. The first bus left the station, and Blankenheim and his white cohort had not been served at the "colored" counter. Not long after, however, the Trailways bus pulled up to the terminal. Jim Peck and Genevieve Hughes walked up to the same counter where Ed Blankenheim had sat alone and tried to place an order. At first they were refused service, but Peck and Hughes engaged the manager in a discussion, and he relented. Peck, Hughes, and Walter Bergman ordered and received refreshments at the Jim Crow counter traditionally allotted to black patrons only.[103] The first challenge had come and gone. There were no arrests, and no violence ensued. Southside intransigence had fallen by the wayside. Massive resistance in the Old Dominion proved to be minor in May 1961 when it came to interstate transportation and its attendant facilities. The Freedom Ride rolled along into North Carolina.

Chapter 5

The Carolinas

North Carolina after the Journey of Reconciliation

If V. O. Key summed up Virginia and its politics as a "political museum piece," he found its Southern neighbor, North Carolina, a "progressive plutocracy" seemingly at odds with the rest of the South due to its advancements in industrial and economic development, education, and race relations. Key quickly asserted that in the Tar Heel State tensions abounded beneath the surface and that on the question of race North Carolina had its share of troubles.[1] Nonetheless, these problems seemed conquerable in a state that one black observer claimed had developed "something of a living answer to the riddle of race."[2]

When asked years later whether Key's observations about North Carolina's progressive traditions were accurate, civil rights activist Floyd McKissick responded, "I think Key was correct."[3] He argued this in 1973 even after a series of recent incidents—Frank Graham's defeat in his re-election bid for the U.S. Senate, the defeat of the two North Carolina congressmen who refused to sign the Southern Manifesto in 1956, George Wallace's electoral success, the emergence of Jesse Helms as a major political figure—cast doubt on the state's alleged progressivism.

If it is possible to credit one man with an entire state's image, North Carolina's progressive reputation is largely owed to the outsized efforts of Frank Porter Graham, longtime president of the University of North Carolina (UNC) and the state's U.S. senator for a short period. Graham, who arrived at UNC in 1915, had developed a reputation as a first-rate teacher. As university president, he defended the right of political dissenters on campus. Graham also served as president of the Southern Committee for Human Welfare (SCHW) during the Great Depression, and he was one of two white members of President Truman's Committee on Civil Rights, which produced the report "To Secure These Rights" in 1947, thrusting, in the words of one historian, "the civil rights question to the forefront of American politics and serv[ing] as a point of departure for the modern era of race relations in the United States."[4] He was also a supporter of union organization. Graham's role on the SCHW in the 1930s and on Truman's commission at the end of the 1940s can be seen as the bookends of his period of greatest influence, as during this period "perhaps no other twentieth-century southerner better exemplified the South's attempt to adapt to . . . changing social and political realities."[5] In the ultimate encomium, Oregon senator Wayne Morse declared Graham "the most Christ-like man I have ever known."[6]

But in 1950 Graham lost a brutal election in which his racial moderation played into the hands of racial demagoguery and bitter invective. Graham was running to take on his first full term in the Senate after his surprising 1949 appointment by Governor Kerr Scott. Graham's opponent, Willis Smith, was a conservative Raleigh lawyer who branded Graham a "nigger lover" and whose supporters picked up on the bullying and vitriol. North Carolina may have been the most progressive state in the South, but it was not immune to the trends of a region that had seen a resurgence of the sort of race baiting that Theodore Bilbo and Ben Tillman had seemingly perfected decades before.

In North Carolina, as elsewhere, *Brown v. Board* had seismic effects. Nonetheless, unlike its neighbor to the north, the state did not develop a holistic program of massive resistance to perceived federal incursions. Some North Carolinians established their own version of the Virginia Defenders, but groups such as the Patriots of North Carolina, Inc. were relatively respectable when compared to Citizens' Councils or Klan-like groups. The Patriots' leaders came from the elite, professional classes and included academics, pharmacists, lawyers, doctors, and others. Even when a more rabid group, the North Carolina Defenders of States' Rights, emerged, it proved to be tepid compared to organizations in states farther south. In any case, neither the Patriots nor the Defenders enjoyed more than fringe status.[7] Similarly, the fulminations of North Carolina's politicians paled when compared with those of their Southern brethren. In the 1956 election for the senatorial seat that Graham had lost in 1950, Kerr Scott ran against Alton Lennon, who had taken Willis Smith's seat after Smith's death in 1953.[8] Scott, a progressive and racial moderate, defeated Lennon, who tried to use demagoguery, racial and otherwise, as Smith had a few years before.[9] This is not to say that most North Carolinians, including the state's politicians, supported *Brown*. But, for example, rather than pass resolutions of interposition, the state's lawmakers settled for a manifesto of protest.[10] Governor William B. Umstead probably summed up the state's response best when he simply announced that he was "terribly disappointed" with the *Brown* decision.[11] The political leadership in Mississippi and Alabama did not respond in such an anodyne fashion.

Thus, it was in moderate North Carolina that a new phase of the Civil Rights Movement began in 1960. When Franklin McCain, Ezell Blair Jr., David Richmond, and Joseph McNeil, students at all-black North Carolina Agricultural and Technical College, sat down at a segregated Woolworth's lunch counter on Greensboro's South Elm Street and asked for service, they embodied a shift in the movement—from piecemeal, intermittent, charismatic-leader-based protest to comprehensive, constant, popular-based struggle.[12] If the boycotters in Montgomery had wanted to open up the bus system, or the black leadership in Little Rock had wanted to integrate the schools, these young activists demanded nothing less than equal access to American society. The Greensboro Four's impromptu but not impetuous actions on February 1, 1960, marked the start of a national civil rights crescendo that would irreversibly change American society.[13] The formation of SNCC at Shaw University's Greenleaf Hall in Raleigh that April formalized this dynamic, youthful, radical, and aggressive brand of activism. While some movement elders, most notably SCLC's Ella Baker, helped the students get their organization off the ground, this new phase was characterized by its grassroots nature.[14] As one observer has asserted, "There was movement by 1960, but there was not yet a Movement."[15] The Freedom Rides would be the central event in this transition.

Although there had been actions similar to the Greensboro sit-ins before, none had so captured public attention and national media. Further, none had spawned comparable successor efforts. As the sit-in campaign escalated in Greensboro, other blacks, usually though not exclusively college students, followed the Four's example. Within just a few months, the "sit-in movement" had spread—first across North Carolina, from Greensboro to Durham, Winston-Salem, Charlotte, Fayetteville, Raleigh, Elizabeth City, High Point, Concord, Salisbury, Shelby, and Henderson. It then crossed borders north and south, reaching up to Hampton, Norfolk, Portsmouth, Richmond, Newport News, and Suffolk in Virginia and down to Rock Hill and Orangeburg in South Carolina. From there it spread farther south and west.[16]

Revealing some of North Carolina's progressive political and intellectual leanings, local newspapers exerted a calming influence, publishing so-ber and reflective editorials as the sit-ins spread. Editorial opinion stopped short of advocating the immediate integration of lunch counters, but in many cases it did not fall far short. In the words of the *Greensboro Daily News,* "The only available course is to find some way to serve all those customers who want to be served."[17] Thus, Key's assessment of North Carolina seemed vindicated. But for all the reason and restraint in some quarters, there were vitriol and violence in others: far from the editorial offices of the state's progressive dailies, the protesting students accepted cigarette burns to their flesh, condiments poured on their heads, and blows rained about their bodies and skulls as the price of achieving liberation. No better embodiment of the true nature of race relations in North Carolina could be found. As William Chafe has written, "North Carolina represented a paradox: it combined a reputation for enlightenment and a social reality that was reactionary."[18] Soon after the sit-in movement began, Freedom Riders would pass through North Carolina, some fourteen years after their predecessors on the Journey of Reconciliation had discovered both the enlightened and the shadowy sides of the Tar Heel State.

"Heads Turned and Eyelids Jumped": Riding through North Carolina

As throughout the South, legally enforced segregation on public carriers and the facilities that served them had not followed an inexorable line from the Old South to the New in North Carolina. The state had not required Jim Crow railroad cars until 1899.[19] Nonetheless, Jim Crow prevailed in the twentieth century, and it extended to buses and the facilities they visited. By 1961 North Carolina ranked ninth in the country in miles of interstate highway, and in keeping with its growth-friendly, business-oriented economy, it was seventh in the amount of new construction of federal highways.[20]

Even after the Journey of Reconciliation, passengers continued to ride Jim Crow. When blacks challenged existing statutes, which did not change as a result of the *Morgan* decision and the subsequent direct action challenges, they usually suffered the consequences. One such challenger was Charles Hauser, who was arrested in Mount Airy on October 19, 1947, when he refused to give up his seat and move to the back of an Atlantic Greyhound bus bound for Charleston, West Virginia, just months after the Journey. Hauser had taken a seat on the bus in Winston-Salem. In Mount Airy a number of white passengers boarded the bus. One stood next to

Hauser's seat, and the two started chatting amiably. The standing passenger asked Hauser if the seat next to him was taken. Hauser responded that it was not, and the white gentleman took the seat, unconcerned with Jim Crow laws or practice. The bus driver, however, took issue with the integrated seating and asked Hauser and another black man to move to the back of the bus. Hauser refused to move. After much commotion, including the congregation of fifty to seventy-five observers who "talked and pointed at" Hauser, the police arrested him. He stayed in jail for two hours, until he was able to secure the one-hundred-dollar bond.[21] Hauser's was one of many individual challenges to Jim Crow in North Carolina in the postwar era, lonely efforts that would culminate in the events of February 1960 and afterward with the sit-ins and Freedom Rides.

What began at the Greensboro lunch counter would have an effect on facilities serving interstate travelers. Almost immediately after sit-ins spread to other cities, train and bus depots became a target for activists. Sit-ins that commenced in Petersburg, Virginia, for example, led to an August 15, 1960, announcement by Bryce Wagoner, the president of Trailways' Bus Terminal Restaurants Inc. (based in Raleigh): not only would the Petersburg facility be integrated, but the company would end segregated policy in all other station restaurants that it controlled in Maryland, Virginia, North Carolina, Tennessee, and Florida.[22]

William Chafe, understanding that North Carolina represented a paradox when it came to race relations, believed Greensboro to be "a microcosm of the state at large."[23] Those inclined to see progressivism could point to Greensboro's (token) integration of public schools, the airport restaurant, the library, public parks, the municipal coliseum, and the city skating rink (including dressing rooms and the stand-up snack bar). But at the same time the city had sold its public swimming pool to private interests in order to avoid integrated swimming; city leaders stalled on acquiescing to integration of other public facilities; and the spread of the sit-in movement was accompanied by the emergence of white hoodlums, the Ku Klux Klan, and other temerarious influences.[24]

Franklin McCain, one of the original Greensboro Four, has always found "rather amusing" the fact that Greensboro's Chamber of Commerce and others "used [the city's experience with the sit-ins] to their advantage" when talking to prospective industry or business, even though "as a matter of fact they were staunchly against" integration. Nonetheless, McCain does not blame the city for trumpeting the sit-ins as further evidence of Greensboro's claimed status as the "Gate City" or the "Gateway to the

New South." "I think that's only smart," McCain has said. "I'm sure if I were the chamber of commerce, I'd do the same thing."[25] James Peck was glad to return to Greensboro on the Freedom Rides, but he too noticed the apparent contradictions between Greensboro's image and some of its realities. "Though reputed for its liberalism," Peck observed, Greensboro "was the first city where the color signs started to become the rule."[26]

The students' actions the year before allowed easy passage through Greensboro and most of North Carolina for the Freedom Riders, who represented the next wave of direct action activism. On the Friday before the Ride passed through the state, the U.S. Supreme Court had agreed to hear two sit-in-related cases. Both derived from the Triangle area, one based on protests by Duke and North Carolina College students in Durham and the other on the actions of Shaw students in Raleigh.[27]

As the Freedom Riders arrived at the Greensboro station, the first thing they saw was large signs everywhere with arrows indicating the location of the colored waiting room. The colored lunchroom, which in Peck's estimation was "no bigger than a good-sized closet and equally gloomy," was closed. Apparently, the closing had happened just a week before their arrival.[28] James Farmer saw this as evidence that "the letters in advance" that they had sent, according to their Gandhian dictates, "did something."[29] Joe Perkins recounted that the Freedom Riders integrated the waiting rooms in their now-accustomed fashion as "heads turned and eyelids jumped but integration ruled the day."[30] One wonders just how shocked many of the observers were. Black patrons had been using the newly integrated lunchroom since the closing of the "colored" waiting room, and Peck recounted that "a Negro in the colored waiting room told me he was amazed when, upon entering the colored lunch room one day, he was advised to walk around to the formerly white restaurant."[31]

They spent the night of May 7 in Greensboro. That same evening, Thurgood Marshall called upon blacks in North Carolina to launch a full-scale assault on school segregation, marking another step toward more aggressive NAACP policies.[32] That night the group held a mass meeting at the Shiloh Baptist Church, the same church where the Journey of Reconciliation had met such a warm reception fourteen years earlier, in the aftermath of the outbreak of violence in Chapel Hill.[33] Although "the church looked exactly the same," Peck noted that the sit-in movement seemed to have transformed the city, at least in terms of its reputation.[34] Farmer warned his audience at Shiloh that "a little of the steam" had gone out of the desegregation fight.[35]

The meeting chair was Dr. George Simpkins Jr., head of the Greensboro chapter of the NAACP, who had phoned CORE to "get the benefit of its long experience in this technique" when the sit-ins first started. Peck noted that the local NAACP sponsored the Riders' stay in Greensboro, even though the Freedom Ride, like the 1947 Journey, received no direct support from the national NAACP office. In Peck's interpretation, "the NAACP rallied to support the Freedom Rides only after they had gained national momentum."[36] A different interpretation might perhaps focus on the disjunctions common between national organizations and their local affiliates. While the national offices of the NAACP and CORE may have conflicted, local organizations usually saw the movement as esemplastic, disregarding theoretical differences, strategic fissures, and political battles as secondary to efficacy on the ground.[37] Simpkins's willingness to engage CORE in Greensboro bolsters this interpretation, as does the warm reception the Journey participants and Freedom Riders received not only in Greensboro but throughout their trips.[38]

On May 8 the group traveled west to Winston-Salem. On their way out of Greensboro, they began to realize that they might be "surrounded by 'enemies' and plain clothes men" who wanted to keep an eye on them. Sometimes this realization that they were being watched had "its lighter aspects." Frances Bergman related one anecdote in a letter: "When we left Greensboro the *Dick* that we had spotted boarded a bus we were lined up to take. Then we discovered this was the 11:30 bus and we were to take the 11:40. So the bus rolled off with our friend frantically trying to get off—but too late."[39]

Winston-Salem, which one close observer called "another city of contradictions," had experienced widespread integration, yet when the sit-in campaign emerged in the city, many residents, businesspersons, and politicians chose to waver and resist.[40] By the time the Freedom Riders arrived for a brief stopover, however, they met with no challenges. The "terminal facilities were available" to all "regardless of race."[41] Moving on to Salisbury, the group similarly faced no difficulties. Early on a coalition of religious leaders, merchants, the mayor, and the president of Livingstone College had agreed that peaceful integration should occur, and all but one drugstore in town had gone along with the removal of discriminatory barriers.[42] While the "color signs" were still in place, the group integrated Salisbury's bus facilities, apparently having a Pied Piper effect on some observers. After watching the group ignore the Jim Crow signs, two black women sat down and received service at the white lunch counter, where they ate their meal.[43]

The "Shoe In": The First Arrest

That afternoon the group ended up in Charlotte, North Carolina's largest city. Charlotte had by and large acquiesced to integration, largely because Charlotte's business and civic leaders understood that some gradual integration was good for both business and politics. They believed "that token and controlled integration, conducted in an environment of 'civility,' could avoid damaging racial demonstrations that might undermine efforts to attract new business and industry to their city." Business leaders in Charlotte, "motivated by economic considerations," rejected the conservatism of some of the civic and professional classes in other Southern cities and "positively influenced the breakdown of racial segregation."[44]

Concerned with their city's national reputation, influential Charlotteans chose to act in the face of sit-in demonstrations when they hit the city's Uptown stores rather than resist or stall.[45] City leaders' goal was for Charlotte to become the "Atlanta of the Carolinas," and racial turmoil would not facilitate achievement of that goal.[46] The city did experience demonstrations. Black students at Johnson C. Smith University engaged in protests against segregated facilities at a number of local businesses. The nascent protest movement provoked Mayor James S. Smith to establish a "Friendly Relations Committee" to address potential racial problems. The committee, headed by former Davidson College president John R. Cunningham, set up a subcommittee of ten members, seven white, three black. The group held meetings with students and merchants at targeted businesses, and eventually the students stopped most of the sit-ins. By and large, Charlotte was able to press forward and maintain its facade of harmony and mutual respect.[47]

The student sit-in movement of 1960 never reached the stage where it spread to Charlotte's city bus or train stations.[48] But in 1961, even as CORE prepared for the Rides, delegates from the still-emerging Student Non-Violent Coordinating Committee prepared to launch a "Drive Against Travel Bias" as the centerpiece of what they called their "School Closing Project." The purpose of this undertaking was to bring attention to the *Boynton* decision and its prohibition of segregation in bus terminal restaurants. SNCC also hoped to apply pressure to ensure that Trailways' announcement that its restaurants would not deny service to anyone based on race would stand. SNCC members believed that if the Interstate Commerce Commission, Trailways' Bus Terminal Restaurants, and the Justice Department enforced their decrees, "the bus and train corporations" would "be forced to integrate all the stations and depots in a few months" because it would not be viable for facility proprietors to pay fines for every violation. Furthermore, unlike national five-and-dime chain stores, terminal restaurants could not afford to close their doors to avoid trouble "because their passengers would be so inconvenienced they would turn to other forms of transportation."[49]

The end of the school year provided an especially apt time for action: "With the closing of the College year and with thousands of students traveling across state lines on public conveyances enroute to our homes, we offer and provide the manpower for a really *MASSIVE REALIZATION* of the promise made in these decisions. Many of us, of course, will not be the hard-core activists who are ready to continue sitting when refused service and to be jailed in a strange city, but we can still be useful if we simply request service, stressing our rights as interstate passengers."[50] SNCC then set out a five-step guideline for students to follow when they implemented the plan. Because SNCC hoped for voluntary adherence, there was apparently no follow-up to evaluate the success or failure of the "Drive Against Travel Bias." Nonetheless, it is important that students were even thinking in these terms prior to the Freedom Ride. The sit-in movement had set matters in motion, so that even those who were not "hard-core activists" realized that they could play a role in forcing the hand of those who would segregate public facilities. Suddenly students saw that a new day was at hand: justice and equality were attainable, and fighting for rights was no longer the province of a radical fringe.

In a note directed at CORE Freedom Ride planners, included at the end of the announcement of the School Closing Project, SNCC observed, "We feel that this is sort of a follow-up to your Bus Trip through the South, and through that it might give further meaning to your efforts."[51] Further, on the eve of the Ride's passage through North Carolina, the Mecklenburg Organization for Political Action, a black organization consisting of both adult and student members, asked Governor Terry Sanford to use his influence to desegregate local restaurants and hotels prior to the International Trade Fair that Charlotte would host in October. As part of its argument, the Mecklenburg Organization pointed out that the local Airport 77 Restaurant had been desegregated without any deleterious effect upon business due to loss of white patrons.[52] There was a confluence between the student sit-in movement and the Freedom Riders, a logical point of conjunction between local protests in various cities throughout the region and the Freedom Ride that connected those points.

And so on May 8, the Freedom Ride arrived in Charlotte.[53] Charles Person, the youngest member of the group, went to the "whites-only" barbershop at Union Station, the location of the Greyhound terminal, and asked for a shoeshine. Minutes earlier he had successfully eaten at the whites-only counter, and as a result of his successful challenge, two local African American women had sat at the counter for the first time.[54]

After being told that service at the shoeshine booth was for whites only, Person rejoined the group. He had sat down only because his shoes needed a shine, and he did not push matters further because integrating the shoeshine stand was not part of the group's mission. After a discussion, however, the Freedom Riders decided to have Joseph Perkins, a veteran of the movement who had been jailed in Florida for his involvement in sit-ins, try his luck.[55] The proprietor of the stand, Grady Williams, denied him service, and Perkins in turn refused to move. The first arrest of a Freedom Rider, thus, was a consequence not of trying to eat at a segregated lunch counter or use a segregated bathroom or drinking fountain (the group had been successful in all these areas), but of trying to get a shoeshine. Perkins was booked on trespassing charges. Such was the potential cost even of fashion in the Jim Crow South.

Jim Peck wryly referred to Perkins's arrest as "the birth of a new 'in,' the shoe-in."[56] Oddly, when Charles Person initially asked for a shine, he had done so simply because he wanted his shoes to look nicer. Only afterward did the group "hastily decide" that when Perkins went back, he should stay in the chair until he was arrested. The police came within minutes of Williams's call. Officers G. F. Lammonds and J. C. Gordon watched Williams ask Perkins to leave three more times before they took him into custody.[57] The police took Perkins first to the city jail, and soon after authorities transferred him to the county jail.[58] He refused to post the fifty-dollar bond that would have secured his release.[59] Initially, his trial was scheduled for the following day, and the group went down to the Charlotte Recorders' Court to support their friend and colleague, but the trial was postponed. Frances Bergman believed this delay was enacted "to wait [to hold the trial] until we are out of town" and thus avoid the potential attendant publicity. She noted that while "we had expected incidents and possible arrests at lunch counters or using other facilities . . . we hadn't expected this."[60] While Perkins languished in jail, the rest of the group spent the night in Charlotte's Alexander Hotel after a mass meeting at Johnson C. Smith University.[61]

Two days later attorney Thomas H. Wyche won Perkins an acquittal based on the principles of the *Boynton* decision.[62] Notably, Wyche was an NAACP lawyer.[63] The sometimes tense but ultimately accommodating relationship among CORE, the student movement, and the NAACP thus continued despite their differences.

When CORE reported the incident, its press release read, "Perkins later said 'my shoes aren't any bigger than a white man's shoes and my money is just as green . . . why can't I get a shine when my shoes are dirty."[64] But as Perkins noted soon after, he "said no such thing." Instead those words came from CORE's Marvin Rich.[65] Apparently, a somewhat controversial new "standard organization procedure" had been put in place—one with which Perkins disagreed—directing that CORE would sometimes put together statements and report them as direct quotations.[66] Thus, the words attributed to Perkins were not his own, instead coming from CORE's national office.

At the last stop in North Carolina, Jim Peck made a small purchase, buying a bottle of fine imported brandy. James Farmer said that Peck did so "to sustain him and possibly me through the upcoming crises."[67] Small stones can cause large ripples, however, and down the road this seemingly minor purchase would prove to have effects beyond the palliative ones that Farmer and Peck imagined.

Crossing the Rubicon: The Freedom Ride Enters the Deep South

The group left Charlotte and crossed into South Carolina. Frances Bergman confided in a letter: "Frankly I am scared, but if I feel this way how must the Negro members of the group feel[?] And they are all such fine people—all so different in background yet we meet on this common problem and work as one. This is a thrilling experience and one I would not have missed. Signing off—keep your fingers crossed."[68]

South Carolina marked the group's passage into the Deep South. V. O. Key has noted the "harshness and ceaselessness of race discussion in South Carolina," attributing this to the very high percentage of black South Carolinians.[69] No progressive plutocracy or museum piece, South Carolina was a state where "preoccupation with the Negro stifles political conflict."[70] In other areas of political life, there could be dissent aplenty, but not on the issue of race. Whereas North Carolina and Virginia had a visible and in some ways proud history of moderation on the race question, South Carolina had an apodictic history of race demagoguery, second perhaps only to Mississippi's.

South Carolina in 1960 was rural and poor. Even among Southern states—overall the poorest in the country and the most denigrated based on most social and economic indicators—South Carolina ranked near the bottom, usually contending for the lowest rung with Alabama, Mississippi, and Louisiana. Low Country, Black Belt politicians dominated the state's legislature, leaving representatives from South Carolina's few densely populated pockets with little access to the levers of power. This rural control gave the Neobourbons a stranglehold on the politics of race.[71]

The political climate went hand in hand with the cultural climate of much of South Carolina. Bob Jones University proved to be a bulwark against integration and just about any other form of social advancement among South Carolina's fundamentalist white denizens. The state's political leadership thus spent a good deal of time courting the Jones dynasty and the student body at the fundamentalist stronghold.[72] Other institutions buttressed Bob Jones to support the segregationism made famous by Strom Thurmond, erstwhile Dixiecrat.

The *Brown* decision caused fulmination, furor, and activity among South Carolina's political elite. As in other states, politicians here proved willing to endanger all of public education in order to prevent even token integration.

Even prior to *Brown*, when the South Carolina portion of the case wound its way through the court system for its inevitable showdown with *Plessy*, state senator L. Marion Gressette headed up a fifteen-member committee in the legislature to address ways to confront what he perceived as the onslaught of integration. The Gressette Committee would be the first body of its kind in the country, its formation coming after the legislature had already passed a series of "preparedness measures." These included authorizing local school authorities to lease public school facilities to private interests and placing hurdles before students who wanted to transfer from one school to another, thus giving local officials the ability to prevent black students from transferring to white schools. Gressette's group further engineered the passage of an amendment to the state constitution that took the responsibility for providing free public schools away from South Carolina. In November 1952, the state's white population passed this amendment by a greater than two-to-one majority. The Black Belt overwhelmingly supported the amendment; the counties in the Piedmont upcountry did not, five actually rejecting it, to no avail.[73]

After *Brown* things got worse. The state was one of the first to pass an interposition resolution.[74] By 1956 the legislature had passed laws to deny state funds to "any school from which, and for any school to which, any pupil may transfer pursuant to, or in consequence of, an order of any court."[75] The legislature repealed mandatory attendance laws, eliminated tenure for teachers, and handed almost all control to local authorities.[76] Segregation had been the coin of the realm in the Palmetto State for the duration of the century, particularly after the onset of World War II. Because the state had mobilized early, there was little need for a wholly new policy or set of policies to respond to the realities *Brown* had wrought.[77] This was especially true because South Carolina had provided much of the impetus for the emergence of the Dixiecrats in 1948, including the party's vigorous presidential nominee, Governor Strom Thurmond.[78] The state's leadership had thus spent most of the 1950s ensuring continued adherence to Jim Crow by further codifying practice into law, tinkering with what worked rather than creating segregation anew.

Perhaps paradoxically, for all of the state's rigorous commitment to segregation, the emergence of hard-core segregationist organizations did not follow. The best historian of the reign of the Citizens' Councils, Neil McMillen, has called South Carolina one of the "weak sisters of the Deep South."[79] Although Citizens' Councils quickly established dominance among those groups that did emerge in South Carolina, the amount of organization paled when compared with their compatriots to the south and west. Part of this can be explained by internal problems within the leadership of resistance groups. Further, the lack of more respectable organizations was largely beside the point in South Carolina: hard-core segregationists, hooded Ku Kluxers, and others engaging in acts of sabotage and terrorism under the cover of night could step into those areas that the state itself had not addressed.[80] South Carolina already had such a quotidian culture of resistance, particularly among the solons in the state government, that such organized groups became superfluous.[81] When the masses are already rallying, there is little need for a pep squad.

And rallying they were. But despite the rage, there was also an active and undaunted civil rights movement going on in South Carolina.[82] It was small, and with the attention thrust upon Greensboro and other locales, sit-in campaigns in towns and cities such as Rock Hill took place away from the glare of all but local media. In the 1940s a local group, South Carolina's Progressive Democratic Party, had proved to be one of the most active and effective black political organizations in the region, serving as something of a precursor to the Mississippi Freedom Democratic Party of 1964.[83] Throughout the 1950s and 1960s, the NAACP had small footholds in the state, and it was in Summerton, South Carolina, not Topeka, Kansas, that the Legal Defense Fund began cobbling together the series of cases that would culminate in *Brown v. Board*. By 1960, however, college students had taken control, engaging in sit-ins throughout the state, including Orangeburg (where substantial violence stemmed from both white onlookers and overmatched police), Florence, Columbia, Denmark, Sumter, and—most relevant for what would happen during the Freedom Rides—Rock Hill.[84]

"Confused Friends": Rock Hill

South Carolina had followed the same historical pattern as most of the rest of the Southern states when it came to the imposition of racial stratification on interstate transport. The state did not require Jim Crow cars until 1898, and even then some observers found the rules foolish.[85] The *Charleston News and Courier*, for example, wrote that "as we have got on fairly well for a third of a century, including a long period of reconstruction, we can probably get on just as well hereafter without it, and certainly so extreme a measure [as Jim Crow railroad cars] should not be adopted and enforced without added urgent cause."[86]

South Carolinians found urgency in the cause of segregation, however, and by the middle of the twentieth century the Palmetto State had as tortured a Jim Crow code as anyplace in the South. By the postwar period there were intermittent challenges to the laws on streetcars, trains, and buses, but these tests found even less recourse than did those in Virginia and North Carolina, where at least occasionally the courts would provide a hint of the impending collapse of separate-but-equal through decisions chipping away at the doctrine. In what the radical journalist Stetson Kennedy called a "typical" case, fifty-five-year-old schoolteacher Fannye Cassanave of South Claiborne, South Carolina, was forcibly removed from a bus by police officers after she refused to move to the back at the driver's command. The police took her to jail in a paddy wagon despite the fact that she was sitting in the section reserved for black patrons. The bus driver had compressed the black section in order to provide more seating for whites. When Cassanave refused to move, the bus driver announced, "You're in the white section now. You're violating the law; so move, nigger!" He then summoned the police.[87]

By the end of the 1950s and the beginning of the 1960s, individuals had lodged a number of complaints protesting Jim Crow, often with the support of the NAACP and the Legal Defense Fund, against South Carolina airports, bus terminals, and rail stations.[88] Segregationist South Carolinians reacted predictably when the Interstate Commerce Commission finally banned segregation in interstate transport in 1955 and when the Supreme Court outlawed segregation on even intrastate public transportation in 1956.[89] In 1957 Rock Hill's black population mobilized a boycott of the city's buses after twenty-three-year-old Allene Austin was ordered to leave her seat next to a white woman.[90] In October 1959, baseball legend and integration pioneer Jackie Robinson encountered South Carolina's unwillingness to accede gently to ICC or court mandates when he and three colleagues were ordered out of the waiting room of the Greenville airport when he was returning from being the guest speaker at a gathering of the South Carolina branches of the NAACP. This led to a prayer pilgrimage and protest by the Greenville Interdenominational Ministerial Alliance and CORE on January 1, 1960, its program including a "sit-down protest" at the Greenville airport's white waiting room. The protest garnered the support of an array of South Carolina's civil rights leaders.[91] Thus, when the Freedom Riders crossed into South Carolina, they were not entering a state unfamiliar with challenges to the Jim Crow system of seating and service, although they were entering a state largely unaccustomed to successful challenges to the status quo.

Rock Hill was the first Freedom Ride stop in South Carolina. A textile manufacturing town of about thirty-three thousand people in 1961, just twenty miles or so south of Charlotte, Rock Hill was one of the few communities in the state that had experienced sustained sit-ins as part of the recent explosion of student activism. The community included an active group of CORE students, who had begun a protracted sit-in campaign on the eve of the first anniversary of the Greensboro sit-in.[92] The first challenges had actually come nearly a year earlier, as Friendship Junior College students engaged in sit-ins beginning on Lincoln's birthday in February 1960 and continuing sporadically throughout the year. The Rock Hill sit-ins were South Carolina's first. January 31, 1961, had marked an intensification of the city's campaign, when ten protesters sat down at Rock Hill's segregated McCrory's lunch counter prepared to go from sit-in to jail-in.[93]

The links between the South Carolina sit-ins and the Freedom Rides were provided by CORE field secretaries and South Carolina natives Thomas Gaither and Jim McCain. Gaither had led a student movement in Orangeburg a year earlier and moved on to Rock Hill to try to aid organization there. When he sat-in with nine black students from Friendship

Junior College at McCrory's lunch counter, it began a series of events that ratcheted tension nearly to the breaking point by the time the Freedom Riders arrived.[94]

The presiding judge in the ensuing case, Billie D. Hayes, seemed momentarily surprised when Lieutenant Thomas first testified that the students had been locked up for "three to 15 seconds" after he ordered them from the premises. He later would change this testimony to three to fifteen minutes. The officer was visibly confused during cross-examination, and he asked for and received a brief respite from testimony before proceeding. Judge Hayes stated that the students clearly had not been granted enough time to leave the store, and the activists began to think that they might actually win a civil rights case in a South Carolina court. The students pleaded not guilty, but Hayes nonetheless found them guilty and sentenced them to thirty days of hard labor or a one-hundred-dollar fine. The fine would go up to two hundred dollars if they chose to go forward with an appeal.[95] Nine of the ten students chose to serve jail time rather than pay a fine, implementing the "jail, no bail" tactic for perhaps the first time in the Civil Rights Movement.[96] At a CORE workshop in Orangeburg the previous December, the group had decided to take this stance if they were arrested in the process of protests. As Thomas Gaither recounted after his Rock Hill arrest: "The only thing they had to beat us over the head with was a threat of sending us to jail. So we disarmed them by using the only weapon we had left—jail without bail. It was the only practical thing we could do. It upset them quite a bit."[97] Eight Friendship College students and Thomas Gaither had served a sentence of thirty days on a York County road gang for their sit-in.[98]

Some parents were not thrilled by their offspring's actions, and many feared for the safety of their children on a Southern road crew. Nonetheless, most of the parents came around when they saw the commitment of the group. John Gaines, one of the protesters, recalled that his grandparents, with whom he lived, were at first filled with trepidation. Gaines's grandmother scolded him for being disobedient when he said that he had to go to jail. "But once I got locked up," he said, "she was quite changed. She came to the jail and asked me if I was all right, or needed anything." His great-grandmother was still mystified when Gaines refused the two hundred dollars bail money she tried to bring. She was afraid that the authorities would work him too hard and that he would be unable to handle it. He puzzled her by responding that "it was a privilege for a Negro to go to jail for his rights." As another student concluded, "If requesting first-class citizenship in the South is to be regarded as a crime, then I will gladly go back to jail again. The whole thing has just strengthened my conviction that human suffering can assist social change."[99] Their time in jail and on the road gang was arduous, but they received tremendous support, including a caravan of visitors. On Lincoln's birthday more than a thousand local citizens undertook a pilgrimage to Rock Hill on behalf of the imprisoned activists. The protestors also relied on one another for support over the course of their weeks in confinement.[100]

Jim McCain too had long been active in civil rights circles in South Carolina and across the South. He had been a CORE field secretary since 1957 and had helped plan and run CORE activities across the South.[101] Furthermore, McCain's cousin Osceola E. McKaine was a major NAACP activist who had founded the Sumter NAACP and was serving as its president.[102] McCain was largely responsible for coordinating CORE's actions throughout South Carolina, and he took a hands-on role in almost anything the organization did.[103] He quickly took an active role in the Rock Hill student protests.

By 1961, with the active support of both Gaither and McCain, Rock Hill had become a focal point of SNCC strategy. The students had picked up the Rock Hill protest from CORE, which had called upon the new student movement across the South to join in the Rock Hill protests. This once again reveals the sometimes uneasy but ultimately inevitable linkages among competing movement groups. At a February meeting of the SNCC coordinating committee at the Butler YMCA in Atlanta, the group unanimously chose to support the Rock Hill protestors and dispatched Ella Baker and Connie Curry to go ahead on a reconnaissance mission. Baker and Curry, investigating the situation, interrogated arrested activists, reached out to their parents, ensured that there was sufficient legal support, and contacted the media.[104]

After Baker and Curry returned to Georgia, four SNCC activists traveled to Rock Hill from Atlanta to try to join those already in jail. The names of the four who arrived in South Carolina that February read like a "who's who" of the student protest movement. Diane Nash, one of John Lewis's colleagues in the Nashville movement, Charles Jones of nearby Johnson C. Smith University in Charlotte, Ruby Doris Smith of Spelman College, and Virginia Union's Charles Sherrod all descended upon Rock Hill to fulfill SNCC executive secretary Ed King's admonition to black students across the South to join their colleagues in sit-ins and in jails. "Only by this type of action," King had declared, "can we show that the non-violent movement against segregation is not a local issue for just the individual community, but rather a united movement of all those who believe in equality."[105]

The Rock Hill movement largely failed when the arrival and subsequent arrest of the four newcomers did not signal the start of a great student awakening and the city's officials refused to yield to protests. However, as the historian Clayborne Carson has argued, Rock Hill did reveal "the willingness of activists associated with SNCC to become involved whenever a confrontation with segregationist forces developed." It further "contributed to the process of building a sense of group identity among militant students."[106] This would prove especially important in the weeks to come on the Freedom Rides, when student activists would provide a frontline phalanx for the continuing struggle. Numan Bartley has gone so far as to assert that the Freedom Rides "provided SNCC with a mission."[107] John Lewis has similarly argued that SNCC demonstrated that it "was organized and aggressive enough to" pull together activists from different protest sites to work together at a flashpoint.[108]

As if to throw the contrasts between the two Carolinas into sharp relief, Frank Porter Graham gave a speech at Winthrop College, a women's school in Rock Hill, in 1961, in the midst of the city's protests, embroiling himself in controversy. At Winthrop, Graham spoke from a general text that he had presented a number of times across the South. Depending on his venue, he veered from his prepared remarks to make relevant asides. At no time had his words caused passionate reaction one way or the other.[109] However, in Rock Hill his deviation from his prepared speech—which generally lauded the ideals of the founding generation of Americans, and which he surely intended as an oblique defense of American traditions of justice, freedom, and liberty, including civil rights—led to a chain of events he could not have anticipated.

Referring to the Rock Hill sit-ins, Graham averred, "The Southern youth movements for the same service for the same price did not have its origin in Moscow but in Carpenters Hall in Philadelphia, on the 4th of July, 1776." This was a less-than-subtle jab at those who baselessly asserted that the Civil Rights Movement was backed by communists. Within days the South Carolina House of Representatives publicly condemned Winthrop for hosting "a known agitator and advocator of circumvention of laws of this state." The censure drew wide commentary, pro and con, across the region, and Graham received letters of support and hate after the rebuke from the Columbia solons. In a column that he sent to his national syndicate and published in his own *Carolina Israelite,* legendary Charlotte editor Harry Golden asked, presumably rhetorically, "What's the matter with South Carolina? What has happened to its great tradition of freedom?"[110]

As Graham and the student protesters had discovered, South Carolina's "great tradition of freedom," in April 1961, did not extend to the civil rights arena. John Lewis observed that the student protests "had the effect of angering the citizens of Rock Hill."[111] Graham's speech and the response to it surely reveal that actions and words in support of civil rights could result in unintended consequences. The effects of this backlash were visible on the afternoon of May 9, when the first busload of Freedom Riders debarked from the bus at the Greyhound station. As Joe Perkins dealt with the legal pillar of segregation in Charlotte, John Lewis and others discovered its twin pillar, the threat of violence, in Rock Hill.

Unbeknownst to the Freedom Riders, a third pillar, federal government inaction, was also at work in Washington. On the morning of their arrival in Rock Hill, scant days after Kennedy's seemingly unambiguous statement of support for civil rights in Georgia, presidential press secretary Pierre Salinger announced that the administration was backing off from legislative action on the putative Democratic agenda of civil rights. Georgia governor Ernest Vandiver also announced that the president had promised that he would not use federal troops to enforce integration in Georgia.[112] This outraged vigilant civil rights activists, who denounced the president's seeming capriciousness. Roy Wilkins claimed that the president's actions in making such deals amounted to "offering . . . a cactus bouquet" to the movement.[113]

None of this had much effect on the Freedom Riders on May 9. Their concerns were more imminent than government waffling and backroom maneuvering. Upon their arrival, Lewis and the others knew almost immediately that the group was in trouble. Local papers had announced the arrival of "CORE tourers" engaged in a "mobile sit-in."[114] The phrase "Freedom Riders" had not yet entered the popular lexicon. Hank Thomas recalls hearing someone announce, "Here come the niggers."[115]

Lewis walked with Albert Bigelow toward the white waiting room, where they ran into young white men pulled directly from central casting. Several of them were recognizable to locals as having recently participated in violence against civil rights activists in Rock Hill.[116] They congregated around the pinball machines and leaned in the doorway, drawing on cigarettes and carrying the insouciant bearing of the aimlessly arrogant. Two of the young men stood guard over the doorway to the waiting room. Both wore leather jackets and ducktail haircuts. One spoke up as Lewis tried to pass. Pointing to a door with the "colored" sign designating the mandates of Jim Crow, he snarled something to the effect of "other side, nigger."[117]

Perhaps as a result of his extensive training and experience in non-violent, direct action protest, Lewis felt neither afraid nor nervous. He responded almost by rote with the justification the group had prepared in Washington: "I have a right to go here on the grounds of the Supreme Court decision in the *Boynton* case."[118] Despite (or perhaps because of), in James Farmer's words, Lewis's "ministerial dignity," the young men were not impressed.[119] "Shit on that," one of them replied.[120]

A group of ruffians descended upon Lewis. One punched Lewis in the side of the head. Another blow struck him square in the face. Before he knew it, he had fallen, and hard kicks were raining on his sides as the taste of blood filled his mouth. At this point Albert Bigelow stepped between the prostrate Lewis and his assailants. The sight of the big ex-navy captain caused the scene to freeze momentarily as the thugs sized up this potential barrier to their plans. Apparently, the fact that Bigelow did not look prepared to fight them emboldened the attackers, who began punching Bigelow. They must have been glad that the older man did not fight back, because it took several of their punches to fell him to one knee.

Bigelow, a strong advocate of the Quaker belief that "there is God in every man," recounted his experience in the assault at a mass meeting later that night. "I think people like" the ones who had attacked him in the station, he said, "are confused friends." "I tasted a little this afternoon," Bigelow said, "of what Gandhi called the sweetness of the opponent's violence." Even as his attackers hit him and brought him to one knee, he attempted to discuss the matter with the most aggressive of the men. He told Moses Newson of the *Afro:* "If this man . . . has that of God in him, there must be some way that I can reach it. I've got to understand that the truth as he sees it is just as real to him as my truth is to me. I tried to surprise him with moral justice." Ultimately, he wanted to tell his attacker: "I understand why you acted as you did but I think we might reach a better understanding to each other by thinking about it. I'd like to enlarge his horizon." Giving it thought for a second, Bigelow conceded, "Under the circumstances, maybe this was not the time to reason with him." But at the same time he truly believed that "they will only understand direct-action," which he understood as the responsibility "to do something you have a right to do, irrespective of the results."[121]

Meanwhile, as Bigelow futilely attempted to engage with the rabble,

Genevieve Hughes became embroiled in the confrontation. As she approached the mass of bodies in an attempt to step between them and forestall more attacks on her peers, the surging whites knocked her down. This seemed to draw a chivalrous reaction from a nearby police officer who, up until that point, had merely been watching the events before him. He began separating the aggressors from their passive victims, saying something to the effect of "All right boys. Y'all have done about enough now. Get on home."[122] Hank Thomas, who was next in line to receive a beating, today recalls: "I didn't relish it. But we were supposed to act nonchalant, like this doesn't disturb me. That's the image we were projecting—my mind is fixed on what I'm supposed to do. The most difficult thing to do is to appear unafraid when you are scared to death."[123]

Almost immediately, more police arrived. One officer sympathetically asked if Lewis, Bigelow, and Hughes wanted to press charges. By this point Lewis was wobbly but back on his feet, feeling sharp pain above his eyes and on his ribs. He later noted wryly, "My lower lip was bleeding pretty heavily. I've always had very sensitive lips. They bleed easily."[124] Following their Gandhian dictates, the group refused to press charges. Bigelow told the officer, "We don't think that's the way to settle these things."[125] This seemed to leave the officer nonplused. Here he was, making an offer to help the group bring charges against white men who had visited violence upon them in the name of Jim Crow, and they were refusing what Taylor Branch has called "his politically risky offer."[126] Lewis later justified their actions:

> Our struggle was not against one person or against a small group of people like those who attacked us that morning. The struggle was against a *system,* the system that helped produce people like that. We didn't see these young guys that attacked us that day as the problem. We saw them as victims. The problem was much bigger, and to focus on these individuals would be nothing more than a distraction, a sideshow that would draw attention away from where it belonged, which in this case was the sanctioned system of segregation in the entire South.[127]

After refusing to press charges, the Riders entered the "white" waiting room and received service. Colleagues attended to Lewis's wounds, applying bandages and attempting to reduce the swelling on his face. A few hours later, when the Trailways bus pulled up to the Oakland Avenue bus terminal, which served all non-Greyhound buses, some of the hood-lums were still gathered in cars. The Trailways terminal was locked up and vacant, the result of the company's response to the Friendship student sit-ins. The hostile locals did not attack the second group, who had missed the earlier drama, but instead followed them a few blocks as they headed toward Friendship Junior College, the locus of the Rock Hill protests a few months earlier. The next day, after mass meetings at the college, the "white" Trailways waiting room reopened. A group went in and success-fully tested the facility. Another group did the same at the Greyhound sta-tion. There was no revival of the previous day's violence.[128] The Freedom Riders had won the Battle of Rock Hill through nonviolent action even though they had suffered the only casualties.

At first this battle was a relatively hidden one. The May 10 *Rock Hill Evening Herald* ran a tiny article at the bottom of page one announcing that no incidents had been reported as the group left bound for points South.[129] However, a longer article inside the paper reported that the "bi-racial tour-ists" had announced at a mass meeting in Rock Hill's New Mount Olivet AME Zion Church the night before that they were unable to use the facili-ties because "a welcoming committee of hoodlums" attacked them.[130] Wit-nesses confirmed the "bus riders' claim" to the *Charlotte Observer.*[131]

That night at New Mount Olivet the group met with another warm reception. The audience wanted to hear from the newest heroes in the freedom struggle, and James Farmer and Elton Cox spoke. Though still a young man, Cox had established himself as quite a powerful orator, who, in Farmer's words, "brought the 'amens' rising to a crescendo throughout his talks."[132] Moses Newson of the *Afro-American* observed that Cox was "a natural for this role" of public speaker and that "the rostrum would not be the same without him."[133] As a consequence of his impressive speaking style, he had earned the nickname "Beltin Elton."

Events in Rock Hill began to change the historical status of this little band of bus riders. Violence seemed to have accomplished what a series of letters to a whole range of local, state, and national officials, and an ar-ray of media outlets, had not: It drew attention. It garnered press. It raised awareness. In short, the beatings in Rock Hill brought the Freedom Rides to the national stage, beginning a run that would last several months, the effects of which would go down in history.

The Rock Hill incident was still relatively minor. The national news media the next day would focus on Alan Shepherd's orbiting of the Earth in NASA's first manned rocket, another step in the ongoing race to put a man on the moon. The space program had captured the imagination of Americans and made them reconsider what was possible. So too would the Freedom Riders challenge the range of possibility and in so doing inspire Americans in a different, more earthbound way.

"This Might Be My Last Day": Winnsboro

On May 10 the Freedom Riders reunited with Joe Perkins after his acquittal in Charlotte. After his bus pulled into Rock Hill, several of the Freedom Riders stepped onto the bus Perkins had taken to meet them, which was bound for points farther south, to continue the trip. In Charlotte, Recorder's Court judge Howard B. Arbuckle had asked three questions pertinent to Perkins's case: Was the barbershop part of the bus station, which dealt in interstate commerce? Was Perkins engaged in interstate commerce? Was Perkins refused service strictly because of his race? To all three questions, the judge answered in the affirmative. Perkins's lawyer, Thomas Wyche, had challenged the arrest on constitutional grounds. Invoking the *Boynton* decision, Wyche asked Arbuckle to decide upon the question that the court had not decided in *Boynton*—namely whether the state could be prevented from using its police powers to enforce private discrimination. Despite the testimony of Grady N. Williams, the shop's assistant manager, who testified that the shoeshine boy at the stand told Perkins "we don't wait on colored people in the barber shop," Arbuckle deferred. He decided that there was not enough evidence to convict Perkins of trespassing.[134]

This was a victory of sorts for Perkins and the Freedom Ride. Perkins left Charlotte that afternoon with Ed Blankenheim, who had accompanied the accused for support, in keeping with the Freedom Ride policy of making sure that anyone who was arrested or otherwise in trouble had someone with them to provide whatever help they could. The two met up with the Freedom Ride in Rock Hill several hours after the day's big events. Perkins's arrest had marked the first casualty of the Ride, and he was welcomed back to the group with a warm, inquisitive reception.

In the meantime, John Lewis was confronted with a dilemma as the Freedom Ride moved on from Rock Hill. After students at Friendship College had found a medical kit and put bandages over Lewis's eyes, he prepared to continue the journey rather than check into a local hospital. He was sore but committed to the mission the group had set for themselves. Bigelow concurred. Upon Lewis's arrival at Friendship, however, he had received an unexpected telegram from the American Friends Service Committee, which had tracked him down by making calls to Nashville. Lewis had almost forgotten, but he had applied for a foreign-service project in Africa through the organization, and the telegram informed him that he was a finalist for the two-year fellowship. He would have to leave immediately for an interview in Philadelphia, using a money order that the Quakers sent with his telegram.

He had to decide quickly. The interview process would take three days, and he would be able to rejoin the Freedom Ride on Mother's Day, May 14, much of the journey still lying ahead. Since he relished the opportunity to work in East Africa and would be able to rejoin the trip soon, he decided to go ahead with the interview.[135] The next morning, after what Taylor Branch has called "soldierly farewells," a Friendship student reversed Lewis's course, taking him back to the Charlotte airport, where an Eastern Airlines flight would shuttle him to Philadelphia.[136]

His interview went well. He also had to take a physical, which he passed, although the doctors had questions about the cuts and bruises. At the end of his interview he received the news. He had been accepted for the program, but he would not be going to Africa. Instead he had been assigned to India. The program would begin at the end of summer. Although he was initially disappointed not to be going to Africa, he realized that there was a certain symmetry to his being sent to India, not only home to Gandhi's nonviolent resistance but also the place where his mentor Jim Lawson had lived and worked after winning the same fellowship in 1954. Lewis accepted the assignment and headed down to Nashville, en route to rejoin the Freedom Ride in Alabama.[137] He had missed epochal events.

In the interim, there had been a great deal more excitement, starting in Chester, a brief stopover between Rock Hill and their next destination, Sumter. As a result of the brouhaha in Rock Hill the day before, the doors of the waiting room in Chester had been hastily festooned with "closed" signs. The group had intended to eat lunch at this stop, but instead they continued on, taking an impromptu respite in Winnsboro, which Jim Peck called "an ultrasegregationist little town." Events in Winnsboro "happened so quickly," according to Peck, "it seemed like a film being rolled too fast."[138]

Upon leaving the bus, Peck followed Henry Thomas to the white lunchroom, where they both sat at the counter. A waitress told Thomas to "go around to the other side."[139] Almost immediately after Thomas refused to do so, the restaurant proprietor rushed off to call the police, who arrived within minutes. One of the officers stepped up to Thomas and told him, "Come with me, boy!" This marked the first Freedom Ride arrest for sitting at a terminal lunch counter. When Peck tried to intervene, he too was placed under arrest. It all happened so quickly that the rest of the Riders did not immediately react. However, Frances Bergman, the designated observer of the day's attempt, "got off the bus and faced the hate filled town alone" in order to find out what was going to happen to Thomas and Peck.[140] At one point, she was told "to get out of town" after inquiring about the arrests.[141] She forged on nonetheless.

In jail the two men were segregated. They were not allowed to communicate with one another while they waited several hours to find out the charges against them. The arresting officers were not even sure whether to post charges and, if so, what charges to make. The officer who had initially taken Thomas into custody wanted to throw the book at the two right away. The officer who had driven them to jail, however, thought it best to wait until they had consulted with the police chief. The driver prevailed. The Winnsboro police eventually levied a trespassing charge against Thomas and booked Peck for disorderly conduct and interfering with arrest. They were initially held on one hundred dollars bond each for trial the next day, though Winnsboro police and the Fairfield County's sheriff's office denied that any arrests had taken place.[142] In keeping with the "jail, no bail" policy of their Rock Hill cohort, the two refused to post bond. The police had also discovered the small bottle of liquor that Peck had purchased in Charlotte. They thus charged him with violating an obscure and little-enforced prohibition against possessing an open container of alcohol not bearing required South Carolina tax stamps.[143] Apparently, local officials realized that recent Supreme Court dictates would cause their case too much difficulty, and they dropped all but Peck's charges for the tax-stamp violation.[144]

The circumstances of the releases of the two men, however, differed considerably. Perhaps in an effort to scare Thomas, the police released him in the dead of night. Segregationists in car and on foot patrolled the town. Thomas, a little concerned by his release and the circumstances surrounding it, would later recall how "all those old movies I had seen about blacks being taken out of southern jails in the middle of the night, they began to come back to me."[145]

When Thomas asked the police where they were going, one said something to the effect of, "Well, you wanted to go to the bus station to get out of town, didn't you? So we're taking you there."[146] It was too late for him to catch a bus, and the station was about to close upon his arrival. Gangs of surly white men were assembled at the bus station when he returned, many more than should have been at a bus station late at night, near closing time, with no buses set to arrive or depart. Many years later Thomas recalled the situation he confronted: "In front of the bus station was a crowd of good ol' boys and I was supposed to be the entertainment for the night. The police took off. I didn't see any guns, but they had sticks and baseball bats. That's when the moment of truth hit me: this might be my last day."[147] When he showed reluctance to get out of the cruiser, one of the cops tapped his gun, as if to tell Thomas he had no say in the matter.[148] Apparently, the law and the lawless had brokered a deal in which Thomas would be given up to send a message to those who would mount a challenge to Jim Crow in Winnsboro.

Thomas somehow managed to collect himself, and with the crowd watching in disbelief, he walked back to the waiting room that had been the scene of his previous transgression and purchased a candy bar. He later explained to Moses Newson, "There was a great deal of pride in it. When I got out of that car everybody was watching to see which way I would go."[149]

Fortunately for Thomas, he had something of a guardian angel watching over him in the form of a local black minister, who at the behest of CORE had been following Thomas since his arrest. Almost as soon as the police left Thomas to his fate at the bus station, the minister pulled up and told Thomas to get in the car: "He didn't have to tell me twice. That brave man . . . he was the only thing that saved me. We hightailed it out of there. We expected gunshots any second, but they didn't come. He told me to stay down. I did."[150] The Reverend Cecil A. (C. A.) Ivory, prominent in local civil rights circles and a longtime NAACP stalwart, got Thomas to Sumter unscathed and relieved. Thus was a potential disaster averted, as the situation had all of the makings of a Deep South lynching under cover of darkness, with the tacit consent of local authorities.

Peck's release was less harrowing. Although one of the segregationists had parked his car so that his lights shone directly into Peck's cell, the white activist did not run the gauntlet that Thomas had faced. Police kept him in custody until dawn, at which point a carload of people, including Farmer, Jim McCain, and attorney Ernest A. Finney Jr., drove over from McCain's Sumter home to pick him up and post the one hundred dollars bond for his liquor violation. His case was never heard in the magistrate's court. Meanwhile, Thomas had arrived at McCain's house earlier, and so when Peck returned, the two men shared a meaningful handshake.[151]

After these frightening incidents the group was relieved to take a scheduled day off in Sumter on May 11. Minus John Lewis, the entire group was finally together again at Morris College, a historically black institution that had been the center of student protests in Sumter since March 1960, where they were quartered during their layover. Attempts to integrate the Sumter station did not materialize because of the chaos that had dispersed the group and made a test risky and logistically difficult. Although most of the events had slipped under the national radar, the Freedom Ride had proven to be the catalyst for volatile reaction that its participants had expected in Washington. On Friday, May 12, the group boarded buses headed for Georgia. Their solemn moods matched their realization of how much had changed since the relatively easy days in Virginia less than a week earlier. They were now in the Deep South.

Chapter 6

"Blazing Hell"

From Georgia into Alabama

Racial Politics in Georgia, 1961

The South Carolina experience added a new level of gravitas to the Freedom Ride. The group continued to sing freedom songs, and they could still laugh and enjoy themselves. But events in South Carolina had brought about the realization that the stakes had been raised. Violence and imprisonment were no longer the theoretical outcomes of a role-playing exercise in a Washington, D.C., Quaker safe house, but real consequences of their actions. In all likelihood, conflicts would grow more intense, menacing, and frequent as the group passed further into the maw of the Deep South.

After their day of rest in Sumter, the group boarded buses for Georgia on May 12. Over the next two days, short tests in Augusta and Athens would precede meetings in Atlanta, a city that proudly proclaimed it was "too busy to hate." The Freedom Riders could be excused if they remained skeptical of this grandiloquent claim.

Georgia, where Robert Kennedy had stated his support for civil rights just a few days earlier, had a somewhat perplexing recent history of racial politics. V. O. Key asserts in *Southern Politics in State and Nation* that Georgia fell under the sway of the "rule of the rustics," with power disproportionately vested in rural areas. Like many of its neighbors, Georgia through the 1940s was a one-party state, marked by factionalism within the dominant Democratic Party. It had for three decades been firmly under the influence of the Talmadge family. Eugene Talmadge, a four-time governor, headed a "cohesive, personal faction" in Georgia politics. Upon his death in 1946, the allegiance of this faction passed as if by primogeniture to his son Herman, who capitalized on his support by winning the governorship in 1948.[1] As a consequence, family demagoguery continued to dominate Georgia politics into the 1960s.

In 1953 Herman Talmadge had anticipated an unfavorable resolution to the Supreme Court's cases on segregated education. He thus proposed to the state legislature a "private school plan" by which an amendment to the state's constitution would allow the legislature to convert public schools to private ones and funnel public school monies into the newly created private schools by way of vouchers for students desiring to attend the newly established private institutions. Talmadge and his supporters staked their reputations on the amendment. Simultaneously, the governor announced the creation of the Georgia Commission on Education, a coalition of public officials and prominent private citizens, which he chaired. The purpose of the commission was to develop strategies to evade integration in the schools.[2]

Opposition groups emerged to fight the proposed changes, arguing that the threat they posed to the public schools was dire and would prove a mistake over the long run. Poorly financed and organized, the opposition nevertheless managed to make the final vote a close one. The balloting broke down largely along geographic and demographic lines, rural voters tending overwhelmingly to support the amendment while urban voters opposed it. The supporters, however, carried the day in a reasonably close referendum held in November 1954.[3] The Georgia legislature eventually repealed compulsory school-closing laws that it had supported, but through 1961 it shifted focus, adopting local-option and freedom-of-choice plans, as well as the tuition-grant system.[4]

The *Brown* decision proved to be a key catalyst in Georgia as across the South. School segregation became the dominant issue in the minds and on the tongues of state politicians, who, in Numan Bartley's words, "maneuvered frantically to occupy the extreme segregationist position."[5] However, with the seeming unanimity that emerged in the wake of the *Brown* decision came an unexpected consequence: the state's two factions, best labeled the "Talmadge" and "anti-Talmadge" groups, nearly disintegrated. Backlash against *Brown* caused the anti-Talmadge group to crumble, and in the process the Talmadgites lost all sense of cohesion, especially as opportunistic politicians tried to out-race-bait one another with indignant fulminations against the Supreme Court and integration. The "dual-factionalism" that Key identifies as having taken hold under Talmadge the elder gave way in the wake of the biggest threat to segregation that Georgia and the rest of the South had yet encountered. Herman

Talmadge was ineligible to run for reelection, so his protégés had to try to outdo one another in order to take his place. Thus, even with the waning force of the anti-Talmadge coalition, the Talmadge faction too ceased to exist as a semicoherent political entity.[6]

Organized resistance in the form of Citizens' Councils and similar groups did not step into the breach created by the transition in Georgia politics. The other "weak sister" of the Deep South, Georgia had an even less vibrant organized resistance culture than did its "sibling" South Carolina. Neil McMillen has argued, "The Peach State stands apart in the history of southern resistance for it alone among the five states of the lower South failed to develop a viable organized segregation movement."[7] The only even vaguely prominent group that emerged, the States' Rights Council of Georgia, Inc., enjoyed a membership of fewer than ten thousand. McMillen does not believe that white Georgians had entered an enlightened phase by 1954 or even that the state was more tolerant of integration than Mississippians or Alabamans. Instead, he argues, the leadership of the groups that did emerge was weak. More fundamentally, the politics of segregation in Georgia made such groups superfluous and secondary to individual and group self-interest.[8]

Another reason why Citizens' Councils did not need to emerge in Georgia was that another kind of watchdog group existed to supplement the apocalyptic rhetoric of the politicians vying to carry on the Talmadge legacy. Georgia continued to be, in the decades-old words of W. E. B. Du-Bois, "the Invisible Empire State"—the home of the revival of the Second Ku Klux Klan in the 1920s and in the 1950s still the epicenter, alongside Alabama, of Klan activity.[9] Historically, the rule of tinderbox, pistol, whip, and rope, the accoutrements of racial vigilantism, was not unfamiliar to a sizeable number of white Georgians.[10] Between 1882 and 1959, according to the Tuskegee Institute, the final arbiter on such matters, Georgia ranked second only to Mississippi in both the total number of lynchings (578 for the Magnolia State compared to Georgia's 530) and the number of lynchings of blacks (538 to 491).[11]

Despite these trends, Georgia was not immune to the changes sweeping across the South in the early 1960s.[12] As elsewhere, in Georgia an active, vocal, and increasingly visible student protest movement had emerged, no longer willing to accede to the demands of the system and anxious to confront Jim Crow head-on. In March 1960, the Atlanta Appeal for Human Rights, an organization formed by students from the six affiliated institutions of the Atlanta University Center (Clark, Morehouse, Morris

Brown, and Spelman Colleges; Atlanta University; and the Interdenominational Theological Center), which was at the center of black intellectual and cultural life in Atlanta and beyond, placed an advertisement in the *Atlanta Constitution* that ran on March 9. The advertisement, "An Appeal for Human Rights," asserted that the students had "joined our hearts, minds, and bodies in the cause of gaining those rights which are inherently ours as members of the human race and as citizens of these United States." They particularly abhorred and could not "tolerate, in a country professing democracy and among people professing Christianity, the discriminatory conditions under which the Negro is living today in Atlanta, Georgia—supposedly one of the most progressive cities in the South." They then went on to provide a list of the "inequalities and injustices . . . against which we protest." These included segregation in education, jobs, housing, voting, hospitals, movies, concerts, restaurants, and law enforcement.[13]

And so the movement spread to Georgia. On March 15, 1960, nearly a week after the "Appeal for Human Rights" ran, two hundred students began a simultaneous sit-in at ten dining facilities, including those at the state capitol, city hall, and the county courthouse.[14] The sit-ins then spread from Atlanta to Savannah, Macon, Columbus, Augusta, and Marietta. By September 1961 more than seven thousand students from the Atlanta University Center, Paine College, local high schools, and the Committee on Appeal for Human Rights had participated in sit-ins, at least 292 having been arrested on a range of charges that included refusing to leave private property, disorderly conduct, loitering, violating ordinances against picketing without a license, violating statutes against disrobing in public, and trespassing. Students from all-white Emory University joined the black students. They engaged in a range of protest actions, including picketing, mass marches, the laying of wreaths at the capitol building, kneelins, stand-ins at voter registries, mass meetings, boycotts, and sitting in the front of city buses. They targeted government offices but also golf courses.[15] One sit-in even included a theatrical performance at Atlanta's Municipal Auditorium.[16]

The protests had some of the desired effects. Atlanta began to hire black drivers for city buses, however slowly and in token fashion. Atlanta's taxis and cars-for-hire also desegregated. The city hired a housing code inspector, and Mayor William B. Hartsfield, a relative racial moderate, told a civic group that segregated hotels, restaurants, and other facilities hurt the city's economic development.[17] According to a Southern Regional Council Report, Hartsfield rejected the development of an interracial committee because he felt that influential whites could not be persuaded to serve on it. The mayor believed "that interracial communication and planning was a normal part of the duties of Southern municipal officers, and that the responsibility for interracial mediation" stood squarely on his shoulders. Despite this official stance, business and civic leaders engaged in informal talks with student groups, usually at the behest of the former.[18] This mediation clearly had a positive effect.

Columbus desegregated the Muscogee County airport. McIntosh County officials appointed an African American man to the board of registrars. Savannah desegregated its golf course, lunch counters, public library, and buses; its citizens also elected blacks to park and recreation bodies.[19] However, stalemate soon set in after a series of arrests and other incidents (including antiprotest picketing by members of a local Citizens' Council) caused a breakdown between white and black representatives on an interracial committee. Further complicating matters were tensions between the NAACP, which vowed to continue protests until a series of demands were met, and a group calling itself the "Negro Citizens Protective League," which claimed to be seventeen hundred members strong and which voted to fight the sit-ins, which some local blacks saw as the actions of outside agitators.[20]

Georgia faced its sternest test in early 1961, when the University of Georgia confronted integration. After more than a year of litigation, Charlayne Hunter and Hamilton Holmes, both from Atlanta, became the first blacks to attend the state's flagship institution in Athens. After Hunter and Holmes had been on campus less than a week, most of it placid, a riot took place. Echoing events of the Autherine Lucy imbroglio at the University of Alabama in 1956, Georgia officials seized upon the riots as a pretense to suspend the two students "for their own safety," setting off another round of court challenges. A new court order returned the two weary students to campus, the state eventually abandoned massive resistance as a way to confront school desegregation, and the University of Georgia had its first black students.[21]

In 1961, Georgia, like the rest of the South, wrestled with the demands of black student protesters and the expectations of white segregationists. The one group demanded integration now, the other resistance forever. Despite Georgia's Deep South pedigree and the ongoing stand of Governor Ernest Vandiver, the student movement by 1961 had made headway in Georgia as it had in North Carolina, Virginia, and South Carolina.[22] The state was not as one on integration, and there was substantial variation from place to place, city to city, and region to region. Little if any progress had been made in the state's brutal Black Belt, a region as entrenched in its outlook as any in the South. But when the Freedom Ride passed through Georgia, its impetus was not entirely alien, especially in the relatively urbane municipalities through which it traveled.

Interregnum: Riding through Georgia

Georgians were among the first to pass Jim Crow streetcar laws in the wave of racial hostility that swept the South in the last decade of the nineteenth century. In 1891 the state legislature passed a law requiring segregation only "as much as practicable," an onerous prohibition for black passengers, to be sure, but hardly up to the standards that future generations of white Georgians would claim to be inviolable social practice etched in history and law.[23] In 1900, however, Atlanta, Rome, and Augusta added their own laws to the books enhancing the state's provisions.[24] In the years around the turn of the twentieth century, protests against Jim Crow streetcars occurred throughout the South, with Georgia's being especially efficacious. Three of the most successful such boycotts of the 1890s came in the wake of attempts to enforce Georgia's 1891 law: Atlanta in 1892–93, Augusta in 1898, and Savannah in 1899. Protesters also staged boycotts in Atlanta and Rome in 1900, in Augusta from 1900 to 1903, and in Savannah in 1906 and 1907.[25] After this fertile period of streetcar protests came an era of relative quiescence as civil rights protest generally declined, what activity there was tending to take place over other issues and about other humiliations.

The first Freedom Ride stop in Georgia came on Friday, May 12, when the group arrived in Augusta, just across the border from South Carolina. CORE had made arrangements for the Riders to meet with Paine College students in this city on the Savannah River. The local contact, Richard Stenhouse of Paine, helped arrange for lodging, as well as for the mass meeting that night.[26] At the bus terminal in Augusta there were no problems when the group mixed and used the facilities.[27] This occasion marked the first time black patrons had successfully eaten at the terminal restaurants. Just a few months before, police had arrested a black serviceman for trying to eat at the facility. The event occurred with little fanfare. Jim Peck noted, "Neither racist hoodlums nor mere curiosity seekers gathered."[28] James Farmer concluded that, as in North Carolina, Augustans "knew we were coming and made appropriate preparations."[29]

Curious as to whether the accommodation was for show after the increasing attention that South Carolina events had brought to unsuspecting facility managers where incidents occurred, a test team went back to the station later that evening to see if those not perceived to be Freedom Riders would receive the same treatment. Herman Harris, an African American who had joined the trip in the past couple of days, accompanied Walter Bergman to both terminal restaurants, where the two received courteous service.[30]

The next day the group again boarded buses in what had become a familiar ritual. The Greyhound and Trailways buses chugged over Route 78 toward Athens. Home of the beloved Georgia Bulldogs and the less beloved but begrudgingly accepted Hamilton Holmes and Charlayne Hunter, Athens was a quintessential university town. The city had seen a few civil rights protests and garnered unwanted attention as a result of the unrest following the appearance of the two black Atlantans on campus, but otherwise Athens enjoyed tranquility. The Freedom Ride did not awaken the city from its somnolence. The group received service at the city's sole bus terminal restaurant with no problems. As Jim Peck recounted, "There were no gapers. A person viewing the . . . desegregated lunch counter and waiting room during our fifteen-minute rest stop might have imagined himself at a rest stop up North rather than deep in Georgia."[31]

Meanwhile, that same day the Fifth Circuit Court of Appeals served to obliterate the distinction between intrastate and interstate transportation when it ruled on a Birmingham case. In Birmingham the train station had one waiting room for interstate passengers and one for black intrastate passengers, an almost comic attempt to maintain segregation while at the same time adhering minimally to the dictates of the courts. Birmingham was not alone in this sort of arrangement.[32] Within a few days the Freedom Riders would enter Birmingham, where they would discover the wide breach between social practice and legal doctrine in the South's Steel City.

The group spent just a few minutes in Athens before continuing on their way. The next stop was Atlanta, gleaming jewel of the New South. "The City Too Busy to Hate" was a model for the region. Led by a progressive business culture that had managed to draw in a number of national businesses, Atlanta seemed able to transcend the quagmire of race relations that had bedeviled most of the rest of the South. It had avoided the sort of school integration crises that had cast aspersion on cities such as New Orleans and Little Rock. It had no reputation for violence like Birmingham and Montgomery. And while Atlanta was the capital of Georgia, which had seen more than its share of race baiters and demagogues in the state house and the governor's mansion, the city managed to transcend the parochial bounds of state politics, unlike such state capitals as Jackson and Columbia. Atlanta had polished itself to a shine that drew the attention of Northerners for all the right reasons.

But a good shine can cover extensive scuffmarks, and Atlanta was not necessarily too busy to hate, just perhaps busy enough covering up the hatred. For one thing, there were two Atlantas, the nexus of which was the intersection of Peachtree Street and Auburn Avenue.[33] One of these Atlantas, which ran along what locals called "Sweet Auburn," was among the most vibrant black communities in America. This area had the highest concentration of black businesses anywhere and an engaged, active political world. The Auburn Avenue elite did not push for a citywide voice, did not push for integration. They had a nice hold on power and status within their insular and insulated world, and at the same time, because of the development of a full-fledged black community, many of the leaders legitimately believed that autonomy was better than integration in a larger society that did not want them. Atlanta also differed from the rest of the South in its consortium of respected black universities, which nurtured the local black elite.

The world presented to Northerners was best represented by Peachtree Street, the glimmering axis of white Atlanta. Peachtree represented the Atlanta of Coca-Cola, which had long maintained its corporate headquarters in the city. It was the Atlanta of skyscrapers. It was the Atlanta of business and industry. It was the Atlanta the Chamber of Commerce touted to outsiders, usually corporate investors looking for a hospitable and stable base of operations in the South. But the Atlanta of Peachtree Street was also an ersatz Atlanta, all folderol and chintz and surface gloss, covering the reality of a city that was as unyielding on segregation as most in the South.

In 1961 Ivan Allen took over from William Hartsfield as mayor of Atlanta. Many saw Allen as a fundamentally sympathetic leader who drew some black Atlantans into the power structure. Others saw him as a paternalist who would use race on a whim, such as when he had a wall constructed on Peyton Road in the southwest part of the city in 1961, when blacks were trying to expand their living possibilities outward.[34] In short, white Atlanta was full of contradictions.

By 1961, Atlanta had proved not to be immune to the sit-ins that had spread across the region. The protests in Atlanta may have been the largest and best organized anywhere.[35] The University Center proved to be a reservoir of protesters, and SCLC and SNCC had their headquarters in the city. Martin Luther King Jr. was from Atlanta, and the student sit-ins would forge a new generation of black leaders, including Lonnie King, a returning veteran, and Joseph Pierce and Julian Bond, fellow Morehouse students who set in motion the events that would lead to the publication of the "Appeal for Human Rights" in the *Atlanta Constitution.* On March 15 two hundred University Center students sat-in at ten downtown restaurants in city, county, and government buildings to protest discrimination. Seventy-six of these students went to jail, released after leaders within the black community came up with their bond money. Atlanta students were active in the formation of SNCC and took leadership roles in various national conferences. The Atlanta movement accelerated in scope and intensity throughout 1960, and while police fought to maintain order, they did not resort to force beyond arrests.[36]

The sit-ins had continued intermittently into the spring of 1961, with no resolution having been reached between the students and the Atlanta powers-that-be when the Freedom Riders entered the city limits on May 13. As usual, Gordon Carey had made arrangements for the group's one-night stay in Georgia's largest city. Ed King, the contact person in Atlanta, had set up a dinner for the group that night with Martin Luther King Jr. The group would also attend a mass meeting with King. This would be the first time the Freedom Riders would cross paths with the man who by 1961 had become the national face of the Civil Rights Movement, although he had little to do with the new student-led direction it had taken. Carey had also made arrangements for James Farmer to meet with radio station WAOH once the group arrived.[37]

Local and state Jim Crow laws were still on the books when the Greyhound and Trailways buses rolled into their respective stations that May day, carrying the traveling sit-in.[38] A large group of students, many active in the ongoing protests, met the Freedom Riders at the Greyhound station.[39] Ed King of SNCC was among them.[40] The restaurant was closed for repairs, but the group used the waiting room and rest facilities with no problems.[41] The ease with which the group passed through Georgia astounded Joe Perkins, the group leader in the Greyhound terminal. His accounts of the tests in Augusta and Athens both simply read: "Terminal desegregated." Atlanta earned the notation "and *more* desegregation," as if it had become commonplace.[42] The Trailways facilities were all open, and the group on that bus used them with no difficulties.

The dinner with King, held at a fancy black-owned restaurant on Auburn Avenue, seemed to go well. King brought along Wyatt Tee Walker, while among the student representatives were Ed King and Lonnie King, who were not related to one another or to the more famous preacher with whom they broke bread. The group toasted a successful journey over some seven hundred miles of sometimes hostile Southern territory, and King lauded their courage and their example.[43] They shared their adventures to that point, and James Farmer recalled that King "listened in a very relaxed and interested fashion and observed that this was nonviolent direct action at its very best." He also beamed with pride about his membership on CORE's national advisory board. He wished the Riders well and offered what help he could provide on the rest of their trip. When the bill came, there was an awkward moment. Farmer waited for King to offer to pick up the check for the dinner he had ostensibly hosted. Farmer then "finally reached slowly for it, certain King would beat me to the punch. He made no move, so to my surprise I found myself picking up the tab." His annoyance was lost on most of the group, however, and after King shook hands and spoke with each Freedom Rider, they returned to their lodgings at one of the local universities, "heartened," in Farmer's words, "by this contact with the man who had become, without question, the symbol of the civil rights movement in America."[44]

Before leaving, King pulled aside Simeon Booker of *Jet* magazine, who was accompanying the group. Despite his relaxed, prideful, and encouraging facade, King had concerns. He had just returned from Alabama, where he had attended the SCLC board meeting in Montgomery. He knew that city well and could surmise the mood of much of the rest of the state. The Freedom Ride had been drawing more attention with each passing day, and attendant with that publicity was a rise in the level of hostility toward an exercise that many Southerners considered provocative. In many ways the increased publicity was a good thing, exactly what the Freedom Riders expected and wanted. But they had no choice as to who took in the newspaper, radio, and television accounts of their impending arrival; the Ku Klux Klan, Citizens' Councils, and others were all reading, listening, and watching.[45] King told Booker, "You will never make it through Alabama." The reporter responded with a joke about how he would stick close to rotund James Farmer, "the only one I can outrun."[46] Fred Shuttlesworth had also sent out warning signals to CORE, and Farmer had his own intelligence sources scouting the scene, reporting dire forebodings.

After the group returned to their housing for the night, they held a meeting to go over last-minute details for the next day's journey into Alabama. Trip organizer Farmer announced that he would lead the tests at each stop that the first bus made. "This was going to be the most danger- ous part of the trip," he later recalled, "and so I appointed myself as the leader of the tests."[47] He assigned the experienced Jim Peck to serve as group leader for the other bus. Farmer reminded everyone that now more than ever they needed to remain disciplined and that there would be occa- sions when impromptu decisions would have to be made. If possible, the group would consult on those decisions. If not, however, the group leaders would choose courses of action, and the rest of the group would comply. Upon adjournment of the meeting, the group huddled and sang "We Shall Overcome."[48]

That night someone awakened Farmer to tell him that he had a long- distance phone call from his mother. Ten days earlier his father had entered a hospital in serious condition from complications that had arisen after surgery to remove a cancerous growth on his tongue. The elder Farmer also suffered from diabetes. While he lay in bed, he had warned his son that the Freedom Ride might be okay through to Georgia, but that in Ala- bama "they will doubtless take a potshot at you. With all my heart, I hope they miss." He asked his son for a copy of the group's itinerary and then said, "Son, I wish you wouldn't go. But at the same time I am more proud of you than I have ever been in my life, because you are going. Please try to survive."[49]

Those were among the last words Farmer heard from his father. He knew even before he picked up the phone receiver in Atlanta the news he was about to hear on the other end—his father had passed away. He would have to leave immediately for Washington for the burial. Farmer experi- enced a range of emotions. He felt the inevitable sorrow and pain and loss. But he also felt "a sense of reprieve, for which I hated myself. Like every- one else, I was afraid of what lay in store for us in Alabama, and now that I was to be spared participation in it, I was relieved, which embarrassed me to tears."[50] His mother would later recount how Farmer's father died after hearing where the group was on its itinerary. She would, for the rest of her life, believe that her husband let himself slip away to save his son's life: "My mother said he willed his death because he had my schedule before him and believed I would be killed."[51]

The next day the group gathered for an early-morning breakfast be- fore their departure. Farmer told the group his news and promised that he would rejoin them in Alabama as soon as he could. He entreated them to keep in contact with him.[52] They agreed unanimously to forge onward.

Meanwhile, a group of students had joined them in Atlanta. Joe Perkins would take over as group leader on the Greyhound bus. Jim Farmer headed for Washington, joining John Lewis as the second original member of the Freedom Ride called away from the group and its rendezvous with destiny. The buses pulled onto U.S. 78 with Freedom Riders, regular passengers, and—unbeknownst to almost everyone—unannounced plainclothes investigators on board.[53] They headed toward Alabama. It was May 14, Mother's Day.

"The Heart of Dixie": The Politics of Race in Alabama

Jim Peck later reflected that the group's experiences in Georgia had provided "clear proof of how desegregation can come peacefully in a Deep South state, providing there is no deliberate incitement to hatred and violence by local or state political leaders."[54] There would be no such restraint on the part of the leadership in Alabama.

Historian E. Culpepper Clark has written: "Nowhere did the images of freedom's struggle or the faces of evil show themselves in sharper relief than in Alabama. Alabama was to the civil rights movement what Virginia was to the Civil War—its significance lending itself to enlargement in the public mind because the most memorable engagements occurred on its soil."[55] In the minds of many, the Montgomery bus boycott marked the beginning of the modern Civil Rights Movement.[56] Martin Luther King had become the most charismatic national spokesperson for the cause of civil rights during that boycott, which led to the formation of SCLC and to a wave of similar campaigns across the South. In a sense, Montgomery served as a catalyst, much as Greensboro would just a few years later. In 1956 Autherine Lucy became the first black person to try to integrate the University of Alabama. The state responded by marshaling its resources to prevent that from happening, foreshadowing the implementation of massive resistance to *Brown* before the events at Little Rock, New Orleans, and the University of Georgia in the years before the Freedom Ride. White supremacy was a powerful force in Alabama, second perhaps only to Mississippi in its intensity and scope. Back in the 1930s the case of nine black boys charged with raping two white women had become a cause célèbre, intertwining many of the white South's favorite bogeymen—black sexuality unleashed on white maidenhood, communism and outside agitation, imperious judgment from the sanctimonious North.[57]

V. O. Key notes that "the political distance from Virginia to Alabama must be measured in light years," and even in 1961 his observation was true. Whereas in the Old Dominion deference to the political and social oligarchy was encapsulated in the Byrd machine, Alabamans were not so easily corralled. Key observes that in Alabama "a wholesome contempt for authority and a spirit of rebellion akin to that of the Populist days resist the efforts of the big farmers and 'big mules'"—Birmingham's industrial power brokers—"to control the state. Alabamans retain a sort of frontier independence, with an inclination to defend liberty and to bait the interests."[58]

Politicians tried to capitalize on this spirit in a number of ways. Some—such as "Big Jim" Folsom and a feisty populist by the name of George Corley Wallace—did so with a brand of country populism that held broad appeal for the state's rural interests. After 1954, however, the quickest way to appeal to the masses was to skip their heads and go right to their guts. Most effective at this was John Patterson, who used a firebrand racism buttressed by the all-but-open support of the Ku Klux Klan to defeat Wallace in the 1958 campaign for governor. That 1958 campaign also marked a change in Wallace, who reputedly proclaimed something to the effect of, "Well boys, they out-niggered me this time. But no other son-of-a-bitch will ever out-nigger me again."[59] And indeed, no one else in Alabama or elsewhere ever would.

Nonetheless, in May 1961 John Patterson was the governor of Alabama, the state that proudly claimed to be "the Heart of Dixie." Alabama had been among the first Southern states whose legislatures called for interposition against *Brown,* and it then went one better by declaring the court's decision null and void.[60] When Folsom tried to hedge, he paid the ultimate political price: Big Jim's attempt to resist the worst excesses of massive resistance lost him his job. For in Alabama there was a groundswell of massive resistance, and the most effective politicians would not be those who resisted the wave, but those who could ride it. Governor Patterson followed sentiment within the state.[61]

Far away from the hustings and the rostrums was the familiar menace of violence. Although Alabama "only" ranked fifth in both the number of total lynchings and the number of lynchings of Negroes in the more than three-quarters of a century since the Tuskegee Institute had begun keeping statistics in 1882, it was nonetheless at the center of postwar Klan activity.[62] The Ku Klux Klan and its associated brethren (such as the "Men of Justice") enforced the orthodoxy of white supremacy throughout the state and region. The secret fraternity had a long history in the state, reaching back to 1916, when the revival of the Reconstruction-era organization spread out from Georgia. For many years the Klan was the refuge of respectable whites, for whom membership in the group was little more than a variant on belonging to the Kiwanis or the Rotary Club, but by 1961 that era had passed. Prominent Alabamans such as Hugo Black had long since renounced their membership in an organization they had earlier seen as giving them access to a certain element of the political and social elite. By the time the Freedom Ride crossed from Georgia into Alabama, the Ku Klux Klan meant but one thing—vigilantism accompanied by violence and aimed squarely at blacks.

Supplementing the Klan and its ilk was what some called the country club Klan: the Citizens' Councils. Although it took Alabama's whites time to mobilize their Councils, once they did, it was with a vigor that only Mississippians surpassed. Unlike in Georgia and South Carolina, Alabama's Citizens' Councils took the lead in pushing massive resistance and stood at the forefront of defiance.[63] The movement began in the Black Belt, and after a series of challenges to segregation, including the Montgomery bus boycott and Autherine Lucy's truncated stay at the University of Alabama, chapters exploded across the state. By the late 1950s, at least one chapter, the North Alabama Citizens' Council, was virtually indistinguishable from the original Ku Klux Klan of the Confederacy in Birmingham.[64] Even after the movement began to wane in the late 1950s, the Alabama Councils held disproportionate sway among some of the state's governing elite, including John Patterson and later George Wallace.[65] Innumerable politicians across the state maintained strong ties with the Councils.[66]

The student movement spread across Alabama despite the state's demonstrable truculence, or perhaps because of it. The first manifestations of the movement came in Montgomery on February 25, 1960, when thirty-five students from Alabama State College took seats in the county courthouse snack shop and insisted upon service. Taking a cue from events in Montgomery, young people in Tuskegee, Mobile, Huntsville, and even Birmingham mounted their own sit-ins and protests. Montgomery saw the worst violence when whites beat a black woman, a black photographer, and a jailed student.[67] There were also incidents in Tuskegee and Birmingham, where the level of protest was relatively mild, largely because of protestors' reluctance to act too boldly in Bull Connor's city.[68] Though there had been protests in Alabama, virtually no desegregation had resulted. The Freedom Riders journeyed into the most hostile territory yet on May 14.

The Mothers' Day Massacre, Part 1: Anniston

Alabama in 1961 was no place for moderates on the race question. Though there had been a brief interlude after the *Brown* decision when moderate politicians tried to forge a route through the segregationist dilemma, the masses resisted, and extremism became the coin of the realm. In its summary report on the Freedom Rides, the Southern Regional Council observed:

> Violence in Alabama, from May 14–25, revealed the truth about "massive resistance." The defiant words hurled by state and community leaders at the law of the land after 1954 received their final definition in the terror of Anniston, Birmingham, and Montgomery. Alabama in May, 1961 reproduced in a few long days a lot of southern history, let loose again a history which most of the South is successfully overcoming. But there it was: the mob and its sadism. The silent, acquiescent "good people"; the inflammatory public spokesmen; the disdain for law; and, the inevitable defeat.[69]

Commenting a few years later on the question of moderation versus radical segregation in Alabama, the journalist Calvin Trillin explained that the moderates were smart segregationists who held sway throughout the upper and border South. But Alabama "was generally agreed . . . the world headquarters for dumb segs."[70] John Patterson fit comfortably into this latter category of "dumb segs," a derisive term for segregationists. The governor had once declared that integration would come to Alabama only "over my dead body." In his inaugural address, he had drawn his line in the sand: "I will oppose with every ounce of energy I possess and will use every power at my command to prevent any mixing of white and Negro races in the classrooms of this state."[71] Of course there were moderates in Alabama. And of course there were those who knew in their hearts that the chosen path of fighting to maintain segregation was an unwise one. But the segregationists ruled the day in the political and thus the social and cultural arenas. Patterson's election demonstrated that beyond a doubt.

On the day the Ride entered Alabama, the *Montgomery Advertiser-Journal* published a special "Vacation, Fun and Travel Guide" touting Alabama as a great location for tourists.[72] While hardly tourists, the Freedom Riders did plan to hit the major Alabama cities of Birmingham and Montgomery before crossing into Mississippi. However, Patterson made it clear that there might be difficulty. Both reflecting state sentiment and stoking it, the governor announced, before the group arrived in Alabama, "The people of Alabama are so enraged that I cannot guarantee protection for this band of rabble-rousers."[73] Such was the state of race relations in Dixie in 1961 that Alabama's chief law enforcement official publicly announced that he would be incapable of keeping order within state borders when a group of unarmed, nonviolent civil rights protesters passed through, exercising rights that the Supreme Court clearly had established they possessed. As a consequence, the most explosive days of the Freedom Ride would come in Alabama.

The last stop in Georgia came in Tallapoosa, where nothing of note transpired. Just across the border, the first Alabama stop, in Heflin, was equally uneventful. Alabama's laws regarding segregation on common carriers extended back to 1891, and by 1961, separation of the races at bus stations and train terminals was simply a given.[74] Nonetheless, the calm in tiny Heflin must have made what occurred just outside of Anniston, some ninety miles from Atlanta and thirty miles from the Georgia border, all the more jarring.[75] In the words of historian E. Culpepper Clark, "Mother's Day, May 14, 1961, signaled an end to segregation's Indian Summer in Alabama."[76] As the Greyhound, the first of the two buses, approached Anniston, a known hotbed of Klan activity, the bus driver made an announcement. Other drivers leaving Anniston and heading east were radioing in warnings that there was trouble brewing up ahead.[77]

Anniston's terminal had been the scene of a horrific incident of violence the previous January. Arthur Bacon, a Talladega College senior, was traveling from his home in West Palm Beach, Florida, back to Talladega aboard the Kansas City Special. When he arrived in Anniston on the morning of January 2, he expected to meet the Talladega College travel service, which would take him the remaining fifteen or so miles to the school. After he arrived, at about 8:30, Bacon tried to use the interstate facility in the station. He would later recall, "The waiting room was one which traditionally had been reserved for white[s] only, but as a result of the Supreme Court ruling [in *Boynton*] it could no longer be thus segregated, and I felt I should exercise my rights as a citizen." Bacon entered and left the waiting room several times to see if the car for which he had been waiting had arrived. A Talladega College employee picked him up, but before the car could leave, five white men set upon Bacon, beating him severely.[78] Earlier that morning, Andrew Lawler Sr., a Talladega employee, had also been attacked.[79] The NAACP inquired about the beating, but nothing came of it.[80]

A few days afterward, Talladega students marched around the police station in silent protest. A gathering crowd of hostile whites jeered, spat upon the students, and shouted at them. A chain-wielding ruffian belted a student in the face. A police car eventually escorted the protesters out of town, though one car carrying students was hit by gunfire and others were pelted with stones. Reflecting on his ordeal, Bacon said: "This was a terrible experience for a loyal citizen to have to go through, but it has made me more determined than ever to fight for justice, decency, and human dignity in America. I have no animosity or hatred for anyone. But it hurt me deeply that one group of men could do such a thing to a human being."[81]

The Freedom Riders were prepared for violence. The foreboding words King had spoken to Simeon Booker; the advance warnings from Fred Shuttlesworth; Farmer's own intelligence gathering, particularly from Gordon Carey and Thomas Gaither—all pointed to an encounter with white supremacists in which people were bound to get hurt. As Jim Peck, who rode the Trailways bus, later recounted, however, "We did not anticipate that the violence would start two hours before we would get to Birmingham."[82]

The Greyhound was the first of the two buses to arrive in Anniston on that morning. It was scheduled for a half-hour layover before continuing west toward Birmingham on Route 78. Hank Thomas was aboard that bus, and upon arriving in Anniston he realized that "if we thought we were having a party" up until then, "we knew the party was over now."[83] He would later liken the scene to Western movies "where a showdown was about to take place between the good guys and the bad guys, and where most of the local people were staying home watching behind closed doors."[84] There were six Freedom Riders on that first bus in addition to Thomas: Ed Blankenheim; Albert Bigelow; Genevieve Hughes; Joe Perkins; Jimmy McDonald; and a recent addition, Mae Frances Moultrie, a black Morris College student from Sumter, South Carolina. Moses Newson and Charlotte Devree continued to accompany the group as journalists. As the bus approached Anniston at about 2:10 in the afternoon, another Greyhound leaving Anniston flagged it down. A man came aboard and warned the group that angry whites were gathering at the station up ahead.

Newson, the *Baltimore Afro-American* journalist, called what transpired next "blazing hell." Almost immediately upon the bus's entry into the station, a mob of "mean-looking, shirt-sleeved ruffians" unleashed their fury. Someone shouted in a "bull voice": "This is Alabama you black bastards. Come on out and integrate." Others called them "yellow," "cowardly," and of course "communists."[85] One member of the mob shouted to Albert Bigelow and Ed Blankenheim: "Down here we teach our niggers to pick cotton. Don't you teach yours how to talk?" Local police flitted among the crowd, chatting with some members of the mob, while others attacked the bus. "There is no doubt in my mind," Moses Newson wrote a few days later, that the local police "would have allowed the mobsters to come aboard the bus and beat us to a pulp had not" two undercover officials "kept them back."[86]

The Greyhound had three officials accompanying it, two of them undercover officers, Harry Sims and Eli Cowling, who blocked the door and made his identity known. The third was a Greyhound official, Roy Franklin Robinson, regional manager of the Southern Greyhound Lines. He had accompanied the bus along with Cowling because he was aware of the potential brewing storm.[87] Members of the mob, which numbered more than two hundred, many recruited by local Klan leader Kenneth Adams, thus did not try to break through the doorway, but they did attack the bus's exterior, banging its side with bricks and pipes and clubs, rocks, chains, and blackjacks, whatever they could gather and use as weapons. They smashed windows with baseball bats. They placed wedges beneath the bus wheels to prevent its departure. And unbeknownst to the passengers, someone slashed its tires with knives. One man, later identified as Roger Couch, lay down in front of the bus to prevent it from leaving.[88] In an interview with the *New York Post* a few days later, Hank Thomas recalled: "I do not think I was scared . . . I felt my idea was more powerful than the mob's. Theirs was white supremacy; mine was equality under law for all men."[89]

In future years, Thomas would concede that maybe he was frightened by what happened next. The bus driver, Odie T. (O. T.) Jones, reacted in the face of the mob by firing up the engine, pulling into reverse, and tearing away from the station. He was able to get away, with some help from Anniston's police chief, J. L. Peek, who finally moved to restrain the crowd.[90] The mob followed the bus down Highway 202. One car, among two or three that had followed the bus into Anniston, pulled ahead of it and then kept slowing down, not allowing Jones to pass.[91] The tires that had been punctured at the station lost air quickly, and the bus clunked to a stop six miles west of Anniston. "I got real scared then," Thomas conceded. "You know, I was thinking—I'm looking out the window there, and people are out there yelling and screaming. They just about broke every window out of the bus. . . . I really thought that was going to be the end of me."[92] Thomas was in the third seat from the front, and before long someone smashed his window out with a baseball bat. Revealing tremendous sangfroid Thomas simply moved to another seat.[93] Charlotte Devree recounted how "they started breaking the windows, but the shatterproof glass kept the glass from flying about the bus. It just hung together, and at one point I saw someone on the outside of the bus trying to cut it out with a large knife."[94] Meanwhile, the bus driver bolted almost as soon as the bus stopped. As Thomas recalled, "He got off, and man, he took off like a rabbit . . . I couldn't very well blame him there."[95]

"Let's roast 'em," a man yelled.[96] Others yelled, "Get off, nigger, get off."[97] A group of white men gathered on the left side of the bus to try to tip it over. Dalford Roberts, a local taxi driver and Klansman, smashed the right rear window of the bus. A fellow Klansman and one of the leaders of the rabble, Cecil Lamar "Goober" Llewellyn, hurled an incendiary device of some sort—most likely a Molotov cocktail, though it could have been some other kind of bomb—through a window. The bus almost immediately filled with smoke. Meanwhile, Jerry R. Eason, a local flower arranger and another member of the Anniston Klavern—whose sole role was supposed to be to confirm the presence of the Freedom Riders on the buses passing through Anniston, not to attack them—tried to block the door to prevent passengers from exiting the smoke-filled bus. At this point Cowling forced Eason to back off by brandishing his pistol.[98] Charlotte Devree would later recount, "I'll smell that smoke for the rest of my life." She and Genevieve Hughes had to squeeze through a narrow bus window to escape. "If I hadn't," Devree told a local reporter, "I would have blacked out in a few more seconds."[99] The two women staggered to a nearby house, whose owners, Mr. and Mrs. K. V. Forbus, took them in and eventually drove them to Anniston Memorial Hospital.[100]

Joe Perkins, who was also aboard the Greyhound, recounted the scene after the passengers were forced to debark from the burning wreckage: "The carrier, emitting dense, black smoke and intense heat[,] burned furiously down to its Greyhound dogs" logo and its "'IT'S SUCH A COMFORT TO TAKE THE BUS . . . AND LEAVE THE DRIVING TO US' sign . . . while all the time the motor continued its steady roar in neutral, the air-conditioner working perfectly."[101]

The picture of the immolated bus, snapped by an intrepid local freelance news photographer on the scene, Joe Postiglione, would become iconic, one of the most famous pictures in American history.[102] The photograph captures the savagery and senselessness of the extremes of white supremacy, showing the burning bus having come to a stop right next to a sign advertising Forsyth & Son Grocers, which proudly sold "Mell-O dairy products." James Farmer, who was still in Washington, first saw the picture on the front page of the *Washington Post.* "I think that photograph was on the front page of every newspaper in the world," he would later claim. He called the CORE office and had them superimpose the photo on the torch of the Statue of Liberty. The composite picture that resulted became the new symbol for the Freedom Ride.[103] All three major networks showed footage of the burning bus.[104]

At first the mob was willing to let the $49,000 bus go up in flames, along with those on board. Some of the passengers, including Larry Hoppe, who had boarded the bus in Atlanta, reacted by trying to hide under their seats. Several of the thugs blocked the door from the outside, but Hank Thomas was able to push his way out. "I knew I was going to die," he said later. "It was a question of whether I die inside the bus where you couldn't breathe or do I go outside and be beaten to death by the mob."[105] Other passengers followed him out the doors, with Albert Bigelow helping to lead the way and quite possibly saving lives.[106]

Moses Newson reflected a couple of weeks later, "When I found myself trapped in that burning bus set on fire by the mob, and the heat leaving me no choice but to go out the door and the smoke preventing my seeing where the mob stood, that cold, chilling realization that this might be it came over me." He went on: "You make up your mind to take whatever is to be. I made one prayer, that my family would be all right, and one wish, that somehow, some miraculous way I could step off that bus and have a machine gun in my hands." He did make it off the bus, and another of the photographs taken that day shows Newson watching the bus burn.[107]

Others braved the crowd by squeezing through the shattered windows. Among these was Genevieve Hughes. Charlotte Devree was injured by shattered glass. Many in the crowd backed off when it became clear that the bus, with its newly full tank of gas, was a bomb waiting to go off. Soon after, the bus exploded into "a thousand rivulets of burning flames."[108] The heat and fire had burned into the gas tank, and there was a concussive blast. By that point, Thomas had successfully gotten away from the bus and found what he thought might be a friendly face among the snarling masses when a white man asked him if he was okay. Thomas was still in a daze, but he managed to nod his head "yes." Far from offering Christian charity, the inquisitor heard this self-assessment and apparently thought it was his responsibility to finish off the job. He clubbed Thomas over the head with a baseball bat.[109] The other Freedom Riders received beatings as well.

Soon a second explosion rocked the hulking shell of the bus and sent the crowd scurrying for cover. At the same time at least one police officer pulled a pistol, and though Thomas feared that one of the slugs might have his name on it, instead the officer fired into the air to clear the mob and provide safety for the Freedom Riders and the other hapless passengers caught up in the maelstrom. Eli Cowling and Harry Sims, the plainclothes investigators for the state of Alabama, had boarded the bus at the request of Governor Patterson and his director of public safety, Floyd Mann, when the bus first entered Alabama. Their mission was almost certainly more one of reconnaissance than of protection, but Cowling did pull out his gun and order the mob to disperse, shouting, "Now you get back and let these people off or some of you are going to die!"[110] He too had been on the bus, so pulling the gun was as much for his own protection as for others'.

Joe Perkins told newspaper reporters that with the explosion, many in the mob "just disappeared. Some of them were standing back in the woods beside the road." The bus passengers probably also benefited from the fact that everyone in the mob did not participate in violence once the bus came to a halt. As Perkins later remembered, "Only about 20 or 25" members of the amassed crowd were active, and the others watched. Perkins claimed that after the explosions, "the crowd was not hostile."[111]

But neither were they exactly friendly. The momentary interregnum provided by the blast enabled Sims and especially Cowling to act and prodded local law enforcement officials to gather up the passengers, most of whom were having serious difficulty breathing. Many were dry-heaving, vomiting, or retching on the ground.[112] Meanwhile, a local woman, Alma Baker, who lived across the street from where the vehicle had ground to a halt, pushed through the mob with a pitcher of water, using it to wash the faces of many of the victims and provide them with drinking water.[113] Local police kept saying, "We'll do the best that we can in getting you to the city limits," and Moses Newson could not help but think back to minutes earlier, when the police and the mob seemed to be on more than friendly terms.[114]

The Anniston Fire Department arrived on the scene and was able to put out the fire using chemical extinguishers. Police and firefighters gathered debris as evidence.[115] Other emergency officials managed to take some Riders to the Anniston Memorial Hospital, where there was yet more difficulty. The hospital staff was reluctant to help the dazed, bruised, and shaken group because Governor Paterson had made it clear that there would be consequences for anyone providing succor to this group of what he perceived to be agitators and troublemakers. At one point hospital officials insisted that the battered aggregation leave the hospital. Only Genevieve Hughes, who had suffered a bloody lip, received help, presumably because the hospital staff did not believe her to be part of the integrationist horde that had descended upon them. Yet another unfriendly crowd was beginning to mass outside the hospital by this point, and the group wisely chose not to heed the requests that they leave. Someone called Birmingham, where Fred Shuttlesworth awaited the group's arrival.

Shuttlesworth arranged for a caravan to fetch the Riders and bring them to Birmingham. The rescue brigade was fifteen cars strong, with Fred Shuttlesworth in the lead. The Freedom Riders were ardent advocates of nonviolent protest, but Shuttlesworth was more of a realist. Each car came with at least one shotgun. Reputedly announcing that he was going "to get my people, I'm a nonviolent man, but I'm going to get my people," Shuttlesworth, with his armed band, arrived on the scene at the hospital. As Hank Thomas recalled, "Man, they came there and they were a welcome sight." There was a dramatic moment when the drivers got out of their cars with their shotguns. "The state police were there," Thomas remembered, "but I think they all realized that this was not the time to say anything because, I'm pretty sure, there would have been a lot of people killed."[116] Shuttlesworth arranged for hospital care for the Riders, many of whom had suffered from severe smoke inhalation.

The Mother's Day Massacre, Part 2: The Trailways Group

Shuttlesworth's cavalry brought the first group to Birmingham. Meanwhile, the Riders on the Trailways bus, an hour or so behind the Greyhound, had no idea what had become of their colleagues or what they were about to ride into at Anniston. Upon their arrival at the station, which was three blocks from city hall, they saw that temporary signs indicated that the restaurant was closed. Walter Bergman went to a nearby restaurant and bought sandwiches and coffee for the group. The sirens of police cars and ambulances taking the first group to the hospital were audible to those anxiously awaiting departure. The station itself was eerily quiet. The Riders did not yet know of the tumultuous events that had preceded them.

The Trailways group did not have to wait long. Eight white men climbed aboard the bus as it prepared to continue toward Birmingham. A uniformed policeman, Captain Harman, approached the bus and spoke to the driver. He also announced to the Freedom Riders that what would happen next "is up to you."[117] The driver informed the group of what had happened in the last hour and said that he would not drive "until you niggers move back where you belong."[118] The black passengers in front remained in their seats. One of the white toughs announced, "We don't want to be burned, niggers get to the back of the bus."[119] They began to attack the black Freedom Riders occupying the front seats.

When James Peck and Walter Bergman tried to intercede and persuade the hoodlums to stop the abuse, they too became victims. "Why don't you white communists stay up North?" one of the thugs asked, apparently rhetorically.[120] Peck received several punches and kicks and blows with Coke bottles and soon found himself facedown on the bus floor with someone on top of him. He was bleeding. Bergman received a cut and a swollen jaw and a blow to the head that would cause permanent brain damage, though at the time the extent of his injury was not known.[121] In Bergman's words, "All were slugged, but not as thoroughly as the two 'white traitors.'"[122] His wife, Frances, was stunned. She screamed, "Don't beat him anymore! He's my husband!" A member of the group of assailants responded by calling her a "nigger lover." Nonetheless, one of the men yelled to his colleagues not to kill Bergman, who by that point was unconscious.[123] Frances Bergman later admitted, "I had never before heard the sound of human flesh being hit. It was terrible."[124] She described the scene to James Farmer, saying, "They used my husband's head for a football."[125]

The thugs grabbed, hit, and kicked the other docile passengers, including Charles Person, who took the brunt of the abuse, and forced them physically toward the rear of the bus. "While I was sitting in my seat at the front of the bus next to the window," Person would testify to FBI special agents a few days later, one of the leaders of the assailants "grabbed me by my tie and hit me with his fist on the left side of my face near the temple. At the same time he pulled me out of my seat and started pushing and pulling me to the back of the bus. At this time I did not . . . attempt to defend myself." Eventually, they threw Person over the seats toward the rear of the bus, and he landed on his side in the aisle.[126] They also assaulted Herman Harris, the Morris College sophomore who had just joined the group, as well as two other newcomers, Isaac "Ike" Reynolds and Ivor Moore.[127]

During the maelstrom the bus driver was outside. The policeman who had entered the bus earlier poked his head in after the commotion, but he was clearly sympathetic to the white ruffians, smiling at them and assuring them, "I didn't see nothing and so I can't do nothing because I did not see nothing."[128] Within days, the political cartoonist Herblock would capture this sentiment, drawing an Alabama policeman (identified as "Gov. Patterson") looking up into a group of white thugs in the front of a bus. The officer is apologizing to the group of ruffians: "Oh. Rioters—At first I thought you said 'Riders!' Go ahead."[129]

Finally, all of the Freedom Riders, along with one black passenger who had not gotten off with the others at the station, were at the back of the bus. The assailants and a pregnant woman who had boarded with them sat at the front. A demilitarized zone of empty seats stood in between. The driver proceeded toward Birmingham while members of the group in back speculated as to whether or not the bus would actually reach its destination or divert to a mob scene at a predetermined destination. For the duration of the ride to Birmingham, the thugs remained vigilant, craning their necks to make sure that the Freedom Riders (whom the toughs had forced to ride in integrated fashion, albeit at the back of the bus) did not try to creep up toward the front.[130] Simeon Booker tried to offer the interlopers a copy of the *Jet* Freedom Ride preview issue. They did not seem too interested.[131] Accompanied by a police escort, the bus detoured through Oxford, Alabama, to avoid the mobs that had reportedly gathered along the regular route. It took two hours to traverse the route to Birmingham, normally a sixty-mile trip that to Walter Bergman and the others "seemed [like] six hundred."[132] They avoided any further problems along the way beyond fear and trepidation, but the Trailways bus and its passengers had not seen the day's last ignominy.

Chapter 7

The Magic City

Showdown in Birmingham

Bull's "Bombingham"

Birmingham in the postwar period liked to call itself the Magic City.[1] Another, more facetious observer preferred to think of it as the "city of perpetual promise," the mocking nickname George R. Leighton had given the city in a 1937 article in *Harper's Magazine*.[2] Civic boosters could boast of the fact that the city had nearly doubled its population in the two decades between 1940 and 1960. The magic stemmed largely from the exhaust of heavy industry, particularly steel. Overseeing the growth was an oligarchy of "big mules," the powerful industrialists who effectively ran Birmingham. Concerned above all with a tranquil climate in which to make money and increase their power, the big mules kept themselves above the fray of day-to-day politics, intervening only when they perceived challenges to their interests. As if to exemplify their power, the steel barons had erected a fifty-six-foot-tall statue of Vulcan, the god of fire, the forge, and industry. The totem overlooked the city from its perch on Red Mountain, the hill that partitioned Birmingham and that was named for the reddish soil, rich with iron-ore deposits, that gave the mountain its coloration. The torch in Vulcan's extended right hand, at the end of a nine-ton arm, glowed green at night, except when there was a traffic fatality, when it shone red.[3]

Outsiders, particularly from beyond the region, saw Birmingham not as an example of the magic of industrial growth or as the result of fastidious boys' club stewardship, but rather as simply the most racist city in America. Many called it "America's Johannesburg." When Carl Carmer, the renowned author (among his more than twenty-five books was *Stars Fell on Alabama*), documentary filmmaker, radio host, musician, and Southerner, wrote of Alabama, "The Congo is not more different from

Massachusetts or California," he could have been describing what many Americans, especially Northerners, thought about Birmingham in 1961.[4] Because of the city's cozy relationship with no fewer than five Ku Klux Klan groups, not to mention its housing the headquarters of the National States Rights Party, there was more than a hint of lawlessness hovering over Birmingham, giving it a nickname evocative of racist atrocity: "Bombingham." The appellation was especially appropriate on "Dynamite Hill," a black neighborhood just west of downtown where a disturbing number of mysterious explosions had occurred at the homes of leaders in the black community.

Birmingham was a city in which, in the words of Harrison Salisbury of the *New York Times*, "Every channel of communication, every medium of mutual interest, every reasoned approach, every inch of middle ground has been fragmented by the emotional dynamite of racism, reinforced by the whip, the razor, the gun, the bomb, the torch, the club, the knife, the mob, the police and many branches of the state's apparatus."[5]

Presiding over this volatile environment like a martinet was Eugene "Bull" Connor, high school dropout, former railroad telegrapher turned cracker-barrel minor-league baseball announcer, and one-time reform legislator in the Alabama House of Representatives. In 1937 Connor had managed to get himself elected to the Birmingham city council and become the city's public safety commissioner. In a city council form of government, this effectively put Bull—so named either for his ability to "shoot the bull" as the announcer of the Birmingham Barons or else for his voice, depending upon whose account one believes—in an authoritative position in the city. His first tenure of sixteen years was often tumultuous, and in 1958, after several years out of power, he made a comeback on a white supremacist platform. Bull wielded control with a sometimes ruthless, sometimes convivial, often controversial style. Connor, an ardent segregationist, was certain to meet any challenge to Jim Crow in law or practice with a firm and potentially brutal hand.[6] And segregation in Birmingham was ubiquitous. The architects of apartheid could not have been much more thorough. Bull and his underlings knew that the Freedom Ride was coming, and once Bull knew, it was not long before the higher-ups in Birmingham's Ku Klux Klan received the intelligence as well. The ugliness that ensued would shock the nation; rock the Civil Rights Movement to its foundations; and, unbeknownst to Bull Connor and the rest of the forces of violent massive resistance, prove to be the beginning of the end of Bull's reign in the emotional heart of American white supremacy.

The Mother's Day Massacre, Part 3:
Birmingham, Bull, and the KKK

Half of the Freedom Riders had gotten safe passage to Birmingham on the early afternoon of May 14, thanks to Fred Shuttlesworth and his caravan of supporters. However, the Trailways band, commandeered by the brigands from Anniston, was still on its way when individuals with bad intentions began to congregate at the Trailways station.

Birmingham was not immune to civil rights activity, though both Bull Connor and the Klan (sometimes in conjunction) had generally seen to it that such rumblings were limited and met with swift reprisal. Episodically, individual blacks fed up with the constant abuse that their skin color invited would fight back. Throughout the 1940s and 1950s, working-class African Americans on public buses challenged vitriolic and mean-spirited drivers and sometimes even white passengers. Historian Robin D. G. Kelley has argued persuasively that organized resistance to Jim Crow from the major civil rights organizations was supplemented with everyday acts of resistance against the status quo.[7] In 1960 Shuttlesworth and others had led sit-ins in Birmingham's downtown stores, meeting with prompt arrest at the hands of Bull Connor. Nonetheless, for all the heroism, bravery, or plain gumption that such actions demanded, by 1961 they had borne little fruit. Connor's hold on power and his willingness to use it, brutally if he deemed it necessary, seemed to be as strong as ever on the eve of the Freedom Rides.

Shuttlesworth, the intrepid Birmingham minister and civil rights leader, was one individual unwilling to be cowed into accepting segregation and maltreatment. Consistently, the pugnacious Shuttlesworth challenged authorities, often frontally and at risk of grave personal harm. His home and church had been burned and bombed. He had been threatened and beaten. And yet he always returned, resolute and unyielding. His tenacity had even begun to earn him the begrudging respect of some in the white power structure.[8] Shuttlesworth was at the forefront of Birmingham's most visible and effective civil rights organization, the Alabama Christian Movement for Human Rights (ACMHR). However, for all of that organization's work, as well as the tentative steps of the nascent student movement, Birmingham was as segregated as ever as the city prepared its welcome for the Freedom Riders. When the student movement had taken its first baby steps in the city, Connor's response was to announce that the city's 443 firemen had started riot training. Not surprisingly, Birmingham's 450 police officers were already prepared for the exigency of racial protests.[9]

Apropos of conditions on the ground in Birmingham, CORE's contact there was Shuttlesworth, who agreed to hold another mass meeting on Sunday night in addition to the ACMHR's regular Monday meeting in order to accommodate the anticipated arrival of the sojourners from CORE. Shuttlesworth also made all other local arrangements.[10] That morning during worship services, Shuttlesworth asked the congregation to pray for the incoming group, understandably worried about them.[11]

The call from Anniston had sent Shuttlesworth into action earlier than he had anticipated, but his advance planning with Gordon Carey, Jim Farmer, and others surely made it easier for Shuttlesworth to pull together a caravan to rescue the stranded and stunned activists at Anniston's Memorial Hospital. Shuttlesworth had also continued the Gandhian practice of giving forewarning of the pending nonviolent action. Knowing full well that the detectives who monitored all of his gatherings and reported to the power structure would rush to Bull Connor with such a disclosure, Shuttlesworth had announced the plans of the traveling civil rights workers at a mass meeting in the days leading up to their arrival. To reinforce this message, at 7:39 Sunday morning, he and a colleague sent a telegram to Connor and his chief of police, Jamie Moore, to tell them details of the group's arrival and to ask for protection.[12] Connor already had this intelligence, but he had helped prepare a greeting party of another kind altogether.

As the Trailways bus passed through the suburbs approaching Birmingham, the Freedom Riders worked to get themselves together as best they could. Jim Peck recalled: "I was pretty bloody from the business in Anniston, and I tried to clean myself up a little. And the others straightened themselves out, too—as if they were going to a party or something. Except we knew it wasn't going to be any party or picnic."[13] It was about 4:15 in the afternoon.

The state-of-the-art bus arrived in Birmingham, where ill-concealed mobs waited. Harrison Salisbury, who the year before had written a profoundly unflattering portrait of Birmingham, described the rabble as "a great number of heavy-set men, wearing sport shirts" and loitering, waiting for excitement to come.[14]

Once the bus pulled in to the depot, Peck first saw a group of white men: "They were all sort of drawn in a sort of semi-circle, maybe 25 or so, all young and grinning at each other. And I swear, almost licking their lips."[15] Hidden out of view were maybe four or five dozen others.[16] The whites who had taken charge of the bus in Anniston scurried off first, likely to blend into the assembled crowd and forestall any potential hassles from the authorities. Perhaps they did not know that in this instance, the authorities were on their side.

Charles Person and Jim Peck had been designated to engage in the scheduled test at the Birmingham station. Committed activist though he was, Peck took pause as they stood on the unloading platform, the mob brandishing their clubs, bats, chains, lengths of hose, blackjacks, and whatever else could serve as weaponry just a few feet away. "I did not want to put Person in a position of being forced to proceed if he thought the situation too dangerous," Peck wrote soon after. "When I looked at him, he responded by saying simply, 'Let's go.'"[17]

Person and Peck entered the waiting room designated for whites and approached the lunch counter. One of the men told Peck, "You're a shame to the white race."[18] In the words of fellow Freedom Rider Joe Perkins, among the group shuttled to Birmingham in the Shuttlesworth cavalry, they approached the waiting room "still feeling their beatings" from Anniston "but undaunted."[19] Peck tried to shield Person, but to no avail. Groups of men grabbed each of them and pushed them toward an alleyway near a loading platform.[20] Six men attacked Peck with fists. But in Walter Bergman's words, "Fists were not enough against this frail veteran of nonviolent protest. Despite odds of two against a mob, Southern gallantry needed lead pipes."[21] A day later, Peck recounted his experience: "They really started slugging me. It was really rough. I put my hands over my face and head, but there were so many of them, and they just kept pounding away. One of them kept shouting, 'Get him, get him. Jesus, get him good.'"[22]

Five or six men attacked Person just a few feet ahead. One individual pushed Person roughly toward the black waiting room. "Hit him!" someone shouted, and on command a fist crunched Person's jaw, dropping him. He stood up, mouth bleeding, only to be hit again and again.[23] Walter Bergman later recounted: "I hadn't reached the station before I saw Charles being ejected and a dozen fists beating down on him. . . . I tried to find the police, but none were visible, nor did they arrive for 15 minutes."[24]

Although the assailants thought they had pulled Peck and Person away from the view of onlookers, at least three media members caught the attack.[25] Howard K. Smith, a CBS news correspondent who would in a few days raise the ire of white Birmingham for his portrayal of race relations in the Magic City in his program *Who Speaks for Birmingham?* (itself a follow-up to Salisbury's scathing *New York Times* feature), witnessed the attacks and was in close proximity to Peck's beating. Smith had been readying his departure from Birmingham when he received a call telling him to "be sure to be at the bus station tomorrow, because you're going to see action."[26] Although Smith and his staff had wrapped up most of their work, the action he saw the next day provided a striking coda to his broadcast.

In Smith's description, after the bus arrived, "the toughs grabbed the passengers into alleys and corridors, pounding them with pipes, with key rings and with fists. One passenger was knocked down at my feet by twelve of the hoodlums and his face was beaten and kicked until it was a bloody pulp."[27] The Rider he so described was Peck. Smith would later compare the events at the bus station to Krisstalnacht, and the mob to the Gestapo. Smith, a native Southerner who had covered Nazi Germany in the 1930s, was profoundly disturbed by what he saw.[28]

Other bus passengers, both Freedom Riders and those remaining travelers who had a bad sense of timing, also received beatings. Among these was George Webb, twenty years old, light of skin, and at the station to pick up his fiancée, Mary Spicer. Several men, including local Klansman (and FBI informant) Gary Thomas Rowe, grabbed Webb and began beating him. One of the white men who had gotten on the bus in Anniston (Spicer recognized him, as she had been adhering to segregated seating when the men commandeered the bus) bashed Webb in the temple and ear with a lead pipe covered by a paper bag. Someone in the crowd warned Spicer to "get the hell out of here unless you want to get the same thing."[29] Webb managed to kick himself loose when the mob released him after their attention turned to the flash and pop of a photographer's camera. Webb somehow emerged with only torn clothes and a bloody, bruised face.[30]

The photographer in question was Tom Langston of the *Birmingham Post-Herald*. At that moment he caught a picture that would become emblematic of Birmingham's savage racist fury.[31] The mob set upon Langston, who thought on his feet quickly enough to remove his film from the camera before it could be destroyed. The mob shattered Langston's equipment, but his photographs from that day survived. Langston took a beating. According to the *Birmingham News*, four of its reporters were also cornered during the brawl, their cameras and film either taken or destroyed, indicating that the mob intentionally targeted media members who could reveal their furor to the world.[32]

Emblematic of this attempt to silence the media was the experience of Clancy Lake, the news director of television station WAPI, who was mobbed as he tried to report the tumult from the front seat of his car. He recounted his experience in the next day's *Birmingham News*, which owned WAPI: "They dragged me out of the car. They tried to blackjack me. And to keep the public from knowing what was happening, they tore the microphone out of my two-way radio unit. They tried to keep me from telling what was happening—in broad daylight, just three blocks from Birmingham's City Hall."[33] The crowd also kicked out the windows of Lake's car. A police cruiser drove by as the attack was ensuing but did nothing.[34]

Others took similar beatings. Some narrowly escaped the worst of the attacks. Simeon Booker, who saw much of the violence in Birmingham, witnessed a bloodied Walter Bergman clawing his way to safety and decided to try to sneak away. He put a newspaper over his face, punching a hole in it large enough to see through. He then tried inconspicuously to sneak around the edge of the building. He was able to get to a cab with a black driver, who brought him to Shuttlesworth's home.[35] After waiting on the bus to gather the group's personal belongings from the overhead racks, Frances Bergman alighted and stood to the side near the luggage compartment beneath the bus, where she witnessed the attacks.[36] Howard Smith, after unsuccessfully trying to hail a taxi for Peck and Person, managed to get three black victims, two of them guilty of nothing more than bad timing, to safety. In all, nine Freedom Riders and a number of bystanders, white and black, suffered injuries.

Freeman Tarth, a black man who operated a shoeshine stand, witnessed the beatings at the station. He sprinted to the front door, but several of the attackers tracked Tarth to his home, aware that he might be able to testify to what he had seen. Several men set upon Tarth and beat him badly, breaking his arm. He would later allege that Birmingham police officers were involved in the attacks and that he had seen several remove their uniforms and change into civilian clothing.[37]

James Peck, meanwhile, had been beaten unconscious. When he awoke he was alone in the alleyway, lying in a pool of blood.[38] He tried to stanch the blood flowing from his facial wounds with a handkerchief that soon became hopelessly saturated. A soldier found Peck soon after and offered aid, but almost simultaneously Bergman, the extent of whose internal wounds was still not known, had managed to stumble and find his fallen colleague. Bergman, still bleeding and dazed from the beating he took in Anniston, had been spared in Birmingham.[39] Nonetheless, his Anniston injuries had already been enough to cause permanent damage. As John Lewis later recounted, Bergman's "bravery matched anyone's on the ride, but his body was not up to the beatings he took that day."[40] Eventually, as a result of the injuries he sustained that day, Bergman would suffer a stroke that would leave him partially paralyzed.[41]

Bergman recalled "stepping over fragments" of a newsman's "shattered camera as I led Peck to the street."[42] The two wounded men managed to summon taxicabs. The first two that they found refused to take them, but a third relented. Peck told the driver to take them to Shuttlesworth's Bethel Baptist Church parsonage.[43] Charles Person had somehow managed to escape on a city bus.[44] When the police finally arrived, in some cases crossing paths with the fleeing Klansmen, in others dispersing those who were still around, the rest of the group was able to get away.

When Peck stumbled from the cab that pulled up to Shuttlesworth's home, the reverend met him and immediately said, "You need to go to a hospital." Peck's gashes went clear through to his skull, and he was, in Shuttlesworth's words, "as bloody as a slaughtered hog."[45] Shuttlesworth called an ambulance. As they waited for it to arrive, Peck found Person, who had also successfully made his way to the house, and the two men shook hands. Person had suffered a gash in the back of his head, and his face was swollen, but he would not need hospitalization.[46] Once again the worst beating of a Freedom Rider was reserved not for a black passenger, although Person and many of the others had been badly beaten, but rather for a white man seen as a traitor in the South.

That evening, Shuttlesworth hosted a mass meeting at his church. Several of the Freedom Riders were able to attend despite their wounds. They described their experiences in Anniston and downtown Birmingham, sitting in a row of chairs lined up facing the congregation. Despite his injuries, Bergman, the former professor, explained to the riveted audience what CORE was and detailed its goals for the Freedom Ride. He told of the attacks that afternoon, showing his wounds to the crowd. Others recounted their stories and implored local blacks to join in the movement for racial justice. One told the group: "We want you to know that we're doing this because we're dissatisfied with the way things are. We need you to take up from this." Many in the crowd were especially impressed by the physical and emotional sacrifices of the white Freedom Riders. By this point the meeting was at an emotional fever pitch, which Shuttlesworth skillfully utilized as he closed the meeting with an oratorical flourish. "This is the greatest thing that has ever happened to Alabama, and it has been good for the nation," he proclaimed, perhaps surprising some who may not have seen the Birmingham violence in such grand terms. "It was a wonderful thing to see those young students—Negro and white—come, even after the mobs and the bus burning. When white and black men are willing to be beaten up together, it is a sure sign they will soon walk together as brothers." By this time, Shuttlesworth, who had seen his share of violence and abuse at the hands of Birmingham's segregationists, had reached his crescendo: "No matter how many times they beat us up, segregation has still got to go. Others may be beaten up, but freedom is worth anything." The meeting ended with prayers and an inspired singing of hymns.[47]

Meanwhile, Peck had not realized the seriousness of his wounds. After he reached Hillman Hospital (the ambulance was turned away from Carraway Methodist), he was on the operating table for hours, partly because his doctor kept being called away to handle other emergencies. "They were nice at the hospital," Peck later reported, "and did their job well, I guess." He didn't really think about much at the hospital, except that "it hurt like hell and I wasn't going to be the handsomest guy in the world." He also thought about his wife, Paula, and his two boys.[48] When reporters arrived, hospital regulations required Peck to sign a paper permitting them to interview him and take photographs. He did so and answered questions as best he could, though he was feeling nauseous and weak. He restated his commitment to continue on to Montgomery.

After eight hours he was released. His six largest gashes required fifty-three stitches, he had lost several teeth, and he was covered with bruises. When he was ready to be released, he first called his family to warn them of the pictures they would see in the morning papers. Next he called Fred Shuttlesworth, who came to the hospital to retrieve Peck. Before leaving the Freedom Riders and their associates behind at his house, he told them to alert the FBI if he did not return with Peck within a half-hour. Shuttlesworth would later call his decision to go and get Peck "one of those divine urges that the Lord interposes."[49] When Peck emerged from the hospital, his head swathed in bandages, it was after two in the morning.[50]

Peck's difficulties, however, were not quite over. As Peck stood outside before Shuttlesworth arrived, a police car drove up, and an officer told Peck that he would be arrested for vagrancy if he did not get off the street. When he went back into the hospital, a guard told him that discharged patients were not permitted in the facility. By the time he got back outside, Shuttlesworth had arrived. The police car then followed Shuttlesworth's vehicle and stopped it a few blocks down the road, even though Shuttlesworth had instructed his driver not to go more than twenty miles an hour. The police started to badger the driver, but from the pas-

senger seat Shuttlesworth defended himself and his passenger. At the end
of his tether, Shuttlesworth snapped at the officer: "I'm Reverend Fred
Shuttlesworth and I'm sure you're familiar with the name. We don't want
any interference from the police tonight." The officer told his partner that
Shuttlesworth was in the car. A short time later Shuttlesworth heard the
dispatcher tell the police, "Oh hell, let 'em go," and they were allowed to
proceed.[51] Shuttlesworth believed that had Peck been left alone outside of
the hospital much longer, he would have been lynched.[52] An emboldened
Shuttlesworth proclaimed after the harassment ended, "They do not want
to get into another tangle with me."[53] Nonetheless, Bull Connor later called
Shuttlesworth, threatening to have the minister locked up for providing
shelter to the white Freedom Riders.[54] That night the Freedom Riders and
the Shuttlesworth teenagers slept in a tangled mass on the floor of the
Bethel parsonage.

"Fear and Hatred Stalked the Streets": Recrimination and Response

No police had been at the scene of the Birmingham assaults even though,
in John Lewis's words, "The whole world knew the riders were coming."[55] Connor had known for days about the pending arrival of the Freedom Riders. Police usually were on duty at or near various bus and rail
stations around the clock. Nonetheless, the beatings went on for a quarter of an hour. When the police finally did show up, the officer in charge
seemed outraged not at the beatings, but that in their zeal the thugs had
exceeded their allotted time. "Goddammit! Goddammit, your fifteen
minutes are up!" he bellowed at the leaders on the spot. "Get 'em out of
here."[56]

When asked later why there had been no police officers at the station, Bull Connor asserted that they were all off visiting their mothers on
Mother's Day. This was, of course, nonsense. A number of Birmingham
police officers had been in the station just moments before the arrival of
the Trailways bus, but they dispersed.[57] Furthermore, the Birmingham police records indicate that on the three o'clock to eleven o'clock shift, the
force had a total of fifty-six supervisors and patrolmen on duty, with one
lieutenant, two sergeants, and twenty-one patrolmen assigned to the Central Patrol Precinct, where the Trailways station was located. Further, these
numbers are comparable to those from the same shift in the weeks before
and after the mob action on May 14.[58] Connor knew the Freedom Riders

were coming to town. He should have been prepared for violence. Instead, he acquiesced to it.

Connor did issue a public statement, however, saying, "I regret very much that this incident had to happen in Birmingham." He did not seem to regret the mob action itself; what he lamented was the presence of the Freedom Riders. "I have said for the last 20 years," he told the press, "that these out of town meddlers were going to cause bloodshed if they kept meddling in the South's business."[59] Connor continued dissembling. Despite the beatings received by local reporters from newspapers, radio, and television, and the presence of a number of well-known local racists among the crowd, Connor insisted that the reports his investigators had given him indicated that "both sides were from out-of-town—the ones who got whipped and the ones who did the whipping."[60]

Connor's pronouncements did not exist in a vacuum. Other Alabama politicians echoed his sentiments publicly. Representative George Huddleston stood up before Congress and denounced the Freedom Riders: "It is difficult for any Southerner who understands the problem confronting our people to sympathize with this radical extremist group which has invaded our state. They got just what they asked for."[61] Governor John Patterson also issued a statement on May 15, placing the burden of events squarely on the shoulders of the victims: "In view of the tenseness of the situation, it is impossible to guarantee the safety of the agitators. Our advice to them is to get out of Alabama as quickly as possible." Patterson had predicted violence days earlier, and as a consequence of the inaction of local officials sworn to uphold the law, his prophecy had come true.[62]

The *Birmingham News* expressed outrage. The traditionally segregationist paper (it had recently endorsed Connor's reelection bid, which he won handily) condemned the previous day's violence in stark terms, festooning the front page with a headline asking, "Where were the police?" In an editorial, the *News* declared, "Yesterday, Sunday, May 14 was a day which ought to be burned onto Birmingham's conscience." Invoking the language of Harrison Salisbury's much-loathed and rejected *New York Times* account from 1960, the editors conceded: "Fear and hatred did stalk Birmingham's streets yesterday. Fear and hatred stalked the sidewalks." The paper laid the blame for what had happened at the feet of Bull Connor, because "the Birmingham Police Department did not do what could have been done Sunday."[63]

Speaking to Alabamans the next day, May 16, the *News* editors opined: "We must demonstrate first to ourselves, our own people, that thuggery will not go unpunished. In so proving to ourselves that, we the people, and not a bunch of thugs are rulers of our city, we will also be showing the nation and the world that, even though matters got out of hand we were properly very swift in bringing about order."[64] Virtually overnight, the *Birmingham News* had gone from ardent support of its city's power structure to utter condemnation. Assessing the *News* coverage a few days later, the *Washington Post* concluded, "The Birmingham News has thrown the full weight of its news and editorial columns into the search for the white hoodlums who attacked" the buses and passengers.[65] In a separate editorial the *Post* announced, "This newspaper is pleased to salute the Birmingham News for a highly effective job of civil responsibility following the brutal attacks upon the 'freedom riders'—attacks that were really assaults upon the dignity and reputation of Alabama."[66]

The *News* was not the only local paper to express outrage. The *Birmingham Post-Herald* similarly faulted Connor and his lawmen: "The police knew the buses were on their way to Birmingham and approximately the time of their arrival. Why then were they not on the job, in uniform and in sufficient number to prevent or to smother any clash or attempted demonstration?"[67]

Outside condemnation was every bit as quick to follow. Speaking in a packed War Memorial Auditorium in Greensboro, North Carolina, Martin Luther King Jr. condemned the savage attacks in Anniston and Birmingham and heaped praise upon the Riders. He called for thousands of people to engage in mass action by descending upon Mississippi and Alabama and praised students across the South who were or had been engaged in nonviolent civil rights protests.

John A. Morsell, assistant to the NAACP's executive secretary, told a crowd at Philadelphia's Lincoln University that Governor Patterson had "read the funeral service for democracy in Alabama" through the state's "failure to protect the bus passengers." Jacob Javits, a Republican senator from New York, condemned the violence in harsh terms and proclaimed that America was "deeply shocked, appalled, and indeed ashamed" by the violence in Alabama against the group "freedom riding through the South." He advocated prosecution of the attackers, adding that he hoped "the country will take note of what these struggles mean and how they are attended by violence, by personal injury, and by disgrace to the good name of the United States throughout the world." Javits also sent a telegram to Robert Kennedy in which he declared the attacks to be "clear violations" of federal laws. "I trust no effort will be spared to bring to justice those who took part in these incidents," the senator wrote the attorney general. Two congressmen, Charles Diggs, a Democrat from Michigan, and Robert N. C. Nix, a Pennsylvania Democrat, also expressed outrage over what Diggs called "this dereliction of duty, of being a part of the red necks and the stupid and vicious people who speak for them."[68]

Birmingham's mayor, James W. Morgan, who was in charge of public improvements as one of the three commissioners who ran the city alongside Connor and Commissioner J. T. (Jabo) Waggoner, received numerous letters expressing displeasure with the city and its leaders after the events of Mother's Day. One man, Barry Cohen from Dallas, Texas, wrote to tell Morgan that he was canceling plans to travel to Birmingham that summer as a result of the riots. "It seems to me," he wrote, "that those CORE people, whoever they were, had a real right to be where they were."[69] Another correspondent from Texas proclaimed: "Those race riots in your city are a disgrace to the great city of Birmingham. . . . Demonstrations are an inherent part of our free system and the right of segregationist and integrationist to express their feeling should not be curtailed."[70] A New York writer echoed the sentiments of many in the press by placing blame squarely on the shoulders of Alabama's leaders. "I am sure many persons are questioning your leadership, your authority, your effectiveness in your position and your worth. I am."[71] And an anonymous Californian invoked the Cold War, arguing, "If ever the Afro-Asian block [*sic*] goes Communist I will blame it on a large part by the actions of Southerners. Lots of luck in your job stoking up the Third World War."[72] Of course, Morgan also received letters like the one from J. A. Reeves of Terre Haute, Indiana, who wrote: "You know and I know that this nigger segregation business is all Communist sponsored and led."[73] In all, Morgan received well over a dozen letters of criticism, concern, and support.[74]

Some observers blamed the mob first and foremost. The *Miami Herald* argued that the Freedom Riders "got their answer" regarding the status of segregation at bus stations in Alabama: "Mob violence reflected a certain level of public opinion which will keep the barriers up for all practical purposes." Moving from this seemingly practical observation, the editors invoked the Cold War imperative: "But the mob itself, if it had any wits, might realize how damaging are these spasms of blind hatred to the country itself. . . . Smashed faces and a burned-out bus in Alabama do the enemy's work." The paper called for better law enforcement, but also called on "experimenters" to "have the good sense—and the patriotism—not to provoke incidents when they jolly well know that what they confront is ignorance rather than reasoned hostility."[75] Apparently, the editors of the *Miami Herald* believed that by testing and exercising constitutional rights, the Freedom Riders were being insufficiently patriotic.

The *Chicago Sun-Times* was one of many papers across the country that blasted Alabama and its leaders at both state and local levels: "The spectacle of their being attacked and beaten, while police made no attempt to arrest the perpetrators of the violence, defies understanding. When police in any community bow to mobs and mob violence, an open invitation is issued to irresponsible white ruffians in other communities to resort to the same tactics."[76]

The *Washington Post* laid the blame squarely on the shoulders of Patterson and the state's law officials: "Alabama has a Governor who encourages contempt for the Constitution of the United States and who preaches incendiary racist nonsense. The plain fact is that Americans cannot be assured in Alabama of the equal protection of the laws guaranteed by the Fourteenth Amendment." Therefore, the *Post* editors reasoned, "They are quite justified . . . in looking to the Justice Department for the protection of their rights as American citizens."[77]

On the local level, away from the media, blacks were furious, while many whites were embarrassed, ashamed, or shocked. Birmingham had earned a national reputation for racism that local white folks insisted was caricature. But the brutality against the Freedom Riders revealed this defense as a chimera. Outside perceptions of white Birmingham would only get worse in the days, weeks, and months to come. As a consequence, for a time matters would also get worse for blacks, who up until that point might not have imagined that their plight could deteriorate.

There is no question that some or most of the violence in both Anniston and Birmingham came from the Ku Klux Klan, with national Grand Dragon Robert Shelton on site and in charge of behind-the-scenes planning. Too, smaller right-wing groups, such as the National States Rights Party, supplemented the Klan presence.[78] But the ringleader was certainly the local power structure, at the pinnacle of which stood Bull Connor, who at one point had said that he wanted the Freedom Riders beaten "until it looks like a bulldog got ahold of them."[79] On Thursday, May 11, Connor dispatched his personal detective, Tom Cook, to determine the schedule for the buses arriving from Atlanta. Cook then provided Connor with the desired information and also passed it along to Hubert Page, an old friend in the Birmingham Klan.[80] In the words of one recent historian of massive resistance, "Connor's response was equally tactical and equally calculated." If the Freedom Riders hoped "to rouse national opinion, Connor was trying to appeal to the only opinions that mattered to him personally: those who belonged to his electoral base in Birmingham."[81] Given the response, Connor appears to have miscalculated, but his reasoning probably seemed sound given what he knew about his city.

Events in Alabama during the Freedom Ride served as strong evidence for Yale Law School dean Eugene Rostow's assertion that in the South the "Ku Klux spirit has not been more active or more effective since Reconstruction days."[82] Well before the end of May, the Kennedy Justice Department gained an injunction against future Klan activity against Freedom Riders and then went to federal court to make the injunction permanent.[83] In 1967 the U.S. District Court for the Middle District of Alabama, Northern Division, would find that:

> On May 14, 1961, certain individuals, some or all of whom were conspirators with or members of the U.S. Klans, Knights of the Ku Klux Klan, Inc., and the Alabama Knights, Knights of the Ku Klux Klan, Inc., by force, threats and violence, intimidated the passengers on one of the buses and destroyed the bus at or near Anniston, Alabama; that said intimidation of the passengers and destruction of this bus by said conspirators was in furtherance of the conspiracy to prevent the passengers on the bus from carrying out their announced and intended purposes. This court further finds that on May 14, 1961, upon the arrival in Birmingham of the Trailways bus . . . [the same organizations and some of its members and other conspirators] unlawfully beat, assaulted, intimidated, threatened and harassed certain of the passengers who had alighted from this bus at the Trailways bus terminal.[84]

In 1975 Gary Thomas Rowe, an FBI informant in Birmingham's Eastview Klavern, told the Senate Select Committee on Intelligence that the police had assured the Klan that there would be a fifteen-minute window after the Freedom Riders arrived when there would be no police presence on the ground and the mob would have an unfettered hand to do what they would with the bus passengers.[85] Rowe had passed this information along both to a Birmingham police officer known to be a Klan collaborator and to Special Agent in Charge (SAC) Thomas Jenkins, who teletyped the information to FBI headquarters.[86] The FBI, however, had not deigned to let the Kennedys in on this intelligence.[87] In fact, much later it came to light that J. Edgar Hoover himself knew about the impending attack.[88] Furthermore, the FBI also suppressed much of what it knew about the attack after the fact.[89]

Nonetheless, Rowe argued that while the steadily increasing media accompanying the Freedom Riders on their way down South drew the attention and ire of the KKK, "the rioting that greeted them in Birmingham was not the brainchild of the Klan. . . . It was instigated by members of the police department." Rowe described the meetings he had attended with high-ranking officials in the Birmingham police department, outlining the plan to provide the Riders—in the words of Lieutenant Jim Collins, one of Rowe's main contacts—with "a little welcome party."[90] When police were milling around before the scheduled arrival of the first bus, the Greyhound that was supposed to arrive at 3:30 (the police station was in the basement of the Greyhound station), Rowe had grown visibly and increasingly nervous until he was assured of getting his fifteen minutes.[91] Too, he had zealously taken part in the violence at the station. Apparently, undercover work was in his blood.[92]

Soon after the events in Birmingham, syndicated newspaper columnist Clarence Mitchell surveyed the situation in Alabama, concluding: "Raw brutal Alabama has become a breeding ground for hoodlums and thugs who whip their victims with tire chains or slug them with sawed-off baseball bats. There is no doubt that this crowd has become a kind of police force."[93] Local reporters had told CBS's Howard K. Smith that many of the men amassed at the Trailways terminal were Klansmen.[94] Later Smith saw several of the attackers standing beneath the window in front of Connor's office, "discussing their achievement of the day."[95] Others collected around Woodrow Wilson Park, both to rendezvous and to revel after extracting their pound of flesh. Appropriating a 1990s term for what happened in Birmingham, John Lewis called the police-authorized fifteen minutes "a wilding—a sanctioned wilding."[96]

Profiles in Caution: The Kennedy Response

And whither the Kennedy administration? Despite Robert Kennedy's speech in Athens days before, and the fact that the president as a consequence had sent an outline of its civil rights proposals to Congress, the administration had not done much to deal with the issue of race. In fact, the president likely would have been happy for the issue to just go away. The New Frontier's horizons often looked outward, toward the far-off lands where the Cold War raged. When the gaze turned inward, the Kennedy program fell comfortably within the range of Cold War liberalism, paying lip service to civil rights while doing its best to placate representatives south of Mason and Dixon's line. By walking the tightrope, by being on the long end of rhetoric and the short end of action, the Kennedy administration hoped to forestall having to do something that would alienate the South while still being able to claim to be a friend of black Americans, or at least a friend of their vote—where they could vote.[97]

Historian E. Culpepper Clark has written of what students entering college on the cusp of the New Frontier saw in the dashing young president and his new administration. These new leaders were "young, charismatic, clarion in their call to serve the future; they were also pragmatic, tough and Janus-faced when it came to race relations. By their reluctance to antagonize the southern wing of the Democratic Party, the Kennedys made it possible for young Alabamans to embrace the party of their fathers while planning their future."[98] This Janus face allowed Kennedy to earn tentative praise not only from enough white Southerners to keep his legislative vision alive (the *Charlotte Observer* was typical in its assertion that the "administration already has shown as much solid interest [in civil rights] as did the Eisenhower administration in all its eight years") but also from a still tentatively admiring black press throughout the first half of 1961.[99]

Many of the architects of Kennedy's administration wished among themselves that Kennedy would push civil rights more aggressively. Kennedy's special counsel and speechwriter Richard Goodwin, who had joined Kennedy's senatorial staff in 1959 and would later be one of the few Kennedy intimates invited into Lyndon B. Johnson's inner circle, later wrote about meeting with Arthur Schlesinger in Schlesinger's Georgetown apartment, where the two men lamented "the excessive caution" the administration was observing with civil rights.[100] In addition to being wary of the political repercussions—given the razor-thin margin by which he had won the 1960 election, and his position as an avowed liberal from Massachusetts, Kennedy was in no position to rouse the South any more than it already was—Kennedy also shared with many of his predecessors a doctrine on the issue of civil rights that embraced federalism—the idea that the states reign supreme except where there is a direct challenge to federal authority and a mandate for federal action. By 1961, it was clear to many observers, and certainly to all those involved with the Civil Rights Movement, that segregation was a direct affront to federal and constitutional law and authority. But in the early 1960s, Kennedy's administration resembled Eisenhower's: the president preferred not to get involved in issues on the ground unless compelled to do so. This would change in the months to come, but as the Freedom Riders passed through the South, Kennedy still adhered to his old doctrine.[101]

Often federalism was a cloak for inaction. In his quadrennial account of the election of 1964, Theodore White, a Boston journalist well-known for his Kennedy sympathies, recounted the administration's and especially Bobby Kennedy's putative predicament. "However devoted" Kennedy and his Justice Department "might be to the cause of human rights—and no more dedicated Attorney General has sat in that office in modern times— the Department was crippled for lack of . . . law and authority to act."[102] White was speaking of the lack of something like the Civil Rights Act, which would emerge in 1964 and change the face of race relations in the United States. Theodore Sorenson echoes this assessment in his book on John Kennedy: the Freedom Rides "tested their ingenuity, for there was no clear-cut federal solution."[103] It would be heedless to understate the importance of the 1964 act and its expansion of government authority and federal power to crack down on Jim Crow. At the same time, however, ever since the late 1930s, the Supreme Court had given the federal government, especially the president, room to act: *Brown* and the cases leading up to it gave the president a legal foundation for desegregating schools. Similarly, *Boynton* and its forebears gave the president leeway on matters of interstate travel. In that sense, federalism and the purported lack of a law enabling action were a fiction, and civil rights activists knew it. That the president would not act did not mean that the president could not act.

Events in Anniston and Birmingham awoke the president, as they had awoken much of the world from its somnolence. John Kennedy and Robert Kennedy would later claim never to have known anything about the Freedom Ride until they found out about it after events in Anniston and Birmingham, but in fact CORE had made sure to send letters to them before the trip.[104] Burke Marshall, Kennedy's chief advisor on civil rights, has noted that although the Freedom Riders did send their itinerary to the Justice Department, the president, and others in the executive branch, they "didn't really demand anything or ask anything. . . . I knew about it, but not in a very dramatic way, until they got in trouble" on Mother's Day.[105] John Seigenthaler, a thirty-two-year-old former reporter for the *Nashville Tennessean* and a special assistant to the president based in Nashville, similarly reported that he "probably forgot about it until I got a phone call this one morning from this reporter . . . in Anniston." The reporter "called and said that they needed help—he was badly shaken. I said 'Alright.'"[106] The reporter who called was Simeon Booker of *Jet* and Johnson Publications, who had gone to Bobby Kennedy before the Ride and to whom the attorney general had said, "OK. Call me if there is any trouble."[107] Well, there was trouble. The Kennedys suddenly had to do something, lest the New Frontier be revealed as more vista than vigor.

"Maybe I Will Die, but Let's Go On Regardless": Forging on to New Orleans

Jim Peck did not sleep well that Sunday night after the riots in Anniston and Birmingham. Staying in Shuttlesworth's guest bedroom, he was too bruised and tired to fall asleep. His blood ruined Ruby Shuttlesworth's beautiful white bedspread, though she had insisted Peck stay there. Ricky Shuttlesworth, Fred and Ruby's daughter, was shocked and intrigued, having never before seen so much blood.[108] She kept peeking into the room and finally gathered up the courage to approach Peck. "How do you feel?" she asked the battered Freedom Rider. "I'm okay," he whispered back, unable to muster much more.[109]

The next morning he looked ill, on top of looking beaten and bloodied, and some members of the group insisted that he should fly home immediately. Peck refused. "I said that for the most severely beaten rider to quit could be interpreted as meaning that violence had triumphed over nonviolence. It might convince the ultrasegregationists that by violence they could stop the Freedom Riders."[110] Peck persuaded the group that he could go on, though first they had to decide among themselves whether or not they should all go on. That morning, all of the available Freedom Riders held a discussion at Shuttlesworth's house. Understandably, some said that they had had enough but that they would go along with whatever the group decided. They took a vote, and those present elected by an 8-4 majority to continue the Ride.[111] Peck believed the trip should continue: "You certainly can't contemplate giving up. If you do that, you're finished. To give up the trip at a time like this would be to surrender to the forces of violence. And it would provoke a lot more violence if these forces thought that by pulling something like they did, they would prevail."[112] As Herman K. Harris, a recent addition to the Rides from Englewood, New Jersey, pointed out, speaking for many in the majority, "Maybe I will die, but let's go on regardless."[113]

The decision to forge on thus made, the group held a meeting to plan for the Birmingham-to-Montgomery leg of the trip. Shuttlesworth and his ACMHR supporters happily provided food and support for the devoted group and shuttled the Riders (who by now numbered eighteen) in cars from North Birmingham to the Greyhound station. There, Jim Peck told a reporter, "It's been rough, but I'm getting on that bus to Montgomery." Meanwhile, an officer tried to remove Shuttlesworth for trying to associate with the group at the terminal without a ticket. Shuttlesworth once again was unwilling to put up with petty harassment. He purchased a ticket to Montgomery and, between conversations with folks in Washington, spent the time with the Freedom Riders.[114]

The Riders decided to travel in a single group on a Greyhound bus that would be leaving at three that afternoon, May 15. This was the result, at least in part, of Shuttlesworth's ongoing conversations with Bobby Kennedy, who believed that one bus would be easier to protect than two.[115] The Mother's Day events had pushed the Kennedys to take a far more active role, and now, Shuttlesworth later said, "Mr. Kennedy told me we would have some kind of protection."[116] From this point matters stalled. Given what had happened to the buses the group had ridden the previous day, no Greyhound drivers were willing to drive them from Birmingham. As one driver told a reporter, "We aren't going to drive it. That's final."[117] Shuttlesworth advised the group to stick it out until someone let them get on a bus, but he left the final decision up to the participants, who agreed with their host.

The only potentially violent incident in the heavily fortified terminal came when a pugnacious drunk approached the group and announced his intention to take them all on. Apparently, Shuttlesworth's infamy had penetrated even the drunkard's addled brain, for he recognized the minister and local agitator and decided he wanted to go mano a mano with the reverend, shouting, "There is the one I want." The police immediately stepped in. Shuttlesworth could not help but chuckle at the entire situation.[118] This aborted brouhaha punctuated an otherwise boring afternoon of waiting.

By this point President Kennedy and his attorney general, who had assumed responsibility for the Freedom Ride, which in his mind had become an embarrassing debacle, had safety first and foremost on their minds.[119] They had been shocked and horrified by the events in Anniston and Birmingham and wanted above all to prevent further bloodshed. After hearing and reading about the events of that fateful Sunday, the president "tersely called for law and order," in the words of Harris Wofford, Kennedy's special assistant for civil rights.[120] Robert Kennedy first placed a call to Shuttlesworth's home and asked for Simeon Booker, possibly under the mistaken impression that Booker was one of the group's leaders. The reporter told the attorney general that the group felt "trapped" in Birmingham. Booker later recalled his conversation with the attorney general: "I said, 'Look, this integrating is dangerous. These people's lives are in danger. This is going to blow up. . . . They have no protection at all down here.'"[121] The phone next went to a couple of the group's leaders before ending up in Shuttlesworth's hands. From this point on, Shuttlesworth would be the local point man in a phone network that ran between his house, the office of the U.S. attorney general, Burke Marshall's apartment (he was holed up with the mumps), and contact people at the FBI.[122]

The attorney general also called a number of Alabama officials. One politician with whom he refused to deal directly was Bull Connor. In the journalist Victor Navasky's words, Kennedy instead called "Patterson, who was mostly unavailable, [and] Lieutenant Governor Albert Boutwell, who was mostly unbelievable," before landing on Alabama's public safety director Floyd Mann, "who was responsible but without much power."[123] Aides had told the attorney general that Governor Patterson had gone fishing, but Mann nonetheless assured Kennedy that Patterson had promised there would be a bus to take the group to Montgomery. Soon, however, Patterson—until then a Kennedy backer, ally, and political friend (in 1960 Kennedy the candidate had called him "our great pal in the South")—backed off.[124]

Apparently, the governor had managed to remove his hip waders long enough to issue his statement condemning the Freedom Riders as "rabble rousers." His pronouncement continued: "We will escort them to the nearest state line; however, we will not escort them to other cities in Alabama to continue their rabblerousing."[125] Patterson knew an opportunity when he saw it, and for an ardent segregationist governor of a Southern state, there could be no greater political mother lode than taking on the federal government in defense of the byways, folkways, and highways of the South. An impasse took hold.

Finally, Kennedy connected with George E. Cruit, the superintendent of the Greyhound bus terminal in Birmingham. Kennedy kept trying to get Cruit to find a bus driver to take the group on to their next destination. Cruit explained that none of the drivers would take the bus under any conditions. Kennedy then tried to get the company to provide a "colored driver," revealing his lack of understanding of the extent of Jim Crow in

Birmingham. Cruit explained, "We do not have any colored or Negro drivers in Birmingham." Kennedy was growing frustrated: "Well, hell, you can look for one, can't you? After all, these people have tickets and are entitled to transportation to continue the trip or project to Montgomery. We have gone to a lot of trouble to see that they get this trip, and I am most concerned to see that it is accomplished."[126]

Cruit continued to insist that none of his drivers would take a bus to Montgomery. Kennedy again tried the tack of finding a black driver, and again this proposal went nowhere. When Cruit told Kennedy, "Only bus drivers who have specialized training can drive these buses," the president's closest advisor seethed, "Well surely somebody in the damn bus company can drive a bus, can't they?" He asked about school-bus drivers. Again Cruit demurred, evoking an amusing, exasperated response: "Well, Mr. Cruit, I think you should—had better get in touch with Mr. Greyhound or whoever Greyhound is and somebody better give us an answer to this question. I am—the Government is—going to be very much upset if this group does not get to continue their trip."[127] Southerners would later use this statement as evidence that the government had masterminded the entire Freedom Ride plot from the outset—a patent absurdity, except in the minds of conspiracy theorists.

Kennedy continued: "In fact, I suggest you make arrangements to get a driver immediately and get these people on their way to Montgomery." He went on: "Under the law they are entitled to transportation provided by Greyhound and we are looking for you to get them on their way. I think you had better call your owner or Greyhound and tell him to get some answer for this question right now. I know there is some way to get a driver for this bus."[128] Kennedy had at turns charmed, cajoled, pushed, threatened, sputtered, fulminated, and even invoked "Mr. Greyhound" in the hopes that it would have some effect. His efforts were of no avail. Mr. Greyhound was not listening to demands from the White House.

More than an hour passed as the group waited first on the loading platform and then inside the station. During that time, a crowd began to amass. This time police provided a protective presence as the group huddled in the white waiting room. Jim Peck later recalled, "We recognized some of their faces."[129] When Robert Kennedy thought he had a deal brokered in which Connor's forces would accompany the bus to the city limits before letting it go on its own, Shuttlesworth expressed concern, reminding Kennedy of what had happened when the bus got outside of the city limits of Anniston. Only accompaniment to the state line would be acceptable.[130]

By this point Gordon Carey had arrived from New York City.[131] The group realized that they would not get to Montgomery and that further delay might mean that they would miss their final mass meeting, scheduled for New Orleans on May 17, the seventh anniversary of the announcement of the *Brown* decision. Reluctantly, the Freedom Riders agreed that they had ridden the last bus of their epochal journey. They decided to fly to New Orleans. Shuttlesworth arranged for cars to bring the group to Birmingham's airport. On the radio they heard updates about their location and status, which had been broadcast throughout the day. These radio accounts were so up to date that they often anticipated events. They also provided intelligence that bands of whites could use to meet the group both at the bus station and at the airport hours later.[132] Some among the group were relieved. Isaac Reynolds, who had been the last of the Riders to debark from the Trailways bus, conceded that were more violence to take place, "I don't think I could stand by again and do nothing."[133] For those for whom nonviolence was a tactic, Anniston and Birmingham had been a test they had passed, but many were not prepared to withstand the onslaught indefinitely.

With some help from the Justice Department, the group secured seats on an Eastern Airlines flight that would leave at 6:50 P.M. for New Orleans.[134] Immediately after the passengers had boarded, an announcement over the loudspeaker informed them that someone had called in a bomb threat.[135] The plane would have to be emptied and all baggage searched. After a lengthy delay, the flight was cancelled. A mob gathered in the airport, overwhelmingly men dressed in jeans and tee-shirts. Jim Peck noted that the men were "clustered in groups" and "were obviously not airline passengers." At one point he heard a young man tell his girlfriend, "We're going to get them as soon as they come through this way."[136] On this day, however, the police were on the scene in large numbers, and they were under orders to deter violence. For all he had endured, Moses Newson found the experience at the Birmingham airport to be his nadir: "The biggest letdown in the whole trip came at the Birmingham Airport. Try to imagine two days full of tension—and yes, fear for your life—and then the good, good feeling aboard a plane that will fly you away from the terrorizing human stalkers. Deep down in your heart you're happy. And like a nightmare comes the voice to say that there has been a bomb threat and everyone must get off and return to the airport. It was pure torture."[137]

One white man did provide some salve to the weary group when he approached them and introduced himself as a native of Birmingham. Peck later recounted the conversation: "He said he was sorry about what had happened to us there and wanted us to know that there were some whites in the city who thoroughly disapproved" of what the Riders had experienced.[138] The next scheduled flight to New Orleans was on Capital Airlines, and the group secured reservations on that flight as well. It too was cancelled, though this time there was no announcement of a bomb scare.

Meanwhile, Bobby Kennedy had dispatched John Seigenthaler to Birmingham. The two men had first met when Seigenthaler wrote a series of exposés in the *Tennessean* on the Teamsters. The young journalist had also helped Kennedy write *The Enemy Within*, on his experiences chasing Jimmy Hoffa. Seigenthaler asked the attorney general, "What sort of help do they want?" and the reply was, "I think they primarily need somebody along just to hold their hand and let them know that we care, and I want to let them know that we care, they've been through a horrible experience." Seigenthaler agreed, but the earliest plane he could get would arrive after the Freedom Ride plane was set to depart. Fortunately, the various delays allowed him to reach the airport in time to find the Riders "all huddled in one corner of the airport." Seigenthaler later described what he saw, encountering "a sad, befuddled group" of Freedom Riders for the first time.[139] "They were bandaged," he said. "Head bandages were bloody and eyes were blackened and they were in terrible shape. I guess they hadn't had a bath or change of clothes since the thing happened to them more than 24 hours before that. I went over and introduced myself to them, and you never really understand what friendship is all about until you see somebody look at you that way—I mean, they literally were scared to death."[140]

By about ten that night, the police had cleared the mob out of the facility and set up a roadblock on the road leading to the airport in hopes of filtering out rabble-rousers. Even as Fred Shuttlesworth led a mass meeting at Kingston Baptist Church, he kept apprised of the situation by phone with Bobby Kennedy. He relayed updates to his congregation, its members thrilled to be at the heart of such momentous events.[141] While Shuttlesworth was bouncing between the church and his office, his trusted ACMHR vice president, Kingston's Reverend Edward Gardner, kept the crowd at a feverish pitch. Pointing to the white detectives sent as spies, Gardner gave no quarter: "Our commissioner sends them here each Monday night, but we can't find them when we need them. I tell you, if the Negroes [*sic*] blood can flow, so can the white blood."[142] The meeting could not have been a comfortable place to be one of Connor's henchmen.

When Shuttlesworth took to the pulpit after nine o'clock, he railed against the lies of the police force, which claimed to have no idea of the events, despite his own ample warnings: "This is the worst city in the world, where Mr. Connor or any other Commissioner of the Police Department will say, 'We didn't know violence would happen.' They are a damn liar [sic]."[143] He had hoped that in providing advance notice, he would see police protection for the group. Instead he had seen "broken heads, broken bones, bloody shirts and such. This is a Democracy? I saw one man with his head laid open," Shuttlesworth fumed, remembering James Peck. "It took fifty stitches to sew his head up. That same man sat in my house before the TV cameras, in my bed."[144]

He then continued his account of the previous day's events and of his ongoing conversations with the attorney general, he and Shuttlesworth by now on a first-name basis. When a call from Kennedy interrupted Shuttlesworth, this simply added veracity to the reverend's narrative. The 350-person throng, solidly Shuttlesworth's people, erupted in jubilation when their leader declared that Robert Kennedy had told him, "If you can't get me at my office, call the White House."[145] By the end of the meeting, the crowd was on its feet in spirited adulation. Ed Gardner announced, "Don't we have a great president who has courage and conviction."[146] Shuttlesworth, long a local hero, had emerged as a national civil rights leader. He was planning a move to Cincinnati, largely because of his frustrations with the local situation—among both the black and the white communities—but the Freedom Rides and subsequent events created an environment in which Shuttlesworth would have to continue his involvement, no matter where his sanctuary was located.

Finally, at 11:39, after more than six hours in the airport, the Freedom Riders lifted off aboard a twin-engine Eastern Airlines flight.[147] Along with them were three black reporters, representatives from NBC in Montgomery, and three other "television men" from New York.[148] John Seigenthaler was in no small part responsible for the plane finally departing. He had identified himself to a Birmingham police officer and explained that the group did not want any trouble. They just wanted to leave. The officer responded by telling the president's aide that Bull Connor wanted them to get out of there: "We want them out just as much as you do." The fear of a bomb or continued bomb threats was still the dominant problem. The police officer took Seigenthaler to speak with an Eastern official. "He looked like he was ready to kiss me," recalled the Kennedy aide. Pulling Seigenthaler away from the policeman, the head of the airline confided, "I think these things are contrived. I know they're contrived." He just wanted to get everyone off safely, but as soon as he announced the flight, there would inevitably be another bomb scare. The two men worked out a system of signals and discrete steps that allowed Seigenthaler to whisk the haggard participants onto the plane and off the ground before anyone realized it.[149]

The flight was uneventful. Several of the group played poker.[150] An hour after departure, at 11:53 P.M., Eastern Airlines Flight 309 landed in New Orleans.[151] The Riders met with a mixed reception. On the one hand, they ran into a group of intransigent police officers. "Gosh the cops were tough," Seigenthaler remembered. "I guess that airport is in another country." He decided to talk to the officer, to introduce himself and tell him, "They're not looking for any trouble, they're just citizens; just be here for a while; they're not going to create any trouble," which seemed to "back them up some."[152] They also encountered a receptive audience of CORE supporters, as well as a gaggle of journalists, many of whom snapped pictures of the beaten but unbowed group. Reporters pulled some of the group aside to interview them. Meanwhile, Seigenthaler "looked up and coming across the lobby is Barry Goldwater in shirt sleeves. Shook hands with every one of them, said what a terrible thing he thought it was and went on. I guess he was just in New Orleans."[153] He told Seigenthaler: "This is horrible. Just horrible. Never should have happened. I'm glad you're with them."[154] They went on to stay in undisclosed homes in the city.[155] The Freedom Ride had ended. Or so most thought. Bobby Kennedy reported back to his brother, referring to Seigenthaler, "They were in bad shape, but he got them out."[156] Both were relieved that the potential calamity was over.

"The Bravest Man in the World": Returning Heroes

In New Orleans the group received the kind of welcome usually reserved for conquering heroes. Fourteen Freedom Riders gathered for a press conference in a dormitory lobby at Xavier University. Peck told the assembled media members that he found it "disheartening to see a city engulfed in such a state of hatred" as Birmingham. He believed that the trip had been a success, though "not completely successful," because it proved "one could not travel freely in this country." He said he hoped that the group's experience "would have a sobering effect on our country." Elton Cox, expanding on this point, declared, "If we are going to live as a Christian nation we are going to have to clean up our own back yard." Albert Bigelow told scribes, "I was ashamed to be a white man in South Carolina and Alabama."[157]

That same day, May 16, police arrested three men for their involvement in the Birmingham beatings. Although local officials knew almost everyone involved in the fray, many had special immunity. Those so anointed were the ones involved with the strong local or statewide Klan chapters. A few members of the virtually defunct U.S. Klans ended up as the fall guys so that local police could point to some activity aimed at bringing to justice someone involved in the beatings. The three arrested men—Jessie Oliver Faggard, a doughnut-machine operator; his father, Jessie Thomas Faggard; and Melvin Dove, a maintenance man—were charged with crimes ranging from assault and battery for the younger Faggard to disorderly conduct for the other two. All three served short jail sentences and paid fines for their actions, though Jessie Oliver Faggard's assault charges were eventually dropped.[158] When the remaining assailants (not among the protected groups) from the Langston photograph of George Webb's beating were finally identified, they too were charged with a series of crimes.[159] One of them, Howard Thurston Edwards, was a surly young foreman in a print shop, as well as a volunteer fireman. He was the man with the pipe in the paper bag. The other was Herschel Acker, a paper-mill worker from Rome, Georgia. As Diane McWhorter has wryly noted, Acker fulfilled the perfunctory role of "the inevitable outside agitator."[160] A jury acquitted Acker of assault with intent to murder after thirty-one minutes. Three times, hung juries could not or would not decide the fate of Howard Thurston Edwards. Both walked.[161]

Gordon Carey and New Orleans CORE chapter chair Ruby Lombard presided over a banquet feting the group on May 17, where "Beltin' Elton" Cox told the assembled crowd, "When we sought equal protection under the law, we did not get it." He asked civil rights supporters to use every "in" they might have with officials in Washington, and he assured them, "We shall overcome, because we shall continue to fight until we win our rights." Reverend Abraham Lincoln Davis, pastor at the host New Zion Baptist Church, gave thanks for the "genuine police protection" New Orleans officials provided that night, especially in light of bomb threats and other threats he and others had received. "I'm happy of one thing," he announced. "We are not afraid any more in this fight." The Freedom Riders received a thunderous standing ovation, and the crowd donated $668 to the cause. One of the highlights of the night was the appearance of a nineteen-year-old local activist, Jerome Smith, a New Orleans resident who had intended to go on the Freedom Ride but missed the event because he was in jail for picketing in his hometown. He was able to secure his release from jail in time to make the meeting.[162] Smith, the project chair of New Orleans CORE, had spent twenty-six days in jail, an institution he called the "new frontier of the freedom struggle," for a charge of "obstructing traffic" during the April 17 picketing of McCrory and Woolworth stores in downtown New Orleans.[163]

The Freedom Riders had grown in number from their start in Washington. Several from the original group could not make the New Orleans meeting. Farmer was still gone as a result of his father's death. Lewis had not returned from Nashville but was in the process of ensuring that the Freedom Rides were not yet a thing of the past. Jim Peck and Hank Thomas had already left for New York on CORE business. Genevieve Hughes and Frances Bergman were in New Orleans but were feeling ill and were not up for the events of the night. Of those who had joined along the way, Mae Frances Moultrie had been forced to leave the trip in Birmingham; Ivor Moore of the Bronx, who had joined the trip at midpoint and made it as far as New Orleans, had to leave because of the death of his grandfather; and Gus Griffin of Tampa, who had joined the group for a short spell between Charlotte and Rock Hill after Perkins's arrest, was also absent.

Many Riders were able to attend the New Orleans meeting, however, and several of them told their stories in the New Zion Baptist church, to the delight of the more than one thousand amassed supporters.[164] Ed Blankenheim amused the crowd when he mimicked a mob member, drawling, "Yawl ain't narth now, yawl in Alabama." Charles Person (who had reported bomb threats against the mass meeting that he had received in New Orleans since returning from Birmingham to the FBI) recalled the moment when he and Jim Peck prepared to debark in Birmingham in the face of the hostile crowd.[165] "We looked at ourselves and said 'are we going to have lunch?' We agreed that's what we'd come for," Person said. Albert Bigelow recalled lying down after the events in Anniston. He was covered with soot from the burned bus: "Joe [Perkins] came in and stuck his hand out and they were the same color and I said 'Joe, I've finally made it.'" Along similar lines, Walter Bergman, the extent of whose injuries was still hidden, remembered seeing "my (injured) eye getting blacker and blacker and I said to myself at least there is one part of my body of which I need not be ashamed."[166] Jimmy McDonald led the congregants in song. Joe Perkins, Isaac Reynolds, and Herman Harris were also present at the final meeting.

For a week or more, the Freedom Riders were celebrities, particularly among African Americans and liberal organizations, who hailed them as returning heroes. *Afro-American* correspondent Moses Newson wrote, "Friendship airport never looked so good to me as it did Thursday afternoon," May 18, when the flight from New Orleans touched down in Baltimore. For Newson, who surely spoke for all of the participants, "traveling with the Freedom Riders on their trip into the Deep South was a shocking and unforgettable experience."[167]

After the group had returned and dispersed, the plaudits continued. In a front-page editorial (almost assuredly written by Moses Newson), the *Baltimore Afro-American* announced that "Operation Dixie-Riders will never be the same":

> The courageous Freedom Riders won't ever be the same. They left Washington, DC in good spirits with high hopes in their country and fellowmen. . . . They held some of the most democratic meetings ever attended. . . . As things got rougher, safety began to take a more important role and every man wanted to have his say and cast his vote on plans. They spoke bluntly. There were no political leaders, just people with feelings about how best to do what had to be done. . . . But the beatings, the shocks, the depth of the hating, the open lawlessness, and the bus riding mile after mile took its toll. . . . As they left for their various homes Thursday some were painfully injured, some considerably nervous, and others just weary. . . . It will be a miracle if all of their physical and psychological wounds ever heal. . . . The Deep South was that tough.[168]

Not all of the original Freedom Riders were fully enamored with everything about the journey. Proud as he was of what he and the group had accomplished, Walter Bergman, en route to Chicago on June 1, wrote a somewhat scathing letter that revealed underlying tensions within the group. For one thing, Bergman, as noted earlier, was adamant that the training in Washington had not been rigorous or disciplined enough. And again, he also believed that participants should have been chosen only after the training sessions and that alternates who joined en route should have gone through training as well. Further, Bergman argued that no one should have been allowed simply to join the group without consultation with "fellow toursmen." Two of the Riders who joined en route were, in Bergman's estimation, "great embarrassments to our project." Bergman did not delve into specifics, but he also had harsh words for a few of his colleagues, including one who suffered from "emotional instability," another who showed "imperviousness to group decisions," and a third who displayed what Bergman found to be galling "exhibitionism." He also believed that at least one member had "flauted [*sic*] group decisions and callously broke promises concerning the topics to be discussed in public." He further condemned the decision to include "CORE staff who have a long-standing reputation for intransigence" and criticized "vulgarity, profanity, and cheap theatrical tricks, no matter how mirth provoking," for cheapening "the excellent impression made by most members of the Ride."[169]

The lack of specifics in Bergman's critique makes it difficult to assess. Certainly, everyone in the group did not always get along well, and there were times when the group deviated from its plans, often because of violence. Movement veterans such as John Lewis had also criticized the Washington training as insufficient. But in the end, most of the Freedom Riders did not echo Bergman's negative assessments, and few today recall who the most troublesome Riders were. Bergman had surely earned his right to speak and criticize, but on the whole, not many of the Riders echo his conclusions.

Paula Peck, meanwhile, was relieved for her husband's safe return. She was one among many who believed her husband "a hero. I know that what he's doing is right." At the same time, however, she couldn't help but admit, "I just wish it was someone else's husband, that's all." Nonetheless, Paula Peck, who had married Jim thirteen years earlier, soon after the Journey of Reconciliation, had "never tried to talk him out of things he wants to do, things he believes in. That wouldn't be right—just as it wouldn't be right for him to try to discourage me from doing something I believed in."[170] Peck recounted how when he had left to take part in the Ride, "my wife had said to me 'be sure and be careful and take care of yourself.' I guess I didn't do too good a job."[171]

A little more than a week after Peck's return to New York, a friend from the Fellowship of Reconciliation, Alfred Hassler, wrote him to "add my word of appreciation and admiration for the way in which you conducted yourself in the Freedom Ride instance and since." He described his thirteen-year-old daughter's response after seeing Peck interviewed on television, when she solemnly said, "I think he must be the bravest man in the world." Hassler added, "I guess she is not far wrong, at that."[172]

Henry Thomas and Jim Peck had left New Orleans almost immediately upon arrival to fly to New York. Within days they and more than a thousand others were in New York City participating in a CORE picket line outside of the Port Authority Trailways bus terminal. More than ten thousand individuals took part in similar protests at Greyhound and Trailways terminals across the country. This coordinated action sought to draw attention to the continuing situation in the South and to make sure that the story of the Freedom Riders did not become merely a transient account that fell off the front page as quickly as it had emerged. But the protest also aimed to pressure the bus companies to take control of the situation by ending segregation where they could, on their buses and in their terminal facilities. One picture that appeared in many newspapers, including on page one of the *Afro-American,* showed Peck and Thomas wearing large signs, almost like sandwich boards, hung from their necks by twine. Peck, who still bore bandages and the scars and bruises of his beating, had a placard reading, "I, James Peck, am a victim of an attempt at lynching by hoodlums." Thomas's sign read, "I, Henry Thomas, was arrested on Freedom Ride in South Carolina." Behind them others carried CORE signs with slogans such as "Segregation is morally wrong." Other organizations, including the National Student Association, seven locals of the New York City International Ladies Garment Workers Union (ILGWU), the Furriers Union, and the Hotel Workers Union, joined with CORE. So too did students from Hunter College, City College, and New York University. During their lunch hours, more than two thousand persons joined the picketing. The protesters passed out leaflets pointing out that the continuing presence of segregation ordinances across the South invited the sort of violence that the Freedom Riders met.[173]

For weeks Peck was "snowed under with TV and radio interviews, meetings and getting out a special Freedom Ride issue of the *CORElator.*" He had his fifty-three stitches removed and was beginning to recuperate. Things had been "tough on Paula, but she too is feeling better now."[174] His beating had drawn so much publicity that he was besieged with requests for speaking engagements and public appearances.[175] Meanwhile, the original Freedom Ride was over, but Peck watched as the students who had changed the nature of civil rights protest through their sit-in campaigns prepared to take over the Freedom Rides. They were ready to take on Alabama and Mississippi. Alabama and Mississippi would prove ready to meet their challenge.

Chapter 8

"I'm Riding the Front Seat to Montgomery This Time"

The Students Take Control

"Backing Away Is Not an Option"

John Lewis, Diane Nash, James Bevel, and the rest of the students who had been active in the Nashville campaign to desegregate public facilities were enjoying a picnic on a gorgeous Southern spring afternoon, celebrating a just-won victory over segregation in Nashville's movie theaters, when a report about the burned Greyhound bus came over the radio.[1] The news bulletins that followed were wrenching. John Lewis remembers his reaction: "I felt shock. I felt guilt. There was my bus, my group. It was devastating to hear this news, and it was torture to hear it in only the sketchiest terms. There were no details—no reports about injuries or deaths. I could only imagine, and imagination coupled with fear is a torturous thing."[2]

Against the protests of even some of the senior activists, the students decided to call an emergency meeting. Lewis, Nash—a veteran not only of Nashville but also of the jails in Rock Hill just weeks before—and Rodney Powell, a medical student and a local veteran of the struggle, had to convince Bevel and several others who were content to finish their picnic that the events in Alabama called for their immediate attention. The meeting that followed lasted all night and into Monday. The students initially considered joining the Riders as reinforcements, before the CORE group had to change its plans. By the time the plane carrying the Riders to New Orleans departed, the young men and women in Nashville had decided that they would carry on with the Freedom Rides from Birmingham. They were going to move from local activism to the national stage.

John Lewis, on his way back from his interview in Philadelphia and en route to join his fallen colleagues when he stopped over in Nashville, believed that CORE had surrendered in the face of violent resistance. He was sickened by what had happened to his friends and colleagues, but he also could not stomach the trip's premature conclusion. As Lewis would later put it, "Once the truth has been recognized and embraced—in this case the truth of the absolute moral invalidity of racial segregation and the necessity of ending it—backing away is not an option. It is simply not a choice."[3] Lucretia Collins believed "that the Rides must continue and that if we did not continue it ourselves, then the purpose of the Rides would have been lost."[4] Diane Nash likewise believed "that the future of the movement was going to be cut short if the Freedom Ride had been stopped as a result of violence. The impression would have been that whenever a movement starts all you have to do is attack it with massive violence and the blacks will stop."[5] For Nash, who had dropped out of Fisk and was a full-time paid staffer for the local branches of SNCC and SCLC, as for the others, it was vital that the Ride continue.

In a church meeting room in Nashville, a group of students began developing strategy to resume the Ride. Diane Nash called James Farmer to let him know their decision and ask for his support. The group was not in search of permission. Farmer at first was taken aback. He told Nash that resuming the Freedom Ride would be suicide and that they were walking into a massacre. Lewis and the others "were all a bit irritated by that kind of warning," which seemed to "assume that we hadn't already considered the brutal reality that lay ahead of us."[6] Having already participated in much of the first phase of this action, Lewis may have rightly felt especially patronized as Farmer lectured the students about dangers he had already confronted.

Farmer had a slightly different perspective. "Well, we had a sort of unwritten law, a gentleman's agreement, in SNCC and CORE and SCLC, that before anyone would come into another's project we'd get permission from them so it wouldn't seem we were usurpers," he later explained. "So they called and asked if I would object to their carrying on the Freedom Ride. Well, my first reaction was, 'Look, you'll be killed. You see what's happened so far in Alabama. You go on to Mississippi, you probably won't survive.'"[7]

Nash responded to Farmer's warnings with a terse, "We fully realize that," and explained her belief that caving in to violence would be the worst thing that could happen to the movement. She told Farmer that she wanted to "send in fresh nonviolent troops to carry the ride on." Then she suggested, "Let me bring in Nashville students to pick up the baton and run with it." The students had called CORE largely because SNCC and the more established organization had established a level of reciprocity whereby each kept the other abreast when their actions intersected and neither, in Farmer's words, would "move in on the other's project without permission."[8] Nonetheless, given the extreme events in Birmingham and the students' level of commitment, it is unlikely that they would have agreed to honor a pact that would prevent them from continuing with the Rides.

Perhaps sensing this, Farmer relented, realizing that he had little alternative. He found the students' argument that they could not allow violence to stop the movement compelling.[9] He agreed to meet Nash in Nashville to provide support as needed. Continuing its planning, the group enlisted the help and support of a man who had served as a mentor and inspiration for many of them—Jim Lawson, a veteran of the freedom struggle who was now ensconced in Ohio. Proud of his former charges, Lawson not only embraced the plan but promised to join in its execution within a few days.[10]

The young advance guard of the movement ran into resistance from some of the leaders of more established civil rights organizations. This led to an awkward situation because for all of their enthusiasm, the students needed at least their elders' financial support. They had to make a number of pleas, some emotional, some rational, some eloquent, some straightforward. Eventually, the Nashville Christian Leadership Conference, an offshoot of Martin Luther King's SCLC, under whose penumbra the Nashville movement operated, relented and provided nine hundred dollars to pay expenses.

When Nash called Fred Shuttlesworth to tell him about their plan, the reverend, who two days before had proclaimed the violence a great thing for America, was flabbergasted. "Young lady," he scolded the young veteran of Nashville's protest battlegrounds, "do you know that the Freedom Riders were almost killed here?" Weary of the old guard's patronizing tone, Nash snapped back, "Yes! That's exactly why the ride can't be stopped." Finally, to let Shuttlesworth know that the decision had been made—that she was calling to ask for support, not sanction—she declared: "We're coming. We just want to know if you can meet us."[11] Shuttlesworth acquiesced in the face of such determination. Perhaps the obstinate, heroic minister had met his match in the former Fisk beauty queen.[12] He quickly jumped on board. Nash was relieved, believing that in contrast to the opposition they had received from some of Nashville's black religious leadership, Shuttlesworth would provide not only an example and inspiration but also tactical support on the ground that would prove invaluable as they carried forth their mission.[13]

The students continued planning logistics by first choosing ten among the group to continue with the Freedom Ride from Birmingham, leaving the Greyhound station. This was a difficult task, and there were many volunteers. Still, there was only enough money to buy ten tickets with some left over, and ultimately the group agreed to let James Bevel, their chair, make the final decision. Bevel chose Lewis to lead the group of ten veterans of what he called a "nonviolent standing army."[14] Of these ten, six—William Harbour, Charles Butt, Paul Brooks, William Barbee, Allen Cason, and John Lewis—were black men. Two were black women—Lucretia Collins and Catherine Burks. Two white Riders—Jim Zwerg and Salynn McCollum—represented both genders.[15] Collins later recounted her assessment of the situation when she decided to join the Ride: "We thought that some of us would be killed. We certainly thought that some of us, if not all of us, would be severely injured. At any moment I was expecting anything. I was expecting the worst and hoping for the best."[16]

This phase of the trip represented a significant shift in the Civil Rights Movement, as this group, unlike those on the racially mixed buses that left from Washington, overwhelmingly represented the new wave of black activists, who had been forged in the crucible of the student struggle. This demographic shift represented the simple realities of the black protest movement in Nashville, but it also reveals that SNCC's members believed first and foremost in black self-empowerment, with help from their white brothers and sisters.

Her peers elected Diane Nash, one of the most visible leaders of the Nashville movement and probably its most popular, to serve as the trip's coordinator, Bevel believing her "too valuable as the focal person in Nashville."[17] To her chagrin, this assessment prevented her from going on the Ride, although it would keep her in regular contact with the Justice Department. She would also serve as media liaison, coordinate action on the ground where SNCC had chapters, and organize recruitment and training for the anticipated successive waves of Freedom Riders to come.[18] Nash enlisted the support of Ella Baker, who provided daily input as Nash dealt with the day-to-day administration of the student phase of the Rides.[19] Bevel did not name himself as one of the Riders, since he had to help a friend move. Nash and the others could not believe that such an excuse would keep Bevel from the Ride, but otherwise they were satisfied with his leadership decisions.[20]

In Washington, James Farmer maintained a proprietary claim on the Freedom Rides. He called the New York CORE office and had them get in touch with members of New Orleans CORE chapters. Farmer wanted CORE to train new recruits to join the students as quickly as possible. Farmer welcomed SNCC's infusion of new volunteers, but "a concern burned within me. I could not let CORE's great new program slip from its grasp and be taken over by others."[21]

Even as the majority of the original Freedom Riders awoke in New Orleans after their difficult and painful ordeal, the ten reinforcements boarded a Greyhound bound for Birmingham. Some of them had given Nash letters to mail to family members in the case of their deaths. Others had written up wills. They were afraid. They were prepared for death. They did not need lectures from their elders for that.

Nash, meanwhile, had developed a code to allow her to communicate with Shuttlesworth and others without their conversations' meanings being readily identifiable to the inevitable eavesdroppers in Alabama or among the feds. The code referred to packages being delivered and various colored chickens. These "packages" were Freedom Riders, and the various kinds of chickens identified their races and genders.

"Y'all Are Freedom Riders": Back in Birmingham

It did not take the Kennedys long to catch word of the machinations in Nashville and Birmingham. When they did, they were apoplectic. At around four in the morning on Tuesday, just a few hours after the Freedom Riders had flown out of Birmingham, John Seigenthaler's phone rang in his New Orleans hotel. It was Burke Marshall.

"Do you know Diane Nash in Nashville?" the president's chief civil rights advisor almost shouted into the receiver.

"Yes, I know who she is," responded a groggy Seigenthaler.

"Well you come from that goddamn town, they started another group down to Birmingham to take over by bus where those others left off; they'll never get them turned back. They were getting ready to leave and they called to warn us they're going. If you can do anything to turn them around, I'd appreciate it."[22]

Marshall gave Seigenthaler a number where Diane Nash could be reached and left him to handle another crisis regarding the Freedom Rides. Seigenthaler called the church, where the students were still meeting. The line was busy. He called people he knew in Nashville, hopeful that someone would pressure Nash and the others to call a halt to their plans. When he finally got through, Seigenthaler practically pleaded with Nash: "You know, it's going to create problems. I came through there. All hell is going to break loose." Nash "was going to get those people killed."[23] After attempts to have them turned around when they arrived in Birmingham proved fruitless, Seigenthaler realized that he was going to have to fly back to the Magic City. His ordeal had just begun.

The Freedom Ride had risen from the ashes of burning bus and bloodied brow. On Wednesday morning the ten activists boarded a Greyhound bus whose destination placard on the upper left-hand corner read "Birmingham." In keeping with Gandhian dictates, Fred Shuttlesworth and Diane Nash had let various authorities know that a new group was coming into Birmingham and that they would be testing Jim Crow. Word soon spread around the bus station to the employees, many of whom were black and some of whom had seen the events of the prior days.

The Freedom Riders themselves had no idea what to expect that day. Lucretia Collins later admitted: "We thought that someone would [be] killed. And we certainly thought that someone would be injured severely."[24] Most were silent throughout the trip. Some rode in an integrated fashion. When they crossed into Alabama from Tennessee that morning, no one seemed to care that Paul Brooks, a classmate of John Lewis at the American Baptist Theological Seminary and one of the group's spokespersons, and Jim Zwerg—white and black respectively—were sitting side by side in a front-row seat. Actually, there was disagreement among some of the students as to whether it was tactically sound to risk confronting accepted racial mores before they could test things in Birmingham and Montgomery.[25] Nonetheless, dissenters' qualms aside, for two hundred miles the two rode with no trouble, until they reached Birmingham's city limits. There they saw several Birmingham city police cruisers parked alongside the highway. An officer standing in the road signaled to the bus driver to pull over. When the bus came to a stop, the officer boarded the bus, took notice of Brooks and Zwerg, and placed them under arrest.[26] He then asked the passengers to produce their tickets. When he saw that all of the young people were headed for the same destination, via the same routes, he chuckled and said, to no one in particular, "Y'all are Freedom Riders."[27] The coinage that Gordon Carey and Jim Farmer had cooked up in planning the Rides had finally entered the lexicon even of the white power structure in Birmingham.

The police officer summoned some of his colleagues aboard, waving the others along, and directed the driver to proceed to Birmingham. Minus Zwerg and Brooks, the Freedom Ride continued into Birmingham, this time with a full police escort, a reception that might have averted disaster three days earlier. When the bus pulled into the terminal, the policeman instructed all of the other passengers, many of whom must have felt timorous about this turn of events in light of what they had seen on the news, to get off. Among these was Salynn McCollum, the lone white female Freedom Rider. Unbeknownst to the officer, McCollum had missed the bus early that morning and had enlisted a colleague, Lester Carr of the Nashville movement organizing committee, to drive her to catch up with her cohort. They had finally caught up with the bus in time to meet it at its stop in Pulaski, Tennessee, some fifty miles down the road. As a consequence, her ticket did not brand her a Freedom Rider, since the others' tickets originated in Nashville.[28]

A crowd had already begun to gather outside the closed bus doors. McCollum took advantage of the misunderstanding and rushed to a phone to call Diane Nash and give her a briefing as to her status and the events that were unraveling. The police would not allow the Freedom Riders off the bus. John Lewis, the group's spokesperson, stood up and addressed the police officer. He stated that they had every right to get off the bus. They had tickets to Birmingham. They had friends and relatives in town. The officer was decidedly undaunted. He poked his nightstick into Lewis's belly, shoved him to his seat, and told him to "sit down and stay there." As the Riders began to wonder about the nature of the congregation outside, the light in the bus started to grow dim—a consequence of the police taping newspapers over the windows to keep the crowd from seeing in or the Freedom Riders from seeing out. "It was strange," recalled Lewis, "very eerie."[29]

They could still hear the crowd outside, which did not alleviate the tension. The group attempted to speak with their captors, hoping that by using this tactic from their workshops they might be able to diffuse some of the worst of what was to come. In Lewis's words, the goal was "to humanize your enemy, break down the barriers, try to connect with him as a person, make him see you as an individual and you him."[30] The officers were not much committed to seeing the Freedom Riders as individuals worthy of empathy. They largely stayed silent, though one did engage with Lucretia Collins for about fifteen minutes.[31]

They remained on the darkened bus for some three hours. When the door finally opened, they were ordered to step off. Police formed a human funnel through which the seven remaining passengers passed into the terminal, the police pushing them through as the expanding white crowd shouted obscenities and epithets. The police made clear to the Freedom Riders that were it not for this protection the white mob would have attacked. Once they had run this gauntlet the students met Salynn McCollum, who by this point was accompanied by Fred Shuttlesworth, the reappearing lead character in the Birmingham drama. The police kept a close eye on the group, allowing them to use the bathroom but giving them little more room to maneuver than that. The terminal was effectively shut off in any case, its restaurants closed, the terminal itself cordoned off to keep the Freedom Riders in and others out.[32] The Riders waited for the five o'clock bus, for which they had tickets. Theirs had been an unorthodox passage, perhaps, but it appeared to the Freedom Riders that they would continue on to Montgomery.

In the interregnum, the group did what they had come to do best in the long and sometimes boring hours spent in sit-ins and picket lines and jail cells. They sang. As Lewis later told it: "So we waited. And we sang. Freedom songs. Songs of the movement. The songs we'd been singing for years now and would be singing for years to come."[33] Perhaps they sang a few verses of "Hallelujah, I'm a Travelin'," one stanza of which went:

I'm paying my fare on the Greyhound bus line
I'm riding the front seat to Montgomery this time.[34]

And it did seem as if they were going to get on that bus to Montgomery, continuing what their immediate predecessors had not. Then in walked a man whom Lewis recognized immediately, though he'd never seen him in person before: "He was short, heavy, with big ears and a fleshy face. He wore a suit, his white hair was slicked back above his forehead, and his eyes were framed by a pair of black, horn-rimmed glasses."[35] For the first time, Bull Connor had arrived at the bus station to see Freedom Riders for himself.

He had also come to arrest them. He did this for their protection, he said smiling.[36] His officers, including Chief Jamie Moore, led the group to a waiting paddy wagon to whisk them off to "protective custody."[37] Shuttlesworth stepped forward to protest, and his old nemesis had the reverend arrested as well. The crowd, which had channeled much of its anger over the past few hours toward the police officers providing the buffer between them and the Freedom Riders, cheered the arrests.[38] On the way to jail, the group continued their sing-in. They reassured themselves that this was no different from their experiences in the jails of Nashville.

At the Birmingham jail, police separated Salynn McCollum from the group because she was white. Eventually, authorities released her into the custody of her father, who flew down from Buffalo. The police segregated the Riders by gender. They were also segregated on a Fred Shuttlesworth and non–Fred Shuttlesworth basis, as police kept the local firebrand from his advisees, perhaps in hopes that he could not instill his rebellious nature in the youngsters any further. Authorities soon released Shuttlesworth on fifty dollars bond after charging him with interfering with an officer.[39]

Meanwhile, the men's cell "looked like a dungeon," John Lewis recalled, with no mattresses or beds, nothing but a concrete floor upon which to sit. So with nothing else to do, they again commenced singing. Freedom songs had become central to the movement. They maintained morale. They kept spirits up. They forged a sense of common identity and common suffering. They provided hope in the face of hopelessness. They served as a soundtrack to a movement and a generation. And on the afternoon and evening of May 17, 1961, in the Birmingham jail, they also annoyed the hell out of Bull Connor and his underlings.[40]

The national headquarters of SNCC quickly moved to let sit-in leaders across the South know about the plight of their peers, the new group of Freedom Riders. SNCC's administrative secretary Ed King sent out a mass mailing to tell members about the detainment in Birmingham and to call for SNCC action. Thus, SNCC demonstrated its belief not only that the Freedom Riders themselves could make a difference but that the entire apparatus of the enthusiastic new wave of activists could apply pressure on individuals and institutions to promote change. King and the Student Nonviolent Coordinating Committee called upon students to do five things: picket Greyhound; send telegrams of protest to Bull Connor; send copies of their telegrams to Fred Shuttlesworth; contact SNCC to volunteer for successive waves of Freedom Rides; and send telegrams to the president and the attorney general, citing the individual rights of those jailed and the deleterious effect on interstate commerce. The hope was that "you can show and prove once again that the south-wide student nonviolent sit-in movement against racial segregation is not a local issue, for just the individual community, but rather a united movement for all freeborn Americans who believe in equality and justice."[41]

The Freedom Riders remained in jail overnight Wednesday and through Thursday. They continued to sing. They also had gone on a hunger strike, refusing all food and even water. Despite all of this, Lewis remembered that throughout the ordeal the police "were very, very nice. They didn't rough us up or anything like that, just very nice."[42] Finally, on Thursday night, Bull Connor showed up at their cell accompanying a group of officers. The time was 11:30, too late for court proceedings. Connor reminded them that he had them in custody for their own protection. Under this protection Connor and his officers would drive them back to Nashville and out of Alabama. Fearing the sort of late-night lynching that was legendary in the black community, the activists extended their nonviolent resistance by going limp. The officers thus had to carry each individual to one of three black, unmarked station wagons. One of the cars carried their luggage. The other two carried the Freedom Riders. Bull Connor took the wheel of one of the cars.[43] Under the cover of darkness, Connor personally escorted this small band of black students from Birmingham.

Lewis and his colleagues felt slightly more at ease soon after the cars headed out of the city and onto the virtually abandoned roads leading north on U.S. Route 31 toward Tennessee.[44] Connor was affable, making idle chitchat with the somewhat stunned group. Catherine Burks told Connor that he was welcome to break bread with them at the Fisk cafeteria for breakfast. The two made small talk for much of the trip, and several of the Riders began to believe that they were going to end up in Nashville, unsuccessful in their attempt to get to Montgomery, but no worse for the wear. In one of the other cars, the Riders also talked with their driver, Lieutenant Holt. Lucretia Collins recalled later, "I thought somehow he was a humanist . . . He was a very kind man," and to some extent she thought that he had been forced to do what he did, that he did not want to be part of these arrests; indeed, to a degree she "got a very positive response" from him "in terms of what we were doing. Sometimes you can just feel kindness," she said, "and I certainly thought he was kind."[45]

Then the three-car convoy came to a stop on the side of the road in Ardmore, a tiny town across the border in Tennessee. After having seen Bull Connor in such a jovial, friendly state, this came as almost as much of a shock as not encountering a hooded mob when they left the jail. A police officer was unloading the car with the luggage, stacking it neatly along the side of the road. "This is where you'll be getting out," drawled Connor. "Y'all can catch a train home from here," he said, nodding toward a small train depot off in the distance. Connor could not help himself. "Or maybe," he added drolly, "a bus."[46]

With that Connor and the other officers jumped back in their cars and drove away. As their taillights faded into the distance, several members of the group came to the same realization: This pitch-dark rural border area was Klan country. The small town would assuredly offer little hope of respite from the night, so they silently trudged on foot in hopes of finding a home with black occupants who might be able to help them solve their predicament. They huddled near the tiny train station while two of the men went to scout the area in hopes of finding a black neighborhood. Once they got their bearings, the two men hurried back to the rest of the group.[47] The students walked along the railroad tracks, moving away from what they presumed to be the white area of town, and went a mile or so until they saw a small, weathered home. The seven approached the front door and rang the doorbell. It was about three in the morning. John Lewis would later say, "I've never been so frightened in all my life" as he was during this time in the haunting backwoods of Tennessee.[48]

An elderly black man answered their knock. "We're the Freedom Riders," Lewis blurted out. "We are in trouble and we need your help. Would you help us?" Likely equal parts dazed, scared, and incredulous, the elderly man shook his head. "I can't let you in. I'm sorry, I can't." Lewis pleaded with the man: "Please sir, we really need your help. If you could just let us make a telephone call." At that moment, a small woman graced the doorframe. Lewis estimated the couple to be in their seventies, similar to the members of his family, who had worked hard their whole lives. "Honey, let them in," she told her husband, who obliged.[49]

It was warm inside, and nine people were about seven too many for the small house. Lewis placed a call to Diane Nash. He spoke to her in the code Nash and Shuttlesworth had designed for the trip to try to flummox the authorities, who no doubt had tapped the phones on one end or another of many of the conversations between the Freedom Riders and home base in Nashville. Nash informed him that eleven other "packages" had been "shipped" from Nashville to Birmingham via train to serve as reinforcements. In the meantime, she would send cars for the group.[50]

The question then became, where would they go from the small home in Ardmore—to Nashville or back to Birmingham? In a short conversation, the group responded unanimously: it was imperative that they continue the trip. Nash should dispatch vehicles prepared to cross back into Alabama. Nash told them that the transport would arrive by midmorning.

By this time it had been nearly two full days since any of them had eaten or bathed. The elderly couple brought two tin tubs into a backroom for the group to wash. At daybreak the man went into town. Using money the students had given him, he went into Ardmore to buy some supplies. Rather than purchase everything at once and arouse suspicion, he went to several stores, eventually emerging with bread, cheese, bologna, and eggs, with which the group broke their fast.

Sometime before noon Leo Lillard, a recent Tennessee State graduate, pulled up in front of the house in a tan Studebaker. The group thanked the old couple, who had clearly risked their own safety for a group of strangers, making their own mark on the history of the Civil Rights Movement in the process. They then piled their luggage into the trunk and themselves into the car, four crammed in front, including Lillard, and four in back. On the way to Birmingham they had to duck down when cars passed to avoid suspicion.

Breaking up the long, uncomfortable ride to Birmingham were periodic radio bulletins. One Birmingham station reported that the Freedom Riders were back in Nashville. The group whooped when they heard that and imagined Bull Connor's reaction when he saw them again. The Studebaker continued to speed in the direction of Vulcan's torch. Then another radio bulletin suspended all laughter. United Press International had somehow managed to find out that the students were not up at Fisk. They were on their way back to Birmingham. Somehow word had gotten out. And there they were, eight young black people crammed into a car with the windows rolled up (which made them feel safer) in the May heat.[51]

Apparently, Connor had not yet managed to fan his troops out along the roads to prevent their arrival. The Riders arrived at Shuttlesworth's house and popped out of the car, sweaty and nervous. There to meet them were the eleven other "packages," including Bernard Lafayette, the young man who had been so jealous of Lewis just two weeks ago and who had driven his tardy friend to catch the bus heading to Washington, D.C. Now Lafayette was one of the Freedom Riders, no longer too young to do his part for the movement. Upon their release from jail, Jim Zwerg and Paul Brooks had also made their way to Shuttlesworth's. Finally, Ruby Doris Robinson from Spelman had flown in from Atlanta to join them on her own. That made twenty-one Freedom Riders total, with Fred Shuttlesworth as their paterfamilias, ready to catch a three o'clock bus to Montgomery that afternoon. The Shuttlesworths fed them chicken and sandwiches, and they then squeezed into a number of cars provided by Shuttlesworth's ACMHR.

At the bus station a huge crowd was awaiting their arrival. Many were newspaper, radio, and television reporters eager for a new Freedom Ride story to grace the front page and the top of the hour. The police were there, though Bull Connor was not. And then there were the masses, many with bad intentions, some three thousand of them. They screamed and shouted at the young men and women. They tried to push through the police phalanx at the terminal to get to the group. Lewis was not frightened: "Partly, I guess, because I'd been through so many situations like this already, and partly, I know, because I had internalized that Gandhian perspective that Jim Lawson had taught us."[52]

If the score of Freedom Riders were ready for the buses, the buses were not ready for the Freedom Riders. A bus sat idling, waiting to depart for Montgomery, but there were no drivers in sight. An announcement went up that the bus was cancelled. The next would depart at five. This met with cheers from the onlookers. The group had to walk back into the terminal and take seats on the benches in the waiting area. Although the police had tried to make sure that no one could get to the students as they waited, some were able to stomp on toes, spray and spill drinks upon the waiting Riders, and otherwise make nuisances of themselves. In what was fast becoming a ritual, the group essayed to block out external annoyances by singing "We Shall Overcome" and other freedom songs and praying. Jim Zwerg led a chorus of the spiritual "Eyes on the Prize." Lewis led the prayers, alongside Eugene Ervin, a church organist.[53] Collins has called the prayer sessions "a beautiful thing! It was unlike any of the other devotional periods that we had had. Because all these kids, they were really in it."[54]

Five o'clock came and went. The crowd outside grew larger. Some threw bricks and stones as well as stink bombs through the terminal windows. The police had to deploy dogs to keep the riotous crowd at bay. In the terminal, the phones had been shut off, and there was no food available. Connor by this time really had no choice but to provide protection—there were no holidays to distract his boys this time—but he also could make life as uncomfortable as possible for the group huddled inside the terminal.

Nighttime came. Unbeknownst to the Freedom Riders, the Kennedy administration was again trying to bargain its way through the labyrinth of white supremacy. After the events of a few days prior, Floyd Mann "knew that we had a tremendous problem on our hands."[55] Governor Patterson knew so as well. Nonetheless, he remained intransigent. Even years later he would assert: "The demand was that we escort them with state police and permit them to do what they wanted to do and then go on unmolested and unrestrained. And, of course, their sole purpose was to violate state laws, to get them tested in court." And so Patterson felt that he "couldn't give a guarantee that I was going to have my police escort and permit and watch these people violate state laws and city ordinances."[56]

Thus, the question for Alabama officials was how to react without seeming to give in either to the Freedom Riders or to the federal government, while at the same time avoiding a repeat of prior fiascoes. After a heated conversation with the attorney general, Patterson finally agreed to meet with representatives from the administration.[57] John Seigenthaler would be the point man. Robert Kennedy called Seigenthaler and said, "Go to Montgomery, the President's going to send you a telegram designating you as special representative to meet with John Patterson."[58]

By the time Seigenthaler got to Birmingham, Connor's forces had arrested the students. Seigenthaler spent most of the day talking to Burke Marshall in Washington and to the people in Nashville, especially Diane Nash, until he was sent to Montgomery. He also let the police know who he was and why he was there. He had heard about the caravan of cars to the state line but could do little about it.[59]

When Seigenthaler finally received an audience with Patterson, who had been avoiding contact with the Kennedys—he was still out fishing in the Gulf of Mexico, according to aides—it was at the governor's office, the Alabama state cabinet seated at a large conference table just across from the governor's desk.[60] Hearing Seigenthaler's Southern lilt, Patterson said, from the head of the long table, "Glad to see you—you're a Southerner." Then he stood up, gesturing toward his cabinet seated around the table: "Now all these people here, they're all with me; . . . so if you've got a tape recorder on you, go ahead and use it." Seigenthaler responded by saying that he did not have a recorder, though he knew the governor probably did. He said that he believed that both sides should say what they felt, that "as far as I'm concerned we won't have any secrets, just have a frank discussion." He then told Patterson, "I'm here to tell you that there is a strong feeling in the Department of Justice that these people have got to have access to interstate transportation, and it makes no sense at all for them to stay here."[61]

Patterson began to lecture. He had already had a testy phone conversation with Bobby Kennedy, and he was still in a fighting mood.[62] He fumed about how "people in this country are so goddamned tired of the mamby-pamby that's in Washington that's a disgrace. There's nobody in the whole country that's got a spine to stand up to the goddamned niggers except me."[63] For fifteen minutes or more, he lectured. He condemned outside agitators. He detoured off into a long-winded tirade against school integration. He vowed that he would not let the federal government step in and determine Alabama's fate. He pounded the table and shouted that this was an Alabama matter and that Seigenthaler and his ilk were the intruders. He raged that he was more popular than Kennedy and that he regretted supporting the president when he was a candidate. In Seigenthaler's recollection, "It was none of my business nor the president's business nor the attorney general's business."[64]

Many cabinet members nodded in clear agreement. Others, like Floyd Mann, were more reserved. Seigenthaler listened, took the abuse, and let the governor say his piece. Then he told Patterson "that my duty as a federal officer was to inform him that if the state could not protect citizens of the United States, either in the cities or on the highways," then protection became "a federal responsibility and we were prepared to assert it, but we hoped we would not have to."[65] The two went back and forth like this for a little while, with Seigenthaler continually returning to the point that, however it had to be done, the Freedom Riders were going to get through Alabama with an escort.

The governor tried to stand his ground. Then Floyd Mann intervened. He knew that Patterson was, as he later put it, "in a terrible political situation because the various people who had so actively supported him strongly and openly were some of the people that were very critical of the Freedom Riders coming into Alabama."[66] Perhaps trying to reconcile Patterson's difficult political logrolling job with necessity on the ground, Mann spoke up: "Governor, as your chief law enforcement officer, I assure you if you give me the responsibility, I can protect them."[67] Seigenthaler used this opening to engage Mann. The two began to work out an arrangement whereby Alabama officials would notify Robert Kennedy of a Patterson declaration: "I can protect all travelers in the State of Alabama, those who are citizens of this state and those from outside."[68] Patterson let Mann handle the details. The plan had state police officers providing an escort between cities, while within city limits, local police would take control.

Seigenthaler called Robert Kennedy from Patterson's office and relayed the text of the governor's message, as well as a glimpse of the plans they were cobbling together. Kennedy asked, "Does he mean it?" and Seigenthaler responded, "I think he does." Seigenthaler then asked Patterson if he intended to uphold his commitment. "I've given my word as Governor of Alabama—let me repeat it to you," and he repeated the statement with Seigenthaler relaying the words across the phone line. Kennedy asked if Patterson wanted to talk to him. Patterson responded, "No, I don't want to talk to him, I talked to him earlier." The two then harangued for a moment about who should issue the governor's pledge to the press. Patterson did not want to do it, but he did not mind if Kennedy issued it.[69] Patterson was playing power politics with the attorney general of the United States.[70]

The last step in the process was to finalize things with the people at Greyhound. The company's officials were more than a bit worried, after having already seen one of their expensive buses go up in flames the previous Sunday. Seigenthaler contacted the president of Greyhound Bus Lines in Atlanta. The official was insistent that without protection for the buses, he was not about to let any leave the station in Birmingham. He wanted federal marshals. Although Nicholas Katzenbach and Byron White were, in Katzenbach's words, "fairly gung ho" to send marshals to Alabama, Sieganthaler and Robert Kennedy were reluctant.[71] Seigenthaler handed the phone to Patterson, who apologized profusely for what had happened to the bus in Anniston and made assurances that the state was perfectly capable of ensuring that nothing would happen to another bus. Finally, Floyd Mann got on the phone with Bull Connor to explain the plan.[72] The die was cast. The federal government had intervened, and the Freedom Ride would continue. Thus far, bringing in Seigenthaler had proven to be either a stroke of genius or a happy accident for the Kennedy administration.

Meanwhile, Alabama officials had a few more tricks of their own. On Friday, May 19, Birmingham sheriff's deputies arrested Fred Shuttlesworth on two charges directly related to his work with the Freedom Riders. Bull Connor signed the complaint. One count charged that Shuttlesworth had conspired with unknown persons to cause a mob to gather in the Birmingham bus station. The other charged him with disturbing the peace in causing a mob to gather. The arrest and charges were related to the mobs that had besieged the Freedom Riders in Birmingham the previous Sunday. Each required one thousand dollars bond. Shuttlesworth was later sentenced to separate ninety-day sentences and fined five hundred dollars for each offense.[73] Bull Connor had decided to hold Shuttlesworth legally responsible for the white mobs that had attacked the Freedom Riders at the Trailways station.

The next morning a bus was waiting, and a driver seemed ready to drive to Montgomery. John Doar of the Justice Department had arrived by this point; he and Seigenthaler stayed in a hotel in Montgomery. Seigenthaler issued a statement about the agreement that had been made. Then Patterson did the same, essentially reiterating the statement that he had given to Kennedy but embellishing it at the end by adding, "We don't tolerate rabblerousers and outside agitators."[74] Seigenthaler and others, at the time, did not see Patterson's bluster as representing a remarkable change in position. By that time a reporter had alerted the Riders to the intrigue between Alabama and Washington.[75] The group approached, relieved but somewhat strengthened in the belief that they were going to take the next step. Instead the stocky driver, Joe Caverno, stepped forward, as if on cue, and made a short statement: "I have one life to give, and I'm not going to give it to CORE or the N double ACP." He then walked away, disappearing through a door reading "drivers only."[76] Once again the bus was driverless. One thing was for certain though—in the public eye the Freedom Rides had put CORE on the map as a significant civil rights force.

Soon Bull Connor, several Greyhound officials, and the head of the bus drivers' union arrived at the terminal. Connor was clearly beside himself with anger. The men met in a back office. Seigenthaler talked with the president of Greyhound, who was able to help cajole his driver to take the bus to Montgomery. A few minutes later, the driver who had announced that he had but one life to give stepped onto the bus without saying anything. Six days after the Mother's Day massacres, the Freedom Riders were heading on to Montgomery.

Chapter 9

"We've Come Too Far to Turn Back"

Montgomery

"It's Terrible. It's Terrible": Montgomery, May 20, 1961

At about 8:30 on the morning of May 20, someone told the students to board the split-level *St. Petersburg Express* for their hundred-mile journey to Montgomery, the Cradle of the Confederacy. As John Lewis later wrote, "It was a surreal trip."[1] The twenty-one Freedom Riders were the only people on the bus. A squadron of police cars with flashing lights and screaming sirens ran interference ahead and followed behind the bus as it headed toward the highway leading south toward Montgomery's Greyhound station. Floyd Mann recalled that this initial stage involved thirty-two patrol cars, sixteen in front and sixteen behind. An airplane followed overhead "to make sure there wasn't any bridges or things blown up or any crowds gathering at any certain place."[2] Behind the police cars were several vehicles with reporters, waiting to see what would unfold next in what was increasingly becoming a significant, bizarre, and potentially disastrous story.

The civil rights activist Virginia Foster Durr recognized the potential for trouble in Montgomery. Writing Burke Marshall the day after the Mother's Day fiascoes in Anniston and Birmingham from the office she shared with her husband, the civil rights lawyer Clifford Durr, she observed: "The Greyhound Bus Station is right across the street from our office and it is full of hard-faced, slouchy men waiting for" the Freedom Riders "to 'come in.' I doubt if the police here will give them any protection either."[3]

At the Birmingham city limits the local police dropped away, and in their place came the state Highway Patrol, just as Seigenthaler and Mann had planned. There were fewer state patrol cars, but every fifteen miles new ones were posted, and like a relay race, the new cars down the road took the place of the ones that had been accompanying the bus. In these exchanges the baton pass occurred at nearly ninety miles an hour, as the bus hurtled straight on through to Montgomery, not making its usual stops, which was "contrary to the understanding" Seigenthaler had with Patterson.[4] Overhead flew the Highway Patrol airplane. For the time being the Freedom Riders rode perhaps the most well-protected bus in the history of automation.

Much had changed in Montgomery since November 1906, when the city street railway system was tied up after the Montgomery Traction Company refused to obey an ordinance calling for separate cars to carry the two races. For almost half a day, the company's stand against the law, which the company found too burdensome, had brought traffic in the city to a standstill. Circumstances only returned to normal when a state court judge granted an injunction restraining enforcement of the separate-cars law. The general public was furious with the city council that had passed the law that led to the traffic quagmire. The mayor, W. M. Teague (who had opposed the law, which passed over his disapproval) and Chief of Police Taylor personally saw to the arrest of the officers of the Traction Company, as well as two-score motormen and conductors.[5]

By 1961, Montgomery's attitude was dramatically different, as the Freedom Riders were about to discover. John Lewis, still the group's spokesperson, sat in the front row behind the driver. Next to him was twenty-one-year-old Jim Zwerg, a native of Appleton, Wisconsin. Zwerg, a Beloit College undergraduate, was spending a year as an exchange student at Fisk. Lewis admired Zwerg, whom he called "one of the most committed people" in the struggle: "And I definitely believe it was not out of any social, do-good kind of feeling. It was out of deep religious conviction."[6]

As the bus made its way to Montgomery, Lewis recalled, "no one on the bus said much. The mood was very relaxed. A couple of our group actually dozed off. It was a pleasant ride, a nice Saturday morning drive."[7] Lucretia Collins and Susan Hermann had a nice long conversation. "We were talking about nonviolence," Collins recalled, "and how wonderful it was . . . And everyone, I think, was in a good mood."[8] Months earlier, Hermann, a twenty-year-old Whittier College student who was at Fisk as an exchange student, had believed nonviolence "a coward's way," but she had soon come to realize that "this is not a coward's way when you can stand there for your beliefs and be punched and kicked and maybe killed."[9]

In just over an hour the bus and its support squadron reached the city limits of Montgomery, and as if in formation, the patrol cars veered from the road. A couple of plainclothes Montgomery detectives continued to follow the bus for a while longer in an unmarked car, and for a few more minutes the plane circled from a distance.[10] At this point, according to plan, the Montgomery police should have taken over with a phalanx of vehicles similar to the one that had seen the Greyhound out of Birmingham. Instead, in the words of Ruby Doris Smith, "When we got inside the Montgomery city limits, it all disappeared."[11] The streets were empty. It was about a seven-minute ride to the station from the city limits.[12]

Once again Lewis "had this eerie feeling."[13] At the same time, he observed, "There was a funny peace there, a quietness."[14] According to Fred Leonard, a freshman at Leo Lillard's alma mater, Tennessee State, at first "everybody was feeling comfortable going into the terminal in Montgomery. We didn't see anybody," but then "we didn't see any police either."[15] By then the airplane had disappeared, and even the police detectives had moved on.

Paul Brooks was among the first off the bus, and he went to call cabs for the group. At first the station seemed virtually deserted, with only a few taxi drivers sitting in their cabs, a number of people who were clearly with the media, and a dozen or so other white men. As he prepared to step off the bus, John Lewis looked to William Harbour and said, "This doesn't look right."[16]

At first the group was bombarded only with questions and the flash of cameras from the members of the media. A reporter and a cameraman approached Lewis and Catherine Burks, who were among the first to debark. Norm Ritter from *Life* magazine asked a question, which Lewis started to answer: "We just got out of Birmingham. We got to Montgomery . . ." and then his voiced trailed away.[17] Seeing a look of horror on Lewis's face, Ritter turned around and saw the white crowd gathering momentum and numbers. What had appeared to be a dozen men turned out to be many more, two or three hundred, including women and even children.[18] Ritter raised his arms high and spread them wide, as if to protect the group from the onslaught to come.[19]

The teeming horde came from alleys and behind doors and around corners. They materialized as if out of nowhere. They carried weapons and everyday items that they could use as weapons. They wielded baseball bats and boards and clubs and pipes and chains and tire irons and bricks and rocks and key chains and blackjacks and hammers and whatever else they could use to gouge or pummel or bludgeon or poleax or maul. At the head of the group was Claude Henley, a local Klan member and an assistant service manager at an automobile dealership. Lewis entreated his colleagues not to run. A woman screamed, "GIT them niggers! GIT them niggers!"[20]

Between the Freedom Riders and the mob stood the journalists. Although it could not have been planned this way, many members of the attacking crowd must have taken great pleasure in taking vengeance upon a group of people who represented the institutions that had made Alabamans look like brutal, racist, animalistic, bullying thugs. And so they attacked the unarmed media members before getting to the mixed-race Freedom Riders.

In the words of John Lewis, "If you had a pencil or a pad, or a camera, you were in real trouble."[21] Moe Levy, the cameraman who had tried to get footage of Lewis and Catherine Burks, took a foot to the gut. His assailant was a fat man with a cigar stuck between his lips.[22] When Levy's big cumbersome camera crashed to the ground, someone picked it up and started beating him with it. *Life* photographer Don Urbrock also found that his lens was turned against him, as someone yanked it from his neck and swung it at his face.[23] They both might have found the situation ironic were they not being pounded senseless by the tools of their trade. Neil Brogden, a *Tampa Times* reporter who happened to have gotten off of a bus from Tampa a few minutes before the Freedom Riders' bus arrived, recounted the violence against reporters in a story he filed for the Associated Press. Brogden took several blows to the face when he interceded to "pull a photographer physically loose" from one of the white attackers.[24] Many more members of the media became part of the story that day, as their blood painted the tarmac of the bus terminal.[25]

But even though the crowd might have found satisfaction in pounding members of the media into pulp, their quarry for the day still stood before them. Behind the Freedom Riders was a small retaining wall with a railing, behind which was an eight- or ten-foot drop to a ramp that in turn led to the basement mailroom of the adjacent federal courthouse building. A "dark-haired woman, primly clad in a yellow dress," screamed, "Get those niggers."[26] Three members of the group decided that there was a fine line between bravery and lunacy and that if they remained on their side of the wall they would find that line crossed. Nonviolent warriors Bernard Lafayette, Fred Leonard, and Allen Cason decided to make the decision to live not to fight another day. They sprung over the wall and jumped down to the ramp. They then ran though the doors to the mailroom, stunning the postal workers sorting the mail on a Saturday morning. "People were in there carrying on their business just like nothing was happening outside," Leonard would recall years later. "But when we came through there, mail went flying everywhere, 'cause we were *running*."[27]

Jim Zwerg did not turn. He did not run. And like Jim Peck before him, he paid a steep price for daring to cross the lines and mix the races in the Deep South. To refrains of "nigger lover!" a group of men wielding the accoutrements of savagery grabbed Zwerg and started beating, kicking, and punching him. He disappeared from the view of the other Riders, who had their own crosses to bear. Dan O. Dowe, the state editor of the *Alabama Journal*, witnessed the attack on Zwerg: "Mr. Zwerg was hit with his own suitcase in the face. Then he was knocked down and a group pummeled him."[28] The prostrate activist fell into unconsciousness somewhere around the time a man took Zwerg's head between his knees while others took turns pounding and clawing at his face. At one point, while Zwerg was unconscious, three men held him up while a woman kicked him in the groin. After it seemed that the worst of the onslaught was over, Zwerg gained semiconsciousness and tried to use the handrails to the loading platform to pull himself to his feet. As he struggled to get upright, a white man came and threw Zwerg over the rail. He crashed to the ground below, landing on his head.[29] He was only the first to be beaten that day, but his beating may have been the most ruthless.

Fred Leonard would later remember Zwerg's actions that day: "He had a lot of nerve. I think that's what saved me, Bernard, and Allen, 'cause Jim Zwerg walked off the bus in front of us and it was like those people in the mob were possessed. . . . It's like they didn't see the rest of us for about thirty seconds. They didn't see us at all."[30] But then, in Ruby Doris Smith's words, "The mob turned from Zwerg to us. Someone yelled 'They're about to get away!' Then they started beating everyone."[31] John Doar could see the events from the federal building adjacent to the bus station. He called the Justice Department to describe the scene: "The passengers are coming off, a bunch of men led by a guy with a bleeding face are beating them. There are no cops. It's terrible. It's terrible. There's not a cop in sight. People are yelling 'Get 'em, get 'em'. It's awful."[32]

The mob tore into the passengers' luggage. Some they threw at the students. Others they wielded as weapons. The rest they simply smashed. Stuart Loory, one of the journalists trailing the buses, described what came out of the suitcases and bags in the next day's *New York Herald Tribune*: "Here a black bow tie, there a religious picture postcard, somewhere else a purple nightgown and a bible."[33] The detritus ended up strewn over the parking lot and on top of the cars on the other side of the railing over which Leonard, Lafayette, and Cason had sprung.

Montgomery's Reverend Solomon Seay, like Fred Shuttlesworth an outspoken proponent of civil rights in a city where speaking out was dangerous, somehow managed to stand "in the midst of" the attackers without getting hurt himself. Seay had been an ardent supporter of the student phase of the movement even when many of his peers and colleagues were reluctant to support the new direction events had taken. At one point after the sit-ins reached Montgomery, Seay admonished his peers: "A lot of our people don't seem to understand what the young people are doing—they say they don't agree with them. Well, that just means they aren't catching the significance of events—it's a case of intellectual sluggishness."[34] The students had redirected the Freedom Rides, and there he was, watching the mob "tearing up the suitcases, throwing cigarette butts in it to set their clothes on fire. . . . I was stepping around trying to put some of it out. They fought and beat everybody passed that way who was black except me—they never touched me."[35]

William Barbee, one of John Lewis's classmates at American Baptist Theological Seminary, took a beating. He had arrived in Montgomery from Nashville on May 18 to help make arrangements for the arrival of the Riders, and he had intended to pick them up from the station that Saturday. Instead the crowd, led by Klansman Thurman E. Ouzts, pulled him from a cab as several Freedom Riders fled the bus station, and before long he, like Zwerg, lay unconscious on the ground after a vicious pummeling. From a hospital bed, Barbee would recount what had happened to him as best he could. Two men had initially been involved in yanking him from the taxi. He got away from them, but "about five or six grabbed me near the loading platform. I pleaded with them to let me go, but they knocked me down and started stomping me. While they were beating and cursing me, I had the uneasy feeling that they intended to murder me. I awakened at the hospital." Barbee's injuries were perhaps even worse than Zwerg's. He was barely able to get his words out to the reporters huddled around his bed. Like Zwerg, Barbee was resolute that the mission continue. He announced to reporters his willingness to "surrender [his] life for the cause of justice. We knew they would probably beat us before we got here. We were willing to give our all so men of every race, creed, and color may be equal before the law. We'll batter your segregation institutions until they crumble to dust."[36] Barbee and Zwerg would never fully recover from their injuries, and Barbee would spend several weeks in the hospital.

The imperturbable Lewis tried to shout directions in the teeth of the lopsided melee, but to no avail. Even with the strict gender roles of the era and region, women crossed the line, swinging purses, pulling hair, screaming, spitting, and lashing out at young men and women trying to ride a bus into Montgomery. Children too got into the act, engaging in a grotesque mimicry of their kith and kin by clawing and scratching and using their little fists and feet to impose a bit more street justice in that Montgomery bus terminal that more closely resembled a war zone.

In addition to the attackers, there were many white onlookers. Stuart Loory witnessed an exchange between "a young father and his blonde, red-faced daughter who was about three" and an interloper. The curious little girl asked, "Daddy, what are they doing?" The father did not respond. "Daddy, what's happening?" Her father finally responded, "Well, they're really carrying on." At this point a man Loory described as "a short-order cook" entered the inquiry, apparently unwelcome. "Those niggers are getting what for today," he said, smiling. The father did not smile at this. "Daddy, what are they doing?" repeated the little girl.[37] Here was a child's introduction to race relations, Alabama-style, and her father had no satisfactory answers to give.

Meanwhile, the Freedom Riders did what they could to get away. Some tried to climb a nearby tree. Others futilely clawed at the sides of a building in hopes of trying to get a foothold and ascend beyond the reach of their wailing attackers. Some of the reporters managed to get away by rushing to their cars. Some removed their ties and pretended to be members of the mob or escaping Klansmen. As the mob grew and closed in, there was no eluding it except by trying to eke a path off to the side toward the cabs, a route that had not quite been sealed off. The men in the group who remained did their best to get the women over to the taxis. The Southern code of chivalry being what it was, the mob had focused their initial attentions on the men in the group. Right away, before hostilities could flare, several of the women had jumped into a cab with a black driver, who told them that he could not allow the white women to ride too. To do so would violate Jim Crow laws. Catherine Burks told the man that she would drive, but to no avail. The two white women, Susan Wilbur and Susan Hermann, stayed behind so a black taxi driver inculcated with the fear and folly of segregation could bring five of their black sisters to safety. Even when the cab drove away, these women were not home free—the car had trouble along the way, and they had to stop at a black home to call Shuttlesworth. They shuttled between a couple of local homes and listened to increasingly worrisome radio accounts for the next half hour or so, until Shuttlesworth's foot soldiers managed to get them to safety.[38]

With the departure of the taxicab carrying their black friends, Wilbur and Hermann were extremely vulnerable to the mob. A group of men and women began closing in, taunting, screaming, and lunging toward them. At that moment, Kennedy aide John Seigenthaler, who had just dropped John Doar at the federal courthouse into which Lafayette, Cason, and Leonard had run, pulled up in his rented car. He thought that he was half an hour early, because he had expected the bus to make its local stops, according to plan. But as he approached the terminal, "There were shouts around the block and there were bags being thrown up in the air, there was screaming, and I thought 'oh my, they've arrived.'" He drove down the street and saw a police officer on a motorcycle driving away. He circled the block to get to the ruckus and saw a young black man "darting out across the bus station area into the street right in front of my car chased by about four people." The sprinting man had a sizeable lead, and his closest pursuer had a limp, so Seigenthaler surmised, "Well, they'll never catch him."[39]

When he got around the block, he saw the riot: "It looked just like an anthill . . . crawling with people and there was an awful lot of hell being raised right in around the bus." He saw the beatings: "They were really giving it to these kids." From there he saw either Susan Wilbur or Susan Hermann trying to get away from the crowd. One woman was hitting the abandoned Freedom Rider over the head with a purse. A young man was dancing backward in front of her, feigning punches "like a golden gloves boxer."[40]

Seigenthaler was able to maneuver his car right next to where one of the young women was trying to avoid the gathering crowd near the curb. Another woman hit the student with her purse, knocking her over the fender of Seigenthaler's car. He got out of the car and grabbed the young victim by the arm and said, "Let's go." The crowd responded: "By this time that anthill was crawling all over that car." Even before Seigenthaler got around to the passenger's side, the Freedom Rider's unseen companion had managed to get into the backseat. Seigenthaler could not get to the driver's door, swarmed as it was by the vitriolic mob, so he went to the passenger side and yelled to her, "Come get in the car!" She seemed to balk. "Mister," she shouted almost plaintively, "this is not your fight. Get away from here. You're gonna get killed." Seigenthaler responded, "Get in the damn car!" She still was worried. "Mister, this is not your fight," she repeated. "Please, don't get hurt on account of me, I don't want anybody to get hurt; I'm nonviolent."[41]

Seigenthaler persisted: "Young lady, get in that car." As she started to move, "two fellas stepped between me and the car" and started screaming at him. One, clad in overalls and a gray shirt, shouted, "Who the hell are you?" Seigenthaler yelled at them to back away. He announced that he was a federal man.[42] Those were probably not the best words to speak at the time. With that utterance he received a blast to the head from a lead pipe that knocked him out. John Seigenthaler, personal aide to the attorney general and representative of the president of the United States, would lie unconscious in a pool of his own blood for the next twenty minutes.

Hermann and Wilbur managed to elude the mob when Seigenthaler went down. They ran through a Christian Science church, where they encountered a woman, Mrs. Edgar McKay, who was working at the sanctuary. McKay heard pounding at the door, and when she answered she encountered the two girls, who told her "they had been beaten and were being chased. . . . They were quite breathless. I didn't know what to do. I didn't agree with them at all, but they were asking for sanctuary." She took them through the church to the back door. From there she led them to an office building, where they called the police.[43]

The police arrived and took the two women to a station house, where they were kept in protective custody. Eventually, the police got the two onto a train that took them back to Nashville. Wilbur, an eighteen-year-old Peabody College student, did not know why the police let them go, though she speculated, "Maybe it was because we were girls." Speaking of Seigenthaler, Wilbur proclaimed, "That man may have saved our lives" because the crowd was "ready to kill anybody." She was shocked to learn of Seigenthaler's identity: "I don't know who he was. All I remember is that I think he told me he was a federal agent, but if he'd had a big revolver it wouldn't have stopped that mob." In any case, Wilbur was undeterred. "We'll go on until we win," she told a reporter, referring to the Freedom Riders, though she admitted, "We were pretty badly beaten today."[44] After she got back home, she told reporters: "I've always felt strongly that segregation is wrong. This was something we could do—it wasn't far away in the Congo. I realized I couldn't stand by and talk about it." Even after all she had been through, she told a reporter, "I would go again, the whole movement has been very rewarding to me."[45]

Back at the station, Lewis's hold on leadership quickly waned: "I thought it was the end. It was like death. Death itself might have been a welcome pleasure."[46] He was holding a briefcase as he departed the bus. Soon someone snatched it from his fingers, despite Lewis's efforts to retain it. "At that instant," Lewis recalled, "I felt a thud against my head. I could feel my knees collapse and then nothing. Everything turned white for an instant, then black."[47]

"I thought it was my last demonstration, really," Lewis would say some years later.[48] Because he was knocked out cold, Lewis did not see what transpired next. Floyd Mann, Alabama's commissioner of public safety and one of Patterson's right-hand-men, was at the terminal alongside his deputy commissioner, W. R. Jones, when the bus arrived, and he soon realized that his public was not especially safe. He called for a hundred state troopers. Mann witnessed the beating of William Barbee and tried to pull the assailants off the prone black man. He realized that given the scope of the violence and the speed with which things were happening, "we had to threaten to take some lives ourselves unless that violence stopped immediately."[49] Like a lawman in the Wild West, he pulled a pistol from under his belt, waved it, and then placed it against the head of one of the assailants, the Klansman Thurman Ouzts. Mann told Ouzts, who was swinging a baseball bat, repeatedly bashing Barbee in the head, that "if he swung that bat one more time, I would blow his brains out."[50] He then personally placed Ouzts under arrest. A black college freshman, Joseph Lacey, was on the scene that day. He saw the beatings and was mashed against a building as he tried to get away from the mobs. He also witnessed Mann's intervention and later noted that Mann "enforced the law as a professional."[51] Lewis would always believe that Mann "literally saved the day. He kept people from . . . being killed."[52] Governor Patterson would concur that Mann had saved lives at the city bus terminal.[53] The mob's carte blanche was over.

Although the rioting must have seemed to last an eternity for those in its midst, within about fifteen minutes or so the Montgomery police showed up. At their head was L. B. Sullivan, who like Bull Connor was Montgomery's commissioner of public safety in Birmingham, in charge of the police and fire departments in Alabama's capital city of 120,000 people. While Sullivan lacked Connor's color and swagger and reputation, he was just as ardent a segregationist. Closely connected with the Citizens' Council, which had the support and participation of some among Montgomery's elite, Sullivan was no more inclined to yield to the integrationists than was his Birmingham counterpart.[54] Sullivan appeared with the state attorney general, MacDonald Gallion, and the assistant attorney general Willard Livingston, son of the chief justice of the Alabama Supreme Court.[55] Some reports had Sullivan sitting in his car around the corner from the terminal during the attack, granting the mob a by-now-familiar window for lawlessness. Sullivan innocently told Stuart Loory: "I really don't know what happened. When I got here all I saw were three men lying in the street. There were two niggers and a white man."[56] These were Lewis, Barbee, and Zwerg.

For the second week in a row, the police in a major Alabama city had somehow managed not to be present at a scene that everyone knew would be violent. And in this case even the transparent shroud of a Mother's Day holiday was not available to them. When they did arrive, the police and mounted sheriff's deputies had to disperse the crowd with tear gas. Even after the rioting ended, members of the fleeing crowd attacked two black men standing in front of the terminal, beating, punching, and stomping them. About a half block away from the bus station, several whites set upon a group of black males. One of the whites threw a bottle at the group, and several retaliated by throwing stones. One of the whites poured flammable liquid on a black youth and set his clothes alight. Police arrived before things could get any worse.[57] In the course of that day, police only arrested five individuals, two of whom, Mr. and Mrs. Frederick Gach, were white passersby who had simply tried to help the victims find medical assistance. They would be charged with disorderly conduct and failure to obey an officer. When they received a fine of three hundred dollars, Judge D. Eugene Loe told Mrs. Gach that she had caused the rioters to become infuriated by telling them that they should be ashamed of themselves.[58]

As Lewis came to consciousness and staggered to his feet, MacDonald Gallion, the state's attorney general, read aloud an order forbidding "entry into and travel within the state of Alabama and engaging in the so-called 'Freedom Ride' and other acts or conduct calculated to promote breaches of the peace." Lewis "hardly listened to those words. My head was spinning, both with thoughts about the carnage that had occurred and with pain. I was bleeding pretty badly from the back of the head. I could not believe how much blood there was."[59] Even as Patterson had been negotiating with Robert Kennedy the night before, Montgomery judge Walter B. Jones was preparing this injunction.

Lewis could see only Zwerg and Barbee, the two most badly hurt of the Freedom Riders. The others had somehow managed to escape on foot or by taxi. Many made their way to a nearby Presbyterian church. Others found temporary shelter in the black community. Lewis stumbled over to Jim Zwerg, who clearly needed medical attention. In the words of one of the officers: "The niggers will have to get out of here in a nigger taxi. The white boy will have to go in a white taxi."[60] Lewis was able to find a black cab driver who would give the two wounded black men a ride, but the driver refused to ferry Zwerg to safety.

Someone led Zwerg to a green Chevrolet, its markings indicating that it was from "Lane's taxi." As he sat there, the white driver refused to come to the car. As policemen blithely looked the other way, two white teenagers left over from the mob accosted Zwerg in the taxi. In the words on one witness, "Mr. Zwerg's eyes were open but expressionless. He hardly moved. The bleeding had stopped." One of the boys said to him: "You're a rotten son of a bitch. Your mother is a dog. You are a dog. You know that? You ride the niggers [sic]." Zwerg just shook his head.[61]

John Lewis approached Loory, the reporter who had witnessed the scene, asking, "Can't you do something to get him out of here?" Loory asked a detective if anything could be done. The detective, "nattily dressed in a brown suit," simply said, "He's free to go." When Loory asked if they couldn't do something to get the taxi driver to take him to a hospital, the detective replied: "We ain't arranging transportation for these people. We didn't arrange their transportation here and we ain't going to take them away." Loory explained the situation to Zwerg, who was so dazed he responded by saying, "You can't get me out of here. I don't even know where I am or how I got here." He was still sitting in the cab an hour later.[62] Finally, a courageous black taxi driver decided to ignore the laws, taking Jim Zwerg to St. Jude's Hospital.[63] Police commissioner Sullivan's explanation for how the three men reached treatment pretty much summed up the attitude of the authorities: "We called an ambulance for the white man but it was broken down and couldn't come, so two policemen took him to the hospital. I don't know what happened to the niggers."[64]

The driver who had taken Barbee and Lewis brought them to the office of a local doctor who treated them both. He shaved Lewis's head near his wounds, then cleaned and bandaged the nasty gashes. Lewis's shirt, tie, and jacket were spattered with his own blood. He checked his jacket pocket for the sizeable amount of money left over from the nine hundred dollars the NCLC had given the group. It was still there. The mob that day had battery, not larceny, on their minds. Meanwhile Barbee's injuries were substantially worse than Lewis's. When a local volunteer from Reverend Seay's church drove to pick up the two men, Barbee was in no shape to go. In the end, his injuries left him partially paralyzed for the rest of his life.[65]

When John Seigenthaler awoke, he had been "kicked . . . up under the car." He had "blood all over my shirt, I had no identification on me when I left; I was just in a sports shirt which I had borrowed from John Doar." He had kept the telephone numbers of officials in Alabama, and of civil rights activists in Nashville and Montgomery and Birmingham, in his pocket. One of the officers was holding this list as he came to. It was a police lieutenant who said to him, "Looks like you got some trouble, buddy." Seigenthaler agreed and asked what had happened. When the cop told him there had been a riot, Seigenthaler groggily asked, "Don't you think you'd better call Mr. Kennedy?"[66] The officer was somewhat perplexed. He shuffled through Seigenthaler's papers, holding the names and addresses of the various people involved in the ongoing drama.[67] He asked, "Which Mr. Kennedy?" To which Seigenthaler responded, "The Attorney General of the US." By this point the officer was nonplussed. "Who the hell are you?" When Seigenthaler explained his relationship to Kennedy, the officer became a great deal more helpful, Seigenthaler's plight less a source of amusement: "Come on get out of there. We'd better get you to a hospital."[68]

Seigenthaler later discovered that the police had initially been on the scene but that when the state patrol called in to let them know the bus was on the way, they just disappeared. The motorcycle officer whom Seigenthaler had seen leaving upon his arrival at the station was probably the last of the evaporating police.[69] When asked if he would have sent a bus to Montgomery had he known there would be no protection for the bus and its riders in Montgomery, Joe Morgan, the president of Local 1314, Amalgamated Street, Electric Railway and Motor Coach Employees of America, AFL-CIO, who had helped encourage Caverno to drive the bus, responded, "No sir." He told a reporter: "We were told we would have protection all the way. We had it right up to the terminal and then it disappeared."[70]

"The Highways of Alabama Are Safe": Reaction

When Seigenthaler got to the hospital, he passed out again. When he awoke, he was on a hospital x-ray table. He had a concussion. Seigenthaler heard Dr. Barton, who ran the medical center, talking to Byron "Whizzer" White, who had been active in the negotiations with Patterson. Barton was telling White, "I don't know how bad it is." When Seigenthaler eventually got back to Washington, he would be reexamined by a doctor and spend a couple of weeks in convalescence.[71]

In all, at least twenty-two were injured. Five went to the hospital.

Eight of the casualties were white; the remaining fourteen were black. Four newsmen spent time in the hospital. The police arrested nine white persons, including a woman, but the majority of the assailants eluded detection—most ran as soon as the police finally arrived.

Patterson responded quickly, taking to the airways about an hour after the police broke up the mob. He began his statement by declaiming: "It is our duty to maintain the law and I will not allow any group to take the law into their hands. The good name of our state and its people is at stake, and I can state frankly that violence of any type will not be tolerated." By this point, Patterson's statements would have seemed cartoonish had they not been so pathetic. Alabama's good name had already been smeared several times over by the preventable acts of violence against which Patterson so cynically inveighed. The charade continued: "The highways of Alabama are safe and state patrolmen will do all in their power to enforce law and order at all times. We have the men, the equipment and the will to keep the public peace, and we use no help—from the federal government, from 'interested citizens' or anyone else." This was Patterson's attempt to proffer a state's rights argument—asserting that local and state law enforcement was a matter for the municipalities and the state and that the federal government did not need to intervene. This argument may have been viable a week before, but it was demonstrably untrue after the Freedom Riders' week in Alabama.[72]

Then Patterson reached a crescendo, making the point he had wished to make all along, something he had said before and that many white Alabamans believed: "While we will do our utmost to keep the public highways clear and to guard against all disorder, we cannot escort busloads or carloads of rabble-rousers about our state from city to city for the avowed purpose of disobeying our laws, flaunting . . . our customs and traditions and creating racial incidents. Such unlawful acts serve only to further enrage our population. I have no use for these agitators or their kind."[73] Never mind that the state had briefly provided the exact protection he said it was incapable of providing and that the Supreme Court had invalidated Alabama's laws and with it any sanctioned recognition of its customs and traditions. The words many Southerners surely heard above all were "rabble-rousers" and "agitators." In just under a week, the Freedom Rides had gone from Anniston to Birmingham and eventually to Montgomery. Yet for all intents and purposes, they were exactly where they had started.

Just as reaction to the brutality in Birmingham had been condemnatory, the response to the mauling in Montgomery was swift and largely scathing. John Patterson and local law enforcement agents took the brunt of the abuse. Almost all observers condemned the mob action. Some provided unwavering support for the Freedom Riders. Others wished they would just call the Ride off, saying that they had proven their point. The Freedom Ride continued to be front-page news, sparking debate and support and getting play not only in America but abroad as well.

Patterson received letters and telegrams from around the country, as did Birmingham mayor James Morgan and Montgomery mayor Earl D. James. One correspondent, Walter Farrar of New York City, sent Mayor Morgan a telegram that asserted, "The southern states and its [sic] people must stand together alongside of Governor John Patterson . . . if they want to help stop the racial elements in their vicious conspiracy to overthrow the southern states." However, most of the letters Morgan received were not so supportive. Organizations such as the American Association of University Women, the city council of San Jose, and the FDR Democratic Club of Hollywood sent letters and passed resolutions in defense of the Freedom Riders and expressing outrage over what had befallen them. One anonymous correspondent pointedly scribbled a note over a copy of an editorial cartoon from the *Minneapolis Tribune* depicting a gleeful Nikita Khrushchev chomping on a giant watermelon labeled "U.S. Race Riots." The note suggested that "the mayor and the Police Chief go to Russia and take the Un-American Governor Patterson with you. It'll smell better in Dixie." Charles T. Beavers, a New York City lawyer who sent copies of his letter to the mayors of Birmingham and Montgomery, was more eloquent: "In the beginning my prayers were with the 'Freedom Riders,' because of the great danger they faced. But now I realize that you and others of your city are in greater danger and in greater need of prayer. Theirs is a physical danger, but yours is a spiritual danger."[74]

At about the same time, Roy Wilkins of the NAACP started receiving Freedom Ride–related hate mail even though his organization had at most an ancillary attachment to the bus action. One anonymous correspondent from Bethesda, Maryland, who signed as "Damned Mad," accused blacks in the United States of being Communist dupes, telling Wilkins, "Had you not been reared in the white man's atmosphere in America you would now probably be gnawing a human thigh bone in Africa. You are a d——d savage and you will never be anything else." This was among the more civil epistles that crossed Wilkins's desk in the last days of May 1961, many of which threatened physical harm and even death not only to Wilkins but to all blacks.[75]

Closer to home, the fifty or so members of the Montgomery Ministerial Association passed a five-point resolution. They expressed "shock and sorrow at events of violence and the mob action that have recently happened in Montgomery." They stated "concern that all necessary steps be taken to prevent future incidents of mob action and bloodshed." They also called for "all authorities and all citizens within and without the state to restrain themselves from actions and statements of an inflammatory nature." They wanted publicly to endorse and support other groups "who do not condone recent events." Finally, they designated the following Saturday, May 28, as a day of prayer.[76]

Similarly, the United Presbyterian Church of the United States sent President Kennedy a letter conveying its "appreciation for the promptness with which the federal government moved to protect the safety of citizens during the recent difficulties in Alabama." The general assembly of the church also issued a formal statement condemning "any deliberate failure of legally constituted authorities to safeguard all persons within their jurisdiction against mob violence" and urged "local judicatories of our Church to speak and act against such breakdown of law and order." It further "commends and encourages those persons who are seeking by nonviolent means to bring about equality for all."[77]

However, there were some who, whatever their reservations about mob action, still blamed the victims. The *Birmingham News* editorialized on May 22, "The right of peaceful assembly has its limitations." Further, "the deliberate rushing of Martin Luther King and his retinue could be construed as nothing but further agitation of an already tense community." Never mind, of course, that it could also be construed as America's most visible civil rights leader going to Alabama to deal with what to that point was America's biggest civil rights crisis. Then, addressing Robert Kennedy, the paper's editors scolded: "The people of Alabama . . . would feel more secure in the efforts to guarantee the rights of all citizens if you found a way to stop those who came here to foment trouble by their actions in the midst of already charged situations."[78] Whatever reason had prevailed in the offices of the *News* a week earlier, status quo ante largely prevailed after the Montgomery riots.

The Rotary Club of Montgomery similarly walked the line between condemnation of the violence and condemnation of the victims, labeling them part of "an invasion of non resident racial agitators." In the end, the most noxious component of recent events, for Rotarians, was the presence of federal marshals. In their May 22 meeting, the 185 Rotarians present unanimously passed a resolution petitioning the Kennedy administration to withdraw the "Federal Marshals and other Federal law enforcement officers." Further, they asked that to "put an end to this deplorable and inflamatory [sic] condition in our state and community," the president and the Justice Department should take an active role in "discouraging, rather than encouraging, the continued invasion and intrusion into our community by the racial agitators who initiated this unfortunate state of affairs."[79]

The Kennedys too were not happy.[80] They were not happy with John Patterson. And they were not happy with the Freedom Riders. Diane Nash had called soon after the riots began to let Robert Kennedy know about the violence.[81] In a telegram to John Patterson, Robert Kennedy wrote, "I am asking the U.S Court in Montgomery to enjoin the Ku Klux Klan, the National States Rights Party, certain individuals, and all persons acting in concert with them, from interfering with peaceful interstate transport by buses." Perhaps more important, Kennedy informed Patterson that he was "also arranging for U.S. officers to begin to assist state and local authorities in the protection of persons and property and vehicles in Alabama."[82] The administration had finally and belatedly realized that it would have to take responsibility for defending the Freedom Riders, because the state of Alabama was not willing to do so or capable of doing so. The president issued a statement to Patterson that indicated his frustrations: "I am deeply concerned that there has been another outbreak of mob violence in Alabama, less than 24 hours after you gave my personal representative assurance that you had the men, the equipment, and the will to enforce the laws; to give equal protection to all persons in Alabama and to resist any attempt to interfere with interstate travel."[83] Robert Kennedy also decided to start waging a public relations battle through the media by calling in a statement to UPI that urged "all citizens of Alabama and all travelers in Alabama to consider their actions carefully and to refrain from doing anything which will cause increased tension or provoke violence and result in further damage to our country."[84]

Courts later found damning evidence of negligence on the part of authorities in Montgomery and elsewhere in Alabama. A U.S. district court case finally decided several years later, *United States v. U.S. Klans, et al.,* clearly established that Spencer Robb of the FBI had informed Montgomery police of the departure of the bus from Birmingham. Further, on May 20, a Montgomery police officer, Detective Snows, had told a reporter from the *Montgomery Advertiser* that the police "would not lift a finger to protect" the passengers.[85] All this occurred despite the fact that Governor

Patterson and Seigenthaler had worked on a plan the night before that putatively guaranteed the safety of the Riders.[86]

Judge Frank Johnson, the legendarily independent Alabama judge, wrote in his opinion in the case: "The evidence is abundantly clear and this court specifically finds that Lester B. Sullivan, as Police Commissioner, was advised by Floyd Mann . . . that the bus in which this group was riding was en route. . . . The likelihood of violence was well known to the Department of Public Safety and [it] . . . had taken the necessary precautions to protect this bus from Birmingham to the city limits." Despite the abundant knowledge the Montgomery police had of the Freedom Riders' arrival on the morning of May 20, the court found, the Montgomery authorities had "willfully and deliberately failed to take measures to ensure the safety of the students and to prevent unlawful acts of violence on their persons." Ultimately, "the willful and deliberate failure on the part of law enforcement officials was also unlawful in that it deprived the student-passengers of their rights without due process of law."[87] There, in the cold, impersonal language of the court, was a most scathing indictment of the behavior of Montgomery's guardians of the public safety.

Johnson's opinion concluded that the Ku Klux Klan had "conspired to and did commit acts of violence upon these interstate student-passengers" on May 20, just as they had in Anniston and Birmingham the previous Sunday. Various Klan organizations had "conspired and acted to interfere with the travel of passengers in interstate commerce . . . and . . . obstructed, impeded, and interfered with the free movement of interstate commerce in and through the state of Alabama and in and through this district."[88] Once again, as in 1947, interstate commerce served as a wedge whereby the courts could assail restrictions on integrated interstate transport.

On the night of May 20, President Kennedy finally spoke publicly about the Freedom Rides. "The situation which has developed in Alabama is a source of the deepest concern to me as it must be to the vast majority of the citizens of Alabama and other Americans," he announced. He explained that he had "instructed the Justice Department to take all necessary steps based on their investigations and information" and called "upon the Governor and other responsible State officials in Alabama as well as the Mayors of Birmingham and Montgomery to exercise their lawful authority to prevent any further outbreaks of violence." Kennedy then spoke words that would serve to alienate many in the freedom struggle and reveal the new president to be equivocal about the ideals he purported to cherish: "I would also hope that any persons, whether a citizen of Alabama or a visitor there, would refrain from any action which would in any way tend to provoke further outbreaks." Kennedy concluded: "I hope that state and local officials in Alabama will meet their responsibilities. The United States Government intends to meet its."[89]

The Freedom Riders, despite the president's admonishment, intended to test the U.S. government's willingness to fulfill its intentions. Diane Nash told the *New York Times:* "We aren't going to stop now. Why, those people in Alabama think they can ignore the President of the United States, and they think they can still win by threatening us Negroes. . . . They beat us and we're stronger than ever."[90] Jim Zwerg similarly told a reporter from the *Montgomery Advertiser,* "You may inform the people of Montgomery and the rest of the Deep South states that we intend to continue our 'freedom rides' until the last vestige of segregation disappears from bus stations." He announced that the group planned to forge onward to Jackson and finally to New Orleans: "We're not doing this just for ourselves, but for all Americans. How can we meet the Communist threat, win the allegiances of African and Asian nations, as long as there is injustice against minority groups in this country?"[91] John Lewis told the *New York Herald Tribune,* "I feel that the Ride must continue in order to accomplish a goal—to fulfill and uphold the Supreme Court decision that people can travel from one part of the United States to another without being discriminated against."[92]

"If We Cool Off Any More, We Will Be in a Deep Freeze": The Mass Meeting

When he finally arrived at Reverend Seay's home after receiving medical treatment, Lewis received cheers and hugs, as had every other Freedom Rider who trickled in that afternoon. Seay's phone rang constantly. Jim Lawson was on his way down from Ohio. Diane Nash was going to head to Montgomery from Nashville. Rumors that Martin Luther King Jr. was coming from Chicago were soon confirmed. The Kennedys had hoped they could convince King not to go down to Montgomery, believing the great man's presence would exacerbate an already tense situation.[93] Jim Farmer was ready to leave Washington, D.C., after his brief mourning period for his father, planning to rejoin the trip that the students had taken up but that he still considered his brainchild.

That night, the Freedom Riders stayed at the homes of various civil rights activists and black supporters. The next day, Monday, May 21, the group participated in its first mass meeting at Ralph Abernathy's First Baptist Church. The group went to the church early—many had warrants out for their arrest as a consequence of their Freedom Riding, which in the eyes of Alabama law enforcement was still illegal—and remained in the church basement library. By five that evening, black Montgomerians began arriving for a meeting that was not to start for another three hours.

Everybody showing up at the church, however, did not have good intentions. Outside, a white crowd had begun to gather. Lewis described the group as "a loud restless mob of white onlookers, many of them waving small Confederate flags, some of them letting loose with Rebel yells."[94] Keeping order were federal marshals whom the Kennedys had finally dispatched in their effort to maintain order where local and state authorities would not or could not. President Kennedy had authorized the attorney general to "take whatever steps are necessary, including the use of marshals, to suppress domestic violence, unlawful conspiracies or combinations in the State of Alabama, which deprive any persons of rights guaranteed by the Constitution and laws of the United States, or which obstruct the execution of laws of the United States."[95] Governor Patterson had earlier threatened to arrest federal officers who attempted to exercise authority in Alabama, but state officials did not intercede against the marshals.[96] Kennedy also called the assistant chief of the Montgomery police, telling him: "I understand there is an ugly situation down there right now and I hope necessary steps are being taken to see that this is taken care of this minute. We are concerned about the situation there and hope there will be no more trouble there."[97]

By the time of the meeting, there were roughly fifteen hundred people in the church. The white mob had at least as many. The three major television networks, UPI, AP, the *New York Times,* and myriad regional, state, and local newspapers also had reporters and cameramen on hand. The congregants within the church were largely undaunted by the mass gathered outside. In Lewis's words: "The people inside, these black men and women of Montgomery, were unfazed by the uproar outside. It was not easy to intimidate them, not with what they had already been through with the bus boycott. They had been through fire. They knew what it felt like. They answered that ominous noise outside with their own sound, the sound of hymns."[98]

The Freedom Riders sat dispersed throughout the crowd, some sitting in the choir stand, figuring that would make them less easily identifiable to authorities. Of course, Lewis acknowledged, "the bright white X-shaped bandage on my head was a dead giveaway."[99] As the Freedom Riders and hundreds of others filled the church beyond its capacity, Ralph Abernathy, Wyatt Tee Walker, and King waited in the basement study for Shuttlesworth to get back from picking up Jim Farmer at the airport. When the Birmingham reverend went outside, the mob lobbed stones, stink bombs, and debris at him.

A small cadre of federal marshals, "gallant but unskilled conscripts . . . who looked overmatched even wearing six-shooters," in the words of reporter Murray Kempton, was just barely able to restrain the surly and growing crowd.[100] The president had sent six hundred marshals down to Maxwell Air Force Base just outside Montgomery upon hearing of the mass meeting. In a phone conversation with John Seigenthaler, Robert Kennedy said, "Sooner or later we're gonna have to have a conflict or confrontation." He urged Seigenthaler not to feel bad about this turn of events and lauded him for his bravery in the face of the mob, saying, "It's just what you had to do, and I'm glad that you're alright." Seigenthaler had some advice for Kennedy: "Don't run for Governor of Alabama; you're not too popular around here." Kennedy laughed.[101]

Later, Kennedy publicly explained his decision to send marshals by first pointing a finger at Alabama's political and public-safety leadership: "If there had been a concentrated effort on the part of the authorities in Alabama, we wouldn't have had to send marshals in there. And I think I would have been derelict in my responsibilities and duties and oath if I had not ordered them in."[102] Further, Kennedy would explain nearly three years later, "The reason we sent marshals . . . was to avoid the idea of sending troops. . . . We thought that marshals would be much more accepted in the South, and that you could get away from the idea of military occupation—and we had to do something."[103] Even with the perspective of time, the hint of near-desperation in the attorney general's tone was palpable.

Martin Luther King snuck a peek outside the church to survey the scene for himself and perhaps to send a message to the mob that he was there and he was not afraid, that this event had grown in scope and importance. At first the crowd did not recognize him, but once someone had, the rocks and epithets, including a chorus of "Nigger King!" followed.

Shuttlesworth and Farmer arrived just before eight. Farmer asked his host, "Can you get me into that church, Fred?" To which the plucky Shuttlesworth responded, "Wrong question, Jim. The only question to ask is: how will I get you in."[104]

They were only able to get Shuttlesworth's car a block or so from the church. The mob set upon them, a number of individuals rocking the car back and forth. Shuttlesworth was able to get enough traction to pull into reverse and get away. They tried another approach to the church, but to no avail. On the advice of black cab drivers at a stand down the road, they finally parked at a nearby cemetery in hopes of outflanking the mob by walking through the graveyard to a side door of the church. But when they got there, the church was already surrounded. Nonetheless, at this point the mob's intentions were not as brutal as they could have been, and Shuttlesworth and Farmer were able to get out of the car and push their way into the church, mostly because Shuttlesworth bravely forged his way through the masses, waving his arms and screaming at the startled crowd, giving him and the closely following Farmer enough berth to eke by.

When they got into the church, Farmer told Shuttlesworth—whom he claimed "didn't know the meaning of the word fear"—that his actions in spiriting them through the mob were indicative of the "crazy nigger syndrome," because when Shuttlesworth acted as he did, members of the mob would say, "Don't mess with that nigger, he's crazy." Farmer later admitted that Shuttlesworth "was a skinny little guy. Here's the mob, people with chains and clubs and guns and everything else, sweating. And he: 'Move out of the way. Let me through. Come on, let me through.' And they all stepped aside. Here I was, big me, you know, trying to hide behind him and I followed him through. I was scared spitless, as it were. But the mob parted, let him through."[105]

As the crowd sat in the pews, local ministers Solomon Seay and B. D. Lambert led prayers and hymns. As the mob outside grew louder and more violent, Lambert prayed for them and for Governor Patterson, albeit perhaps not as much in the Christian spirit of forgiveness as he could muster: "Bless all those cowards standin' outside that can't fight unless they have a mob to come with them. Bless that stupid Governor of ours."[106] Soon after, the official meeting commenced, with Wyatt Tee Walker speaking first, followed by Ralph Abernathy, and then finally Martin Luther King Jr. The crowd gathered in the church sat waving fans provided by the Ross Clayton Funeral Homes.[107] King invited Farmer and Lewis down to the front, where they embraced. The two original Freedom Riders were now in Montgomery, the connecting links between CORE's challenge to Jim Crow and the student movement's. King warned the crowd that they had some decisions to make that night: "But we aren't going to become panicky. And . . . we are going to continue to stand up for [what] we know is right."[108]

Even as King got rolling, the mob outside was growing more unruly, flipping one car over, setting alight another owned by British writer Jessica Mitford, who was there to witness the meeting in the church. At one point, the mob pushed forward enough to force a church door open, and some thugs momentarily gained entry into the church. Several marshals were able to jam the door shut. James Farmer later recalled that the marshals just seemed to materialize: "It seemed almost fictional. *There they were* suddenly, the marshals confronting the mob. They had arm bands on, U.S. Marshals. . . . They didn't draw their guns, but they used their clubs" and were able to keep the mob from the church.[109] A brick crashed through a stained-glass window, evoking screams. Lewis described the familiar "rhythm of a mob, . . . how its temperature rises as the hours pass, how it is timid and careful at first but then grows bolder as its size and restlessness increase. And then the sun sets, bringing the twisted kind of courage that comes with the cover of darkness."[110] This mob fit the model precisely.

King had written his formal address to the group on a plane from New York to Atlanta. He could not help but juxtapose the amazing technology that "lifted our head to the skies" with the fact that "our feet are firmly planted in the muck of barbarism and racial hatred." This was "America's chief moral dilemma. And unless the Nation grapples with this dilemma forthrightly and firmly, she will be relegated to a second rate power in the world. The price that America must pay for the continued oppression of the Negro is the price of its own destruction." Invoking the Cold War imperative, King reminded his audience, "America's greatest defense against communism is to take the offense for justice, freedom and human dignity." Then he spoke more clearly to and about the Freedom Riders and the resistance they had encountered:

The Freedom Ride grew out of a recognition of the American dilemma and a desire to bring the nation to a realization of its noble dream. We are all deeply indebted to CORE for this creative idea. These courageous Freedom Riders have faced ugly and howling mobs in order to arouse the dozing conscience of the nation. Some of them are now hospitalized as a result of physical injury. They have accepted blows without retaliation. One day all of America will be proud of their achievements. . . . Over the last few days Alabama has been the scene of a literal reign of terror. It has sunk to a level of barbarity comparable to the tragic days of Hitler's Germany.[111]

King ultimately blamed Governor Patterson for the attacks and brutality. He would prove not to be alone in the days and weeks to come. As for the federal government, King believed they had a responsibility to act. In the face of those who claimed that you cannot legislate morals, King had one of his most famous retorts: "It may be true that morals cannot be legislated, but behavior can be regulated. . . . The law may not be able to make a man love me, but it can keep him from lynching me."[112]

Even as King spoke, and the Freedom Riders felt confident enough to reveal themselves and lead the congregation in singing movement songs, the mob surged. The federal marshals responded with tear gas, some of which they released into a breeze, causing the gas to blow back into their faces, doing more harm than good. It did not help matters much that the marshals, in the words of Floyd Mann, "were just about as inexperienced at handling a crowd like that as some of the police were in Alabama."[113] Mann also remembered that "different cars were burning in different places . . . it was just a chaotic situation."[114] Reverend Seay told the congregation to remain calm, and by and large it did.[115]

Sometime before midnight, as the mob continued to rage, Reverend Seay introduced two men. The first was Mann, the state public safety director, who had been one of the few Alabama officials to acquit himself well in the last week or so. Even as Mann sat in the church, Robert Kennedy sent him a telegram commending him for being "most helpful" and for handling "yourself and those serving under you with great vigor and skill."[116] Seay echoed the attorney general's sentiments. "I choose my words when I talk about white folks," Seay confided to the crowd, "but there is a Christian soul in Mr. Mann. I think we ought to stand on our feet and thank him," and the crowd stood. The second introduction was for Henry V. Graham, the Alabama adjutant general, who had been sent to the church to read a proclamation from Governor Patterson declaring martial law. Murray Kempton described the governor's decree and Graham's reading of it as "a horrid, pompous mash blaming the victims for the crime." When Graham finished, the crowd, those "gracious, patient people," in Kempton's words, stood and applauded their guest. Seay admonished them: "I don't think that was a document for cheering. I want to be respectful to our leaders and to the government of Alabama but if John Patterson hadn't been playing cheap politics we wouldn't be here now. I think you ought to take those cheers back."[117] Lucretia Collins later commended Seay's leadership throughout the ordeal in the church as being "wonderful," in that he "directed the people" so that they did not "become panicked or hysterical in any way."[118]

As the situation grew increasingly tense, King was relieved to receive a telephone call from Robert Kennedy.[119] Kennedy heard the mob through the telephone. Trying to defuse the tension, Kennedy made a lame joke: "As long as you're in church down there, you might as well say a prayer for us." King was not amused. Kennedy asked if it might be possible for the group to engage in a cooling-off period to give the administration time to act. King consulted with Farmer, who responded by telling King, "I won't stop it now. If I do, we'll just get words and promises." King tried to argue the other side: "Maybe the Freedom Ride has already made its point and now should be called off as the attorney general suggests." Farmer consulted with Diane Nash, who was also adamant that the Ride continue. Finally, Farmer approached King: "My objective is not just to make a *point*, but to bring about real change in the situation. We will continue the Ride until people can sit wherever they wish on buses and use the facilities in any waiting room available to the republic." Then Farmer responded colorfully to Kennedy's "cooling-off" metaphor, telling King to tell Kennedy "that we have been cooling off for 350 years. If we cool off any more, we will be in a deep freeze. The Freedom Ride will go on."[120]

Chastened, Kennedy told King that he was sending in the National Guard. Soon King relayed that message to the audience. Meanwhile, as the mob violence escalated, the leaders in the church decided to bring all of the children downstairs to safer shelter. The adults dropped to the floor to lessen their chances of being clobbered with projectiles or glass. The church was almost unbearably hot. First Baptist Church member Joseph Lacey, the college student who had witnessed the riots at the bus terminal, was present that evening: "At that time our church was not air conditioned. . . . The gas was coming in, and eventually we had to close the windows up and imagine how hot it got with a church full of people."[121] The tear gas wafted in the air. Gwen Patton, a Freedom Rider from Nashville who had entered Alabama in the second wave that Nash sent, remembers the meeting that night, after things grew chaotic: "There would be periodic reports. 'Don't leave the church. Stay here. If you're sleepy just lie down. . . . God is with us and we will get out of this, and we will get out of this with victory.'"[122]

King's phone call had convinced the attorney general to send reinforcements for the struggling marshals. Kennedy got into a shouting match with the increasingly temerarious governor, who finally acceded to Kennedy's blandishments to declare martial law. The president federalized the Alabama National Guard, which then had to carry out what was surely a reluctant duty, but a duty nonetheless. By this time a full-fledged battle raged outside, and it took the National Guard some time to quell the inflamed mob. One observer, Mark Gilmore, witnessed the crowd outside: "They were burning crosses and hollering 'niggers, niggers, niggers,' you know. 'Niggers you ain't no good . . . get off welfare.' You could hear them hollering to the top of their voices. Throwing at cars and things that was passing."[123]

King promised the assembled crowd that they would triumph over this adversity. He excoriated the state's officials. "Alabama will have to face the fact that we are determined to be free," he said, to assent from the assemblage. "Fear not," he continued. "We've come too far to turn back."[124] The meeting came to a conclusion at about midnight. Everyone was ready to go home. Adults gathered their bleary-eyed children. Suddenly, however, their protectors had become their captors. The Alabama National Guard blocked the doors, not allowing anyone to exit. The troops could not let them leave, those inside the church were informed, because it was too dangerous. There was no way to get so many people safely through the mob, and there was no transportation in any case. Once again the Freedom Riders were under effective arrest for their own protection. This time they had several hundred supporters for company. Abernathy's First Baptist Church became a shelter for the night. Children slept downstairs. The elderly slept on the cushioned pews. The rest attempted to steal forty winks on the floor. Abernathy asked Joseph Lacey to sneak outside and get to his house and send out calls to enlist help, to let people know what was happening and so forth.

This was not what Robert Kennedy had planned. Once again he and Patterson debated over the phone. Patterson went over his well-rehearsed litany of reasons opposing both the Freedom Riders and the federal government's support of them. The end result was that Kennedy had a squadron of the National Guard arrive at the church at 4:30 with a full complement of jeeps and trucks. In small groups they shuttled fifteen hundred people from the church to their homes in and around Montgomery. Earlier, Governor Patterson had arranged to have sandwiches and coffee sent to the church. Gwen Patton recalls: "None of us took it because we just knew it was poisoned. . . . I mean, how could a governor who unleashed that white terror turn around and then provide us with sustenance?"[125] The Freedom Riders went to various homes in the city. At Dr. Dean Harris's expansive house, John Lewis had his first taste of beer.[126] He had earned it.

"The Time and Place of My Golgotha": Sparring with De Lawd

The next morning was quiet outside of the church. Patterson had declared martial law, and virtually the only people on the street were members of the Alabama National Guard, riding in jeeps and wearing steel helmets and carrying rifles. There would be a curfew in Montgomery, and it appeared that the worst mob behavior had been suppressed.

On Monday, May 22, in the court building next to the bus terminal, Judge Frank Johnson listened to arguments that would help him determine whether to override Judge Walter Jones and lift the injunction against the Freedom Ride and, if so, whether to issue a new injunction guaranteeing protection as the Ride advanced.[127] A day earlier, Johnson had issued a federal restraining order against Alabama's various Klan factions, including bitter rival Klan leaders Robert M. Shelton and Reverend Alvin C. Horn, as well as the U.S. Klans, Knights of the Ku Klux Klan Inc., Federated Ku Klux Klan Inc., and two other Klansmen, Lester C. Hawkins and Thurman Ouzts. The Kennedy administration's justification for going to Johnson to seek a restraining order was twofold. In the words of Burke Marshal, "If we could get a restraining order then we would have two powers: one would be the enforcement of a court order directly, we could probably do that without a proclamation; and the other would be to make a finding that there was a breakdown of law and order such that the right to travel interstate was not being protected and he could act on that basis independently of the court order."[128]

John Lewis and others testified before Johnson, convincing the judge, and in two quick swoops he removed the legal hurdles to the continuation of the Freedom Rides, though at the same time he denounced the Freedom Riders and acceded to an injunction request preventing future Freedom Riders from entering Montgomery.[129] This injunction would not prevail.

That night the Freedom Riders met. By this point Jim Lawson, Jim Bevel, and Diane Nash had arrived. The youths sat on the floor. King, Abernathy, Farmer, and Walker sat in folding chairs. The meeting was to determine how best to proceed into Mississippi. Farmer stood before the group, proclaiming his own importance and that of CORE. The students, who by now had earned their stripes, were growing weary of such self-aggrandizement. John Lewis and the others had a hard time taking seriously Farmer's proprietary pronouncements that the Freedom Rides were "CORE's Rides," given that the students had by now put their own lives on the line.

There had been much behind-the-scenes maneuvering in the CORE offices in the preceding couple of days. On Monday the CORE National Action Committee had met in Washington to discuss how to deal with the Freedom Rides, which they still thought of as a CORE endeavor. The committee decided that at least one CORE staffer should accompany the Freedom Ride through to Mississippi. Most on the committee thought Farmer was the logical person to go on the trip, since he was the senior staff member already in Alabama at the time, the Freedom Ride had in large part been his doing, and he had already ridden for a good bulk of the previous trip. Wary of volunteering Farmer for a job he may not have wanted, Marvin Rich spoke up, pointing out that it would be embarrassing for all involved should Farmer decide not to go. At this point Joe Perkins volunteered to Freedom Ride with the students if for any reason Farmer could or would not.[130] In fact, Farmer had not planned to go, and only guilt would push him back onto the buses.

Back at the Montgomery meeting, Diane Nash cut to the heart of another issue that many within the student movement wanted to have resolved: King's participation. Nash asked King if he would be jumping on a bus with them to ride into Mississippi. At first King protested that he was on probation and could not participate. This argument seemed absurd to many of the young veterans, who chimed in with their own probation status, which they would not allow to keep them from participating. Then King took another tack, one that would lead to one of the most unfortunate utterances of his life. Clearly exasperated with what he saw as insolent badgering from the young men and women, King snapped, "I think I should choose the time and place of my Golgotha."[131] The students were taken aback. As James Farmer put it, "They roared at that one."[132] To them it was unseemly for King to compare his situation with that of Jesus Christ. This solipsism was emblematic of why so many students derisively referred to King, with his sometimes imperious style, as "De Lawd." King may have been justified in his stance, and he was hardly alone among members of the movement in invoking the Bible, but his pronouncement was simply too much for many of the young activists to take.

Jim Farmer sympathized with King. The students probably assumed that Farmer was going with them, and he had given them no indication otherwise. "I don't know what was going through Martin's mind at that time, but I know what was in mine," Farmer later wrote. "I was frankly terrified with the knowledge that the trip to Jackson might be the last trip any of us would ever take. I was not ready for that. Who, indeed, ever is?"

Therefore, Farmer could not think critically of King's decision not to go. Only student pleading convinced Farmer himself to join the students on the way to Mississippi.[133]

Irrespective of the dithering of the elders, as Lewis put it, "We had to go. To stop now would be disaster. There was too much commitment, too much momentum. This Freedom Ride had taken on a life of its own. For the same reasons that we had picked up the reins after Farmer and CORE set them down, we all agreed that we had to carry on now." Even when individuals such as Roy Wilkins started to pressure the students to forgo continuing the trip, it was to no avail: "We considered the adults' advice, but the decision was in our hands, the students' hands, and there was no question. We were moving on."[134] The students were bound for Mississippi. The federal government seemed to be on board.

Chapter 10

Mississippi

"That Irreducible Citadel of Southernism"

The Closed Society

V. O. Key perhaps best summed up Mississippi's role in the region and nation when he wrote: "Northerners, provincials that they are, regard the South as one large Mississippi. Southerners, with their eye for distinction, place Mississippi in a class by itself." Whereas North Carolinians might "consider Mississippi to be the last vestige of a dead and despairing civilization," Virginians might look to the state and "rank [it] a backwards culture, with a ruling class both unskilled and neglectful of its duties." Meanwhile, the rest of the South found "some reason to fall back on the soul-satisfying exclamation, 'Thank God for Mississippi!'" Yet in the end, "Mississippi only manifests in accentuated form the darker political strains that run throughout the South."[1]

In his inimitable way of phrasing things, C. Vann Woodward once called Mississippi "that irreducible citadel of Southernism."[2] Even when placed next to its neighbor and partner in white supremacy, Alabama, the state of Mississippi stood alone. Its racists—Theodore Bilbo, James K. Vardaman, James Eastland—were larger than life. Its crimes—the murder of Emmett Till, just the most prominent of the state's hundreds of lynchings—were the most disturbing. Its institutions—Parchman Farm, Mississippi's Citizens' Councils and State Sovereignty Commission—were the most grotesque.

It came as a surprise to no one that Mississippi had moved to the forefront of massive resistance. Responding to *Brown*, the state's legislature asserted interposition and went further, declaring the decision null and void. Perhaps nowhere was the fight against integration so visceral and vicious. The state's politicians, media, business and social institutions, and people spoke seemingly as one: integration will never happen here, in Mississippi. A subtext came across equally clearly to some: we will shed blood to ensure as much. Within days of the *Brown* decision, Judge Tom P. Brady wrote a manifesto that would prove to be the Magna Carta of massive resistance, a pamphlet he titled "Black Monday." A curious blend of law, history, political science, anthropology, and propaganda, the pamphlet roused many to action, including Robert "Tut" Patterson, former Mississippi State University football star and World War II paratrooper and now manager of a nearly sixteen-hundred-acre plantation in LeFlore County, some eighty miles northwest of Jackson.

Even prior to the Supreme Court's decision, Patterson was "confused, mad and ashamed" at the possibility that the courts would eradicate segregation. At that time he sent out a clarion call to his fellow Mississippians, urging them to "stand together forever firm against communism and mongrelization." Until May 17, 1954, he had received a tepid response. However, that all changed with "Black Monday," and within weeks of the court's decision, Patterson had successfully organized the first chapter of Citizens' Councils in Indianola. The Councils spread like kudzu and within months had gained a place of prominence in Mississippi. Soon they would represent a regional phenomenon of massive resistance with a patina of respectability that the Klan could never hope for even if they had wanted it. The Citizens' Councils fast became the most prominent organizations of their type, and Mississippi thus became, in the words of historian Neil McMillen, the "Mother of the Movement" of Citizens' Councils and indeed of massive resistance across the South.[3]

In an effort to counteract Mississippi's national reputation for racial atrocity and destigmatize the state, as well as to take the initiative away from the Councils, which had become a political juggernaut, Governor James P. Coleman developed the "State Sovereignty Commission," which would implement what he liked to call a policy of "friendly persuasion."[4] However, the far right wing of the state legislature, which by 1955 seemed to hold a majority, had another idea in mind for the commission, one that it embraced: rather than supplant the Citizens' Councils, the State Sovereignty Commission would supplement them, and thus both would receive support from the state legislature. The space for discourse on racial politics in the state, always narrow, had closed substantially. The State Sovereignty Commission (which served as a model for other states, including Alabama) now had virtual carte blanche "to do and perform any and all acts and things deemed necessary and proper to protect the sovereignty of the State of Mississippi, and her sister states." It had nearly unlimited powers of investigation and often collaborated with private organizations, such as the Councils, to fight the integrationist threat.[5]

Under Coleman this organization was somewhat benign. But that changed with the ascension of millionaire lawyer Ross Barnett to the governor's seat in 1960. He had campaigned on a platform of unrelenting support for segregation, and he pledged his willingness to go to jail to prevent integration's arrival in Mississippi. He was an ardent supporter of both the State Sovereignty Commission and the Citizens' Councils, and he ensured generous financial support in the state budget for both. In the months after July 1960, for example, the Sovereignty Commission contributed more than sixty thousand dollars to the Citizens' Council Forum's national radio and television activities.[6] An otherwise unexceptional politician, Barnett had fully embraced the cause of segregation. In the words of Walter Sillers Jr., a New Dealer, Delta planter, and the speaker of the Mississippi House, Barnett stood "head and shoulders" above his gubernatorial cohort in Dixie on the race question.[7]

Although Mississippi continued to be a state with a geographic divide—the Delta planters at odds with the hill country dwellers and the relatively moderate folk down by the Gulf of Mexico—by 1960 this schism had long been overwhelmed by the consensus of white supremacy. Historian James Cobb has described Mississippi's Yazoo Delta as "the most southern place on earth," but in the minds of many both in Mississippi and out, he could have been describing the entire state, especially with regard to race relations. By May 1961, orthodoxy was not only established but effectively enforced by both a stifling demand for conformity and the ubiquitous threat of violence. On the eve of the arrival of Freedom Riders, a group bound to bring the blood of Mississippians to a boil, the state had become what Ole Miss professor (and, for his racial views, pariah) James Silver would come to call "the Closed Society."[8]

"I'm Travelin' to Mississippi on the Greyhound Bus Line": Crossing the Line

Even with its deserved reputation for intolerance of breaches of racial etiquette, there had been periodic challenges to Jim Crow transportation in the Magnolia State.[9] In the mid-1950s, a furor had arisen over the 1955 *Keys* decision, the ICC moving to end segregation on trains and buses that crossed state lines.[10] In December 1956, Governor-Elect Coleman announced sternly that there would be no rail integration in Mississippi; that the ICC was an administrative agency, not a judicial one; and that there would be no intermingling of the races in rail and bus depots, cafes, and rest rooms within the state.[11] On January 9, 1956, the day before the ICC order was to take effect, the *Jackson Daily News* issued one of its trademark front-page editorials: "We must resist that order with every force at our command. That means exercising our police power to the utmost. The NAACP and its Communist backers must not be allowed to put a foot in the door of Mississippi." The paper issued a dire warning. "A failure to fight against mixing of races in waiting rooms of common carriers will mean that we are no longer on record against admitting Negroes to our schools, churches, clubs, homes, and all other places where human beings assemble."[12] White Mississippians as much as black saw transportation as a key battleground for the race question.

When the day of the decision's implementation arrived, nothing changed in Mississippi. The Jackson police took over the city's depots to ensure that the situation remained under control.[13] On January 12, the Jackson city council reaffirmed its stance on segregation by introducing and passing unanimously a Jim Crow law setting for violators a fine of twenty-five to one hundred dollars, a sentence of thirty days in jail, or both. In the words of the ordinance, the council passed the bill because "a sudden intermingling of the races necessarily involved in the common use of such waiting room and restroom facilities would likely result in disturbances, breaches of the peace, disorder, and confusion."[14] Within a few weeks, the Mississippi House of Representatives took up and passed similar statewide bills. The issue effectively ceased to be of concern, as the state had taken its stand, and the Eisenhower-era Interstate Commerce Commission was not about to push enforcement of the order.

Challenges occasionally arose after this storm had passed. A few months later, when the Montgomery Bus Boycott had taken on national significance, Mississippi officials from the governor down to the Jackson mayor vowed that there would be no integration of buses in the city.[15] In October 1957, the Ministerial Improvement Association of Hattiesburg, an all-black organization, issued a prepared statement of objectives that they hoped to attain, including "first-class citizenship for all people of Mississippi regardless of race, color, or creed"; action to promote voting rights for Negroes; and the integration of bus and railway stations. The Reverend W. H. Hall of Hattiesburg's Zion Chapel AME Church issued this statement to reporters, explaining that the group would "use every peaceful means and method" to achieve its goals.[16]

Medgar Evers, the NAACP activist whose 1963 death would mark one of many notorious Mississippi incidents during the civil rights era, engaged in his own brave if futile challenge to Jim Crow transportation in the spring of 1958. Perhaps emboldened by his experiences at an NAACP conference in North Carolina over the previous few days, Evers was on his way back from that meeting when he changed buses in Meridian and knowingly violated Jim Crow by taking a front seat and then refusing an order to move. The driver called the police, who arrived and took Evers in for questioning. They chose not to arrest him. When he got back on the bus, Evers returned to the same seat, but this time the bus pulled out. Three blocks down the road, Evers confronted Mississippi's other form of justice, less formal but in some ways just as systematized. A taxi driver waved down the bus, which stopped and let him on. The white man punched Evers in the face. The civil rights worker did not flinch and did not budge. He also did not fight back. Unsure of what to do, the driver ordered the white man off the bus, and the trip continued without further ado.[17] For one brief moment in time, at the cost of a slug to the face, Medgar Evers had integrated an interstate bus in Mississippi. The victory was fleeting.

Mississippi was prepared for the Freedom Riders to descend upon its highways. Ross Barnett had offered his "moral support" and assistance to Alabama governor John Patterson after the federal government sent U.S. marshals and the National Guard into Montgomery. Barnett had further announced that his commissioner of public safety, General T. B. Birdsong, who also served as head of the Mississippi Highway Patrol, would be instructed to move any Freedom Riders across the state without a stop if they crossed the border from Alabama. Similarly, O. A. Booker, the chief of police in Meridian, a city not far from the border and on the same route that Medgar Evers had ridden between Montgomery and Jackson, placed his department on twenty-four-hour alert. "We don't know exactly what they plan to do," Booker told a reporter, referring to the possible plans of the civil rights activists, "but we aren't taking any chances."[18] Attorney General Joe Patterson, who had conferred with Barnett, announced cryptically, "We have plans, but to reveal them would be bad strategy."[19]

In a joint statement issued that same day, Tut Patterson and William Simmons, the head of the national Citizens' Councils of America, chided the federal government for "sponsoring and shepherding this expedition of black and white agitators whose sole purpose is to break all local laws and stir up strife and discord." They blamed the recent crises in Alabama on "the provocations to violence on the part of invading integrationists." Patterson and Simmons labeled federal support for the Freedom Riders "Reconstruction with a vengeance" and asked, "Would the federal government show the same solicitude for a Citizens' Council expedition to the heart of Harlem for the widely-advertised purpose of openly violating Northern customs and breaking laws?" They commended Patterson and other officials "for their firm stand to protect the racial integrity of their sovereign state."[20] Predictably, Mississippi's two senators, James Eastland and John Stennis, blamed the "cold blooded plan of a group of outside agitators" for the violence on the trip to that point, pointing out that "people who look for trouble can usually find it."[21] No one seemed to notice when Aaron Henry of the Mississippi Conference of the NAACP announced the NAACP's support for the Freedom Riders and commended the Kennedys "for the action taken in behalf of the 'Freedom Riders' and America in their efforts to insure safe travel for all people on public conveyances."[22]

Responding to the violence in Montgomery and subsequent events in Mississippi, but also to what he and his colleagues had experienced on the first Ride's entry into Alabama and to the ongoing resistance of Mississippi officials, original Freedom Rider Jimmy McDonald wrote in *Freedomways* after he returned from his harrowing time in the South: "We can see how, if state executive officers, or just the chief of police, were to use their positions in a responsible manner, there would be a complete change of atmosphere. Instead of being thrown into segregated jails, the Freedom Riders could peacefully—and lawfully—sit together in integrated waiting rooms. And not one Southern white would lose the slightest shred of dignity by it. In fact, he would gain immeasurable stature by simply acknowledging the law of God and, incidentally, that of the United States of America."[23]

McDonald recognized the culpability of Governor Patterson, the consequences of whose intransigence he had experienced firsthand, and of other leaders at the state and local levels. Nonetheless, Mississippi's leaders, with Ross Barnett in the foreground, continued to resist the changing tide.

Indeed, Barnett's predecessor, James Coleman, had warned Robert Kennedy in the days after the Montgomery violence that the group would never reach Jackson, that they would be killed, and that Barnett was not to be trusted. It was this sense of doubt about Barnett that ultimately fueled federal willingness to broker a deal with Senator Eastland, whom the Kennedys did trust.[24] "The assurances that [Eastland] gave me," Kennedy later said, "that this was what was supposed to happen: that they'd get there, they'd be protected, and then they'd be locked up."[25] Given their trepidation about working with Barnett and their reluctance to bring in troops, dealing with Eastland must have seemed the most palatable option, although the administration also received Barnett's assurances that he would keep the peace.

Meanwhile, the Freedom Riders vowed to forge onward into Mississippi. At a news conference in Montgomery, John Lewis, Martin Luther King Jr., Ralph Abernathy, and James Farmer fielded questions. Lewis still had the bandages on his scalp from his Montgomery beating. When asked if a police escort, which Ross Barnett had promised, would make for a successful Freedom Ride, Farmer responded: "It would not be successful, because one of our purposes is to test unsegregated facilities. If it were made under escort or without stops it would be in a sense a frustration." While an escort by marshals would be "a real victory," he maintained that the group would prefer to make the trip on their own. King told the assembled media throng: "We feel the moment has come for a full-scale assault on segregation. I conceive of a massive non-violent attack on segregation—through sit-ins, stand-ins, wade-ins and the like." King played the role of the one truly national civil rights leader well, providing a long-term vision for the current activity. King acknowledged that even if the Freedom Ride into Mississippi proved successful, it would not mean a speedy end to segregation on interstate transport and facilities: "It will serve to break the back of segregation in interstate commercial travel, but there will still be some problems. It will bring the issue to the front so that the good will of this nation and the Federal Government will stand ready to see it will not develop again."[26] King was well aware of the violent potential of the impending trip. But he encouraged the group to forge onward. "Freedom Riders must develop the quiet courage of dying for a cause," he told the reporters. "We would not like to see anyone die, but we are well aware that we may have casualties. I'm sure these students are willing to face death if necessary."[27]

Byron White, deputy U.S. attorney general and the administration official in charge of the marshals in Montgomery, who was also at the conference, was elusive as to specifics.[28] He said that he had not received any requests for an escort by the marshals, that he hoped that Mississippi officials could handle whatever came up, and that in any case he would consult the state's authorities. He refused to go much further in answering reporters' queries.[29]

Burke Marshall had a phone conversation with Mississippi attorney general Joe Patterson on May 22 in hopes of ensuring the Freedom Riders' peaceful passage into Mississippi. While asserting that he had no control over the Riders, he also insisted, over Patterson's protests, that they must have safe passage. Patterson kept returning to the idea that his state was calm and that the Freedom Riders would only make things difficult: "Mississippi is quiet and peaceful today. We haven't got one iota of trouble in it. I wouldn't advise the Governor of this state to let 12 wild-eyed radicals in here to have them spit in the faces of the people of Mississippi. That's what they're coming here to do." Nonetheless, Patterson agreed that they would find a way to get the Riders across the state to Jackson. But he did not want to provide them a forum "to come in here and spit in the faces of the people in our state. I think they ought to go home and quit their darned Communist conduct. . . . They are not coming in for a good purpose. Why should we put guns around them and protect them when they are here to create trouble. They've got no business in Mississippi." Marshall indulged Patterson's complaints, but ultimately he told the state attorney general: "That is not the point we are concerned with. It isn't something that you or I can do anything about." The conversation went on in this fashion, with Marshall trying to secure guarantees of the buses' safe passage and Patterson trying to argue against the very presence of the "wild-eyed radicals." In the end Marshall got a concession that probably was not sufficient to put his worries to rest. "First, we hope they do not come," Patterson reiterated. "Next, if they do come," he hoped that "they come out of the state as soon as they can and we will see to it that they get out of the state." Patterson closed by saying that he appreciated the call and that he had "tried to be absolutely frank."[30]

The next day, Robert Kennedy spoke with Governor Barnett. Their conversation was brief. After asking if there was any way to stop the buses of Riders from passing through and being assured that there was not, Barnett told the attorney general, "What I had in mind was to escort them through the state with every protection in the world."[31] The administration hoped to cover its bases by speaking to all sides in hopes of averting the sort of disaster that had befallen the Freedom Ride in Alabama.

Barnett placed the Mississippi National Guard on alert the next day and wired Robert Kennedy that Mississippi would be capable of maintaining law and order without the assistance of the federal government. In the meantime, Highway Patrol officers had begun stopping buses crossing the border from Alabama in search of Freedom Riders, and Jackson mayor Allen C. Thompson announced that his city would be ready and that he had received overwhelming support for the city's preparation.[32] That night Joe Patterson went on television to ask Mississippians to "keep our heads and be calm."[33] Even John Wright of the Citizens' Council of Jackson, which claimed as members nearly every major city official and many state officials as well, issued a statement urging people to let the authorities handle things despite the fact that "these apostles of discord" hoped to foment a violent response. The police authorities would "see to it that Mississippi does not provide any grist for the Northern propaganda mills!"[34] All indications were that Mississippi had learned from the debacles in Alabama.

On the morning of Wednesday, May 24, Barnett asked the public to stay calm: "I earnestly solicit the cooperation of all the citizens of Mississippi and plead with them to let our well-trained state and local officers handle any situation that may arise. The laws of Mississippi must be enforced." This last statement may have given an indication of what was to come, and M. B. Pierce, chief of the Detective Bureau of the Jackson Police Department, amplified this aspect of Barnett's statement when he said that the Freedom Riders would not be bothered—unless they violated a state law. Mayor Thompson similarly asserted that the city had plans in place and that he did not "anticipate . . . trouble" but that any attempt by Riders to violate city laws by occupying the white waiting rooms would bring prompt arrest. In his television statement the night before, Attorney General Patterson had also said that any such violations of state and local law would lead to arrests. The arrests would have to happen because Mississippi officials adhered to the line that, as Patterson put it, the Freedom Riders were not interstate passengers, but "a group of wild-eyed fanatical troublemakers who went to Alabama to create confusion."[35]

In a page-one editorial that morning, the *Jackson Daily News* assured its readers that "the law will maintain." The editorial began by condemning the "ridiculous conduct" of the Freedom Riders, which left "an open question whether they should be in jail, at the Whitfield Mental Hospital or the Jackson Zoo." The editors nonetheless placed their faith in Governor Barnett and declared their belief that the whole state would "endorse and support" his "clear and appropriate" statements.[36]

In the strange-bedfellows department, NAACP leader Roy Wilkins, an initial supporter of the Freedom Rides, effectively took the side of Barnett, the *Daily News,* and other critics, trying to warn the group against going into the bowels of Mississippi. Medgar Evers, the NAACP field secretary who had challenged Jim Crow on the bus in Meridian three years earlier, concurred with Wilkins. He told reporters he was against the Freedom Riders coming to Mississippi. Evers believed that civil rights workers needed to build more of a foundation in the state before such a confrontation would be viable.[37]

In the midst of all of this fanfaronade, the first band of more than two dozen Freedom Riders arrived at the heavily fortified Trailways station in Montgomery early on the morning of May 24. They came in from the "makeup point" at Dr. Dean Harris's Montgomery house, where they had all met, loading into taxicabs and private automobiles and departing with a National Guard escort of six jeeps. Alabama National Guard troops lined both sides of the street in front of the terminal. Another group stood vigil from the second floor of a garage across the street. King, Abernathy, Walker, Ed King, Diane Nash, and others met the students at the terminal. They entered the "white" waiting room, where the students bought tickets, checked their luggage, and walked together to the white snack bar where they placed food orders. The group ate breakfast together. According to the manager, this marked the first time blacks had ever been served at that counter.[38]

The mechanics of carrying out the Ride had garnered so much attention that the actual mission had seemingly been lost. Nonetheless, integrating an establishment at the scene of such recent violence was a small victory in anticipation of what must have been a harrowing prospect: Freedom Riding into Mississippi. Many of those on board were not optimistic that they would actually end up at the night's planned destination, Tougaloo Southern Christian College on the outskirts of Jackson.

Tougaloo had provided the brunt of the support for the sit-in campaign that began at Jackson's City Library in March 1961.[39] Tougaloo students began the sit-ins, and after their arrests, students from Tougaloo and Jackson State sat-in at the city courthouse protesting their arrests and trials. This brought out Jackson police with German shepherds.[40] In early summer 1961, civil rights activity was still the foremost concern among many students in Jackson.

Tougaloo, however, must have seemed far away, and the ultimate destination, New Orleans, a mirage. King shook hands with some of the Riders as the bus prepared to depart. "This is a dramatic moment," he told them solemnly. "Good luck." After the bus was loaded, Major General Henry V. Graham went aboard and explained the precautions that were being taken to "prevent trouble." Although he believed that major difficulties would be remote, he acknowledged, "The trip is a hazardous one."[41]

At about 7:15 the first bus rolled out of the station to begin the 250-plus-mile journey to Jackson. It carried twelve Freedom Riders. Three non–Freedom Riders who had bought tickets refused to board after discovering the nature of the bus they were scheduled to take.[42] Also aboard were six National Guard members and nearly twenty reporters. A police motorcycle convoy followed the bus to the city limits and then peeled off. From there, three L-19 reconnaissance planes, two helicopters, and seventeen Highway Patrol cars, as well as National Guard jeeps and trucks and trailing reporters who had not gotten on the bus—some forty-two vehicles in all—took over. At strategic checkpoints, FBI spotter cars were in place. Kennedy, Eastland, and Barnett had agreed that there would be no federal marshals accompanying the bus.[43]

Jim Lawson, the inspirational thirty-two-year-old leader of so many of the students, did not find the armed guard ideal: "We appreciate the government's concern, but protection does not solve the problem of segregation."[44] "This is not a normal situation," he argued, and as such it did not "carry out the purposes of our project. We are not traveling as private citizens, but as protectees of a government. We would rather be without all this protection." Reaffirming his understanding of the potential trouble ahead, Lawson told reporters, "We are not seeking violence, but if it is coming, we are prepared to accept it, and absorb." The Riders were similarly concerned about the media presence.[45]

On the bus Lawson led a mini-workshop for the new Freedom Riders. James Farmer greatly admired Lawson, much as the students whom Lawson mentored did. Later Farmer mused, "Courage, after all, is not being unafraid, but doing what needs to be done in spite of fear." He thought of this as he watched Lawson "leap . . . onto the bus, with a grim gladness."[46] Lawson expected a riot, and on the bus he prepared his charges accordingly: "If we get knocked down, I think the best bet is to stand where we are if we can—or kneel where we are."[47]

The bus made three stops before it reached the Mississippi line. General Graham explained that the first stop, in Selma at 10:30, was a stretch break. The second was unexpected—Freedom Rider Alex M. Anderson, one of the Nashville contingent, became ill with stomach pains, and General Graham and several National Guard troops formed a circle around him while he vomited off the side of the road. A third stop was also unexpected: five miles from the state line, in the little town of Scratch Hill, the bus pulled to the side of the road. It remained there for thirty-five minutes. No one explained what was happening.[48]

The administration had received information that there were two attacks planned against the bus on either side of the Mississippi border, one in or around the little town of Cuba, Alabama, and one just across the border. Allegedly, white men with dynamite were waiting among roadside crowds. "I think those [reports] were real," Burke Marshall later remarked. "There were whites that were intending to ambush this bus and waylay it, and hurt or to kill the occupants."[49] Nonetheless, when the National Guard investigated the woods near the highway, they found nothing. At 11:40 the bus reached the Mississippi state line, where 260 Mississippi National Guard troops took control.[50] All of the regimentation led one Freedom Rider to comment, "I'm going out of America into a foreign country."[51]

The bus route took the Riders across U.S. Route 80. Claude Sitton of the *New York Times,* who covered the Southern beat for the paper and had long been engaged in covering the integration struggle, described the part of the state through which the journey passed. Route 80 "leads through the heart of the Black Belt, an area of dark soil and a large Negro population. Militant segregationists hold the reigns of power throughout much of this strip and race relations have made relatively little progress."[52] The Freedom Riders may not have known the geographic and demographic breakdown of the state, but they knew by reputation that they were not entering friendly territory as the bus worked its way toward Jackson.

In Meridian, twenty or so miles past the border, a phalanx of some 130 National Guard troops surrounded the bus station, and the area was cleared to make way for the double-decked red, silver, and white bus to pass through. A fire engine and a fog machine were on hand. The bus bypassed its expected Meridian stop, and military officials refused to allow even a break for the passengers to relieve themselves. Both Lawson and Nashville's Reverend C. T. Vivian tried to persuade Lieutenant Colonel Gillespie V. Montgomery, who was also a state senator, to allow the bus to pull aside so the passengers could go to the bathroom, but to no avail.[53] There would be no stops in Mississippi.

In Meridian a relatively passive crowd of a thousand or so gathered to watch. Along the sides of the road, crowds were beginning to congregate. Someone threw a rock at the bus, but most people seemed inclined just to take in the spectacle. A few snapped pictures. Some waved sarcastically.[54] At the little towns in Mississippi between Meridian and Jackson, in Newton and Forest and Morton, where the bus would have stopped on its normal route, crowds gathered. At Newton, a large group congealed at the intersections of Highways 15 and 35 and Highway 90. There were angry shouts, and a man shook a fist as the bus passed through about an hour before its Jackson arrival. In the town of Pearl, a man in an automobile leaned out of his car and shouted at the caravan, which had forced him off the road to pass.[55] According to Jackson's WMAG reporter Barbara Goodwin, many of the onlookers "seemed amused."[56]

A crowd was gathered some distance from the bus terminal in Jackson, but the police were there in full detail. They had cleared out a two-block radius, sweeping away individuals on foot as well as waiting taxi drivers. A crowd gathered as close as possible on Lamar Street, which ran alongside the station. Onlookers leaned from the windows of nearby buildings to get a closer look. The bus had taken an hour and a half to cover the ninety miles from Meridian, and Jackson police met the caravan at a cloverleaf on Highway 80, just outside of Jackson, and escorted them through town and to the terminal. The bus pulled in at 2:55 P.M. Mississippi time.[57]

Lawson readied his charges, who had broken down into teams of two. They departed the bus in pairs and headed toward the white waiting room. Even if they had wanted to, the Freedom Riders could not have gone to the section designated for "colored" passengers. That waiting room was closed, a sign on the door reading "out of order."[58] Clearly, the state authorities wanted to push the Freedom Riders into breaking segregation laws. A Jackson police officer approached two young black women and politely asked them to move on from the white waiting room. They refused, and he arrested them immediately for causing a disturbance. As more Freedom Riders approached the waiting room, a police captain told them, "You all have to move." When no one moved, he asked, "You all going to move?" Someone replied, "No," and so the officer directed them to the waiting patrol wagons.[59] Three of the men were allowed to use the white restrooms. All twelve Freedom Riders on this bus—eleven black, one white—went to jail. Chief of Detectives M. B. Pierce announced that they were being charged with breach of peace, disobeying an officer, and inciting a riot.[60] Eight had made it as far as the verboten waiting room. The trip to the jail was a quick one—the bus station was just two blocks from the city jail.

James Meredith—a native Mississippian who in the summer of 1961 was in the midst of his own legal struggle with Ole Miss officials, which would lead to a rendezvous with destiny involving the Kennedys, Ross Barnett, and the forces of white supremacy in Mississippi—was present when the Freedom Riders arrived in Jackson: "The radio was giving a blow-by-blow account of the activities and I knew the minute the bus was in town. I drove to downtown Jackson to watch. The bus station area had been cleared and behind the police lines were hordes of Mississippi whites. . . . The main street going past the bus terminal was open to traffic, and I drove by about five minutes after the Freedom Riders' bus had been stopped. They were already putting the Freedom Riders into the waiting police vans."[61]

Even as Meredith watched events unfold, another busload of Freedom Riders, this time on a Greyhound, was en route to Jackson. John Lewis served as group leader for this second bus holding fifteen Riders. Hank Thomas was also part of this group, alongside New Orleans CORE worker Jerome Smith. So was James Farmer. He had not intended to be. He and King had stood outside of the first bus, shaking hands and waving goodbye from the loading platform. Then Doris Castle, another young CORE member from New Orleans, plaintively addressed Farmer. Farmer had shaken her hand and said something about his prayers being with her, that when it was over they'd talk about what would come next. "Jim, you're going with us aren't you?" Castle said. Farmer mumbled something about CORE paperwork and obligations, but Castle stared at him. "Jim, please!" she pleaded. Perhaps chastened by what had happened to King at the meeting with the students and certainly more personally committed to the Freedom Rides than King, Farmer relented. He had his luggage placed on the bus, and he joined the group, though he was, by his own admission, "scared shitless" about the prospect of heading west into Mississippi.[62]

The police and troop arrangements reminded Farmer of "a military operation." Initially, Kennedy had hoped that there would be only one bus, but he received word from Byron White via Martin Luther King that there would be a second leaving by 11:30.[63] The infrastructure would still be available for the subsequent buses. The National Guard was still in place. The police Highway Patrols in both Alabama and Mississippi were prepared for other groups. The presence of all the officials, the police and National Guard, did not put Farmer at ease: "If anything, it increased [our fear]. We didn't know which way" they "would point their guns in the event of a showdown."[64] Like the first bus, the second also held National Guard troops and media members, a half dozen of each. The former were simply doing a job that was surely distasteful to many of them. The latter were not about to miss the story of the day, maybe of their lives. The students, meanwhile, were writing. They had slips of paper on which they wrote the names and addresses of their next of kin, small wills, and in some cases messages to be passed on—just in case. The men put the slips of paper in their pockets. Some of the women slipped them into their brassieres.

Just inside the Alabama border, a transfer between the Alabama and Mississippi authorities took place. The bus rolled safely through to the Mississippi state line, where a highway sign reading "Welcome to the Magnolia State" greeted it. Before crossing the line, the bus stopped, and the Alabama protection fanned away. The driver got off; another replaced him. Floyd Mann got on the bus and whispered something to one of the reporters, who then passed his intelligence on to the other five. They got off the bus. When Farmer asked the lone holdover what had happened, he was told that an ambush awaited them over the border and planned to destroy the bus. Farmer feigned calm.[65]

Replacing the Alabamans was a similar convoy of Mississippi State Highway Patrol cars and National Guard troops. The Mississippi National Guard had bayonets on their rifles.[66] Freedom Rider Frank Holloway later remarked, "Behind all these escorts I felt like the President of the United States touring Russia or something."[67] When they crossed into Mississippi and saw that unintentionally ironic highway sign welcoming them, Farmer later remembered, "Our hearts jumped into our mouths."[68] John Lewis had never been to Mississippi before, but all of the horror stories had him scared. He remembered that he "found it unsettling seeing crowds of onlookers standing by the roadside, held back by those armed troops." Lewis thought it odd that some of the National Guard wore bushy beards "that made them look like Confederate soldiers." As it turned out, they were playing Confederates in a Civil War reenactment that was interrupted when they were summoned to emergency National Guard duty.[69]

The bus lumbered through steamy rural Mississippi. The threatened ambush never materialized, but the National Guard troops on the sides of the highway kept their rifles pointed toward the big oak trees flanking either side of the road, just in case. Before too long, the Southern countryside began to give way to Jackson's periphery, and anxiety began to rise. One of the Freedom Riders broke into the newest verse of "Hallelujah, I'm a Travelin'":

I'm taking a ride on the Greyhound bus line,
I'm a-riding the front seat to Jackson this time.[70]

The rest of the group joined in at the chorus as the bus pulled into Jackson.

When the bus arrived at the Greyhound station at 5:47 P.M., the passengers saw a crowd of white men and stiffened. Then they realized it was only Jackson police and media members. "Oh, we stuck our chests out then," Farmer recalled, "'cause we didn't see a mob."[71] The police made a path for them from the bus to the inside of the terminal. Farmer marched arm-in-arm with Nashville movement veteran Lucretia Collins.[72] They effectively went straight from the bus to the white waiting room and, after a stopover at one of the white drinking fountains, on to the waiting police paddy wagons and into jail.

Farmer recalled Captain J. L. Ray pointing them toward the wagons. Farmer later likened Captain Ray's stabbing finger to "that of the little Dutch boy of legend vainly trying to plug a breach in the dike of segregation in order to hold back the floodwaters of resistance—to save his city, his state, his way of life."[73] Frank Holloway, a SNCC worker from Atlanta, compared the policemen waiting for them in Jackson to "the doorman of the Waldorf Astoria. . . . I guess the crooks in the city had a field day because all the Jackson police were at the bus station . . . opening doors for us."[74]

John Lewis had managed to make it to a urinal in the whites-only restroom. An officer caught up to him, poked him in the ribs, and demanded that he move. "Just a minute! Can't you see what I'm doing?" shouted an annoyed Lewis. "I said move! Now!" the officer replied. Lewis zipped up and moved along, joining the rest of his group on the way to jail.[75]

For all of the fears of deepest, darkest Mississippi, there was no violence in the capital city that day. In the words of James Farmer: "It was all very civilized; the nation was watching through newsreel cameras. Bigotry had many faces, and unlike Alabama, where Klan hooliganism had been allowed to run amok, Mississippi was putting its best face forward."[76] The *Memphis Commercial-Appeal* called "the reception" that the buses of Freedom Riders received "short and snappy" and added, "It couldn't have been smoother if it had been practiced a dozen times."[77] This was not unintentional. Ross Barnett was ready for the Freedom Riders: "We saw what a terrible scrap they had in Alabama. They had a world of trouble . . . so we got ready for it here. I had the cooperation of the Highway Patrol, the Jackson Police, the Mayor, Allen Thompson, and we had meant to meet them at the Alabama line, and bring them in, and when they'd violate our laws we would just put them in jail, one after another."[78] Barnett had weighed several options for dealing with the Freedom Riders. One was to declare martial law. Another was to have them detained and sent to Whitfield Mental Hospital rather than have them arrested. A meeting with Mayor Thompson encouraged him that the police could handle the job in Jackson.[79]

The Jackson police arrested twenty-seven Freedom Riders that day.[80] Two of these were white men. On the first bus was Paul Dietrich, a twenty-nine-year-old office worker from Washington, and on the second bus was Peter Ackerberg, a twenty-two-year-old history major from Antioch College in Ohio.[81] The rest were a mixed-gender group of black Riders. The police were polite to a fault. Everything was orderly. In the end, Jackson prosecutor Jack Travis charged all of the members of the group with refusing to obey an officer and breach of the peace—the charge of attempting to incite a riot was dropped. All of the accused refused to post the one thousand dollars bond, so they remained in the city jail to await trial on the charges, each of which carried, on conviction, a maximum fine of two hundred dollars, a sentence of four months in jail, or both.[82]

Meanwhile, Robert Kennedy was keeping himself apprised of every move via a sophisticated communications network that allowed him to follow minute-by-minute accounts from police radios as well as via telephone. Byron White, Kennedy aide Joe Dolan, Burke Marshall, FBI assistant director Al Rosen, and James McShane—a colorful former New York City police officer, Golden Gloves boxer, Rackets Committee investigator for Bobby Kennedy, and JFK bodyguard—all served as point men on the ground, sending in dispatches. Robert Kennedy had one primary concern, and he would place it above any principles he may have had, including those seemingly clear assertions he had made in his speech at the University of Georgia Law Day, and that was to avoid violence at all costs. Unbeknownst to almost everyone on the ground, Kennedy had brokered a deal with Senator Eastland, the powerful chair of the Senate Judiciary Committee. Whatever the Mississippi senator's faults, Kennedy trusted him. "He always kept his word," Kennedy later said, "and he always was available, and he always told me exactly where he stood and what he could do and couldn't do. He also told me who I could trust and couldn't trust in Mississippi."[83]

Eastland had promised that Mississippi authorities would ensure that there would be no violence in exchange for the Kennedy administration not enforcing the Supreme Court decision forbidding Jim Crow at the Jackson station. By Kennedy's estimate, he spoke to Eastland "seven, eight, or twelve times each day about what was going to happen when [the Riders] got to Mississippi and what needed to be done."[84] "I think Jim Eastland really took a responsibility for" ensuring that things ran smoothly, Kennedy later recalled.[85] When Eastland told Kennedy point blank that the Freedom Riders would face arrest as soon as they arrived in Jackson, Kennedy told him "that my primary interest was that they weren't beaten up," though he believed he had little immediate say about the arrests.[86]

Throughout the night, Kennedy also kept up communications with Ross Barnett, Mayor Thompson, and other officials to ensure that there would be no repeat of the Alabama imbroglios. Kennedy was comfortable brokering deals through backroom channels. While this is often an appropriate and effective means of getting things done, in the case of civil rights and the Freedom Rides, this backroom approach "made Negroes feel like pawns in a white man's political game," in the words of historian John Dittmer.[87]

On the morning of the departures from Montgomery, Robert Kennedy issued a statement asserting his belief that officials in Mississippi would ensure public safety. President Kennedy, about to embark upon a trip during which he would meet with France's Charles de Gaulle and that would culminate in June at a summit meeting in Vienna with Nikita Khrushchev, clearly linked this upcoming meeting with U.S. events, stressing the importance of avoiding anything that would "bring or cause discredit" to the reputation of the United States.[88]

That night Kennedy again issued a plea for a cooling-off period. This time he did so publicly, hoping to put pressure upon the movement. He urged those traveling through Alabama and Mississippi to delay their trips "until the present state of confusion and danger has passed and an atmosphere of reason and normalcy has been restored." He warned that continued Freedom Rides could result in injury to regular passengers not affiliated with the protest.[89] As he later told an interviewer: "I thought that people were going to be killed, and they had made their point. What was the purpose of continuing with it?"[90] As Leslie Dunbar, head of the Southern Regional Council in 1961, once asserted, in the Kennedy administration there was "a great reluctance . . . to accept the fact that you had to be on somebody's side in the South."[91]

The leaders of the movement rejected this request with equal strength, believing there was ample reason to continue, using some of the same language and metaphors they had when Kennedy had made the same request to the leaders in the Montgomery church three days earlier. Farmer publicly issued his "deep freeze" comment.[92] Montgomery activist Uriah J. Fields sent Robert Kennedy a telegram with a focus similar to Farmer's: "Had there not been a cooling-off period following the Civil War, the Negro would be free today. Isn't ninety-nine years long enough to cool off, Mr. Attorney General?"[93] The editors of the *Afro-American* commended

Kennedy for all that he had done in Montgomery but then likened his call for a cooling-off period to "a man who kicks over the pail after milking the cows."[94]

Robert Kennedy and Martin Luther King Jr. squared off in a testy conversation. Kennedy made an offer whereby the federal government would arrange for payment of bail for all those who had been arrested if the Rides stopped. King demurred. "It's a matter of conscience and morality," he explained to the attorney general. "They must use their lives and their bodies to right a wrong." Kennedy remained unimpressed: "That is not going to have the slightest effect on what the government is going to do in this field or any other. The fact that they stay in jail is not going to have the slightest effect on me." Ignoring the fact that Kennedy's comment was a patent absurdity—the administration was and had been acting solely because the Freedom Riders had gone South, and he was on the phone at that time because of the very events he said would not have "the slightest effect"—King then touched a nerve by asking whether it might make a difference if students across the nation headed down South by the hundreds, or perhaps by the hundreds of thousands. Kennedy's frustrations were mounting: "This country belongs to you as much as to me. You can determine what's best just as well as I can, but don't make statements that sound like a threat. That's not the way to deal with us." This met with silence. Rather than press a point on which he had the moral and constitutional high ground, King rephrased his argument: "You must understand that we've made no gains without pressure and I hope that pressure will always be moral, legal, and peaceful." King continued, stating his belief that the "creative and nonviolent" approach "can save the soul of America." Kennedy countered by saying that the problem wouldn't be solved "but by strong federal action." King turned gracious, telling Kennedy: "I'm deeply appreciative of what the administration is doing. I see a ray of hope, but I'm different from my father. I feel the need of being free now." It was Kennedy's turn to back off. "Well," he sighed. "It all depends on what you and the people in jail decide. If they want to get out, we can get them out." King settled things simply: "They'll stay."[95]

King was exasperated. In addition to his tête-à-tête with Kennedy, he had also been holding regular conversations with Burke Marshall, who had similarly tried to encourage King to use his influence to call a halt to the Rides. He turned to his colleagues in Montgomery and said, "You know, they don't understand the social revolution going on in the world, and therefore they don't understand what we're doing."[96]

Robert Kennedy, meanwhile, called upon Harris Wofford, special assistant to the president for civil rights, to vent his own frustrations. Wofford was probably the administration official most sympathetic to the Civil Rights Movement, its aims, its approach, its tactics and means. "This is too much!" Kennedy shouted. "I wonder whether they have the best interest of their country at heart. Do you know that one of them is against the atom bomb—yes, he even picketed against it in jail! The President is going abroad and this is all embarrassing him."[97] Even in the midst of a serious domestic crisis, when large groups of civil rights activists felt that the interest of their country might just lie in upholding the Constitution and the Supreme Court, the Cold War prism shaped the Kennedy administration's views. In addition to feeling dumbfounded that anyone could oppose the most destructive weapon humankind had ever developed, Kennedy emphasized his worry that America's racial troubles, especially the ongoing Freedom Rides, would embarrass the president in his upcoming meetings, especially with the Soviet premier. In the end, even the Cold War–liberal, staunchly pro-Kennedy group Americans for Democratic Action rejected the plea for a cooling-off period, its vice chairman urging Freedom Riders to stay the course on May 27.

In his speech that night, Kennedy repeated that the federal government was obligated to protect interstate travelers and to protect law and order when local officials were unwilling or unable to do so. Kennedy also said that he had no comment about the arrests in Jackson and announced that the Justice Department had already asked for federal district court injunctions to prevent Birmingham and Montgomery officials from interfering with interstate travel—even as he was helping the Jackson authorities do the same. This last step was actually an amendment to the injunction against the Ku Klux Klan that the Justice Department had gotten from Judge Johnson a few days before. This amendment charged that the Birmingham police "deliberately withheld" protection for the Freedom Riders and that the Montgomery police "took no measures to preserve their safety."[98] The federal government had acquiesced in a plan that led to the arrests of the Freedom Riders—arrests that, in the words of Burke Marshall, "were unconstitutional . . . without any question."[99] All in all, observers on both sides of the segregationist divide had reason not to trust the Kennedys' Janus-faced approach to civil rights.

Away from Mississippi, the Greyhound Corporation ordered disciplinary action against Montgomery employees who had denied food service to blacks. In LaGrange, Georgia, authorities arrested five men attempting to organize resistance to Freedom Riders.[100] These events indicate that the Freedom Ride was having positive national effects even as Kennedy was authorizing Mississippi to violate the Supreme Court's clear dictates. Robert Kennedy would later claim that his brother was "very concerned about what could be done" for the Freedom Riders in Mississippi but that the consensus in the Justice Department was that "our authority was limited." The belief was that "it's better not to impose things from above because people resent it."[101] The Justice Department was the chief law enforcement arm of the executive branch, which itself had a constitutional obligation to ensure adherence to the Constitution. The Supreme Court had been quite clear in *Boynton* in establishing the rights that the Freedom Riders were trying to secure. This—not avoiding feelings of resentment of Mississippians—was the federal responsibility.

The *Jackson Daily News* issued kudos to everyone "involved in connection with the immoral, ugly, un-American conduct of our unwanted, undesired visitors." While its editor, James C. Ward, hoped "that none of these kind words are premature," he went on to congratulate "all Mississippians" for "maintaining a dignified, typically Southern hospitable atmosphere in the face of unfortunate, but not unbearable, insult from groups of mentally deranged people who deserve a nitwit net more than physical challenge." The editorial then congratulated Ross Barnett and all state and local officials, the "responsible press, radio and television media," and the leaders and troops of the Mississippi National Guard and Mississippi Highway Patrol, and extended "a most generous word to the citizens of Jackson, who, except for their good-natured, entertaining window-peeking from office floors paid no other attention to our disappointed guests." Finally, the *Daily News* commended "the lint-headed, diabolical, inconsiderate, sadistic-thinking leadership of CORE, the gang of New York crackpots who sponsored this mission."[102] The editor explained this seemingly disjunctive praise as follows:

We congratulate CORE and its NAACP brotherhood in their excessively ambitious love for strife and hatred that has left all of them naked to the nation searching for their goal of deceit and fraud. Unwitted [*sic*] supporters now, finally see them in the true light. . . . The whole story of this insane visitation is turning out to be a Southern blessing in disguise, exposing these so-called victims of minority "discrimination" to be the wild-eyed money-raising social bandits they are. We wish for these vulgar, restroom-loving quacks a pleasant journey home. Thanks to them for favors done in their illegal, scummy mission.[103]

Other members of the "responsible press" of Mississippi weighed in as well. The *McComb Enterprise-Journal* praised Jackson and Mississippi law enforcement officers "for the effective and forthright manner in which they handled the so-called 'freedom riders' who came to Mississippi knowing well that they were laying the foundation for trouble.[104] The *Jackson Clarion-Ledger* portentously noted that "almost every member of the so-called 'freedom riders' . . . admitted having past police records."[105] Of course, those arrests had come in the process of fighting segregation across the South, something that was no mark of shame in the movement. The *Vicksburg Sunday Post* echoed the praise of most of the rest of the state's newspapers for "the manner in which officials of our state met the challenge": "Outsiders, bent on creating a situation of strife and turmoil, made their much publicized entry into our state. They were frustrated in their main objective. They had hoped for violence and thus would be pictured as martyrs. There was no violence in Mississippi. Instead there was the calm and efficient execution of the law, with a maximum of protection given even to those who deliberately and flagrantly violated the law of our state."[106]

The *Clarksdale Press Register* had perhaps the most humorous response of all. First, it did not condemn the Freedom Riders in the way that other outlets did. It did have some unkind words for Bobby Kennedy, to whom it "respectfully suggest[ed] that he tie his tie and get his feet off the desk and remember that he is responsible for running the Justice Department of the United States of America and is no longer bulldozing his brother's campaign from the backroom of a precinct headquarters." However, the best line from the wags in Clarksdale came toward the end of the opinion piece: "Then, too, is the humorous fact that very few bus station lunch counters or the menus they provide are worth making an issue over, much less getting a two by four laid up beside you[r] head. A gastronomic problem, yes! But hardly a national issue."[107]

It was not only the Mississippi print press pulling out all of their rhetorical guns against the Freedom Riders. Prominent national media were starting to weigh in as well, and many of them did not side with the Riders. The *New York Times* and the *Washington Post* gave their support to Kennedy and his call for a "cooling-off" period. More damning, however, was David Brinkley's nationally televised NBC editorial on May 24. Brinkley was fed up with the whole thing: "It's time for these so-called Freedom Riders to stop this. They are accomplishing nothing whatsoever and, on the contrary, are doing positive harm. Aside from the physical injuries caused to a number of people, all of this is humiliating the United States all over the world."[108] Actually, what was humiliating the United States all over the world was the fact that in a country that preached the superiority of its democratic system, which supposedly valued human rights, black and white passengers could not travel together into certain parts of the country without being beaten nearly to death.

Brinkley then deigned to acknowledge the plight of black Americans. "There is no doubt," he continued, "the Negro people in the South need and deserve better schools, jobs and a better deal in many respects. But the kind of exhibition now in progress is not going to get it for them." Brinkley believed that "on the contrary," the Freedom Ride was "more likely to inflame the southern opinion still further and make these advances more difficult than they already were." Choosing to weigh what should matter to blacks and where they should focus their energies, Brinkley, from his news reader's chair, asserted that he "couldn't help believing that schools, jobs and the right to vote are a lot more important than who sits where at the bus station. That particular aspect of segregation could wait until last." Even Brinkley could not deny the glaring fact that "the bus riders are, of course, within their legal rights in riding anywhere they like." But in his mind, "the results of these expeditions are of no benefit to anybody—white or Negro, the South or the North, nor the United States in general."[109]

The civil rights community thought that Brinkley was being willfully blind, ignorant, or worse. The *Baltimore Afro-American* made a simple rejoinder to Brinkley, who, as they pointed out, "has never been segregated in the back of a bus or denied service at a public lunch counter and been barred from using a public restroom." The newspaper's weary response to Brinkley's fulminations? "Ho Hum."[110] Marvin Rich, acting on behalf of CORE in his position as community relations director, telegrammed NBC asking for an opportunity to respond to Brinkley's editorial. In the telegram he asserted that CORE "support[s] the right to editorialize but also feel[s] [the] right to respond is properly guaranteed by FCC." He sent a similar missive to Newton Minnow, chair of the Federal Communications Commission, sending copies to the eight major New York newspapers.[111] Not surprisingly, NBC did not agree that CORE deserved equal time to respond to Brinkley, though they did "continue to be interested in covering the story" and had used CORE to contact Jim Peck to appear on the program *Monitor* on May 27.[112]

On May 26, the day the *New York Times* ran two editorials on the Rides, including the one supporting the cooling-off period, the NAACP issued a clear statement: there would be no cooling-off period for the Freedom Riders. Whatever its previous reservations, the NAACP was now fully in line with the leaders of the Rides. They were not about to abandon the Freedom Riders imprisoned in Mississippi.[113] That same day, Marvin Rich wrote a letter in response to the *Times* editorials. Rich acknowledged that what the Riders, what the movement, were asking "is difficult—not easy." Nonetheless, they asked "that the prejudiced put aside their prejudices: that those filled with hate return to sanity. We ask that every American be given equal impartial service on the highways of the nation." After affirming that "the right to this service is given us by the constitution and also by the moral law," Rich asked, "If [we] were to suspend the constitution and morality for a month would the Cooling-off period then result in a more favorable atmosphere? Or would [we] . . . once again at the end of that month's time find that peaceful travelers were arrested for doing that which they had every right to do?"[114]

Marvin Rich knew the answer: "No, we in America must do the hard thing. We must get rid of segregation root and all, and we must do it now." Rich knew that "'long held customs' will be held the longer if there is a cooling-off period. I would suggest that at the end of such a period any group that then attempted to assert their constitutional rights would meet substantially the same situation that prevails now." In the end, Rich wrote, "We in America must be true to ourselves."[115] This was a clear if subtle reminder that American values were only important inasmuch as Americans actually continued to stand up for those values and that a summit meeting abroad provided pretty poor subterfuge for denying moral and constitutional rights.

The editors of the *Afro-American* entreated the Freedom Riders to ignore Kennedy's request and continue on with their journey. "Chicken-hearted individuals, north and south have urged the Freedom Riders to quit and go home," they wrote, but "these advocates of freedom have said 'no.'" The federal law was clear on this question, and the editors were confident that the Kennedys would back the Freedom Riders with troops: "Once having begun the test, the Freedom Riders MUST continue to ride the buses and defy the mob. . . . They will be accused of provoking disorder and 'rocking the boat.' Some boats were made to be rocked. This is one of them."[116] The Freedom Rides would continue, but the locus of the struggle would largely shift from buses and stations to jail cells. Mississippi had been ready for the Freedom Riders. Would the Freedom Riders prove ready for Mississippi?

Chapter 11

Jailed In

From Jackson City Jail to Parchman Farm

Comes the Deluge: The Freedom Riders in Jail
and More on the Roads

Robert Kennedy was not happy with the news he heard next. On the same day as the first arrests in Mississippi, seven men from Connecticut had departed the Nutmeg State and were bound for Mississippi. At the head of this delegation of four whites and three blacks was Yale University chaplain William Sloane Coffin Jr. Accompanying him were Reverend Gaylord Noyce, an associate professor at Yale's Divinity School; Dr. John Maguire and Dr. David Swift, both religion professors at Wesleyan University; Clyde Carter and Charles Jones, theology students at Johnson C. Smith University; and George B. Smith, a Yale law student.[1]

After the events in Anniston and Birmingham, John Maguire and the others realized how serious matters had become: "It really did appear to us that this ride could be terminated by bombs." Before the chaos in Montgomery, Maguire later recalled, "we were speaking very bravely, that if anything happened to the Freedom Riders, we would go down and keep this thing going, which was, in a way, real bravura because up to that point, no representative white clergy members had gotten into it."[2]

Coffin, Maguire, and the others flew to Atlanta, where they boarded a bus bound for Montgomery. "The hostility was incredible!" according to Maguire. "The people were just glaring at us." The bus left just after noon with a police escort that disappeared by the time the bus reached the Alabama border. Crowds gathered at various points along the route. Some were curiosity seekers. Others shouted epithets at the passengers and even assaulted the bus in some of the towns along the way. Coffin, who had no formal training in nonviolent direct action, grew agitated and, according to Maguire, "wanted to take these guys on." The Greyhound arrived safely in Montgomery after linking up with a National Guard caravan outside the city.[3]

It was nearly five o'clock when the seven new arrivals debarked at the Montgomery greyhound terminal. Hundreds of National Guard troops were there to protect them, but the scene was still fraught. "We were out there about twenty minutes in this extraordinarily tense situation, with bricks occasionally being lobbed over," Maguire later remembered. The group spent that duration "sort of trying to smile, and very frightened."[4] Two vehicles arrived before long to collect Coffin's group. A reporter shouted a question about whether the Freedom Rides might embarrass the president on the eve of his summit meeting with Khrushchev, and Ralph Abernathy, one of the drivers, responded, "Doesn't the Attorney General know that we've been embarrassed all our lives?"[5] Someone threw a rock at Abernathy's car as it sped from the Montgomery bus station with the new arrivals.

Soon after, Coffin called both McGeorge Bundy, the president's chief advisor on foreign affairs and soon-to-be national security advisor, and Harris Wofford, in hopes of convincing the president to use "a little moral suasion" that would serve to "clear up the confusion in this country."[6] He also talked to Burke Marshall, who tried to dissuade them from continuing their planned challenge at the bus station in Montgomery.[7] The almost universal response from the administration was to pressure the group to reconsider, which left Coffin and the others shaken.[8] When doubt crept into the minds of the new arrivals, they held a prayer meeting with Martin Luther King Jr. and elected to sleep and tackle matters again in the morning. Kennedy, who had spent his undergraduate years at Harvard, tried to make light of the situation, quipping, "Those people at Yale are sore at Harvard for taking over the country, and now they're trying to get back at us."[9] Behind the joke, though, was a seething attorney general.

While May 25 was something of an interregnum in the Jackson phase of the Freedom Rides, Montgomery had returned to the fore. Reverend Seay was shot in the wrist by a bullet from a passing car, presumably in retaliation for his prominent role in working with the Freedom Riders. Meanwhile, Coffin and his friends had decided to continue on with the Montgomery challenge despite the increasing pressure from the Kennedy people.

With the media in full attendance, Coffin and the others, accompanied by Abernathy, Shuttlesworth, Wyatt Tee Walker, and King associate Bernard Lee, arrived at the station, bought tickets for the journey to Jackson, and made purchases at the lunch counter. As they waited for the scheduled bus departure, Sheriff Mac Sim Butler arrived, arrested all eleven men, and carted them to jail, charging them with breaching the peace after they started eating in the white side of the Trailways terminal. The group accepted bail, quickly raised by friends as well as students and faculty at Yale and Wesleyan upon hearing news of the arrests, after twenty-nine hours in the segregated jail. Coffin called the detentions "blatantly illegal and a travesty of justice."[10]

The group did not continue on to Mississippi, and Reverend Abernathy and the Riders filed suit immediately in federal district court asking for invalidation of Alabama's bus terminal segregation laws. The Department of Justice promptly filed an amicus brief at the prompting of the presiding judge; it also asked for an expedited hearing. That same day the New Orleans city council looked ahead to the likelihood of Freedom Riders crossing into their city and requested that the police escort any Riders nonstop through and out of the city.[11] CORE kept up its publicity barrage, sending Joe Perkins and other Freedom Riders on another junket of speaking engagements about CORE and the Freedom Rides.[12] The arrest of Coffin's contingent garnered massive media attention, becoming more fodder for an increasingly fierce media debate in the South and across the nation. The Freedom Ride experience turned Coffin, a previously obscure thirty-seven-year-old university chaplain, into something of a phenomenon, and he would continue to be active in political and social causes for the remainder of his life.[13]

That same day, fresh from his negotiations with Robert Kennedy, Senator Eastland lambasted the Freedom Rides from the Senate floor. Calling the Freedom Ride "part of the Communist movement in the U.S.," Eastland asserted that the Riders' visit to Mississippi marked the first time the people "of my state have come face to face with this world conspiracy." The senator made a connection between events down south and the impending summit meetings, claiming that civil rights activists intended to embarrass the United States and the president. He then went on to detail the arrest records of many of the Freedom Riders, including those in the first group, who had disbanded a week earlier after the nightmare in Alabama. In the end, Eastland argued, "the day has come when these agent provocateurs must be stopped, and I salute the governor and the officials of my state for the prompt, efficient and peaceful treatment that they extended to these riders who entered the state of Mississippi for the deliberate purpose of violating the laws of Mississippi and fomenting strife and discord."[14]

James Farmer had sent word to Jackson's sole black attorney, Jack Young, to contact CORE and keep the Freedom Riders "coming into Jackson as fast as possible on every bus . . . every train . . . and recruit madly and train." By this time, CORE "didn't have to do much recruiting because . . . the volunteers were barraging us."[15] At this stage of the Freedom Rides, CORE played a secondary role anyway. Diane Nash and other student leaders in Nashville had already taken care of assuring a steady flow of reinforcements long before Farmer tried to take charge again from jail. They had been training recruits, they had sent out a call for volunteers, and they were coordinating efforts to continue the Freedom Rides and deluge Mississippi with civil rights activists.

The twenty-seven Freedom Riders went to trial in Jackson's municipal court at four in the afternoon on May 26, with Jack Young and Wiley Branton, an NAACP lawyer from Pine Bluff, Arkansas, as their defense lawyers. By this point Roy Wilkins had yielded on his opposition to the Freedom Rides, and he provided Legal Defense Fund support for the group. Eventually, he even visited Freedom Riders in jail. He brought Jim Farmer a couple of books to read, including *To Kill a Mockingbird*.[16] The prosecutor, Jack Travis, barely made a case, simply announcing the charge, including the fact that the city was dropping a charge of refusing to obey a police officer, and telling the court: "They came to Mississippi to violate the laws of Mississippi and for no other reason. They were here under the most obvious circumstances—to breach the peace of this community and they did it." Travis then made an incredible statement: "If they had observed our laws they would have been welcome."[17]

Young tried to make an impassioned speech for his clients based on their desire to be treated like human beings. Judge James Spencer turned his back on Young and Blanton and stared at the wall while the lawyers vainly pleaded the case of the twenty-seven accused. Almost summarily, the judge found them guilty, sentenced them to sixty days in jail, suspended, and fined them two hundred dollars. He told them he believed they sought to "inflame the people," instead of letting the courts decide their rights, and he asserted that "we are not here trying any segregation laws or the rights to sit any place on buses or eat any place."[18]

The Freedom Riders chose not to pay their fine and thus accept guilt, meaning they would have to serve jail time, adopting the "jail, no bail" tactic. At a rate of three dollars per day, that meant that they faced sixty-seven days in jail. As more Riders joined them, the locus of the struggle effectively moved from the highways and bus stations to the courts and jails.

That day, CORE, SNCC, SCLC, and the Nashville movement joined forces to form the Freedom Ride Coordinating Committee (FRCC) to oversee the ongoing activities.[19] This marked a vital moment both for the Freedom Rides and for the Civil Rights Movement generally. With the formation of the FRCC, the mainline grassroots civil rights organizations had committed themselves to continue to take the challenge directly to Mississippi, to scoff at cooling-off periods, and instead to devote themselves to filling up Mississippi's jails, keeping national attention focused on Jim Crow in the realm of public transportation—and by extension public facilities—and forcing federal officials to act. Further, the establishment of the FRCC showed that rather than compete for resources and attention, the various civil rights organizations could instead combine forces. While territorial skirmishes would continue to haunt the movement at times after the Freedom Rides, the model of the FRCC would reemerge with the formation of the Albany Movement in Georgia a few months hence and with the Conference of Federated Organizations, a similar confluence of groups, in Mississippi during the intense struggle for voting rights.

That day Robert Kennedy addressed much of the world on Voice of America radio. He discussed the Freedom Rides, acknowledging that people worldwide were aware of what had happened in Alabama in the preceding weeks. He asserted that the American government was "disturbed about the fact that beatings took place and about the fact that people's rights were not being protected." The rest of the world heard the attorney general claim that those who participated in the attacks were part of a "small group" that "certainly [did] not represent the attitude of the U.S. Government or the American people." Then Kennedy began to stretch credulity for the purpose of public relations in the disputed battlefields of the Cold War. In "many areas of the United States," he boldly proclaimed, "there is no prejudice," an idea apparently validated by the fact that "Negroes hold high positions in the U.S. Government." One example of this was that "some of our leading judges are Negroes." Then, to justify American civil rights failings within the Cold War context, Kennedy told his listeners: "You have problems and difficulties in your areas. We have them here. Our society is set up so that everyone knows about our successes and they know about our failures." In his talks with civil rights activists, Kennedy had emphasized how disturbances down south might disrupt President Kennedy's important upcoming meetings. Robert Kennedy reiterated this concern in his radio address, though this time he seemed to be speaking to potential vigilantes as well as the Freedom Riders themselves when he practically pleaded that in light of the president's important trip, "whatever we do in the United States at this time, which brings or causes discredit on our country, can be harmful to his mission."[20]

Ross Barnett used his bully pulpit to keep up state resistance. As new Freedom Riders made their way toward Mississippi, Barnett declared that the state would maintain its segregation laws in the face of a new onslaught. In a press conference in the Mississippi Senate chambers before about forty-five visiting news reporters and photographers, the governor announced that new groups of Riders would find a police escort at the state line and that the police would arrest them if they broke state segregation laws. Barnett also praised the citizens of his state. "I am grateful to all of the people of Mississippi, including local and state officers, for their splendid and usual cooperation," he said. "It clearly demonstrates that Mississippi can certainly handle its own problems without aid from outside sources." Barnett rejected offers from Robert Kennedy and Whizzer White of federal troops or marshals, and he lamented "that all the people of Mississippi, both white and colored, cannot be permitted to live in peace and harmony, as we all want to do in order to better the educational standards and living conditions of all." In the end, he believed, "There is too much work to be done in Mississippi for us to have to put up with outside agitators trying to stir up our people for no good cause whatsoever."[21]

Barnett welcomed the visiting news people and announced that Mayor Thompson invited them to take a guided tour of the city that afternoon. Reporters had come from cities as far-flung as London, Toronto, New York, Washington, Miami, and Minneapolis.[22] About one-third of the reporters accepted Thompson's offer, prompting the *Memphis Commercial-Appeal* to run a wry headline: "Trailers of 'Freedom Riders' Taken on Bus Trip of Own." For the journalists who accepted the hospitality, there was quite a bit of emphasis on the progress of black Jacksonians, including a visit to a black junior high school where they talked to teachers and students. They also saw black housing developments and recreation facilities along with their public relations tour of white Jackson. The affable mayor, known for his sense of humor, sent his audience into paroxysms of laughter on several occasions. Of the city jail, where the Freedom Riders were ensconced even as the tour passed, Thompson told the media tourists: "One of our visitors said it was the prettiest jail he ever saw. We have some who keep coming back all the time." In all, the reporters were impressed with the tour and with the mayor, about whom an English newsman remarked, "What a wonderful guy. What a salesman."[23] The next day the Jackson Chamber of Commerce took the journalists out for a steak dinner.[24]

Mississippi officials realized that they were engaged in a war of public relations, among other things, and they were determined to put their best foot forward. Later in the summer, before a Rotary Club luncheon in Pocatello, Idaho, the State Sovereignty Commission's public relations director Erle Johnston declared that, far from bringing shame to Mississippi, the Freedom Riders had "actually done the state a service," because rather than bringing embarrassment or violence, "they brought many representatives of the news media into Mississippi who were able to learn firsthand how the two races live and work in harmony" in the Magnolia State.[25]

On May 27, Lucretia Collins allowed for her bond of five hundred dollars to be paid so that she could graduate with her class at Tennessee A&I. Once she bonded out, four other Freedom Riders—Julian Aaron, a student at Southern University; Jerome Smith, a former Southern student; Doris Castle, the CORE worker who had harassed Jim Farmer into taking the Freedom Ride from Montgomery; and David Dennis of Shreveport, a former Dillard University student—followed, leaving twenty-two of the second group still in jail.[26] The four Louisianans flew into New Orleans to deal with legal affairs and decide what to do next.

The next day eighteen new Freedom Riders showed up in Jackson on buses from Memphis and Montgomery. Seventeen of them went through the perfunctory arrest and court process and joined their cohort in jail. The eighteenth, Louis Jordan, a twenty-eight-year-old black man, rode into Jackson as a show of solidarity but did not participate in the challenge that led to the arrests, as he had to return to Brooklyn for work. The first group, which arrived at 5:30 that morning on a Greyhound, consisted of nine black students from Tennessee A&I College in Nashville. Catherine Burks, of Birmingham, led that group. It was a regularly scheduled bus and had no National Guard or other accompaniment. Twenty-year-old Nashvillean Pauline Edith Knight led the second team, which included two white students from historically black Central State College in Wilberforce, Ohio—David Myers and David Fankhauser. It arrived from Montgomery on a regularly scheduled Trailways bus at 2:00 P.M.[27]

David Fankhauser was a nineteen-year-old chemistry student at Central State.[28] He had seen the events in Alabama from afar on the news and in the papers, and when he saw a SNCC call for volunteers, he shaved his beard, cut his hair, put on his best clothes, and flew into Montgomery, where he was taken to Ralph Abernathy's house. At Abernathy's, the whites were instructed to stay away from the windows because knowledge of whites staying in a black home could lead to Klan retaliation. Fankhauser and Myers went to the train station the next day to meet new white Freedom Riders who were arriving in Montgomery by train, sent because it seemed wiser not to send blacks to pick up whites. On Sunday, May 28, the group got up early to go to the bus station, where there was already a police presence. On the bus were three National Guard troops, a small escort of a couple of Highway Patrol cars in front and in back. Some media members followed in their own cars. At each station where the bus stopped between Montgomery and Jackson, only passengers ticketed for that destination were allowed off the bus; the National Guard did not permit the Freedom Riders to debark at any point. As they entered Mississippi, a small convoy of Mississippi highway patrolmen took over the escort. There was a crowd at the Jackson Trailways station, but the police kept them at bay. The blacks entered the white waiting room, while the whites entered the black area. Upon arrest, the police took the blacks to the Hinds County jail and Myers and Fankhauser to the city jail.[29]

Both of the buses that day made their regularly scheduled stops, and none encountered violence. For the first time in Mississippi, Freedom Riders rode with regular passengers. On the bus from Nashville, Pauline Knight, one of the A&I students, sat next to Esther Crosby of Montgomery, who was on her way to visit a friend in Selma. After the trip, the middle-aged white woman told a reporter, "I didn't like it a bit." She and Knight did not speak. On the second bus, two men elected to stand in the aisle for about ten miles along the route. They refused to sit next to black passengers and refused to take seats near the rear, associating those with the Jim Crow seats in which blacks were supposed to sit.[30] The next day Judge Spencer convicted the seventeen Riders of breaching the peace and meted out two-hundred-dollar fines, which fourteen of them chose to work off at the three-dollar-a-day rate. Three bonded out for five hundred dollars. It must have struck Robert Kennedy that he could try to coerce the Freedom Riders all he wanted, but it would be to no avail.

On May 29, Freedom Riders took to the rails. A group of eight integrated travelers—five black, three white—led by James Kent Davis, a twenty-one-year-old black student leader from Claflin College in South Carolina, arrived aboard the Illinois Central Railroad from New Orleans. The ubiquitous Captain Ray was on hand to arrest them at the train station, as small groups of both whites and blacks gathered a distance from the station in what the *Memphis Commercial-Appeal* described as "a more or less gay mood." Jack Young stepped in as their lawyer and requested an expedited court date for that afternoon. Spencer gave the expected sixty-day suspended sentence and two-hundred-dollar fine, which most of the train passengers refused to pay, thus heading to Hinds County jail.[31] Within just a few days, fifty-two Freedom Riders had been arrested in Jackson.

Some among the new Freedom Riders were not as emotionally and mentally prepared as those who had come before them. James Farmer recalled how "many of the people who rushed in, including some of the SNCC people, were not prepared for this sort of thing." When they first arrived, they would be firm in their commitment, saying things such as, "We're gonna stay in 'til hell freezes over," but then, Farmer remembered, "after two days" they would be asking, "You got money to bail me out?"[32] Soon after arriving in the Jackson jail, a number of the Freedom Riders staged a hunger strike to protest both their arrests and their treatment.[33] This began a wave of dissension among the Freedom Riders, for while John Lewis knew that, among the new people, most "came with all their heart and soul and courage to put their bodies on the line for the cause of racial and human justice," there were many who "were not necessarily familiar with nor committed to the way of nonviolence." One Freedom Rider proved so difficult during the first day or two in jail that the group arranged to have him bailed out early so as not to destroy the group's morale.[34] In the end, James Farmer convinced his colleagues that a hunger strike was not the best tactical decision, and soon they relented.[35]

The jailed Freedom Riders were committed to remain imprisoned for forty days, which was the maximum time that they could stay in jail and still file an appeal. The purpose of doing this was to make their imprisonment as expensive as possible for Mississippi, while still getting the Freedom Riders their day in court and hopefully an appeal to the Supreme Court. The whole endeavor did cost Mississippi a great deal. As Farmer later put it, "they were spending barrels of money" on police, on the costs of using the Parchman unit, on feeding the Freedom Riders, and on a whole range of other expenses.[36]

Writing in the *CORElator*, James Farmer made the point that while "jails are no new experience for most of the Riders . . . the Riders were definitely a new experience for Mississippi jails."[37] In the jail cells, the Freedom Riders, separated by race and gender, sang. They developed special songs for Mississippi. One, sung to the tune of the old labor anthem "Which Side Are You On," went:

They say in Hinds County,
No neutrals they have met,
You're either for the Freedom Ride
Or you Tom for Ross Barnett.[38]

The jailers hated the freedom songs. They hated the Freedom Riders. So they started to play psychological games with the imprisoned men and women, denying them anything extra, such as the ability to purchase chewing gum or candy or—even more problematic for some of the activists— cigarettes. They denied them afternoon snacks. They refused to allow them any books or newspapers. The Freedom Riders were like alien creatures to the wardens. As James Farmer conceptualized it, "They tried to extract from each one of us a confession that we were Communists, drug addicts, homosexuals, we didn't know what we were doing, or we were being paid by some organization to do it." Dumbfounded prison guards kept saying, "Niggers don't do things like this."[39]

The whites were as much of an enigma to the jailers and to many in the outside world. At one point, authorities asked David Fankhauser to meet with a journalist, who turned out to be the right-wing columnist Westbrook Pegler. Pegler's line of questioning to Fankhauser culminated with, "Do you believe in money?" in an apparent effort to draw out communist leanings in the Freedom Ride and thus to discredit the movement. Fankhauser did not take the bait, and Pegler waved him away dismissively.[40]

The Freedom Riders persevered. John Lewis described how Jim Bevel "took center stage with his voice and his passion, preaching to whoever was within earshot while we sang in between his impromptu sermons."[41] The singing continued throughout the summer, and even some of the regular prisoners, convicted of assault and murder and robbery, joined in the movement songs.

Many of the Freedom Riders were transferred to the Hinds County jail, which was directly across the street from the city facility. The transfer occurred late at night under an overwhelming police show of force. This was done in part to prevent any outside interference from the Klan or other vigilantes, but it also served to reinforce the power of the Jackson officials to the civil rights activists. Freedom Rider Frank Holloway recalled that "when we went in" to the county jail, "we were met by some of the meanest looking, tobacco-chewing lawmen I have ever seen. They ordered us around like a bunch of dogs and I really began to feel like I was in a Mississippi jail."[42]

Whereas the city jail facilities were relatively modern, the county jail was decrepit and poorly ventilated. The black male Freedom Riders found themselves occupying one cell block, with a series of two-bed bunks and a common room. They shared a commode in the sleeping quarters and a single washbowl in the common room. The body odors soon became virtually noxious. When Farmer wondered aloud how their white counterparts were doing, one of the first hints of interracial antagonism cropped up, as one Nashville student sneered, "Oh, they probably have a suite of rooms with hot and cold running maids." The student then invoked an aphorism: "If you're white you're right; if you're brown, stick around; if you're black, get back."[43]

If the student expected his comments to meet with a wave of support and substantiation, he was sorely disappointed. Rather than pile on with speculation about the possible privileges of their white brethren, the more experienced people spoke at once to defend their white colleagues. Bernard Lafayette derided the speaker: "Man, you gotta be from the North; you don't know nothing about the South. If they're on our side, they'll get their asses kicked more than us. They always do. Man, the whites caught more hell riding through Alabama than the Negroes did. They almost got killed." Jim Farmer agreed with this observation and others that followed.[44]

One student talked about his experience on the picket lines in Memphis: "We got pushed around by the red-neck cops, but the whites got their heads split open." Another pointed out the differential treatment at a Nashville sit-in in March: "When they got through with us, all we needed was some Band-Aids and some rubbing alcohol. But man, the whites had to go to the hospital." In the end, the black students and their colleagues agreed with the student who said, "Yeah, man, the whites are looked at like traitors to their race, on top of everything else."[45] Throughout the Civil Rights Movement, blacks and whites cooperated in fighting injustice, but the Freedom Rides represent the apogee of this collaboration, and the spirited defense of the white Freedom Riders in that black cell block represents an understanding among the participants that white civil rights activists had earned their stripes on the battlefield. In the decades since 1961, most black Freedom Riders have continued to emphasize the importance, earnestness, and sacrifice of their white friends and fellow soldiers.

The student who suggested that the white Freedom Riders might have it easy having been chastened, thoughts turned to the women in the group. Some worried about girlfriends. Others tried not to think about matters in the women's wing. Actually, the women were in pretty good spirits, all things considered. In a letter to CORE's Gordon Carey, Betsy Wyckoff, one of about ten female Freedom Riders from the New York City area in the Hinds County jail, wrote, "All goes on swimmingly—in more senses than one, as we sure do swelter." She explained how most of the Freedom Riders were college aged, with the exception of "one old married woman of 26" and the occasional appearance of "an interesting local tossed in with us." The white and black women were segregated, but the black women were in two cells on the same corridor, and they often sang songs. The presence of the other group of women "is very nice for us," explained Wyckoff, "especially as we haven't a decent voice in the bunch, but we can enjoy listening to them and chiming in—not too loud." A hint of the stress they were under was that "those of us who smoke have all started smoking like chimneys recently," but in general "everyone's spirits are good," even though "we were sad last night when some of our friends left." There was not much for them to do in the jail, so showers had become "a principal diversion." In all, "we are not badly off," she assured Carey, "what with plumbing that works and plenty of mattresses." Things improved markedly later that day when the women received clean new shirts, shorts, underwear, and toiletries from a local church group, "all of which caused morale to soar."[46]

Freedom songs continued to bond the group, men and women. At two in the morning on one of their first nights in the county jail, Jim Bevel began singing another freedom song:

If you can't find me in the backa the bus
You can't find me nowhere,
Oh-h, come on up to the fronta the bus,
I'll be ridin' up there.

I'll be ridin' up there—up there
I'll be ridin' up there.
Oh-h come on up to the fronta the bus,
I'll be ridin' up there.[47]

They continued to sing. Soon their voices merged with the sounds of song from other wings and other floors. Women's voices came through from one wing. White male voices came through from another floor. White women joined in as well. A fellowship of song pervaded the whole Hinds County jail, white and black voices, those of men and women, ignoring the menacing threats of the guards, ignoring the fact that it was the middle of the night. Within days the Freedom Riders had recruited the regular prisoners. The activists taught the regulars their protest songs and spirituals in exchange for learning work songs, prison songs, and even new spirituals and protest songs. Music brought people together.

Parchman Farm

Before long word came down from an old black trustee who whispered a message: "They're gonna send you to the prison farm. That's where they're gonna try to break you. They're gonna try to whip your ass."[48] In the dead of night, the paddy wagons came and brought the Freedom Riders to the Hinds County prison farm, where they stayed for just over two weeks. Frank Holloway recalled arriving at the penal farm. "When we got there, we met several men in ten-gallon hats, looking like something out of an old Western, with rifles in their hands, staring at us."[49]

Conditions worsened out in the country. Part of the reason for the transfer was simply that the Freedom Riders had filled the jails in the city, and there was no more space. But from the state's perspective, the county work farm offered the prisoners extra hardships. The cells were smaller than in the city jail, and there were not enough beds for all of the prisoners, so many slept on the floor or benches or wherever they could sprawl. Although at a work farm, the Freedom Riders were not allowed to labor like the other prisoners; their only exercise was the rigorous cleaning of their cells with mops and brooms that the guards supplied. They were confined to their cells, their food rations barely enough to survive.

Sometimes the abuse became physical, such as when a guard gave Reverend C. T. Vivian a beating with a blackjack for refusing to preface remarks to the guard with "sir." He emerged from the confrontation with blood gushing from his head.[50] Vivian had been a particular thorn in the side of the guards for his unwillingness to sacrifice his dignity in the face of the epithets and intimidation that the guards daily presented.

Richard Haley of the CORE office in Chicago arrived in Jackson to investigate the assault on May 28 and filed a complaint with the FBI, which promptly began an investigation.[51] This fray led to the brief suspension of Max Thomas, superintendent of the county penal farm, but he was back in place within a few days after an internal investigation found that Thomas had been hurt in the process of defending himself in a scuffle with Vivian.[52] Vivian was a committed nonviolent activist, and a number of Freedom Rider witnesses refuted the assertion that Vivian had engaged in any sort of violence, but this did not matter in the eyes of the Hinds County officials. The assault and subsequent investigations led to a dilemma for the state. Thus far they had managed to avoid the negative publicity that had so tainted Alabama. Mississippi authorities were not about to yield to the Freedom Riders, but they also could not allow police brutality to destroy the finely honed system that had served them so well. Officials chose not to send any more Freedom Riders to the Hinds County work farm. Instead, Freedom Riders would go to Jackson's city jail or the Hinds County jail in the short-term and then on to Parchman Farm.[53] As James Farmer put it, "Washington was watching now," and so the Mississippi authorities "had better not take liberties with the hated Kennedys."[54]

Despite the prison-imposed news blackout, news filtered through of the flood of new Freedom Riders pouring in from the North, South, East, and West, from college campuses and churches and labor unions and all walks of life. Some were members of CORE or SNCC, responding to calls from those organizations to fill up the jails.[55] Most were not. Local NAACP chapters held various fund-raisers and got the word out about the ongoing rides into Mississippi.[56] The Fellowship of Reconciliation, CORE's partner in the Journey of Reconciliation fourteen years earlier, solicited both support and participation in the Rides from its members after the first wave of Jackson arrests.[57] The Southern Regional Council also voiced its support and dedicated resources to helping the cause.[58] The Freedom Rides had spawned a genuine and enduring movement. In all, 328 persons were jailed in Mississippi in the summer of 1961, with dozens more meeting resistance at other points across the South. There were many more who could be called "Freedom Riders" in the three months after the first students went to jail in Jackson.[59]

Of those arrested in the state capital, two-thirds were college students, three-fourths were men, and more than half were black. The Freedom Riders had set in motion something that had become, in James Farmer's words, "a different and far grander thing than we had intended."[60] Even as Martin Luther King Jr. somewhat bizarrely announced a "temporary lull but no cooling-off" in the Freedom Rides, a statement bound to alienate many and please none, the new wave of Riders ensured that there would be neither a lull nor a cooling.

At the same time, unprecedented contributions poured into CORE's coffers to provide much-needed financial support for the Freedom Riders. CORE gradually emerged as the most powerful and important of the

FRCC sister organizations, and it used its resources to handle much of the training, travel arrangements, financing, and logistics of the summer's deluge of protesters into Mississippi and Alabama. The FRCC established training centers in Atlanta, Nashville, and New Orleans, and CORE took primary responsibility for training volunteers for the challenges ahead. Many others traveled independently from colleges and universities, providing a model for Freedom Summer in Mississippi a couple of years down the road.

The *Jackson Daily News* encouraged Mississippians to stay the course in the face of new influxes of "misguided young people." The newspaper urged its readers to "permit the officers of the law [to] handle this group without hindrance." The editors believed that the new group came from CORE; if they tried "to create a violent incident," the editors, urged, "let's do not be provoked by their unlawful acts into lawlessness of our own. Let's just let the officers show the invaders quietly to our jails."[61] Governor Patterson of Alabama continued to chastise the Kennedys for letting the "racial extremists" engage in an "all out 'invasion' of Mississippi, our sister state."[62]

Only a handful of the newcomers joined the group at Hinds County's prison farm, which proved to be merely a way station en route to the place that had for generations inspired fear in black Mississippians: Parchman Farm, a place that historian David Oshinsky has described as presenting dreadful conditions that some have called "worse than slavery."[63] On the fifteenth of June, well after midnight, guards rousted the male Freedom Riders from their cramped, uncomfortable cells and marched the forty-five of them like cattle out into big trailers with no windows and no seats. The guards closed and locked the doors, leaving the Freedom Riders in total darkness as the truck pulled out for its journey up Highway 49. For a couple of hours, the prisoners stumbled into one another as the truck bounced and jostled over country highways and curves, the driver periodically slamming the brakes or taking a corner a bit too quickly, smashing the Riders against one another or into the walls of the trailer. One of the vehicles broke down, and a pickup truck carrying the group's luggage had to tow it the last few miles of the journey. When the guards finally opened the door again, the group was more than a hundred miles from Jackson, in northwest Mississippi, at Parchman State Penitentiary.

John Lewis had "heard about Parchman in the same way I'd heard about Mississippi—in tones of horror and terms of brutality. In a South filled with nightmarishly inhuman prisons and work farms, Parchman Penitentiary was infamous for being the worst." Fred Jones lorded over Parchman as its superintendent. He met the Freedom Riders as they stepped off the truck. "We have some bad niggers here," he sneered as he chewed on an unlit cigar. "We have niggers on death row that'll beat you up and cut you as soon as look at you." Then one of the guards began herding the group toward the prison gates. "Go ahead and sing your goddamned freedom songs now," he said. "We got niggers here that will eat you *up*. So you go and sing your songs inside now."[64]

Just at that moment two of the white Freedom Riders, Terry Sullivan and Felix Singer, went limp, forcing the guards to drag them by their legs from the truck. "What you actin' like that for?" one of the guards asked, amused at the antics of the young men. "Ain't no newspapermen out here." John Lewis later acknowledged that the guard had a point: "There was nothing out there but them and us—and, oddly, a small flock of ducks and geese waddling around near the barbed-wire fence." The fence seemed to stretch forever in both directions, serving as the perimeter of the 21,000-acre prison farm. Lewis mused that he "imagined the birds as some form of barnyard warning system, quacking and honking at the sound of escapees in the night."[65]

Their fellow Freedom Riders watched as guards threw Sullivan and Singer from their van onto the sand and gravel drive and dragged them through wet grass, muddy puddles, and across a rough cement walkway. Sullivan replied to the guard's query by saying, "We refuse to cooperate because we have been unjustly imprisoned." Eventually, the guards used a cattle prod to try to move the two men, but to no avail. The guards finally stripped the two men naked and threw them into a cell.[66] The rest were told to strip as well. Then they stood there for two and a half hours, waiting to see what was next. John Lewis "could see that this was an attempt to break us down, to humiliate and dehumanize us, to rob us of our identity and self worth." By the time they "were finally led, two by two, into a shower room guarded by a sergeant with a rifle, I thought of the concentration camps in Germany. This was 1961 in America, yet here we were, treated like animals for using the wrong restroom."[67] In the showers, those men with facial hair were told to shave.

The Freedom Riders hoped to be able to work at Parchman, but instead they found themselves confined to the maximum-security wing of the vast prison complex, which held not only the most dangerous and incorrigible prisoners but also the electric chair. The guards herded them into six-by-ten compartments, which each housed two prisoners, and gave each prisoner a tin cup and a toothbrush. The cells were segregated. The horseshoe-shaped cellblock was not. A tall, burly guard passed shorts and tee-shirts through the bars to the men. These scanty clothes would be the male Freedom Riders' uniform while at Parchman. As if this was not humiliating enough, the guards often gave the bigger men tiny undershorts and the smaller men big, baggy shorts. James Farmer later remembered that the "big guys were trying to hold theirs shut and the little guys were trying to stay in theirs and keep 'em from falling down." The guards further arranged things so that big guys shared cells with big guys, small with small, to prevent clothes swapping.[68] Someone complained, and James Bevel's booming voice rose above the crowd: "What's this hang-up about clothes?" He demanded from his colleagues: "Gandhi wrapped a rag around his *balls* and brought down the whole British *Empire!*"[69]

About a week later the state shipped its first truckload of women Freedom Riders up to Parchman. The young women were split almost equally between white and black. The guards brought in the women in groups of three or four at about seven P.M. on June 23. From that point on, the goal in Jackson was to process arrests as quickly as possible and shuttle Freedom Riders from Jackson to Parchman "as soon as possible after their arrests," according to Sheriff J. R. "Bob" Gilfoy.[70] Upon arrival in Parchman, the women were issued skirts with stripes and then put into the maximum-security unit of the women's side of the prison.[71]

Carol Ruth Silver, a recent University of Chicago graduate, was among this initial group of women to arrive at Parchman Farm, as part of the new group of Riders to head in the direction of Mississippi after the first wave of Jackson arrests. They had arrived in Jackson, tried to use the bus facilities, and found themselves first in the Jackson city jail and then in the county jail. When they first heard about the men being transferred to Parchman, some of the women engaged in an ill-fated hunger strike that almost divided the women when a number of them, prompted by their lawyer Jack Young's admonition that a hunger strike would not be an effective protest measure, called a halt to the strike without consulting the whole group. On June 23, the women, by now numbering twenty-three, heard the news: they were going to Parchman Farm.[72]

Silver recalled the four-hour trip to Parchman as the most frightening aspect of the jail experience. The women, wearing shorts or slacks and, in the estimation of one journalist, "looking surprisingly fresh" given their time in the county jail, were packed into a hot, sweaty truck with bad shocks that Carol Ruth Silver felt "bounced along towards an unknown future."[73] As they were loaded onto the bus, many of them joked and teased the police. The officers loaded black and white women together, prompting one of the Freedom Riders, a "wispy blonde," according to a reporter, to comment, "Glory be, the cops are putting us on an integrated bus."[74] The mood was far less jocular on the way to Parchman. Three times the vehicle jolted to a stop, and the women could not help but "imagine . . . every horror from a waiting ambush of Ku Klux Klan to mined roads."[75]

Meanwhile, earlier that same day, four black Jacksonians brought a new approach to the Freedom Ride movement when they walked into the Trailways station in Jackson and announced that they wanted to buy tickets to leave. Then they walked into the white waiting room and refused to move when told to do so, leading to their arrests. CORE representative Haley told reporters later that the action proved "that Negroes in Jackson have graduated from the wish for freedom to the act."[76]

The Freedom Riders sang at Parchman as they had everywhere else. The warden threatened and cajoled the Freedom Riders to stop. These efforts just made them sing louder. The warden told them their singing bothered the cooks. David Fankhauser remembered that this complaint "seem[ed] hilarious to us, since the cooks were black trustees who clearly were getting a kick out of our spirit and defiance."[77] The warden then threatened to take their toothbrushes away, which similarly got him nowhere. Finally, on June 24, the singing got to be too much for the guards, who stormed the cell block and took the mattresses out of the cells, leaving only the cement floor or the steel bed frame upon which to sleep. The deputy had threatened to remove the mattresses earlier in the night, and Hank Thomas had shouted back, "Take my mattress! I'll keep my soul!" With that, almost everyone took their mattresses off their beds and leaned them against the cell walls so that they were right there when the guards came to seize them.[78] The Freedom Riders responded with good humor at first, continuing to sing and even making up verses and songs about their newest hurdle.

The guards returned the mattresses the next night, but when the group started to sing again, the guards returned, this time with some of the other, non–Freedom Rider inmates in tow. Fred Leonard shared a cell with Stokely Carmichael, who would go on to achieve fame for his leadership in the Black Power movement.[79] Leonard told Carmichael, "I'm not letting my mattress go," even as his colleagues sang, "Freedom's coming and it won't be long." The guards came again and started taking mattresses. Most let go peacefully, but true to his word, Leonard held on tight to his.

The guards dragged him and his mattress out into the cell block. One of the guards called to an inmate, "Peewee, get him." Peewee was a short, muscular black inmate, and what he had to do next clearly devastated him. Leonard recalled, "Peewee came down on my head. *Whomp, whomp*—he was crying. Peewee was crying. And I still had my mattress. Do you remember when your parents used to whup you and say, 'It's going to hurt me more than it hurts you'? It hurt Peewee more than it hurt me." Leonard held tight, so the guards came by "and clamped these things on my wrists like handcuffs," called "wristbreakers," "and they started twisting and tightening them up—my bones started cracking . . . and finally I turned my mattress loose."[80]

The guards blasted the cell block with fire hoses and then turned on exhaust fans full blast, bringing in the cool night air. Many of the Freedom Riders came down with colds.[81] Most had no idea that it could seem so cold on a summer night in Mississippi. At the other extreme, on especially hot days, of which there were many, the guards kept the windows closed, and the Freedom Riders stewed in the suffocating heat. Lights stayed on around the clock. Sleep could be virtually impossible. The guards banged on cell doors with billy clubs at all hours. They removed screens from the windows, allowing the voracious Delta mosquitoes and other pests to ravage the Freedom Riders. The presence of the bugs provided a pretense for the guards to call in exterminators to spray DDT with what looked like a fire hose, drenching the prisoners with the toxic fumes and liquid.[82]

The women faced similar difficulties. When they sang, they lost their mattresses. They tried to sing the "Star-Spangled Banner," and they lost their sheets. Then the guards took their towels and toothbrushes. At one point Ruby Doris Smith faced physical abuse from the prison guards when she refused to take a shower without sandals. The women guards forced her into the shower area in handcuffs, scrubbed her forcefully with a brush, and knocked her down several times while holding on to the handcuffs.[83]

Smith and nine other black women were eventually taken to live in the prison infirmary. Conditions were much better there, but through the windows they could see the prison work detail out in the fields: "There were fifty, sixty Negro men in striped uniforms, guarded by a white man on a white horse. It reminded you of slavery."[84] One of the Freedom Riders miscarried while a prison guard watched and did nothing. The two months Smith spent imprisoned for her activities with the Freedom Riders proved to be profoundly transformative, helping her to grow as a political and tactical movement leader and instilling strength and confidence within her. At one point during Smith's incarceration, Ella Baker wrote Smith a letter in which she expressed her "continued pride in the courage you have manifested on more than one occasion." She hoped that Smith's "present experience has not been too trying for you" and "that your health will not suffer" as a result of her jail experience. Baker's biographer Barbara Ransby has argued, "In seeking to strengthen the resolve and confidence of Smith and other young women, Baker wanted them to rise toward leadership roles in the larger movement."[85]

As a consequence of all the travails, the mood inevitably turned sour in the cell block. When a group of Freedom Riders braved the wrath of the guards by singing further, several of the authorities tightly slapped the same sort of "wrist breakers" on them that they had used on Fred Leonard and dragged the students down the hall by these clamps, tossing them in six-by-six-foot solitary confinement boxes for two days. Some of the students sang "I'm Going to Tell God How You Treat Me" as they were pulled to their confinement.

Meanwhile, as the days and weeks passed, more Freedom Riders, men and women, rolled into Parchman, past the razor-wire fences and guard towers, past the endless acres of prisoners laboring. They usually came in on gray prison buses with metal seats and bars on the windows.

At one point Ross Barnett paid a visit. Many of the Freedom Riders recognized the governor from his pictures. He stopped at James Farmer's cell, and after exchanging introductions, he asked, "Are they treating you all right here?" Farmer responded by saying, "Well, there's been no brutality, no physical brutality. We haven't been beaten or anything." Barnett responded, satisfied, "You got no complaints?" Farmer was shocked: "I didn't say that. The biggest complaint is that we are here." Barnett just nodded and walked off.[86] Barnett had instructed the Parchman authorities not to engage in brutality against the prisoners, although the guards had a pretty long tether.

Soon after, Farmer went before the prison superintendent to protest their treatment. Accompanied by two guards, he desperately tried to keep his undershorts, which he could not button, from falling. When he got to the office of the director of prisons, he was forced to stand nearly naked while a well-dressed man sat smoking a cigar.[87] Farmer pleaded his case, hoping for some sort of compromise, but instead he was told that things would get worse for the group if they did not start to cooperate. Farmer asked for a written list of rules to clarify what was meant by cooperation, but he was rebuffed there as well. The Freedom Riders then worked together to develop their own list of rules based on the principle that they wanted to respect the authorities but deserved to be treated as human beings.

Some of the Freedom Riders resumed fasting. Price Chatham lost about thirty-five pounds. He was one of a handful who, in the words of Freedom Rider and Parchman detainee William Mahoney, "fasted until there was a thin line between life and death."[88] Chatham, a twenty-nine-year-old white man from East Rockaway, New York, continued his hunger strike for more than twenty days before relenting and taking food. At one point Chatham's young son, Rhys, wrote the Kennedys in scrawling penmanship. "My father is in a big prison. He is a Freedom Rider," Rhys Chatham pleaded, "not a criminal. I can't get in touch with my father any more. My mother is worried. He wasn't eating for 20 days now. Please get him out of prison." On June 30, Rhys received a response from Harris Wofford. "Dear Mister Chatham," wrote the President's Special Assistant. "The President wants me to thank you for your letter about your father. I am happy to hear your father is now eating. When your father comes home he will talk with you about the reason he stayed in prison." Wofford also sent the young boy a copy of the petition the attorney general had filed with the Interstate Commerce Commission.[89] The New Frontiersmen, it is clear, had a deft way with children.

Others did not fast, and some behaved ignobly by gorging themselves in front of those who did, many of whom gave in after a few days or less. Then again, the food was atrocious. Even those who did not fast often ate as little as possible. Sometimes the authorities saturated the food with salt. Sometimes it arrived cold or even uncooked. Portly James Farmer lost thirty pounds, and he did not even fast.[90] David Fankhauser remembered the Parchman meal regimen: "Breakfast every morning was coffee strongly flavored with chicory, grits, biscuits and blackstrap molasses. Lunch was generally some form of beans or black-eyed peas boiled with pork gristle and cornbread. Evening was the same as lunch except it was cold." Nonetheless, "after fasting for twelve days," Fankhauser "ate everything with gusto."[91]

The activists persevered. They carried out group devotions in which they prayed and sang. They used the tunes of spirituals, work songs, and union songs and made up lyrics based on their experiences as Freedom Riders. The only reading material they were permitted was the Bible— except for the whites, who were also given copies of Carleton Putnam's pseudoscientific anthropological quackery, *Race and Reason—A Yankee View*, a publication popular among the Citizens' Council crowd. They did their best to fight off boredom. Often they argued over tactics and philosophy. Given the constraints under which they operated, disputes occasionally grew heated. Twice a week they left their cells to shower. Once a week they were allowed to write a letter. Unlike Lucretia Collins, Lewis elected not to post bond to attend his graduation from American Baptist Theological Seminary that summer. "It was unreal in a way to be sitting in a Mississippi penal farm's maximum security cellblock while many of my classmates were marching in procession in their commencement caps and gowns," Lewis later wrote. "But I really felt there was no better place for me to be than right where I was."[92]

Eventually, outsiders with a certain amount of influence began to look more closely at what was going on in Parchman. One morning the warden was clearly in a conciliatory mood. He claimed that they had all gotten off on the wrong foot and gave the prisoners back their bedding, Bibles, toothbrushes, and everything else he had confiscated. In return he asked them to keep the singing down and restricted to certain times. This largesse did not come from a change of heart or a spirit of reconciliation. Delegations from various states were beginning to express interest in the plight of the Riders.

The activists had gotten the word out to their connections in the civil rights community, and in July a group from Minnesota visited Parchman on behalf of that state's governor.[93] A few of the Freedom Riders came from that Northern bastion of progressivism, and the visiting delegation wanted to see firsthand what sort of treatment the civil rights workers were receiving. The authorities confined the Minnesotans to one section, and when the visitors came, the guards did not allow them past the cells into which the Minnesota Freedom Riders had been shifted. For whatever reason, when asked about their treatment, the students understated the level of deprivation and maltreatment. David Fankhauser, in a cell adjacent to one of the Minnesota cells, called out that he was sure other Freedom Riders would have information that they would want to hear. One of the guards tried to intervene, infuriating some of the dignitaries and causing them to threaten that they would report that the Parchman authorities were uncooperative. After lengthy negotiations, the delegation visited the whole wing and got a more complete picture of conditions in the prison. Soon some things improved—the window screens were put back in place and the bedding returned. They were even granted the right to receive correspondence, though this was a Pyrrhic victory, as most letters were severely censored. Fankhauser remembered getting one letter that said, "Dear David," and then "the whole rest of the letter was cut out leaving a hole," with the closing "good bye" left intact.[94] Nonetheless, according to at least one Freedom Rider, the visit of the Minnesota delegation and the resulting improvements "raised morale considerably"; it was his hope that CORE might be able to arrange more such outside contacts and shows of concern.[95]

At five o'clock on the afternoon of July 7, those remaining from the first groups of Freedom Riders were released on appeal bonds of five hundred dollars provided by CORE. They had served their forty days in jail and wanted to preserve their right to appeal their sentences. The guards handed the haggard new releases the things with which they had arrived, returned their clothes, and accompanied them to the front gate. There a small group of friends and lawyers waited to greet them. There were solemn hugs, and the group piled into a line of cars that drove them away. When this first group left, there were still one hundred Freedom Riders—the reinforcements sent in by the Freedom Ride Coordinating Committee—confined at Parchman, and these numbers continued to grow. In the next few days, another group was released. This pattern continued through the summer, with new Freedom Riders coming in, about to face whatever Parchman Farm had to offer, while grizzled veterans departed after forty days.

When David Fankhauser left Parchman Farm on Sunday, July 9, just two days after the release of the first group, one of the most hostile of the guards approached him as he dressed. The guard "came up to me and said that he hoped there were no hard feelings. He said he was only doing his job, didn't I understand, and that he didn't personally hate us. I thought that was a very positive statement for him to say."[96]

The Freedom Rides and the subsequent events in Mississippi's jails, especially Parchman Farm, were, in the words of imperturbable civil rights activist Reverend C. T. Vivian, "a national action." Vivian argued: "Now we were challenging states' rights, we were challenging the laws across state lines and people came from all over the country. That's the first time people had come from all over the country into a major movement." Jail merely served to reinforce everything the activists believed in. In Vivian's words: "The feeling of people coming out of the jail was one that they had triumphed, that they had achieved, that they were now ready, they could go back home, they could be a witness to a new understanding. Nonviolence was proven in that respect. It had become a national movement and there was no doubt about it, for common people in many places in the country. And there was a new cadre of leaders."[97]

The summer progressed, and the Freedom Riders did not relent. The Kennedy administration would finally and unequivocally have to intervene as the Civil Rights Movement forged inexorably onward.

Chapter 12

Conclusion

Legacies of the Freedom Rides

Justice, the Kennedys, and the ICC:
The Movement Rolls On

They kept coming. Even as the first groups of Freedom Riders arrested in Jackson dispersed, heading back to their homes—some to regroup and return to the civil rights struggle right away, others to go back to their colleges and universities, pulpits and jobs—volunteers kept coming. Ministers came from out west. College students flocked in from Wisconsin and New York and Massachusetts and all across the North. Black students across the South joined their colleagues in the jails. Most went to Mississippi, but others found the chance to stand up to Jim Crow in New Orleans and Nashville, Tallahassee and Tuscaloosa, and all points in between. Many Americans did not understand why the activists had to persist in their challenge. A June 1961 Gallup Poll indicated that 64 percent of respondents voiced disapproval when asked the question, "Do you approve or disapprove of what the 'Freedom Riders' are doing?" This negative sentiment was one that a majority of whites would continue to express when polled about civil rights demonstrations for the next few years.[1] Nonetheless, the movement progressed undaunted, activists realizing full well that all gains in eradicating Jim Crow had come over the protestations of whites.

But Mississippi remained front and center, and as those who were released prepared to move on, Mississippi had one last surprise for them: each of the cases would have to be adjudicated individually. CORE, which had taken responsibility for the defense, the posting of bond, and the appeals in the Freedom Ride cases, had expected that the state would handle the matter by arguing a few test cases that would speak for the whole. The state remained firm on its policy, however, not only for the first groups but for all of the subsequent Freedom Riders, more than three hundred in all. CORE would lose its bond money, a sacrifice that the organization feared would bankrupt it. CORE had to track down every one of the Freedom Riders and ensure that they got back to Mississippi. This time, however, they were forbidden to break laws, as legal fees, bail bond, transportation fees, and ancillary expenses were mounting. Just when the Freedom Rides seemed over, their hangover seemed ready to hit and hit hard.

On May 29, the same day that Patterson declared the end of martial law in Montgomery, the government began to flex its muscles in the legal arena. In that city, the trial began in federal district court on the government's complaints against the Birmingham and Montgomery police officials. Continuing the frenzy of activity from Washington, Attorney General Kennedy requested that the Interstate Commerce Commission pass regulations banning segregation in interstate bus terminals. Although the ICC and the Supreme Court had already spoken on this issue, renewed ICC regulations would give the ICC impetus to enforce integration throughout interstate transport on conveyances and on the ground.

The ICC conducted hearings on Kennedy's request on August 15. Kennedy made some proposals on behalf of the Justice Department, and Carl Rachlin, general counsel for CORE, similarly presented the ICC with a series of requests.[2] Five weeks later, on September 22, ICC officials issued an order banning segregation in interstate terminal facilities.[3] On October 16 three major railroads serving the Deep South announced that they would end segregation in both trains and terminals. The ICC order went into effect on November 1, followed by tests to determine compliance. These tests often came from ICC workers, but groups from the civil rights community also conducted tests. For example, the day after the ICC ruling went into effect, CORE dispatched people on buses to determine the level of adherence to the decree.[4] Furthermore, the ICC investigated complaints from individuals across not only the South but the country for the remainder of the decade. Although Mississippi, parts of Louisiana, and much of southern Georgia still remained intransigent in the months after the ICC enforcement decision, ICC responsiveness to Kennedy's request proved to expedite desegregation of Southern transport and revealed that Kennedy had been utterly off-base when he told King and the civil rights community that their actions in Mississippi would not make a bit of difference. Taylor Branch points out that many observers found the attorney general's ability to expedite the ICC action to be "a bureaucratic miracle."[5]

As Kennedy began to push for a renewed commitment to voting rights, most of the rest of the summer, for the Freedom Riders and their supporting organizations, was as much about the dreary details of legalese as about frontal challenges to Jim Crow. With Mississippi's decision to make each Freedom Rider stand trial individually, the FRCC, with CORE at the forefront, had to track down every arrested activist no matter how they had gotten to Jackson, no matter what their affiliation. Trial dates ran from August into the New Year, with more scheduled with each wave of releases from Parchman Farm.[6] The civil rights organizations had to track down those who had slipped through the cracks, and at times, after their release, Freedom Riders sought help with things such as getting jobs, in addition to the legal support provided by CORE, the NAACP's Inc. Foundation (part of the Legal Defense Fund and run autonomously by Thurgood Marshall), and the FRCC.[7] This was all on top of trying to maintain some semblance of control over the ongoing Freedom Rides, reassure antsy parents, pressure the Kennedys, keep a watchful eye over the authorities in Mississippi and Alabama, develop future strategy, and instigate future civil rights programs.

Perhaps the most pressing concern of all was the squeeze for money. Up to July 27, CORE had spent $138,500 on the Freedom Rides. This included $72,700 in bail in Jackson, as well as in Tallahassee and Ocala, Florida, where Freedom Riders had also been arrested. About $32,400 had gone to travel for the Freedom Riders, and the rest had gone toward legal fees, travel expenses to stand trial, the training of Freedom Riders, hospital bills, phone and telegram expenses, and various office costs, including printing fees. None of this took into account overhead, regular office expenses, fund-raising costs, or the expense of other concurrent activities. CORE expected to spend another $148,000 by Labor Day.[8] As James Farmer put it, while CORE "tried to break" the city of Jackson, "they tried to break us."[9] The Freedom Riders had caused the city of Jackson and the state of Mississippi to overextend their means.[10] By raising each Rider's bond from $500 to $1500 cash, Jackson almost succeeded in overextending CORE, but fund-raising, help from other organizations (most notably the Inc. Foundation), and clever allocation of resources, as well as substantial borrowing, kept CORE afloat.[11] The LDF also used its "Committee of 100" lawyers to defend the Freedom Riders engaged in fund-raising efforts for the cause.[12] Local and regional groups, such as the Bay Area Freedom Riders Fund, also engaged in extensive fund-raising to help defray the costs of locals who had gone to Mississippi to join the freedom struggle.[13] CORE maintained a resolute public face, and as costs added up and expenses became an issue, Farmer told reporters, "We were not under any illusions that freedom would come quickly."[14]

Furthermore, many of the individual Freedom Riders fell on hard times, particularly some of those who were not among the early Freedom Riders, who enjoyed the glow of semi-celebrity that America periodically grants even the most unlikely individuals. Reverend James E. Warren, who had been arrested eleven times for violating segregation laws since joining the Freedom Rides in late May, was one such neglected activist. A photographer from *Look* magazine had captured one of Warren's arrests in Tallahassee's airport. Warren went to the NAACP to try to get help in paying his legal expenses for a trial in Jackson that was to take place in January 1962, as well as in getting him back to his hometown of Los Angeles, where on November 1, 1961, he would start a job as a teacher. He had gone on several CORE speaking tours, but these generally did not generate enough money to allow speakers to live very comfortably, and many of them barely recouped much revenue even for CORE's coffers. In Arkansas, when Warren was asleep on a bus en route to Los Angeles, someone stole what money he had, and he felt compelled to go to the NAACP for help. That organization's Little Rock chapter raised funds to get him a ticket back to California, bought him lunch, and provided dinner for him at the home of a Little Rock NAACP stalwart. They also gave him the change, amounting to $13.13, from the money they had raised for bus fare.[15] Warren was not the only former Freedom Rider to have to seek support from the NAACP, CORE, SNCC, and local organizations affiliated with the Freedom Rides and the renewed wave of activism they had spawned nationally.

The Freedom Riders received little relief in the Mississippi courts. They did not expect to. At every turn of appeal, Mississippi judges upheld the guilty verdicts and the attendant fines and prison terms. Given that many of the terms had been served, the fines paid through jail time, and a good many of the sentences suspended, there was little at stake except perhaps the most important issue of all: principle. Segregationist judges were willing to subvert the stubborn fact of constitutional law for the principle of state's rights. Even mediocre first-year law students know about the Supremacy Clause and what it means for state-federal relations. Yet in Mississippi, interposition was and would be the modus operandi, whether it was articulated as such or not. Judge Sidney Mize, a federal judge and unreconstructed segregationist, made effective alliance with the state by refusing to grant the Riders a writ of habeas corpus, thus forcing them to carry their case through the state courts.[16]

When original Rider Hank Thomas appealed to the Mississippi Supreme Court, he was afforded a glance at the willfulness of the state's officialdom. In 1964, with Justice Henry Lee Rogers writing the unanimous opinion, the court determined that "the jury was warranted in deciding" that Thomas "intended to create disorder and violence which was imminent at the time when he refused to obey a police officer's order to move on." Rogers used the standard accusatory language in describing the Freedom Rider as intending "to show disapproval of segregation laws and to incite violence rather than . . . to prove his right to travel unhampered in interstate commerce." Thomas and his companions "obviously realized," Rogers wrote, "that such a publicized invasion might create a holocaust and a race riot."[17]

Also sitting on the Mississippi Supreme Court was Justice Thomas Brady, who had used his powers of vituperation to pen the famous "Black Monday" pamphlet that had served to mobilize much of the South's leadership against *Brown*. Not surprisingly, Brady issued a blistering concurring opinion that was more screed than legal argument. Brady colorfully labeled the Freedom Rides as "strife-fomenting junkets" that were "planned by individuals and groups erroneously called Freedom Riders and poorly disguised as an exercise in constitutional guarantees." For Brady, they were "nothing more than harbingers of government operation, not under law but under groups of men or committees, the highest expression of which is represented by the Communist order throughout the world."[18]

For the Freedom Riders the principle at stake was self-evident—the right to ride across the South and use its facilities as the Supreme Court had mandated. The Riders were willing to take the case to the U.S. Supreme Court—and they would. Hank Thomas challenged his conviction to the highest level, where it was ultimately overturned based on *Boynton* and the body of law that had really begun with Arthur Mitchell, Norvell Lee, Elmer Henderson, and Irene Morgan and their challenges back in the 1940s. Thomas's case thus connects multiple generations of struggle together and provides a reminder of the continuity of the long-range struggle for equality that the Freedom Rides embodied.

The Hate Bus, the Reverse Freedom Ride, and Organized White Resistance

Percolating beneath the surface of all the Freedom Rides was the discontent of organized massive resistance groups, from the Citizens' Councils

to the Ku Klux Klan. Because of the front-and-center role of the state
in Mississippi, these organizations did not actually get the chance to do
much save wring their hands and preach to the choir, though they did those
things ceaselessly.

On May 22, an American Nazi Party "Hate Bus," led by the party's
leader, Lincoln Rockwell, had bombastically launched from Washington.
Lincoln Rockwell's "Hate Bus" planned to follow the path of the Freedom Ride. The next day the bus, plastered with signs affirming the group's
hatred of, among other things, "race mixing" and "Jew-Communism,"
passed through Montgomery, escorted by federal officers. Later that day
the bus arrived in New Orleans, where its occupants had a difficult time
finding lodging. They carried more signs declaring that they desired the
"Gas Chamber for Traitors" and "America for Whites, Africa for Blacks."
They hated the "Communist, nigger-loving" Freedom Riders. On May 24,
the "Hate Bus" participants were promptly arrested for "unreasonably"
alarming the public.[19]

As always in Mississippi, the state's leading newspapers, particularly
Jackson's *Daily News* and its sister paper the *Clarion Ledger,* seemed a
virtual mouthpiece for the Citizens' Councils and their ilk. Indeed, in a
summer when organized groups were reduced to sarcastic editorials and
propaganda, the *Jackson Daily News* produced an editorial cartoon in the
form of a recruitment pitch from the Department of Tourism:

>   Editor's note—The following is offered as a facetious edito-
> rial cartoon for the benefit of potential "tourist" traffic from the
> North and East:

ATTENTION: RESTLESS RACE MIXERS
WHOSE HOBBY IS CREATING TROUBLE

>   Get away from the blackboard jungle. Rid yourself of fear of
> rapists, muggers, dopeheads, and switchblade artists during the
> long, hot summer.

FULFILL THE DREAM OF A LIFETIME
HAVE A VACATION ON A REAL PLANTATION
Here's All You Do

>   Buy yourself a Southbound ticket via rail, bus or air.
>   Check in and sign the guest register at the Jackson City Jail.

Pay a nominal fine of $200. Then spend the next 4 months at our 21,000-acre Parchman Plantation in the heart of the Mississippi Delta. Meals furnished. Enjoy the wonders of chopping cotton, warm sunshine, plowing mules and tractors, feeding the chickens, slopping the pigs, scrubbing floors, cooking and washing dishes, laundering clothes.

Sun lotion, bunion plasters, as well as medical services free. Experience the "abundant" life under total socialism. Parchman prison fully air-cooled by Mother nature.

(We cash U.S. Government Welfare checks.)[20]

Usually the editors and news staff of the Jackson dailies were more interested in sending blacks out of the state, an interest that coincided with various programs of the Citizens' Councils. Oddly, such an idea often had the support of liberals in the North and was sometimes even pushed by them. In the wake of the Emmett Till trial, *Life* magazine editor (and New York City councilman) Earl Brown had proposed the formation of a refugee committee to "move all of the Negroes out of Mississippi." While Brown's proposal was clearly intended as an indictment of the way people of color were treated in the deepest of the Deep South states, the *Daily News* enthusiastically embraced the proposal as something to which to aspire.[21] Using the Mississippi secretary of state's figure of 986,707, the *Daily News* did some calculations. It would have taken nearly $80 million "to haul all our good Negroes to the Nawth," asserted a September 1955 headline. That figure was based on the cost of one-way plane tickets. The state could expend just under $40 million if it was willing to use trains. The logistical hurdles would have been tremendous, as a train of twenty cars containing 17,000 passengers would have to leave every hour on the hour for thirty-four days in order to send the state's black population northward. Brown even explicitly announced that his idea was intended to be a counter to the Citizens' Councils, which "put economic pressure on Mississippi Negroes to force them into submission." By removing all of the blacks from the state, Brown believed that Mississippi's whites would "then be a victim of their own doing." William Simmons of the Citizens' Councils asserted that Brown had "his facts wrong in at least two cases. One, the Citizens' Council puts economic pressure on no one, and two, the white people are not economically dependent on the Negro in Mississippi."[22]

Acting governor Carroll Gartin (both Governor White and Governor-Elect Coleman were out of town at the time) claimed that the whole idea was "ridiculous. It is just another case of northern radicals trying to stir up confusion in Mississippi."[23] Yet less than two months later, State Representative Upton Sisson announced that he would ask the 1956 legislature "to appropriate the sum of $1000 to be used in the purchase of one-way transportation from any place in Mississippi to the City of Chicago for any and all members of the Negro race who are citizens of this state and wish to leave Mississippi because of the alleged mistreatment but who are financially unable to make the exit." Sisson's proposal was a response to the "unjust criticism" the state faced after the Till case. Sisson, who had lived in the North, believed that the region was full of hypocrites who "hate the Negro with a purple passion, and when they can tolerate the Negro no longer, the result is mass slaughter."[24] He was referring to race riots he had seen in Detroit and that had occurred in other cities in the North. He did not believe that the $1000 would be used, but if it were depleted, he would ask for it to be replenished. Certainly, the North was vulnerable to charges of hypocrisy on the matter of race, which made the Reverse Freedom Ride all the more compelling in the minds of many.

By 1960, what Carroll Gartin had accusingly called "ridiculous," the result of instigation by "Northern radicals," had become a central part of the Citizens' Council program. The Council was pleased to note that in the decade from 1950 to 1960, Mississippi had gone from being second in the country in total number of Negroes to eighth and that over the same period the state was fiftieth in terms of increase in the Negro population. Mississippi had lost 706,751 blacks over the course of the decade, only one of four states to lose black population over the ten-year period. The Citizens' Council believed that the migration of blacks to the North would "do more to promote the cause of racial separation among white Yankees than all the written logic on earth."[25]

Once the demonstrations in the South spread to the point of becoming a concern for whites desirous of maintaining Jim Crow, the Association of Citizens' Councils developed a seven-point "Community Plan to Counteract Racial Agitators." The various points included organizing auxiliary police, advising Negroes not to affiliate with agitators, advising white citizens to ignore Negro demonstrators, ensuring that attorneys informed all (white) citizens of their rights, identifying the agitators and their supporters, registering all white citizens over twenty-one years of age, and encouraging voluntary Negro migration to the North and West. Of this last point (actually listed sixth of the seven), the association noted:

Immediate steps combined with long-range plans should be made to encourage voluntary Negro migration from the South. Our disproportionate Negro population has become an unbearable economic and political liability. Because of our large Negro population, the future looks dark indeed when one contemplates the years of political, economic, and social struggle that lie ahead. Logic and reason should indicate that voluntary Negro migration and resettlement is the best solution to the race problem.[26]

Before long this plank in the Citizens' Council platform became a primary answer for the state, the South, and the United States. Migration suddenly became "the only reasonable answer."[27] This was a plan that Georgia's senator Richard Russell had developed in 1958. The "Russell Plan" was legislation aimed at "bringing about a better nationwide balance of the country's Negro population."[28] Russell's program would be voluntary, but support for it would come from federal funding. The Citizens' Councils quickly took up the proposal. A variation on the old "back to Africa" approach, which had developed pockets of support among both radical blacks and vicious white supremacists, the migration argument was based on the idea that "we have comparative racial peace when we have 10% or less Negroes in the state's population."[29] Using the 10 percent figure and the 1960 census, the councils then came up with a chart indicating the "Negro surplus or deficit for each state." With the exception of Delaware, Maryland, and the District of Columbia, every state running a "Negro surplus" was in the South. On the whole, only thirteen states plus the District ran a surplus. Every other state was ripe for the reception of the South's black population. With surpluses of more than 600,000, Georgia, Louisiana, Mississippi, North Carolina, and Alabama stood to lose the largest black populations. Meanwhile, by the same calculations, California, Minnesota, Wisconsin, Pennsylvania, and New York would absorb the most, each requiring an influx of 300,000 or more in order to achieve the Citizens' Councils ideal equilibrium of racial makeup.[30] Apparently, Richard Russell and the Citizens' Councils were among the original supporters of racial quotas.[31]

This plan to "send the problem to the people who are so sure they have the answers" gathered momentum with the Freedom Rides.[32] The Citizens' Councils were quick to capitalize on the Rides to support reverse migration.[33] By 1962, less than a year after the start of the Freedom Rides, the Councils had issued broadsides advertising a "FREEDOM BUS to any city in the North or West." The Councils offered free transportation plus five dollars for expenses to "any Negro Man or Woman, or Family (no limit to size) who desire to migrate to any city in the north or west of their choosing." By sending their names to local contacts, those blacks who desired to take advantage of the offer would "be notified at an early date when you will leave." On the back of the broadside were listed the names, addresses, and phone numbers of the NAACP; the Urban League; and the Welfare Departments of Pittsburgh, Chicago, New York, Detroit, and Washington.[34]

The Citizens' Council even developed a "Freedom Ride–North Society," which served to pull together finances and support for the movement. Those who contributed to the cause received membership cards certifying that the bearer had "contributed to the Freedom Rides–North Fund which finances voluntary Negro migration from the South to the North and West."[35] This was not a joke, even if the broadsides and publications regarding the Freedom Ride–North evidenced the same sort of sarcasm, bluster, and condescension as did much of the group's other propaganda.

On May 5, 1962, members of the Citizens' Council of Greater New Orleans watched and waved as eleven blacks boarded a bus with one-way tickets to either San Francisco or Los Angeles that the Council had provided. That same day the Louisiana Citizens' Council similarly financed seven blacks bound for the Midwest. No state money up to that point had been used to support the program. Those blacks who participated in the Councils' Reverse Rides gave several reasons for their participation. Some were using the opportunity to go North in search of better employment; others wanted to get away from the discrimination in the South. By the one-year anniversary of the CORE Riders' departure from Washington, the Louisiana Citizens' Council—the parent organization of all the Pelican State's Councils—claimed that 161 Reverse Riders had left Louisiana courtesy of the Freedom Ride–North program. Journalists who had done the research could account for only 58 such departures, and although the Louisiana Council claimed that 100 had left for Chicago secretly in April, Chicago officials denied such an influx into their city. Still, Citizens' Council authorities gleefully predicted an exodus as a consequence of their latest brainchild."[36]

New Orleans segregationist and Citizens' Council leader George Singelmann was the founding father of the Reverse Freedom Ride.[37] He had gotten the program off the ground, and it had gone so well that the Citizens' Council of America soon embraced the relocation program, believing that

shifting all dissatisfied blacks to the North and West and all segregationists to the South would be a good "democratic solution of the integration
controversy."[38]

The Reverse Freedom Ride received sharp criticism from many quarters in the North. Edward J. McCormack Jr., attorney general of Massachusetts—a state that was receiving more than its share of the Reverse
Riders—condemned the "inhumane segregationists' project." McCormack,
who was running against Edward Kennedy for the Democratic nomination
for the U.S. Senate, asked Robert Kennedy and the federal government to
"step in—and step in now—to halt this callous, degrading game."[39] Twice
Ted Kennedy had promised that jobs would be waiting for anyone who
moved to Massachusetts as a result of the Citizens' Council project or
otherwise. As the Councils ironically and cynically dispatched busloads
of blacks to Hyannis, Massachusetts, home of the famous Kennedy com-
pound, their supporters derived pleasure in the fact that those jobs were not
immediately forthcoming.[40]

The Councils quickly came to realize that Cape Cod and Hyannis in
particular were especially ripe for an exploitation of what they saw as
Kennedy hypocrisy on the race issue. By May 20, when the Little Rock
Citizens' Council provided one-way bus tickets for two black women and
their combined twenty children, Hyannis officials were in crisis mode,
debating whether to ask Congress to step in and stop the Reverse Rides.
At almost the same time, a Hyannis restaurateur announced that emigrant
families were not welcome at his establishment anymore. He claimed that
his decision was not discriminatory, but based on his shortage of employees. Nonetheless, more than one Southern newspaper reveled in reporting
such details, further evidence of rank Northern double-dealing on matters
racial.[41]

Within days Robert Kennedy had stepped into the emerging controversy in the affluent Cape Cod village where he and his family had spent
so much time developing the image that later would come to be known as
"Camelot." Kennedy conferred with Massachusetts governor John Volpe,
promising the federal government's help "in every way" to deal with what
had become a steady procession of black Reverse Riders. The summer
resort village, with 4,200 permanent residents, had established a Cape Cod
Refugee Fund to deal with the more than 50 largely penniless blacks, including more than 30 children, who had arrived up until June 1962. The
relief committee, which had been arranging food and housing for the new
arrivals, denounced the "fanatical bigots bringing disgrace on their state

and our nation." The committee's statement continued, asking the "decent citizens" of the South "to stop these miserable men and the 'castaway caravans' they sponsor."[42]

The segregationists responded by justifying the Reverse Rides. Little Rock arch-segregationist Amis Guthridge, a lawyer and the president of the Capital Citizens' Council, had sent thirty-two of his area's black citizens to Hyannis and now said that he would keep sending them until Northerners told their politicians to "stop this foolishness about civil rights." Guthridge believed that he was engaged in a "perfectly legal, moral and honorable campaign," the Reverse Ride intended not to embarrass the North but rather to educate the people of the North, East, and West about the South's problem. "We're going to find out," he declared, "if the northern politicians really do love the Negro and have an interest in him, or if they are just a bunch of hypocrites using the South as a whipping boy to corral the Negro vote."[43]

When a white moderate on the race question, Robert Chandler of Stamps, Arkansas, asked Guthridge and the Citizens' Council for a one-way ticket to Hyannis, based on the fact that he could not find work in Little Rock because he was not a staunch segregationist, Guthridge punted. Guthridge told Chandler that he had to discuss the matter with the Capital Citizens' Council's board of directors. Chandler thought that this was "passing the buck"—that if the Council really wanted to help people, as it claimed, its members would be happy to give him the ticket with no questions. "I would have been happy to pay back the Citizens' Council's money when I earned it," Chandler told reporters. "I don't want anybody to give me anything."[44] Chandler apparently never got his ticket north.

The Reverse Freedom Ride certainly succeeded in one area: it drew substantial media attention. Every major newspaper in the country ran articles about the event. In early May, *U.S. News and World Report,* never especially sympathetic to civil rights activity to begin with, carried a two-page article including "Negro Migration" charts and maps that could have been obtained directly from the Citizens' Councils.[45] One of the Freedom Rides' goals had been to draw media attention, and segregationist groups were savvy enough to realize that favorable national media play could yield fruit even while they rhetorically purported to reject national opinion.

Before long, Robert Patterson, the secretary of the Citizens' Council, asked that the nation's major newspapers poll readers regarding a migration of blacks from the South to the North.[46] In fact, George Gallup, the director of the American Institute for Public Opinion and the premier pollster in the United States, was already at work on such a project. Gallup discovered that the Reverse Freedom Ride met with disapproval in the North, but as much because of concern with the economic burden caused by such a migration as because of any rejection of the plan on principle. Showing the extent to which the Citizens' Council program had entered the culture at large, three out of four people polled (extrapolated to represent eighty-one million Americans) had heard of the Citizens' Council plan to provide free transportation to the North for unemployed Negroes. In the thirty-seven states outside of the South, only 9 percent of respondents had a favorable response to the plan, while 71 percent reacted unfavorably. The remaining 20 percent had either had a mixed response or no opinion. However, for many of those who responded negatively—black and white—their opposition was based on "honest and outraged indignation over a move which seems to offend human dignity." Additionally, many seemed concerned with what such an action did to the United States' image abroad. As the twenty-five-year-old Brooklyn wife of a newsmagazine analyst commented, "It's morally wrong and can only lead to another international discrediting of our so-called democracy." Just as common, however, was opposition based on the pocketbook. Some were worried that "we'd have to pay their relief money." Others responded with comments such as, "It would burden us," and "There aren't enough jobs now." Many Northern blacks agreed with this sentiment, demonstrating that economics was at least as important as race throughout much of the rest of the country.[47]

A day later the Gallup organization followed up by trying to determine whether the North or the South offered a happier life and better work opportunities for blacks. Not surprisingly, white response varied by region. A quarter of Southern whites polled believed that blacks would be happier in the North, but 45 percent thought the South was the place blacks would be happiest. Among Northern whites, 34 percent of respondents thought the North was the best place for blacks to find happiness, while 38 percent believed that the South was still the best. Among both groups, a sizeable portion—28 percent of Southern respondents, 30 percent of Northern—was undecided.[48]

Many Southerners in fact opposed the Citizens' Council's ingenious but disingenuous attempt to turn the tables. Admittedly nonscientific man-on-the-street-type interviews produced mostly critical comment. Attorney Henry H. Ware said, "Freedom Rides either way are absurd," branding both kinds of Riders as publicity seekers, adding, "If newspapers would lay off them . . . they would stop." Presbyterian pastor Dr. Merle C. Patterson believed that the Reverse Rides did "not represent the attitude of most of the people in Atlanta," calling them "a passing thing that will disappear within two months." Rose Fox, an Atlanta restaurant cashier, said, "It is very wrong for us to send Negroes on reverse freedom rides. We should make a place for them in the South . . . give them good jobs and a decent salary."[49] The Little Rock Ministerial Association condemned the Reverse Freedom Rides as "un-American and un-Christian" and "utterly degrading to our religious and national concepts of the inherent dignity of the human person."[50]

So how did the Reverse Freedom Riders fare? Early indications were that they did not do especially well. A United Press International survey of nearly one hundred of the men, women, and children who had uprooted their lives and moved to the North or West revealed that approximately a half dozen had returned to the South—two at the expense of Harry Golden, the North Carolina newspaper columnist and critic of the Reverse Rides—but the remainder intended to stick it out in the North. Reporting for UPI, Jack Fox wrote: "In the first flush of publicity, the one-way riders got red-carpet welcomes from welfare and civic groups and help in finding work. But jobs and job promises folded quickly." Hyannis in particular had grown "very resentful" at being targeted, especially after the two women with twenty children arrived in the Cape.[51]

The first of the Reverse Riders, Louis Boyd of New Orleans, garnered a lot of attention from news sources when he landed a one-hundred-dollar-a-week job in Jersey City, New Jersey, in April. That job lasted but one week, while his wife and eight children were cramped for three weeks in a Harlem hotel. Although an apartment was eventually found for Boyd, he remained jobless as June approached. Similarly, after Peola Denham of Baton Rouge rode the "Sunset Limited" to Los Angeles with his wife and ten children, he received "a celebrity's reception" and landed a job as a construction worker for three dollars an hour. But when work slowed a few weeks later, he too found himself jobless. His children were happy in the Jordan Hills housing project in San Pedro, which had two hundred units and only four white families. "The kids like the school here," Denham told a reporter, "but I ain't getting along too good right now. I'm off work. They [the L. M. Matthews Realty Company] laid me off. I don't know why. I don't know what I'll do next." Ted Kennedy had been on hand to greet David E. Harris of Little Rock, the first Reverse Rider to arrive in Hyannis. As the influx mounted, however, things grew tough, and only three of the new arrivals landed jobs. Residents were furious when Fred Calvin, an unemployed laborer from Little Rock, showed them a circular reading: "Freedom Rides North. Free airplane tickets for two large Negro families to Hyannis Port, Mass. Grand reception assured by the President's brother. Good jobs. Good homes."[52] If anyone still granted the benefit of the doubt to the Citizens' Councils, the rank duplicity of this circular should have shattered that presumption of goodwill. As dozens more followed, taxing the small community's affluent but seasonal economy, the residents of Hyannis and the surrounding communities began to wring their hands, coming to realize that they were targets of Southerners with points to prove and axes to grind.

In all of the Northern cities that received Reverse Riders, no family went without housing, even if only in the form of a hotel roof over their heads. However, jobs proved difficult to provide. Most of the Reverse Riders—victims of regional tensions, Southern racism and discrimination, and some Northern hypocrisy—nonetheless did not plan to return. When a reporter asked him if he was thinking of returning to the South, Peola Denham, struggling with his family in the Los Angeles area, did not hesitate. "Oh no," Denham replied. Similarly, Little Rock's Victoria Bell, who had arrived in Hyannis with her eleven children, said: "I came North for the children. I know the lord is with me." Toward the end of May, a Bellingham farmer offered Bell a home and a job.[53]

Just as Freedom Riders had continued to flow into the South and especially into Parchman Farm the previous year, throughout the summer of 1962 Reverse Riders deluged Northern communities, moving into Maine and elsewhere along with the cities that had been targeted from the onset. In its own assessment, a month and a half after the first Reverse Riders pulled into Northern terminals, the Citizens' Council had a bright outlook. In a speech before the Magnolia Kiwanis Club in Columbus, Mississippi, Tut Patterson announced that the Reverse Rides were "an act of desperation" meant to dramatize "the fact that the South's problems cannot be solved by theorists." Focusing on the "economic liabilities that Negroes present," Patterson contended, "We haven't gotten any attention in Massachusetts until there were reversed freedom rides up there." Noting that the presence of fifty-three newly arrived Negroes in the town of Hyannis was creating a severe problem, Patterson contended that his concerns had finally "gotten into Massachusetts politics. If 53 Negroes came into" Mississippi's "LeFlore County, they wouldn't even be noticed." Patterson mentioned the Gallup poll and argued that Northerners did not cite moral reasons, but economic ones, in their criticism of the Reverse Rides. Patterson told his audience, "It may not solve it, but I believe this migration will eventually alleviate our problem." Blacks in Mississippi were becoming "an economic and political liability," largely because of policies in Washington, and so "the only thing for the Negro to do is to voluntarily migrate." Unless migration occurred, present trends would "only lead to chaos, hatred and misunderstanding."[54]

A white Baton Rouge shipyard worker did not buy any of the Northern protestations, arguing that the South was just "doing the same thing they did to us" the year before in the Freedom Ride: "What's good for the goose is good for the gander."[55] But was it? It seems willfully ignorant or worse to compare the Freedom Rides and the Citizens' Councils' grotesque response. The Freedom Rides were about mixed-race interstate travelers testing their constitutional rights by riding through the South and integrating buses and terminal facilities. The apostles of massive resistance, meanwhile, found the most vulnerable members of their society, gave them one-way tickets and five dollars, and sent them to the North to fend for themselves. No one in the North challenged the Reverse Riders' right to travel or use facilities. They received warm receptions. No one beat them, cracked their skulls, or hauled them off to prison farms. And while many Southerners wrongly accused the federal government of organizing the Freedom Rides, the fact remains that while the Freedom Rides' participants and organizers had substantial overlap, the organizers of the Reverse Ride were not themselves participating in a noble experiment or test. Furthermore, the fact that so many blacks were willing to uproot themselves and their families for so little, either to find employment or to avoid white supremacy, hardly speaks well of the environment they chose to leave.

Patterson asserted the very presence of blacks as an economic problem, as if the Southern economy would otherwise have been thriving, as if the economy did not rely on black labor for a range of jobs, and as if the debilitating policies of white supremacy played no role. Furthermore, Patterson and his ilk went under the assumption that black Southerners should have to abandon the land of their birth, the places where they had developed roots and communities and lives of their own. And on top of all of this, assuming that blacks in the South had ever gained voting rights (admittedly far from guaranteed in 1961), why should or would they dilute whatever voting concentration they had by dispersing in order to appease those exact people who had dedicated their lives to preventing black equality? Whatever hypocrisy the Reverse Rides may have revealed, and there certainly was some, claiming moral parallelism between the Freedom Rides and the Citizens' Councils' bastardized concoction is absurd and vacuous at best.

After the Freedom Rides: The Movement Continues

When the Freedom Ride saga came to a conclusion, CORE and the other elements of the movement were not finished addressing Jim Crow on the nation's highways and byways. CORE looked north from Washington after the Freedom Rides and saw the largely segregated restaurant and hotel infrastructure flanking Route 40 across Maryland and into Delaware.[56] In the words of Stokely Carmichael, these Jim Crow facilities along Route 40 represented "a constant irritant."[57] On October 20, 1961, CORE's National Action Group announced a planned Route 40 Freedom Ride that would consist of a motorcade of more than one hundred cars that would test segregated restaurants along the roadsides on November 11. The catalyst for this particular challenge was directly related to the Cold War imperatives that so pervaded the relationship among civil rights workers, their detractors, and the federal government: in the months leading up to October, at least ten African diplomats had been refused service when they stopped at restaurants on their way to or from Washington.[58]

Even as CORE officials looked forward, they looked backward too, in a sense. On November 1, the day the ICC decree mandating the end of Jim Crow in interstate transport went into effect, CORE sent test teams across the South to gauge adherence to the decision. After a week of tests, James Farmer and Gordon Carey issued a report. In most locations, the report was based on one attempt to use facilities, so while a successful test did not mean "that discrimination or segregation" did not continue in a facility, it did indicate that no discrimination "was encountered on the basis of one survey."[59] The tests started off auspiciously in Mississippi, where, perhaps not surprisingly, Captain Ray met Levert Taylor and Glenda Jackson of CORE and arrested them within seconds of their entering the white waiting room at 7:30 on the morning of November 1. While at least two Mississippi cities, Winona and Grenada, had announced that they would adhere to the ICC mandate, a state judge had issued an injunction against Greyhound forbidding the company from desegregating their facilities.[60] It would take further Justice Department action to force the state's hand, and even then, compliance behind the Magnolia Curtain remained spotty at best.

Across the rest of the South, the decision seemed to have taken hold. Despite Farmer and Carey's warnings that one test did not necessarily ensure continued compliance, the signs were positive. In Alabama, Arkansas, Florida, Georgia, North Carolina, Texas, and West Virginia, all of the tests met with no resistance, although in many locations signs explaining the ICC ruling were not posted, as the decision required. In Oklahoma, South Carolina, Tennessee, Louisiana, and of course Mississippi, at least one and in some cases multiple facilities intransigently maintained the caste system.[61] Pockets in Mississippi would continue to resist. In 1963 and even beyond, the Justice Department filed suit in a number of civil actions in an attempt to force the hand of stubborn local authorities who refused to accede to integration at bus terminals. Two years after the Freedom Rides, a front-page editorial in the *Winona Times* laughably whined, "Winona and Montgomery County officials are fully capable of keeping the peace in this city IF Federal authorities will keep their meddling fingers out of the pie!"[62] This despite the fact that authorities in much of the state, including Winona, had proven themselves incapable of ensuring peace, and more to the point, the law, for more than two years.

In February 1962, CORE issued a plea to college students across the South to test further bus terminals, to ensure continued compliance both at those places that seemed to have relented and at those places that kept up the fight against Jim Crow. Ongoing CORE tests had revealed further adherence in the South and even challenged locales across the North, where they had no difficulties.[63] The entreaty to students revealed that CORE understood what a powerful and committed resource they had in the student civil rights struggle. SNCC's actions in the preceding year and a half clearly had made them the prime force for change.

The Route 40 challenge saw CORE win a preemptive victory when thirty-five Maryland and twelve Delaware restaurants agreed to integrate their facilities. The CORE pressure, which would have involved a series of tests and protests at individual restaurants, had borne fruit. CORE called the decision of the forty-seven restaurants "a Thanksgiving present for the American people" but warned that it would "continue to test the other restaurants along this major federal highway."[64] Robert B. Jones Jr., vice president and general manager of radio station WFBR in Mulberry, Maryland, read an editorial on November 9 and 10 in which he opined that "a giant step has been taken in behalf of integrated service in public places here in Maryland." He commended both the restaurant proprietors and CORE, stating that though he realized there was "a long and perhaps difficult road yet to travel," he urged "all Marylanders to join hands now to reduce" bias and prejudice "to a more livable level."[65]

The Route 40 Freedom Riders were set to go when the announcement of the restaurant integration came down. CORE had prepared extensive documents for Riders that outlined which establishments each carload would test and provided contact information for the group leader and the passengers in each car. The Riders were to take note of whether or not they had been served in each of the places they tested.[66] With each major event, movement activists had developed more sophisticated and cunning programs, learning from the successes and failures that had come before.

Instead of undertaking the Route 40 Freedom Ride, on November 11, CORE conducted a massive sit-in and picket demonstration in Baltimore, the beginning of a campaign to desegregate a city that bore resemblance to places farther south. Meeting as scheduled at Howard University (two hundred of the anticipated one thousand participants were Howard students), the Route 40 Freedom Riders proceeded to Baltimore's Cornerstone Baptist Church and then dispersed to segregated restaurants in the city. CORE officials hoped that a civil rights bill pending before the Maryland legislature would pass, but in the interim, the organization planned to continue boycotts.[67]

By autumn 1961, the Civil Rights Movement had found the next challenge that it hoped would draw national attention to the fight against Jim Crow. Albany, in southwest Georgia, was fully segregated, and after a confluence of circumstances, SNCC, Martin Luther King and SCLC, and others joined with local black organizations to form the "Albany Movement." As in other prominent civil rights activities, students quickly asserted themselves in Albany, many arriving by bus from Atlanta and elsewhere as "Freedom Riders." Indeed, according to one of the participants in Albany, "some historians have called the Albany Freedom Ride the 'Rosa Parks' incident that incited the Albany Movement to begin massive direct action demonstrations. I don't know. But I was an Albany Freedom Rider."[68]

The Albany Freedom Rides actually stemmed directly from their CORE forebears. In the process of testing the ICC pronouncement, some activists, including Jim Forman, realized that there had been no formal tests of train facilities, which were also subject to the ICC ruling that had gone into effect on November 1. Since a number of the tests had taken place in Atlanta, where there was a solid core of activists, that city became a center from which testers went out to determine compliance across Georgia and other parts of the South. Thus, a group of eight Freedom Riders, black and white, plus a designated observer, Sandra Cason "Casey" Hayden, boarded a train on December 10, 1961, that was bound for Albany, where they would meet Charles Sherrod, Cordell Reagon, and Charles Jones, the three SNCC field secretaries who had originally gone to southwest Georgia to conduct a voter registration drive in Terrell County. When Terrell proved too difficult to breach, they moved on to nearby Albany in hopes of inspiring local blacks to challenge the city's rigid segregation. Soon after, the Albany Movement was born.[69]

The group bound for Albany enjoyed their train trip. Of the eight Riders who would test the Albany station, four were black, including trip organizer Jim Forman, the charismatic SNCC leader; SCLC's Bernard Lee; Atlanta University graduate student Lenora Taitt; and Norma Collins, another SNCC activist. The four whites were Tom Hayden, a student activist and writer who was on his own crash course with history; Bob Zellner, who along with Hayden had just returned from the sit-in movement in McComb, Mississippi; Per Laursen, a Danish journalist; and Joan Browning, the only white woman in the group, who was about to embark on her first civil rights challenge.

As the train chugged along toward southeast Georgia, the group joked and sang freedom songs, and veterans shared their experiences in the movement and passed on wisdom to newcomers. Upon arrival in Albany, Casey Hayden immediately separated from the group so that she could call Julian Bond and otherwise take care of things in the case of an arrest or any other difficulty. Meanwhile, the eight Riders walked into the white waiting room, lingered for a few minutes, and crossed through the station, where they encountered a crowd of about fifty cheering black people, as well as a vocal but small group of jeering whites. Moments later, even as some of the group managed to find taxis to depart, the police arrested eleven people, including the eight who had come from Atlanta, as well as SNCC field secretary Charles Jones and two students from nearby Albany State College, Bertha Gober and William Henderson.[70] Just as when the Freedom Riders encountered arrest in Jackson, hundreds of new activists entered Albany, many by bus or train, and within days Martin Luther King Jr. had embraced the southwest Georgia campaign. The Albany Movement was under way in earnest, a Freedom Ride having served as an important catalyst.

Not surprisingly, given the emotional appeal and clear narrative tug of the Freedom Ride story, it was not long before someone developed the idea of making a movie about the Freedom Riders. Within months of the Jackson arrests, a filmmaker by the name of Dick Bruner had devised a treatment and sent it off to CORE's Marvin Rich for his comments. Rich generally liked the idea and hoped the project would get off the ground (apparently it never did). The film was to have a series of narrators—Jim Peck the most prominent among them—and narrative voiceover moments, such as the voice of John Patterson, the sounds of riots, speeches by Martin Luther King and Robert Kennedy, comments from journalists, and the like. Bruner's idea was that "the film should build toward the final climax in Jackson through a series of smaller episodes: the burning of the bus in Anniston; the beatings in Birmingham; and the mobs outside the church in Montgomery. . . . After each crescendo there should be an abrupt change of mood. The narration" was to "make clear . . . that the Ride has not yet served its purpose of directly confronting segregation."[71]

Rich sent back commentary to Bruner, providing some insights about the Ride. He took issue with Bruner's assertion in his introduction that the Freedom Rides were intended to confront: "The purpose of the ride was not merely to confront. It was to confront and to overcome." He reminded Bruner that along the way, early in the first Ride, the group had successfully integrated terminals such as the one in Augusta, Georgia, and that the ICC decision had served to desegregate many more. Rich hoped that Bruner could find a way, if possible, to convey the sense of the Riders overcoming fear among Jackson's black population. He averred that the Rides had initially met with resistance from local blacks, but that before long the previously docile black population was providing "aid and succor" to the Riders. When new arrivals entered the state from all across the country, Mississippians eventually joined in. Rich also had some suggestions as to who should be providing narration, believing that in the section where Bruner planned for Jimmy McDonald to explain the training process and team method, Cox, Thomas, or Charles Persons might better serve as spokespersons, as they were "essentially more articulate than McDonald." Rich also made a couple of "factual" corrections, including an assertion that the students who joined the group later "had no training at all" in nonviolence—a patent falsehood, given that the original wave of Nashville students were all veterans of that city's nonviolent movement and that many successive groups did receive some training, however truncated.[72] Some of Rich's comments indeed seem to indicate the continuing tensions underlying the relationship between CORE and the assertive young activists from SNCC.

Even with the potential for success on the silver screen, the Congress of Racial Equality did not see the Freedom Rides as an end point, a Hollywood story, nor did they see them as a metaphor. Civil rights organizations in 1962 were still fully immersed in the struggle to defeat Jim Crow. In 1962 CORE undertook the unpublicized "Freedom Highways" project, taking the struggle to integrate the nation's highways to private hotels and restaurants, including the Howard Johnson chain. The project focused on the Southeast, from Maryland down to Florida. As soon as CORE announced the campaign, Howard Johnson's integrated its sixty or so restaurants in Florida "to try to head off trouble," in the words of Jim Farmer.[73] Howard Johnson's used its decision not to fight the integration battle to draw considerable publicity, and newspapers across the country carried headlines that the restaurant chain's advertising staff could not have concocted. The *Binghamton Press* in upstate New York was not atypical in splashing boldly across its pages, "Howard Johnson's Stands against Racial Bias."[74] Clearly, the experience of the Freedom Rides had taught the corporate masters of Howard Johnson's a lesson in the power of direct action protest. Freedom Highways garnered virtually no national press; what little coverage it received did not credit CORE or link the Freedom Highways project with the Freedom Rides, even though the lineage was clear.

Outside of Florida, some Howard Johnson's and Holiday Inn restaurants and hotels were not so quick to respond, spokespersons claiming that many of these businesses were franchises and thus beyond the control of the national offices. Even as some of the nation's newspapers lavished praise on seemingly forward-thinking HoJos, some individual restaurants did not acquiesce, particularly in South Carolina, where local proprietors of Howard Johnson's establishments in Columbia and Charleston refused to serve blacks. While the national corporation owned and operated 297 restaurants, 359 were owned locally, and many of those in the South ignored national directives.[75] As Vermont's *Bennington Banner* wryly noted in a headline, "Howard Johnson Says Chain Doesn't Discriminate—Much."[76] So CORE began a campaign of sit-ins focused on the state of North Carolina. The goal became to integrate not only the restaurants alongside the highway but, according to Farmer, "all public accommodations in the state of North Carolina and all of the cities."[77] Once again the sit-in movement merged with the Freedom Rides. The result was a massive campaign in which thousands filled jails in cities across the state, particularly in Greensboro.

This time, however, there was no press, no outrage. The police would not allow the students and their colleagues to fill the jails. Instead, when the students refused to post bail, state officials simply took them from the jails and bused them back to various campuses. Farmer has said that he believes that city editors, who wanted to bury these stories, told their reporters to bring their copy to the city editor desk. He believed that the editors wanted to protect Greensboro's image, and with no violence and with students ultimately never facing conviction, there was no story. Farmer has asserted that Terry Sanford, North Carolina's moderate governor, was responsible for suppressing the Freedom Highways story.[78]

Legacies: "Freedom Ride" as Civil Rights Movement

In September 2002, the gay rights group SAVE Dade worked to defeat a referendum to repeal Dade County's law banning discrimination against gays and lesbians. Lorri Jean, the executive director of the National Gay and Lesbian Task Force, which had contributed volunteers and substantial financial support to the Miami-area effort, told reporters what the battle against discrimination meant to the gay community. "It's sort of our version of the Freedom Riders," she explained.[79] She went on to provide historical context for the conflict in South Florida, but she did not explain her comment on the Freedom Rides. Nor did the reporter from the *Washington Post* find it necessary to expand any further upon this reference.

More than forty-one years after the Freedom Riders first left Washington, a gay and lesbian political coalition that had no apparent direct connection to buses or even interstate commerce invoked the Freedom Rides as an analogy, a metaphor, for the struggle for freedom. This was hardly the first time the Rides were so invoked. In fact, in many ways the use of the words "Freedom Ride" or "Freedom Rider" has a history as interesting as the event they recall.

The Freedom Riders even captured the imagination and inspired the spirits of activists on the other side of the globe. By the 1960s, a committed group of activists in Australia had come to fight a civil rights battle of their own. The indigenous people of Australia, commonly known as Aborigines, faced an uphill battle for civil, political, and economic equality that was the rival of what blacks faced in the Mississippi Delta. In February 1965, a group of thirty Sydney University students boarded buses to begin Australia's Freedom Ride, which involved a tour of towns in New South Wales to investigate and protest discrimination against Aborigines.[80]

There were two Aborigines aboard the caravan, which would travel thirty-two hundred kilometers, including Charles Perkins, who along with Jim Spigelman was one of the two leaders of this trip, which some have called "the most significant act in Aboriginal-European relations in the twentieth century."[81] Perkins would go on to become a legendary leader in Australia, with a career trajectory eerily similar to that of John Lewis. Australian writer and filmmaker John Pilger has called Perkins, who died in October 2000, "Australia's Mandela."[82] Perkins was the first Aborigine to graduate from an Australian university, in 1965, and he was also the first to become head of an Australian government department when he was named head of the Department of Aboriginal Affairs in the 1980s.[83] In an interview on Australia's ABC television network, Perkins later said of his Freedom Rides: "Off we went, in full ignorance of what was ahead of us and not too much courage and not too much knowledge, but we thought, 'Well, let's do it.' And so, we did it."[84] The Australian Freedom Ride met with resistance and tremendous opposition, yet it is seen as a landmark in Australian race relations.

Thirty-five years later another group of Australian activists invoked the Australian Freedom Ride and the American experience on May 4, 2000, when—thirty-nine years after the first Freedom Riders left Washington—a group of Australian activists announced the first "Drug War Freedom Ride," an odd agglomeration of the Sydney-based prisoner advocacy group Justice Action and the Nimbin-based Australian Cannabis Law Reform Movement. This group rode a "Peace Bus," a motley vehicle intentionally evocative of that ridden by the unintentional "Freedom Riders" the Merry Pranksters. The goal of this Freedom Ride was "to bear witness to the inexorably rising prisoner population that is a consequence of the drug prohibition policies into which our governments federal, state and local had been locked in by the US alliance."[85] Four decades after the Merry Pranksters rolled into New Orleans and were mistaken for Freedom Riders, a group of far more politically active but spiritually akin free spirits boarded a bus not dissimilar to the drug-inspired *Furthur,* the "magical mystery tour bus," and invoked the Freedom Riders. What a long strange trip the last four decades had been for the bus rides that had become inspiration, epithet, invocation, and metaphor for a movement. In 1991 a group of students at the University of North Carolina took a bicycle tour modeled after the 1961 Freedom Rides, aimed at addressing racial discrimination by focusing on the underlying causes of racism and poverty in the United States.[86] And in 2001, many of the Freedom Riders themselves attended reunions in Washington, New Orleans, and Jackson. Many of the Riders in Washington boarded a bus and traveled down to Atlanta, attending a reunion there as well.[87] It had been many years, but the Freedom Rides still resonated for these remarkable men and women and anyone who was there with them.

Conclusion: Paul Revere and the Freedom Rides

Sometime after the Freedom Rides, an admirer, S. Ralph Harlow, composed a poem, "Paul Revere and the Freedom Riders," borrowing generously in form and theme from the famous work that most children in America once read and committed to memory alongside the "Gettysburg Address," in a synergistic linkage of history and civics. One of the closing stanzas of Harlow's double homage reads:

Yes, whether on Greyhound or steed of black,
For Riders Freedom shall never lack:
So once again America stirs
At the hoofs of a horse o'er the bus wheel's whirs.[88]

Ignoring the literary merit of Harlow's derivative doggerel, the Freedom Riders do belong alongside the historical actors, real and mythologized, who fought for freedom at all costs and who markedly improved a country with so much promise that so often fell short of its grandiloquent standards.

The Freedom Rides were vital in ending Jim Crow in interstate transportation. After the Rides and Robert Kennedy's reluctant intervention, the stigmatizing signs pushing "Colored" into inferior facilities began to disappear. Mississippi continued its intransigence, naturally, but across the South adherents outnumbered holdouts: it had become clear that segregation was untenable after the Freedom Rides forced change. The Justice Department further ensured that patrons of railroads and airlines benefited from what the Freedom Rides had wrought. In 1963 the Justice Department could announce, "Systematic segregation of Negroes in interstate transportation has disappeared." This was not merely wishful political thinking.[89]

CORE realized what a powerful movement it had channeled with the Freedom Rides. So too did outside observers. Many future organizers modeled their direct action protests after the Freedom Ride in the wake of the bus rides through the South. CORE used the Freedom Rides as a springboard into the Freedom Highways and Route 40 projects. New arrivals to Albany, Georgia, the movement's next hot spot, self-consciously referred to themselves as "Freedom Riders." In November 1961 James Farmer wrote in the Workmen's Circle *Call*, "The Freedom Rides are a major factor in the Non-violent Revolution occurring in America."[90] The use of the present tense was appropriate. The Freedom Rides, the Freedom Riders, had changed America. They had changed the struggle for racial justice in America. But as important, the movement that they had helped to reinvigorate, and for which they served as a model, forged onward, drawing inspiration and tactical approaches from the Rides.

In an essay memorializing three recently deceased heroes of the Civil Rights Movement—Little Rock's Daisy Bates, the independent-minded judge Frank Johnson, and Freedom Rider and movement leader James Farmer—historian Douglas Brinkley asked readers of the *New York Times Magazine* why these individuals and masses of others were not considered in the gauzy hagiography of the "Greatest Generation" that anchorman Tom Brokaw had foisted upon America in the final decade of the twentieth century. Brinkley raises a good question. If standing up for democracy and fighting injustice, risking bodily harm for natural rights and for those rights imbued in the Constitution, braving evil and the armed hordes whose intent is to undermine human justice and dignity, embody the reasons why we rightfully admire the World War II generation, then certainly those on the front lines of the domestic war for civil rights should be front and center when the prose gets purple and the heroes are accounted for. As Brinkley wrote: "Farmer, Bates and Johnson were a part of 'the greatest generation' that happened to serve the country at home. We are rewarded by their efforts every time a teenager walks into an integrated high school or protesters march freely or an elderly woman takes the first available seat on the bus."[91]

Within a couple of years after the Freedom Rides, Hank Thomas found himself in Vietnam: "In 1963 I was in the South. I couldn't go in certain restaurants . . . couldn't vote" when the U.S. Army "decided to take me in to help the Vietnamese gain their freedom." When he went back to Anniston with a CBS news crew in 1991 for the thirty-year commemoration of events in that town, three of the old mob members would not shake his hand.[92] In 1994 he returned to Vietnam as a guest of that country's government, where he received a warm welcome and was greeted with hugs, conversation, meals, and generosity of spirit. It dawned on a reporter at the time that, as he told Thomas, "In Vietnam they tried to kill you because of the color of your uniform. In Alabama they tried to kill you because of the color of your skin."[93]

Thomas returned from Vietnam, where he had earned medals as a medic. He took a job at an Atlanta-area McDonald's restaurant, where he was told that he could not handle the food or money or work at the front counter. Years later he became a McDonald's franchisee and bought that restaurant and six others. "Mine is a good old American story," he says. He is now retired and lives with his wife in Stone Mountain, Georgia, one of the historical strongholds of the Ku Klux Klan. "I have absolutely no complaints. I've had," he understates, "an interesting life." Not surprisingly, the Freedom Rides stand out for him, but his role in the movement as a whole is rightfully a point of pride. "I'm proud of what I did, gosh, yes. I'm proud of the small part I played in the big battle. I call it the Second American Revolution."[94]

In just a few short weeks in 1961, CORE's brainchild, "Freedom Ride 1961," went from an obscure challenge to segregation to a national and international event that galvanized the Civil Rights Movement and changed the course of American history. To echo what a young woman told some of the participants on the Journey of Reconciliation, these men and women in 1961 did a brave and wonderful thing. They risked their lives for justice and human dignity. They challenged Jim Crow. They became Freedom Riders.

Notes

Prologue

1. R. Wright, "How Bigger Was Born" (1940), in R. Wright, *Native Son* (1993), 509.
2. R. Wright, "How Bigger Was Born," 509.
3. See S. Kennedy, *Jim Crow Guide,* 178.
4. Barnes, *Journey from Jim Crow,* 1–10, passim.
5. Myrdal, *American Dilemma,* 634.
6. Myrdal, *American Dilemma,* 635.
7. Myrdal, *American Dilemma,* 635; S. Kennedy, *Jim Crow Guide,* 179.
8. Myrdal, *American Dilemma,* 635.
9. Myrdal, *American Dilemma,* 1340 n.6.
10. R. Wright, "How Bigger Was Born," 509–10.
11. R. Wright, "How Bigger Was Born," 518.
12. *New York Post,* Sept. 27, 1935, quoted in Margolick, *Beyond Glory,* 111–12.

Introduction

1. There are a number of recent important historiographical essays and assessments of the field of civil rights. Among the best are Steven F. Lawson, "Freedom Now, Freedom Then: The Historiography of the Civil Rights Movement," in his vital collection of essays *Civil Rights Crossroads,* 3–28; Eagles, "Toward New Histories"; Hall, "Long Civil Rights Movement"; Gaines, "Historiography of the Struggle"; Chafe, "'Gods Bring Threads.'"
2. *Look for a Kool Place,* video, courtesy of Richard Dodgson (1999). See also Kesey, "Merry Pranksters Meet Jim Crow," 92, 157.
3. Kesey, "Merry Pranksters Meet Jim Crow," 157.
4. It is inevitable that historians and others will compare *Freedom's Main Line* to Raymond Arsenault's *Freedom Riders: 1961 and the Struggle for Racial Justice.* Arsenault's splendid book is a welcome and long-overdue contribution to the field, but our projects are different in scope and focus.

I began this project as a graduate seminar paper in 1999, when I decided to write a dissertation and eventually a book that I thought would be the first full treatment of the Freedom Rides. Upon discovering that Professor Arsenault was working on a similar project, I decided nonetheless to forge ahead with *Freedom's Main Line*. In a world in which entire libraries exist on Gettysburg and D-Day and *Brown v. Board*, Ray and I agreed that ample room existed for two books on the Freedom Rides. This book, eight years in the researching and writing, must stand or sink on its own merits. While it is inevitable that our volumes will be compared, that reality does not mean that they must be pitted against one another.

In addition to being significantly shorter than *Freedom Riders*, *Freedom's Main Line* follows a different path to the same destination. Historians must address two countervailing yet essential issues in their writing: continuity and disjunction. It is a cliché to say that history is about change over time, but it is true that history is about those strands that maintain themselves even as things change. In the nature of the Oxford University Press series in which it appears, "Pivotal Moments in American History," *Freedom Riders* depicts its subjects as agents of a turning point in history. I have no wish to argue this point, but one of my goals here is to reveal the Freedom Rides in the context of a larger struggle for black equality that reached back before World War II and continued long after the Rides themselves ended.

Furthermore, this project seeks to place politics, broadly defined, at the center of the struggle for civil rights. If *Freedom's Main Line* is about anything beyond the Freedom Riders, it is about the ways in which politics at the local, state, and national levels served to harm or help the cause of civil rights. Politics, however, is not merely about officeholders and politicians. The movement itself was beset by politics. Infighting, turf wars, clashes of ego—these were part and parcel of the Civil Rights Movement, and they came to the fore during the Freedom Rides. By understanding conditions on the ground at the various places where both the Journey of Reconciliation and the Freedom Rides stopped, we can develop a better sense of how the fight against white supremacy played out across the South, as well as how the forces of massive resistance mobilized against civil rights.

1. "We Challenged Jim Crow"

1. On the Civil Rights Movement in the generation before *Brown*, see Feldman, *Before Brown*; Egerton, *Speak Now against the Day*; A. D. Morris, *Origins of the Civil Rights Movement*; Savage, *Broadcasting Freedom*; Sitkoff, *New Deal for Blacks*; and Sullivan, *Days of Hope*.

2. On the case, see *Morgan v. Virginia*, 328 U.S. 373 (1946); *Morgan v. Virginia*, "Brief on behalf of the Commonwealth," Record No. 2974, a copy of which can be found in the Leon Ransom papers, 173, box 5, folder 16, Moorland-Spingarn Research Center. See also *You Don't Have to Ride Jim Crow!*; Arsenault, *Freedom Riders*, 10–22; Barnes, *Journey from Jim Crow*, 44–51; Palmore, "Not-So-Strange Career"; Wallenstein, *Blue Laws and Black Codes*, 96–98; Miller, *Petitioners*, 367–68. Of recent interest, see "Freedom Rider"; Richard Gold-

stein, "Irene Morgan Kirkaldy, 90, Rights Pioneer, Dies," *New York Times,* Aug. 13, 2007.

3. Virginia Code of 1942, 4097dd, quoted in *Morgan v. Virginia,* 375.

4. *Hall v. DeCuir,* 95 U.S. 485. For the best exposition of the path from *De-Cuir* to *Morgan,* see Palmore, "Not-So-Strange Career," 1773–1817, passim.

5. See Palmore, "Not-So-Strange Career," 1773, 1776, 1816–17. It should also be noted that the Court ruled unanimously in *DeCuir* and nearly so in *Morgan,* which can be seen as affirming Palmore's argument about the Court's adherence to its reading of the Commerce Clause or as revealing the changes in attitudes toward segregation over the intervening century—or, oddly enough, perhaps both.

6. *Hall v. DeCuir,* quoted in *Morgan v. Virginia,* 384. See also Palmore, "Not-So-Strange Career," 1777–82.

7. *Morgan v. Virginia,* 376.

8. *Morgan v. Virginia,* 383.

9. *Morgan v. Virginia,* 386.

10. *Morgan v. Virginia,* 389. On the dissent, also see Palmore, "Not-So-Strange Career," 1814–15. In one of the many ironies attendant in the *Morgan* and *DeCuir* cases—one that shows how Supreme Court justices often (though not always) keep their personal opinions out of the cases they judge—Justice Burton, by all accounts, was far more sympathetic to civil rights and equal protection claims than was Reed, even though Burton wrote the dissent and Reed the opinion for the court.

11. *Morgan v. Virginia,* 391.

12. *Morgan v. Virginia,* 394.

13. *Morgan v. Virginia,* 388.

14. *Morgan v. Virginia,* 386–88.

15. It is worth noting that as early as June 10, 1946, just a week after the reading of the *Morgan* decision, Texas railway officials acknowledged that the state's segregation statutes were likely invalid as a result of the ruling. See Osborn, "Curtains for Jim Crow," 416.

16. Bayard Rustin, "Nonviolence vs. Jim Crow," *Fellowship: The Journal of the Fellowship of Reconciliation,* July 1942, reprinted in Rustin, *Down the Line,* 5–7. For biographies of Rustin, see D'Emilio, *Lost Prophet;* D. Levine, *Bayard Rustin and the Civil Rights Movement;* J. Anderson, *Bayard Rustin.*

17. Rustin, *Down the Line,* 5–7.

18. Rustin, *Down the Line,* 5–7.

19. See D'Emilio, *Lost Prophet;* D. Levine, *Bayard Rustin and the Civil Rights Movement;* J. Anderson, *Bayard Rustin.* See also C. Vann Woodward's introduction to *Down the Line* for an assessment of Rustin's role as a champion of nonviolent civil rights leadership, his role as an advisor to King, and his career up to March 1963. On Rustin's early embrace of Gandhian nonviolent direct action, see Kapur, *Raising Up a Prophet,* 113–15, 138–39.

20. Salmond, *"My Mind Set on Freedom,"* 3–4.

21. Others also challenged Jim Crow laws on buses in the states that would encompass the Journey of Reconciliation in the period between announcement of the *Morgan* decision and the Apr. 1947 commencement of the journey. Some of the legal papers for these cases can be found in the Leon Ransom papers, 173, box 1, folder 18. Many of these challenges involved passengers riding between northern Virginia and Washington, D.C. In some cases there were threats of violence. It is unclear whether the individuals involved knew of the *Morgan* decision at the time of the breach of local Jim Crow codes.

22. For insight on the history of CORE, see Meier and Rudwick's seminal *CORE*. See also Bell, *CORE and the Strategy of Nonviolence,* and George M. Houser's booklet "CORE: A Brief History," July 1949, Meier-Rudwick Collection of CORE records, 1943–1969, box 3, folder 3, State Historical Society of Wisconsin.

23. George M. Houser, "A Personal Retrospective on the 1947 Journey of Reconciliation," 3, Swarthmore Peace Collection, DG 13, series E, box 16.

24. Memorandum Number 2, n.d., signed by Bayard Rustin and George Houser, Fellowship of Reconciliation Papers, Swarthmore Peace Collection, DG 13, series E, box 16.

25. George Houser and Bayard Rustin, "We Challenged Jim Crow!" 2, Swarthmore Peace Collection, DG 13, series E, box 16.

26. Quoted in J. Anderson, *Bayard Rustin,* 114.

27. See Houser and Rustin, "We Challenged Jim Crow!" 2; J. Anderson, *Bayard Rustin,* 114–23; Peck, *Freedom Ride,* 14–27; D. Levine, *Bayard Rustin and the Civil Rights Movement,* 53.

28. See, e.g., Igal Roodenko's Apr. 14 and 19 letter to an unknown recipient in which he relates his experiences on the buses, especially the Chapel Hill confrontation and its aftermath (CORE Papers, series 3, box 4, folder 8, "Discrimination in Interstate Transportation," State Historical Society of Wisconsin).

29. Peck claims that it was in early April; D'Emilio confirms that they met two days before the ride commenced; Anderson wrote that it was toward the end of March; Daniel Levine, Houser, and Rustin do not provide a date.

30. Memorandum Number 2 argued that "both men and women can be used in the test groups, but there should be no mixing of the sexes in any one group. There is less likelihood of violence if women happen to be present, although this is not taken for granted."

31. Houser, "Personal Retrospective," 6; D'Emilio, *Lost Prophet,* 133–34; *You Don't Have to Ride Jim Crow!*

32. FOR Fliers, Fellowship of Reconciliation Papers, DG 13, series E, box 19.

33. On the issue of not allowing the police to intimidate participants, see Peck, *Freedom Ride,* 16.

34. Quoted in J. Anderson, *Bayard Rustin,* 114–15.

35. J. Anderson, *Bayard Rustin,* 116–17. For more on Marshall's ambivalence, see also D. Levine, *Bayard Rustin and the Civil Rights Movement,* 52.

36. The first and second quotations are from Houser, "Personal Retrospective," 6; the third is from D'Emilio, *Lost Prophet,* 134. FOR and CORE also mailed out a number of letters to raise funds for and awareness of the Journey of Reconciliation. One of these listed some of the challenge's prominent supporters. Examples of such letters can be found in the Fellowship of Reconciliation Papers.

37. The group had been sure to send out press releases about the trip through the Religious News Service, Apr. 4, 1947, JOR Scrapbook, Swarthmore Peace Collection, DG 13, series E, box 16. Newspapers as far away as Texas informed their readers about the trip (*Fort Worth Defender,* Apr. 10, 1947).

38. Houser, "Personal Retrospective," 9–10.

39. Quoted in Houser and Rustin, "We Challenged Jim Crow!" 3.

40. Houser and Rustin, "We Challenged Jim Crow!" 3–4. See also Peck, "Not So Deep Are the Roots," 273; *Baltimore Afro-American,* Apr. 19, 1947.

41. Quoted in Houser and Rustin, "We Challenged Jim Crow!" 4. See also Houser, "Personal Retrospective," 10; Peck, "Not So Deep Are the Roots," 273.

42. Quoted in J. Anderson, *Bayard Rustin,* 117.

43. Quoted in Houser and Rustin, "We Challenged Jim Crow!" 4. See also Peck, "Not So Deep Are the Roots," 273.

44. Houser and Rustin, "We Challenged Jim Crow!" 4.

45. Peck, *Freedom Ride,* 18–19.

46. Peck, *Freedom Ride,* 20. See also J. Anderson, *Bayard Rustin,* 117–18.

47. Quoted in Houser and Rustin, "We Challenged Jim Crow!" 5.

48. Houser, "Personal Retrospective," 11. See also *Resistance,* May 1947. As far back as the nineteenth century, it was clear that the Supreme Court had left open the possibility that while states themselves could not impose laws that would violate the Commerce Clause, individual carriers had a great deal of leeway in enforcing their own seating policies, including segregation if they so chose. See Palmore, "Not-So-Strange Career," 1782, 1804–7, 1815–16.

49. Greyhound, in a memo released after the *Morgan* decision, left a great deal of discretion to drivers. The memo did not specifically refer to *Morgan* and in fact gave broad guidelines for accepting Jim Crow mandates, but it also warned against "undue discrimination" and admonished drivers not to use force in handling those customers who refused to give up seats they had taken (Greyhound Memo, Aug. 1, 1946, Leon Ransom papers, 173, box 1, folder 18).

50. *Pittsburgh Courier,* Apr. 19, 1947.

51. Graham would continue to be an important Southern spokesperson on racial moderation. See, e.g., the written text of a standard address on civil rights that Graham made, "The Negro in North Carolina and the World," and other papers on the Interracial Commission of North Carolina and Graham's appointment

to the President's Committee on Civil Rights, all in the Frank Porter Graham Papers, 1819, subseries 1.2, box 30, folder 68, "1946 Negroes and Race Relations," Southern Historical Collection. See also Pleasants, "Frank Graham and the Politics of the New South."

52. Quoted in Peck, "Not So Deep Are the Roots," 274 (Peck here also provides the description of the taxi driver who hit him); Houser and Rustin, "We Challenged Jim Crow!"; J. Anderson, *Bayard Rustin*, 118; D. Levine, *Bayard Rustin and the Civil Rights Movement*, 54; Peck, *Freedom Ride*, 21.

53. *Pittsburgh Courier*, Apr. 19, 1947; *New York Times*, Apr. 14, 1947. See also *Greensboro Daily News*, Apr. 15, 1947; *New York Post*, Apr. 15, 1947; *PM*, Apr. 16, 1947; *Asheville* (NC) *Citizen*, Apr. 15, 1947; *Asheville* (NC) *Times*, Apr. 14, 1947.

54. Peck, "Not So Deep Are the Roots," 273–74.

55. Roodenko to unknown source, Apr. 14 and 19, 1947.

56. Roodenko to unknown source, Apr. 14 and 19, 1947.

57. Roodenko to unknown source, Apr. 14 and 19, 1947.

58. *Pittsburgh Courier*, Apr. 19, 1947; *New York Times*, Apr. 14, 1947. See also *Greensboro Daily News*, Apr. 15, 1947; *New York Post*, Apr. 15, 1947; *PM*, Apr. 16, 1947; *Asheville Citizen*, Apr. 15, 1947; *Asheville Times*, Apr. 14, 1947.

59. Quoted in Houser, "Personal Retrospective," 13. See also Peck, "Not So Deep Are the Roots," 274; Egerton, *Speak Now against the Day*, 422–23. For a critical assessment of Jones, see the rabid editorial in *Textile Bulletin*, Apr. 15, 1947.

60. Quoted in Houser and Rustin, "We Challenged Jim Crow!" 5–6. See also Peck, "Not So Deep Are the Roots," 274.

61. *Pittsburgh Courier*, Apr. 19, 1947; *New York Times*, Apr. 14, 1947. See also *Greensboro Daily News*, Apr. 15, 1947; *New York Post*, Apr. 15, 1947; *PM*, Apr. 16, 1947; *Asheville Citizen*, Apr. 15, 1947; *Asheville Times*, Apr. 14, 1947.

62. Quoted in J. Anderson, *Bayard Rustin*, 119–21. See also Peck, "Not So Deep Are the Roots," 274.

63. *New York Times*, Apr. 14, 1947. See also *Greensboro Daily News*, Apr. 15, 1947; *New York Post*, Apr. 15, 1947; *PM*, Apr. 16, 1947; *Asheville Citizen*, Apr. 15, 1947; *Asheville Times*, Apr. 14, 1947.

64. *Greensboro Daily News*, Apr. 16, 1947. For a response to this editorial, see Eugene Stanley to *Greensboro Daily News*, Apr. 16, 1947, JOR Scrapbook, Swarthmore Peace Collection, DG 13, series E, box 16.

65. On the racial climate in North Carolina, see, e.g., Chafe, *Civilities and Civil Rights;* Douglas, *Reading, Writing and Race.* On the nature of massive resistance, see Numan Bartley's essential book *The Rise of Massive Resistance.*

66. *Greensboro Daily News*, Apr. 17, 18, 1947; *Carolina Times*, Apr. 26, 1947; *Chicago Defender*, May 3, 1947.

67. See Peck, *Freedom Ride*, 23; Houser, "Personal Retrospective," 14. As Peck points out, the Shiloh Baptist Church in Greensboro was also the site of the mass meeting during the 1961 Freedom Ride.

68. Houser, "Personal Retrospective," 14.

69. "Journey of Reconciliation," *Common Ground* (Autumn 1947): 23, quoted in Houser, "Personal Retrospective," 14.

70. George Houser to author, June 6, 2003.

71. Quoted in Houser and Rustin, "We Challenged Jim Crow!" 6. See also Houser, "Personal Retrospective," 15.

72. Houser and Rustin, "We Challenged Jim Crow!" 6. See also Peck, "Not So Deep Are the Roots," 273; Houser to author, June 6, 2003.

73. *Asheville Times*, Apr. 18, 1947.

74. Quoted in Peck, *Freedom Ride*, 25. See also Peck, "Not So Deep Are the Roots," 274; *Pittsburgh Courier*, Apr. 26, 1947; *Baltimore Afro-American*, Apr. 26, 1947.

75. Houser and Rustin, "We Challenged Jim Crow!" 6–7; *Asheville Citizen*, Apr. 19, 1947; *Asheville Times*, Apr. 18, 1947; Peck, "Not So Deep Are the Roots," 274; *Pittsburgh Courier*, Apr. 26, 1947.

76. "Journey of Reconciliation," 23.

77. Houser and Rustin, "We Challenged Jim Crow!" 7.

78. Houser and Rustin, "We Challenged Jim Crow!" 7; Houser, "Personal Retrospective," 16.

79. *Lynchburg* (VA) *News*, Apr. 23, 24, 28, 1947.

80. J. Anderson, *Bayard Rustin*, 123.

81. Quoted in J. Anderson, *Bayard Rustin*, 124.

82. In Apr. 1947 there were several incidents in the South in which individuals challenged Jim Crow on interstate transport independent of the Journey of Reconciliation. In Greensboro, N.C., Municipal Judge E. E. Rives held that the North Carolina law requiring the segregation of races on public carriers was unconstitutional. At issue was the case of Mrs. Leona Parker, who refused to sit according to Jim Crow laws while traveling from Richmond to her home in Winston-Salem. Rives took three weeks to render his decision. He concluded that the *Morgan* decision was as valid in North Carolina as it was in Virginia. This would not prove helpful to those accused in Chapel Hill, however. In another case, an all-white jury ruled that the Louisville and Nashville Railroad had to pay $800 in damages to James E. Stamps and Ennis L. Powell, who were returning from a meeting of the Fisk University Alumni Association when they were refused service in a segregated dining car because the two allotted (and curtained-off) seats for Negro passengers were filled. The two successful businessmen made it clear through their lawyers that their $25,000 suit was a stand on principle and that they would be willing to have the damages reduced to $500. A third incident did not see such successful and peaceful resolution. A coroner's jury released C. A. James, conductor of an Atlantic Coast Line train, without charges, finding that he had fired shots at black passenger Fletcher Melvin in self-defense. Melvin, a twenty-four-year-old orderly at Provident Hospital in Baltimore, was traveling to

his home in Dunn, N.C. According to black witnesses, Melvin had been asleep for most of the trip and was sleeping when James ordered all black passengers to move forward to the colored coach. James insisted that at Enfield, N.C., he had nudged Melvin and told him to go to the Jim Crow coach and that Melvin had responded with "disorderly conduct." James told the coroner's jury that Melvin had marched up and down the coach loudly, objecting to being sent to the Jim Crow coach. He then explained that he shot Melvin in self-defense. No one ever explained why none of the railway employees was called to assist James, nor could anyone explain why neither James nor any other employee called police in either Rocky Mount or Wilson, two towns through which the train passed during the period of alleged disorder. See Social Science Institute at Fisk University, *Events and Trends in Race Relations: A Monthly Summary,* May 1947, Fisk University, Nashville.

83. C. J. Gates to Bayard Rustin, Sept. 18, 1947, CORE Papers, series 5, box 62, folder 14, "Journey of Reconciliation Freedom Ride."

84. Houser and Rustin, "We Challenged Jim Crow!" 9, Peck, "Not So Deep Are the Roots," 274, 283; *Raleigh News and Observer,* May 21, 1947; *New York Amsterdam News,* May 31, 1947; *Durham Morning Herald,* Mar. 18, 1948; *Chicago Defender,* Mar. 27, 1948; *Pittsburgh Courier,* Mar. 27, 1948; *Baltimore Afro-American,* Mar. 27, 1948. See also Bayard Rustin to George Houser, telegram, Mar. 17, 1948, JOR Scrapbook, Swarthmore Peace Collection, DG 13, series E, box 16.

85. CORE, press release, May 27, 1948, CORE Papers, series 3, box 4, folder 8, "Discrimination in Interstate Transportation."

86. Houser and Rustin, "We Challenged Jim Crow!" 9; Peck, "Not So Deep Are the Roots," 274, 283; *Raleigh News and Observer,* May 21, 1947; *New York Amsterdam News,* May 31, 1947; *Durham Morning Herald,* Mar. 18, 1948; *Chicago Defender,* Mar. 27, 1948; *Pittsburgh Courier,* Mar. 27, 1948; *Baltimore Afro-American,* Mar. 27, 1948. See also Bayard Rustin to George Houser, telegram, Mar. 17, 1948, JOR Scrapbook, Swarthmore Peace Collection, DG 13, series E, box 16.

87. *New York Herald Tribune,* Apr. 12, 1948; *PM,* Apr. 8, 1948; *Pittsburgh Courier,* Apr. 17, 1948; *American Unity,* Apr.–May 1948.

88. The correspondence regarding the interaction among the three civil rights organizations and the lawyers from 1947 to 1949 can be found in the CORE Papers, series 5, box 62, folder 14, "Journal of Reconciliation Freedom Ride."

89. Quoted in the *Asheville Times,* Dec. 14, 1948.

90. *State v. Johnson, et al.,* NC 723—(Orange).

91. Quoted in Percy Wood, "India Welcomes Negro Pacifist from New York," *Chicago Tribune,* Jan. 13, 1949.

92. C. E. Boulware to George Houser, Jan. 18, 1949, CORE Papers, series 5, box 63, folder 1, "Journey of Reconciliation, 1949, Chapel Hill Case."

93. Robert L. Carter to George Houser, Feb. 8, 1949, CORE Papers, series 5, box 63, folder 1.

94. Carter to Houser, Feb. 8, 1949.

95. *New York Times,* Mar. 9, 1949. Chapter 3 explores the Lee case more thoroughly.

96. *Norvell Lee v. Commonwealth of Virginia,* Virginia Supreme Court, 1949, Record #3558. See also Martin A. Martin to George Houser, Oct. 12, 1949, CORE Papers, series 3, box 4, folder 8, "Discrimination in Interstate Transportation."

97. See "Minutes," Feb. 11, 1949, meeting, and George Houser to Nelle Horton, Feb. 12, 1949, both CORE Papers, series 5, box 63, folder 1.

98. Quoted in *New York Post,* Jan. 14, 1949.

99. Conrad Lynn to Andrew Johnson, Feb. 14, 1949, CORE Papers, series 5, box 63, folder 1, "Journey of Reconciliation, Freedom Ride."

100. Andrew Johnson to George Houser, Mar. 12, 1949, CORE Papers, series 5, box 63, folder 1.

101. FOR, press release, Mar. 20, 1949, CORE Papers, series 5, box 63, folder 1.

102. George Houser to James Robinson, Mar. 23, 1949, CORE Papers, series 5, box 63, folder 1.

103. Felmet faced quandaries similar to Johnson's. He aspired to go to law school, ironically enough in Chapel Hill, at the University of North Carolina. However, Felmet's arrests as a consequence of his peace activism—including violation of the Secret Service Act of 1940 for resisting the draft, a 1944 arrest as a result of his attempt to secure affidavits from black workers who had been arrested for refusing to work and were fined and given sentences without having been tried and convicted, and of course his Chapel Hill arrest and conviction—made attainment of this goal problematic. For more information see the Joseph Felmet papers, 4513, Southern Historical Collection, series 1, folder 1, "Correspondence with Board of Law Examiners, 1948," series 1, folder 7, "Transcript of Interview with North Carolina Law Examiners, July 1948," and series 2, folder 11, "FBI Files—Fellowship of Reconciliation."

104. See Rustin, *Down the Line,* 22–49. See also Rustin, "A Report on Twenty-Two Days on the Chain Gang at Roxboro, North Carolina," Bayard Rustin papers, Library of Congress, box 19, folder 9. Although they were sentenced to thirty days, the three men served twenty-two, as they had eight days subtracted from their sentences for good behavior. Rustin's blistering account led to an investigation of conditions in North Carolina's prison camps. See Arsenault, "'You Don't Have to Ride Jim Crow,'" 67.

105. George Houser to "CORE members and friends," Apr. 1, 1949, Fellowship of Reconciliation Papers, DG 13, series E, box 19.

106. Quoted in Rachi Marshall to Jessie (last name unknown), Apr. 4, 1949, CORE Papers, series 5, box 63, folder 1. See also other letters in same folder—Bayard Rustin to A. J. Rustin (Bayard's brother), Mar. 27, 1949; George Houser

to Wally and Juanita Nelson, Mar. 29, 1949; Mrs. F. M. Felmet to George Houser, Apr. 9, 1949—and Rustin, "Report on Twenty-Two Days on the Chain Gang." Rustin gives no indication as to whether he was the victim of any "sexual malpractice" during his ordeal. One wonders if he was himself victimized and if his homosexuality came to light during his imprisonment. Daniel Levine avers that "there was no homosexual incident" during Rustin's time on the chain gang, as the potential consequences were too dire and Rustin's arduous routine too exhausting (*Bayard Rustin and the Civil Rights Movement,* 63–64). Nonetheless, his sister's letter leaves room for doubt.

107. *Baltimore Afro-American,* Apr. 26, 1947.

108. Houser, "Personal Retrospective," 17.

109. Houser to author, June 6, 2003.

110. Houser, "Personal Retrospective," 17.

111. "Free and Equal," script, WMCA, New York, Nov. 18, 1947, Swarthmore Peace Collection, DG 13, series E, box 20.

112. "Free and Equal," 18.

113. *New Republic,* May 5, 1947, quoted in Houser, "Personal Retrospective," 1.

114. Houser, "Personal Retrospective," 19.

115. Peck, "Not So Deep Are the Roots," 273.

116. Peck, "Not So Deep Are the Roots," 19–20.

117. Meier and Rudwick, *CORE,* 39.

118. Houser, "Personal Retrospective."

119. Houser to author, June 6, 2003.

120. Peck, *Freedom Ride,* 14–27, passim.

121. See, e.g., James Peck, interview with James Mosby, Feb. 19, 1970, Civil Rights Documentation Project, Ralph Bunche Oral History Collection, Howard University, Moorland-Spingarn Research Center.

122. Quoted in J. Anderson, *Bayard Rustin,* 129.

123. Farmer, *Lay Bare the Heart,* 196.

124. It is worth noting, e.g., that the future activist Allard Lowenstein, a student at the University of North Carolina in the 1940s, and his friends followed the case of Rustin and the others in Chapel Hill. See Ruth Michaels to Allard Lowenstein, Apr. 18, 1947, Allard K. Lowenstein papers (#4370), Southern Historical Collection, series 1, subsection 1, folder 41, "Correspondence—Apr. 1947."

2. Erasing the Badge of Inferiority

1. Perhaps the best overall treatment of public accommodations law in the law reviews is Singer, "No Right to Exclude."

2. Houser to author, June 6, 2003.

3. *Mitchell v. United States,* 313 U.S. 80.

4. For more on the Mitchell case, see *Mitchell v. United States,* 313 U.S.

80. See also Barnes, *Journey from Jim Crow,* 20–31, passim; Palmore, "Not-So-Strange Career," 1807–9; Miller, *Petitioners,* 365–67.

5. *Mitchell v. United States,* 313 U.S. 816, at 97.

6. Palmore, "Not-So-Strange Career," 1809.

7. Howard University Athletic Hall of Fame, http://www.cldc.howard.edu/~cotton/HalloFame/nll.htm (transcript in author's possession).

8. *Norvell Lee v. Commonwealth of Virginia,* Record No. 3558.

9. *Norvell Lee v. Commonwealth of Virginia,* Record No. 3558 (my emphasis).

10. *Norvell Lee v. Commonwealth of Virginia,* Record No. 3558. Among the decisions that the Virginia court quotes are *Matthews v. Southern Railway System,* 157 Fed. 2d, 609; *Washington B. & A. Electric Railway Company v. Waller, supra,* and *Bob-Lo Excursion Company v. Michigan,* 33 U.S. 28, 68 S. Ct.

11. Martin to Houser, Oct. 12, 1949.

12. George Houser, memo to Igal Roodenko, Joe Felmet, Conrad Lynn, A. J. Muste, Jim Peck, and Connie Muste, Oct. 28, 1949, CORE Papers, series 3, box 4, folder 8.

13. George Houser to Sue Watts, May 5, 1950, CORE Papers, series 3, box 4, folder 8.

14. Sue E. Watts to Fellowship of Reconciliation, Apr. 16, 1950, CORE Papers, series 3, box 4, folder 8.

15. Houser to Watts, May 5, 1950.

16. CORE, press release, Dec. 1, 1949, CORE Papers, series 3, box 4, folder 8.

17. *Henderson v. United States et al.,* 339 U.S. 816.

18. See Reed, *Seedtime for the Modern Civil Rights Movement,* 215.

19. For a good treatment of the *Henderson* case, see Barnes, *Journey from Jim Crow,* 66–80, passim. See also Miller, *Petitioners,* 368–72; Osborn, "Curtains for Jim Crow," 418–19.

20. In a footnote the court observes that while the incident occurred while the train was in Virginia, "no reliance is placed in this case upon any action by any state" (*Henderson v. United States et al.,* at 818, fn. 1).

21. *Henderson v. United States et al.,* at 818–20. Footnote 2 at 819 provides the text of the rules in effect on May 17, 1942.

22. Barnes, *Journey from Jim Crow,* 66–67. The case was *New Negro Alliance v. Sanitary Grocery Co.,* 303 U.S. 552 (1938). For more on Lawson and the case, see also Pacifico, "'Don't Buy Where You Can't Work'"; Catsam, "New Negro Alliance," 514–15.

23. Barnes, *Journey from Jim Crow,* 67.

24. 54 Stat. 902, 49 U.S.C. § 3 (1), quoted in *Henderson v. United States et al.,* at 818.

25. *Henderson v. United States et al.,* at 820.

26. *Henderson v. United States et al.,* at 821.

27. *Henderson v. United States et al.*, at 822.

28. On Truman-era civil rights policies, see Berman, *Politics of Civil Rights in the Truman Administration;* Gardner, *Harry Truman and Civil Rights;* McCoy and Ruetten, *Quest and Response.* On presidential civil rights policy from Truman onward, see Shull, *American Civil Rights Policy.*

29. Anthony Lewis, "'Imposing on Them a Badge of Inferiority,'" *New York Times,* Jan. 22, 2000. On *Henderson* and Elman, see also Berman, *Politics of Civil Rights in the Truman Administration,* 172–77; Gardner, *Harry Truman and Civil Rights,* 178–80, 183–85; McCoy and Ruetten, *Quest and Response,* 218–20.

30. Quoted in A. Lewis, "'Imposing on Them a Badge of Inferiority.'"

31. See Gardner, *Harry Truman and Civil Rights,* 178–79.

32. *Henderson v. United States et al.*, at 824–25. See also Gardner, *Harry Truman and Civil Rights,* 179–80.

33. One other important case is worth addressing at this point. On May 28, 1951, the Supreme Court refused to grant a writ of certiorari to the Atlantic Coast Line Railroad Company (341 U.S. 941). The refusal to grant cert meant that the Fourth Circuit Court of Appeals ruling in *Chance v. Lambeth,* 186 F2d, 879, 4th Circuit, was upheld. In that case, William Chance had been arrested in Virginia for refusing to change his seat to a segregated railway coach. (In addition to the two cases cited, see also H. Long, "Racial Desegregation in Railroad and Bus Transportation," 215.) The court sided with Chance, effectively assuring that the decision in *Morgan* also held on segregation on interstate trains. Thus, *Mitchell, Morgan, Henderson* and the Court's willingness to let *Chance* stand provided a pretty solid wall of defense for those committed to integrating Southern transport. Nonetheless, the questions that Houser raised in his May 5, 1950, letter to Sue Watts, in addition to the still-unresolved question about bus and train facilities along bus and train routes, meant that for all of the Court's clear direction, there were many unresolved issues before Jim Crow would be invalid on the ground.

34. At least one observer in 1954 explicitly linked *Brown* to the question of segregation on interstate transport. In a special Summer 1954 issue of the *Journal of Negro Education,* titled "The Next Steps in Racial Desegregation in Education," Herman H. Long's "Racial Desegregation in Railroad and Bus Transportation" appeared. However, Long, the director of the Race Relations Department for the American Missionary Association and a member of the Board of Home Missions for the Congregational Christian Churches, saw definite linkages between transportation and other areas subject to Jim Crow's pervasiveness, including education.

35. Bartley, *Rise of Massive Resistance,* 67. See also Belknap, *Federal Law and Southern Order.*

36. Bartley, *Rise of Massive Resistance,* 68.

37. Congress of Racial Equality, press release, Mar. 21, 1951, and "Memo on Greyhound Situation," Apr. 3, 1951, both CORE Papers, series 3, box 4, folder 8.

38. Quoted in Congress of Racial Equality, press release, Mar. 21, 1951.

39. "Memo on Greyhound Situation," Apr. 3, 1951.

40. *James Peck v. Securities and Exchange Commission,* 97 Fed. Supp. 679.

41. *James Peck v. Securities and Exchange Commission,* Brief for the Petitioner, CORE Papers, series 3, box 4, folder 8.

42. "Statement by 13 Shareholders owning 282 shares to be presented at the Greyhound Corp. Stockholders Meeting on May 20, 1952," CORE Papers, series 3, box 4, folder 8. There were some familiar names among the petitioners. The thirteen (as they signed) were Mrs. Anna Ames, David Berkinghoff, Par Danforth, Mrs. Margaret Eberhard, Leon Henkin, George Hogle, Mrs. Lois Hogle, Mrs. Eula Morrow, James Peck, Bayard Rustin, Mrs. Caroline Urie, Samueal Wolfson, and Mrs. Frances Wolfson. One cannot help but wonder if the absence of single women among the petitioners was intentional.

43. *James Peck v. The Securities and Exchange Commission,* Brief for the Petitioner.

44. CORE, press release, May 20, 1952.

45. *Pittsburgh Courier,* Dec. 13, 1952.

46. *Pittsburgh Courier,* May 16, 1953.

47. *Pittsburgh Courier,* May 16, 1953.

48. *Pittsburgh Courier,* May 16, 1953.

49. George Houser to Mary Weaver, May 18, 1953, CORE Papers, series 3, box 4, folder 8.

50. Robert Carter to George Houser, Mar. 22, 1954, CORE Papers, series 3, box 4, folder 8.

51. Robert Carter to Billie Ames, Oct. 22, 1954, CORE Papers, series 3, box 4, folder 8.

52. Billie Ames to Robert Carter, Oct. 26, 1954, CORE Papers, series 3, box 4, folder 8.

53. Ames to Carter, Oct. 26, 1954.

54. *Keys,* 64 MCC 769, and *NAACP,* 297 ICC 335. For a Southern response, see *Birmingham News,* Nov. 25, 1955. Two years later, the American States Rights Association (ASRA), Inc., gave its own assessment of the state of the law when it came to interstate transportation. See "American States Rights Association, Inc. Memorandum on Bus Segregation Prepared by our Expert on Constitutional Law," Birmingham, Feb. 5, 1957, Alabama Department of Archives and History, Subject Files, Segregation, SG 6985–6980. Suffice it to say that ASRA proposed a rather tortured and anachronistic reading of the law, relying on a 1910 court decision (*Chiles v. Chesapeake & Ohio Railway Co.,* 218 U.S. 71) to buttress arguments that the courts had clearly made moot over the previous decade and more.

55. Gaillard, *Cradle of Freedom,* 61–65 (quotation on 62).

56. *Boynton v. Virginia,* 364 US 454 at 455–56. See also Greenberg, *Crusaders in the Courts,* 269–70; Barnes, *Journey from Jim Crow,* 144–45.

57. Greenberg, *Crusaders in the Courts,* 270.

58. *Boynton v. Virginia,* at 456–57.

59. Tushnet, *Making Civil Rights Law,* 308.

60. Greenberg, *Crusaders in the Court,* 275.

61. Greenberg, *Crusaders in the Court,* 280–81. Greenberg makes Boynton out to be considerably more colorful than he comes across in the Supreme Court opinion. Greenberg suggests that Boynton may have been drunk when he asserted that he could defend himself and that he changed his mind suddenly and capriciously, storming out after pounding his fist on the table and announcing, "Okay, you all argue it. I got me a chick outside and I don't want to waste any more time here with you." Greenberg also reports that Boynton became a practicing attorney in Alabama and Tennessee, but he had "next to nothing to do with the LDF" (281).

62. *Boynton v. Virginia,* at 457.

63. Tushnet, *Making Civil Rights Law,* 308.

64. *Boynton v. Virginia,* at 457.

65. *Boynton v. Virginia,* at 459.

66. *Boynton v. Virginia,* at 460–61.

67. *Boynton v. Virginia,* at 463.

68. *Boynton v. Virginia,* at 463–64.

3. "The Last Supper"

1. "Three Questions of Law," 16.

2. Farmer, *Lay Bare the Heart.* See also "Higher Education of James Farmer," 79.

3. Joe Perkins, "My 291 Days with CORE," Meier-Rudwick Collection of CORE Records, 1943–1969, box 3, folder 3.

4. Meier and Rudwick, *CORE,* 136.

5. Gordon Carey, in Hampton and Fayer, *Voices of Freedom,* 74. See also Niven, *Politics of Injustice,* 39.

6. Quoted in Laue, *Direct Action and Desegregation,* 98–99.

7. Farmer, *Lay Bare the Heart,* 196.

8. James Farmer, interview, in Williams, *Eyes on the Prize,* 145.

9. Farmer, *Lay Bare the Heart,* 196.

10. Farmer, *Lay Bare the Heart,* 196.

11. "Freedom Ride, 1961—preliminary draft," CORE Papers, series 5, box 20, folder 10. See also "CORE to Test Bus Bias in 'Freedom Ride, 1961,'" CORE Papers, series 5, box 20, folder 10.

12. "Freedom Ride, 1961—preliminary draft."

13. "Freedom Ride, 1961," press release, Mar. or Apr. 1961, CORE Papers, series 5, box 62, folder 11.

14. "Freedom Ride, 1961—preliminary draft."

15. "Freedom Ride, 1961—preliminary draft."

16. "Freedom Ride, 1961," press release, Mar. or Apr. 1961.

17. A number of letters, e.g., went to individuals in Sumter and Rock Hill, S.C., on Mar. 17, 1961. See CORE Papers, series 1, box 2, folder 8.

18. An announcement for the Ride appeared, e.g., in the Mar. 1961 issue of SNCC's publication *Student Voice.* See CORE Papers, series 5, box 26, folder 4. Of course, SNCC had become a vitally important actor in the new phase of direct action civil rights protest, and a number of the Freedom Riders—both those on the original Ride and those who joined in Mississippi—had gained experience in SNCC activities.

19. Freedom Ride Application Blank, CORE Papers, series 5, box 20, folder 10.

20. Marvin Rich to Harold Keith, Apr. 17, 1961, CORE Papers, series 5, box 20, folder 8.

21. James Peck, Freedom Ride Application Blank, CORE Papers, series 5, box 62, folder 11.

22. James Farmer, Freedom Ride Application Blank, CORE Papers, series 5, box 62, folder 11.

23. Peck, *Freedom Ride,* 115.

24. On the Nashville movement, see Halberstam, *Children.* For Lewis's background (and his own impressive account of his role in the movement), see J. Lewis, *Walking with the Wind.*

25. John Lewis, Freedom Ride Application Blank, CORE Papers, series 5, box 62, folder 11.

26. For representative acceptance letters, see Gordon Carey to Edward Blankenheim, John R. Lewis et al., Apr. 25, 1961, CORE Papers, series 5, box 62, folder 11.

27. See Gordon Carey to Thomas Gaither, Apr. 22, 1961, CORE Papers, series 1, box 2, folder 8.

28. "Arrangements for FREEDOM RIDE," reports, Thomas Gaither, Apr. 23–27, 1961, CORE Papers, series 1, box 2, folder 8.

29. Farmer, *Lay Bare the Heart,* 197 (quotation). See also Farmer, interview, in Raines, *My Soul Is Rested,* 110; J. Lewis, *Walking with the Wind,* 139. Before he led his Salt March in 1930, Gandhi wrote British authorities declaring his intentions. See Wolpert, *Gandhi's Passion,* 144–51, passim.

30. Oates, *Let the Trumpet Sound,* 168.

31. James Farmer to President Kennedy et al., Apr. 26, 1961, CORE Papers, series 5, box 20, folder 10.

32. Farmer to Kennedy et al., Apr. 26, 1961. On the question of the Civil Rights Movement and the Cold War, see Dudziak, *Cold War Civil Rights;* Borstelmann, *Cold War and the Color Line;* Romano, "No Diplomatic Immunity." See also Krenn, "Unwelcome Mat"; Dudziak, "Birmingham, Addis Ababa."

33. Quoted in Raines, *My Soul Is Rested,* 110 (emphasis in original).

34. John Seigenthaler, interview with Robert F. Campbell, Nashville, July 10, 1968, 22, Civil Rights Documentation Project.

35. Seigenthaler, interview, July 10, 1968, 23. See also Branch, *Parting the Waters,* 412–13.

36. Burke Marshall, interview with Robert Wright, Feb. 27, 1970, Civil Rights Documentation Project.

37. Letter, itinerary, and participant list, papers of John F. Kennedy, White House Central Files, "HU 2–6 Transportation" folder, box 374, John F. Kennedy Presidential Library (hereafter JFK Library).

38. See *Washington Post* editorial "Southern Hospitality," Apr. 25, 1961. See also Dudziak, *Cold War Civil Rights;* Romano, "No Diplomatic Immunity"; Krenn, "Unwelcome Mat"; Dudziak, "Birmingham, Addis Ababa."

39. Woods, *Black Struggle, Red Scare.* See also G. Lewis, *White South and the Red Menace;* Borstelmann, *Cold War and the Color Line;* Dudziak, *Cold War Civil Rights;* Plummer, *Rising Wind;* Von Eschen, *Race against Empire;* Meriwether, *Proudly We Can Be Africans;* Plummer, *Window on Freedom.*

40. J. Lewis, *Walking with the Wind,* 136.

41. "Freedom Ride, 1961—Participants," Apr. 26, 1961, CORE Papers, series 5, box 20, folder 8, indicates that there would be sixteen Riders, and this list does not include two of those who would depart from Washington.

42. Perhaps out of a sense of self-defense, partially because its members knew critics would accuse them of being communists, and undoubtedly out of a belief that communism was wrong for the United States, CORE had made its opposition to communism clear as far back as 1948: "We are opposed to the undemocratic tactics which Communists and Communist-front groups use in order to attain their ends" ("Statement on the Communist Issue," Adopted by the Congress of Racial Equality, June 1948, CORE Papers, series 4, box 1, folder 1, "Conventions").

43. For brief biographical sketches, see "Freedom Ride, 1961—Participants," Apr. 26, 1961. See also J. Lewis, *Walking with the Wind,* 136–39; Farmer, *Lay Bare the Heart,* 197; Branch, *Parting the Waters,* 412–13; Halberstam, *Children,* 237–50, passim. See also Meier and Rudwick, *CORE,* 136–37.

44. See Catsam, "James Peck."

45. On Detroit CORE and the Bergmans, see Anderson-Bricker, "Making a Movement," esp. chap. 8.

46. "Freedom Ride, 1961—Participants," Apr. 26, 1961; Halberstam, *Children,* 249.

47. *Washington Post,* May 5, 1961.

48. Charles Person to author, e-mail, Jan. 24, 2004.

49. J. Lewis, *Walking with the Wind,* 134.

50. J. Lewis, *Walking with the Wind,* 132–33.

51. Halberstam, *Children,* 248–49.

52. J. Lewis, *Walking with the Wind,* 136.

53. *Fellowship*, Sept. 1947, and "Interracial Workshop: Progress Report," 1, both Swarthmore Peace Collection, DG 13, series E, box 19. See also Murray, *Song in a Weary Throat*, 200.

54. On the New Negro Alliance, see Pacifico, "'Don't Buy Where You Can't Work'"; Catsam, "New Negro Alliance," 514–15.

55. For Randolph's account of his justifications of the march, see A. P. Randolph, "Why Should We March." See also "Excerpts from Keynote Address to the Policy Conference of the Mar. on Washington Movement," Detroit, Sept. 26, 1942, in Grant, *Black Protest*.

56. "You Don't Have to Ride Jim Crow," Swarthmore Peace Collection, DG 13, series E, box 19.

57. For the best firsthand account of the events at Howard, see Murray, *Song in a Weary Throat*, esp. chap. 17, "Jim Crow in the Nation's Capital" (198–209). See also Brown, "NAACP Sponsored Sit-ins."

58. Rustin, *Strategies for Freedom*, 23–24. Also quoted in Fairclough, *Better Day Coming*, 252–53.

59. Viorst, *Fire in the Streets*, 141.

60. Farmer, quoted in Williams, *Eyes on the Prize*, 148.

61. James Farmer, interview, in Hampton and Fayer, *Voices of Freedom*, 75.

62. *U.S. News and World Report*, Apr. 5, 1961.

63. Wolpert, *Gandhi's Passion*, 66.

64. Wolpert, *Gandhi's Passion*, 59.

65. For a theoretical, social-scientific approach to the question of nonviolence in the U.S. direct action civil rights context, see Laue, *Direct Action and Desegregation*, 59–74, passim.

66. Southern Christian Leadership Conference, "The Philosophy of Nonviolence and the Tactic of Nonviolent Resistance," Civil Rights Documentation Project, Vertical File Collection, box 12, folder 26. The Civil Rights Documentation Project's Vertical File Collection has a number of documents on nonviolence, many of which inform this section of the chapter.

67. Peck, interview, Feb. 19, 1970.

68. "Student Nonviolent Coordinating Committee Statement of Purpose," in Carson et al., *Eyes on the Prize Civil Rights Reader*, 119–20.

69. J. Lawson, "On Nonviolence," 31.

70. Quoted in Viorst, *Fire in the Streets*, 136.

71. James Farmer, interview, Sept. 28, 1968, Civil Rights Documentation Project.

72. Richard Haley, interview, Aug. 12, 1969, Civil Rights Documentation Project.

73. On Williams, see Tyson, *Radio Free Dixie*. See also Robert F. Williams, "'Is Violence Necessary to Combat Injustice?' Williams Says 'We Must Fight Back,'" in Carson et al., *Eyes on the Prize Civil Rights Reader*, 110–12.

74. Quoted in *Baltimore Afro-American,* Apr. 29, 1961.

75. *Baltimore Afro-American,* Apr. 29, 1961.

76. Jimmy McDonald, interview with James Mosby, Nov. 5, 1969, 21–28, 22–29, Civil Rights Documentation Project.

77. Motley, *Equal Justice . . . Under Law,* 132.

78. See Marvin Rich, interview with James Mosby, Nov. 6, 1969, Civil Rights Documentation Project.

79. Farmer writes about these early meetings in *Lay Bare the Heart* (197–99).

80. Viorst, *Fire in the Streets,* 141.

81. Farmer, *Lay Bare the Heart,* 198.

82. Farmer, *Lay Bare the Heart,* 198.

83. Farmer, *Lay Bare the Heart,* 198.

84. J. Lewis, *Walking with the Wind,* 138.

85. Halberstam, *Children,* 250.

86. J. Lewis, *Walking with the Wind,* 138–39.

87. McDonald, interview, Nov. 5, 1969, 24-11.

88. Walter Bergman, "Appraisal of Freedom Ride," June 1, 1961, CORE Papers, series 5, box 63, folder 3, "Correspondence."

89. Farmer, *Lay Bare the Heart,* 198–99.

90. J. Lewis, *Walking with the Wind,* 139–40.

91. Halberstam, *Children,* 250.

92. Lewis mentions the "Last Supper" in all of his interviews and writings, and he spoke of it to me in a conversation, as well as in a speech he gave at the Washington Court Hotel, at a fortieth-anniversary Freedom Rider reunion in Washington, D.C. (both on May 10, 2001).

93. J. Lewis, *Walking with the Wind,* 140.

94. *Washington Post,* May 5, 1961.

95. Farmer, *Lay Bare the Heart,* 199.

96. Seigenthaler, interview, July 10, 1968, 412–13.

97. *Baltimore Afro-American,* May 6, 1961.

98. J. Lewis, *Walking with the Wind,* 140; Morrison and Morrison, *From Camelot to Kent State,* 28; Lewis, interview, in Hampton and Fayer, *Voices of Freedom,* 77.

99. McDonald, interview, Nov. 5, 1969, 25-12.

4. "Hallelujah, I'm a Travelin'!"

1. *Baltimore Afro-American,* May 6, 1961.

2. *Baltimore Afro-American,* May 13, 1961. Note that the *Afro-American* was a weekly newspaper, so the stories from May 13 reflected events from the week of the Freedom Ride's departure.

3. *Baltimore Afro-American,* May 13, 1961.

4. For more on this theme, see Dudziak, *Cold War Civil Rights;* Borstelmann, *Cold War and the Color Line,* 164–71.

5. *Washington Post,* Apr. 25, 1961.

6. James Robinson to *Afro-American,* May 13, 1961.

7. J. Lewis, *Walking with the Wind,* 140.

8. Dunbar, "Annealing of the South."

9. For perhaps the best treatment of white supremacy in Virginia, see J. D. Smith, *Managing White Supremacy.* See also Lechner, "Massive Resistance."

10. For an assessment of the literature on civil rights in Virginia, see Pratt, "New Directions." Pratt argues that "events taking place in Virginia" during the Civil Rights Movement, "even though they were not always in the national spotlight, were no less pivotal in the remaking of an American society committed to the ideals of racial equality and social justice" (149). On the legal challenges to Jim Crow, see Wallenstein, *Blue Laws and Black Codes.*

11. See Meier and Rudwick, "Boycott Movement against Jim Crow Streetcars."

12. Palmore, "Not-So-Strange Career," 1793.

13. See Meier and Rudwick, "Negro Boycotts of Segregated Streetcars."

14. See Meier and Rudwick, "Boycott Movement against Jim Crow Streetcars."

15. See Crofts, "Warner-Foraker Amendment."

16. Key, *Southern Politics in State and Nation,* 19.

17. For the best treatment of the Byrd Organization, see Ely, *Crisis of Conservative Virginia.* For a series of reflections on Byrd upon his 1966 death, see Vertical File: Harry Flood Byrd, 1887–1966, Virginia Historical Society.

18. See Sullivan, *Days of Hope,* 204–5.

19. Bartley, *Rise of Massive Resistance,* 108. For a series of essays exploring the New Deal and the New South, see Badger, *New Deal/New South.*

20. Frederickson, *Dixiecrat Revolt,* 23–24; Freidel, *FDR and the South,* 72–73.

21. On black political mobilization during the Byrd years, see Randolph and Tate, *Rights for a Season,* 111–62.

22. Bartley, *Rise of Massive Resistance,* 109.

23. See Bartley, *Rise of Massive Resistance,* 108–49, passim; Lassiter and Lewis, *Moderates' Dilemma.* See also G. Lewis, *Massive Resistance;* Lechner, "Massive Resistance." Perhaps the best of the older treatments is Muse, *Virginia's Massive Resistance,* but also see Peters, *Southern Temper,* 60–61, 154–59; Gates, *Making of Massive Resistance.* A final source worth examining is James Rawlings Sydnor's unpublished paper "When Virginia's Public Schools Were Closed," Nov. 15, 1994, James Rawlings Sydnor Papers, Virginia Historical Society.

24. Sherman, "'Last Stand.'" See also J. D. Smith, *Managing White Supremacy,* 76–106. On issues of "racial purity" in Virginia in the 1920s, see J. D. Smith, "Campaign for Racial Purity."

25. Quoted in Sherman, "'Last Stand,'" 84.

26. Gates, *Making of Massive Resistance,* 48–49, quoted in McMillen, *Citizens' Councils,* 106. See also McMillen's treatment of the Defenders and Council-type organizations in Virginia (105–7); J. D. Smith, *Managing White Supremacy,* 76–106.

27. Lechner, "Massive Resistance," 632, 633.

28. See the "Almond Biographical" sketch in the guide to the J. Lindsay Almond Papers, Virginia Historical Society. As an example of Almond's views on civil rights prior to 1959, see "The Achilles Heel of America," address by J. Lindsay Almond Jr., South Carolina Bar Association, Columbia, May 2, 1958, Almond Papers, section 2, box 13. See also "Almond Scrapbooks," Jan. 1960–June 1963, section 4, box 34, Almond Papers; clippings file, James Rawlings Sydnor Papers.

29. See Don Murray, "Lindsey [*sic*] Almond Was a Prophet," transcript of July 7–8, 1970, radio broadcast, WRVA Radio, Richmond, VA, J. Lyndsay Almond Papers, section 2, box 18. On the day the Freedom Riders left Washington, however, Harry Byrd Jr., son of the former governor and senator and himself a staunchly conservative Democrat state senator, announced that Almond had backed off somewhat by opposing federal intervention in the case of the Prince Edward County school integration case. Almond saw the folly of massive resistance. He was, however, no integrationist. See *Richmond Times-Dispatch,* May 5, 1961. Two useful treatments of the still-prominent role Byrd could play in the 1960s can be found in James R. Sweeney's articles: "Whispers in the Golden Silence" and "New Day in the Old Dominion."

30. For a good early treatment of white moderates in the Old Dominion, see Hershman, "Rumbling in the Museum."

31. See Boyle, *Desegregated Heart.*

32. See J. D. Smith, "'When Reason Collides with Prejudice.'"

33. Eddy, "Alexandria Council Seeks Improved Race Relations," 6.

34. Sydnor, "When Virginia's Public Schools Were Closed." See also "Organizing to Save Public Schools," pamphlet, James Rawlings Sydnor Papers.

35. Senator Henry L. Marsh III, from panel "Explorations in Black Leadership," Sept. 13, 2000, University of Virginia Television, http://www.virginia.edu/uvanewsmakers/newsmakers/marsh.html (transcript in author's possession).

36. Netherton et al., *Fairfax County,* 662–63, chap. 3.

37. Barnes, *Journey from Jim Crow,* 56–57.

38. 85 F. Supp. 545 (E.D. Va. 1949).

39. See Christina A. Samuels, "Rare View of School Integration Day," *Washington Post,* May 12, 2001.

40. Eddy, "Alexandria Council Seeks Improved Race Relations," 9.

41. Dion Diamond, interview with Kay Shannon, Nov. 11, 1967, 14–17, 21–22, passim, Civil Rights Documentation Project.

42. "Hallelujah, I'm a Travelin,'" 33.

43. Goldfield, *Black, White and Southern,* 125.

44. McDonald, interview, Nov. 5, 1969, 26-13-27-14.

45. Frances Bergman to "CORE Friends," May 9, 1961, CORE Papers, series 5, box 20, folder 8.

46. Frances Bergman to "CORE Friends," May 9, 1961.

47. James Peck, "Freedom Ride," *CORELator,* May 1961, "Special Freedom Ride Edition," 2, Swarthmore Peace Collection, DG 13, series E, box 19 (also in Peck, *Freedom Ride,* 116).

48. Frances Bergman to "CORE Friends," May 9, 1961. See also J. Lewis, *Walking with the Wind,* 140.

49. Quoted in J. Lewis, *Walking with the Wind,* 140; Farmer, *Lay Bare the Heart,* 199.

50. See Pratt, *Color of Their Skin;* Randolph and Tate, *Rights for a Season.*

51. Wynes, *Race Relations in Virginia,* quoted in Woodward, *Strange Career,* 33.

52. L. A. Randolph, "Civil Rights Movement in Richmond," 63.

53. L. A. Randolph, "Civil Rights Movement in Richmond," 64.

54. Alfreda L. Madison to J. O. Gilliam, July 16, 1947, Leon Ransom papers, box 1, folder 18.

55. For a general treatment of race in Richmond during the civil rights era, see Randolph and Tate, *Rights for a Season,* 163–204.

56. L. A. Randolph, "Civil Rights Movement in Richmond," 64.

57. See clippings file, John Aubrey Brown papers, series 2, folder 3, Virginia Historical Society.

58. See Aubrey N. Brown Jr. to family members, Feb. 24, 1960, John Aubrey Brown papers, series 2, folder 1, "Correspondences"; "Searching for a Sense of Direction," John Aubrey Brown papers, series 2, folder 4.

59. L. A. Randolph, "Civil Rights Movement in Richmond," 66–68, passim.

60. *Baltimore Afro-American,* Apr. 29, 1961.

61. On these Cold War questions, see Dudziak, *Cold War Civil Rights;* Borstelmann, *Cold War and the Color Line.* On the question of the treatment of African diplomats, see Romano, "No Diplomatic Immunity." See also Dudziak, "Birmingham, Addis Ababa"; Krenn, "Unwelcome Mat." On the question of the Cold War, communism, and civil rights in the South, see Woods, *Black Struggle, Red Scare.*

62. The location of the former Trailways station where Boynton was arrested is the current site of the Library of Virginia. See John Kneebone, "Freedom Rides in Virginia," va-hist listserv, July 14, 1999, http://www.listlva.lib.va.us/oldarch/va_hist/1999/jul99/msg00029.html (transcript in author's possession).

63. Frances Bergman to "CORE Friends," May 9, 1961.

64. J. Lewis, *Walking with the Wind,* 140.

65. Perkins, "My 291 Days with CORE," 14.

66. Frances Bergman to "CORE Friends," May 9, 1961.

67. Peck, "Freedom Ride," 2; Peck, *Freedom Ride*, 116.

68. Frances Bergman to "CORE Friends," May 9, 1961.

69. Perkins, "My 291 Days with CORE," 14.

70. Walker would be one of the lead tacticians for SCLC and would develop most of the strategies of the Birmingham movement in 1963.

71. J. Lewis, *Walking with the Wind*, 141.

72. J. Lewis, *Walking with the Wind*, 141; Branch, *Parting the Waters*, 413.

73. Frances Bergman to "CORE Friends," May 9, 1961.

74. Peck, "Freedom Ride"; Peck, *Freedom Ride*, 116; J. Lewis, *Walking with the Wind*, 141.

75. Branch, *Parting the Waters*, 413.

76. Peck, "Freedom Ride"; Peck, *Freedom Ride*, 116.

77. Frances Bergman to "CORE Friends," May 9, 1961.

78. *New York Times*, May 7, 1961; *Charlotte Observer*, May 7, 1961. See also Bryant, *Bystander*, 256–60, Brauer, *John F. Kennedy and the Second Reconstruction*, 95–98.

79. Bryant, *Bystander*, 257.

80. E. Thomas, *Robert Kennedy*, 127.

81. On the integration of the University of Georgia, see Pratt, *We Shall Not Be Moved*; Trillin, *Education in Georgia*.

82. *Charlotte Observer*, May 7, 1961.

83. Bryant, *Bystander*, 257.

84. *New York Times*, May 7, 1961.

85. "Address by Honorable Robert F. Kennedy Attorney General of the United States," Law Day Exercises at the University of Georgia Law School, May 6, 1961, Robert F. Kennedy Papers, Attorney General Files, Speeches 1961–1964, "UGA Law Day Speech, May 6, 1961" folder, box 1, JFK Library. Text quoted in *New York Times*, May 7, 1961.

86. "Address by Honorable Robert F. Kennedy." See also Brauer, *John F. Kennedy and the Second Reconstruction*, 95–98. Somewhat curiously, Dudziak never refers to Kennedy's University of Georgia speech in *Cold War Civil Rights*, despite the fact that this was his first major speech as attorney general; despite the fact that Kennedy so clearly linked the struggle for civil rights with Cold War imperatives; and despite the fact that even as Kennedy spoke, the Freedom Riders were about to head into a maelstrom that would hurt Americans among precisely those people in the rest of the world about whom Kennedy spoke. Arthur M. Schlesinger Jr. quotes one line of the speech without providing much context in *Robert Kennedy and His Times* (316).

87. "Address by Honorable Robert F. Kennedy."

88. "Address by Honorable Robert F. Kennedy."

89. "Address by Honorable Robert F. Kennedy."

90. "Address by Honorable Robert F. Kennedy."

91. "Address by Honorable Robert F. Kennedy."

92. Branch, *Parting the Waters,* 414.

93. *Baltimore Afro-American,* May 6, 1961.

94. Branch, *Parting the Waters,* 415.

95. *Pittsburgh Courier,* June 12, 1943. Carrie McCray, Wilson's cousin, later recalled of Danville, "In this town segregation was carried out to a 'T.'" McCray believes that Wilson "was very brave to do that there way back in 1943 with no movement behind her" (Carrie McCray to author, Apr. 18, 2003).

96. See "Background Information on Danville, VA," Student Nonviolent Coordinating Committee, 1963, and "Background Information: Danville Protest Movement," Danville Christian Progressive Association, July 9, 1963, both in Civil Rights Collection, Buford W. Posey Papers, box 3, folder 2, Special Collections Library at the University of Tennessee-Knoxville. See also the series of articles on the Danville protests published in the *Danville Register & Bee,* June 7, 2003 (four articles: "Summer of 1963 Marked by Tensions in Southeast," "Student Marched to Protest Injustice," "The Face of Segregation," "Whites Reflect on Civil Rights Attitudes"), June 11, 2003 (two articles: "A City Remembers," "'A New Era' Begins in the River City"), and July 8, 2003 (one article: "Bloody Monday, 40 Years Later"). Finally, see Branch, *Parting the Waters* 822, 834; Belknap, *Federal Law and Southern Order,* 120–21. Belknap tells of Danville's pistol-packing Judge Archibald Aiken, who sentenced many of the Danville protesters to prison.

97. See Rise, *Martinsville Seven;* Rise, "Race, Rape and Radicalism."

98. On Scottsboro, see D. Carter, *Scottsboro.*

99. For an astute assessment of the state's role in taking the lead in massive resistance and forestalling the emergence of vigilante groups, see Hershman, "Massive Resistance Meets Its Match."

100. In 1950 and 1951, the Civil Rights Congress led what one historian would later call "Freedom Rides" to Virginia in hopes of saving the Seven. See Gerald Horne, "Civil Rights Congress," 322.

101. Peck, "Freedom Ride," 2; Peck, *Freedom Ride,* 117.

102. Perkins, "My 290 Days with CORE," 14.

103. Peck, "Freedom Ride," 2; Peck, *Freedom Ride,* 117; Perkins, "My 290 Days with CORE," 14.

5. The Carolinas

1. See Key, *Southern Politics in State and Nation,* chap. 10 (205–28).

2. *Raleigh News and Observer,* July 17, 1947, quoted in Key, *Southern Politics in State and Nation.*

3. Floyd McKissick, interview with Jack Bass and Walter De Vries, Dec.

6, 1973, Southern Oral History Collection, #4007: A-134, McKissick, Southern Historical Collection.

4. Pleasants, "Frank Graham and the Politics of the New South," 195. See also Chafe, *Civilities and Civil Rights,* 5.

5. Pleasants, "Frank Graham and the Politics of the New South," 177. The Frank Porter Graham Papers (1819) provide ample evidence of Graham's progressive spirit. The papers contain a number of folders of speeches, letters, and other documents revealing Porter's relative liberalism on race.

6. Quoted in Chafe, *Civilities and Civil Rights,* 5.

7. See McMillen, *Citizens' Council,* 111–15.

8. Kerr and Willis Scott were not related.

9. Bartley, *Rise of Massive Resistance,* 72–73.

10. Bartley, *Rise of Massive Resistance,* 144.

11. Bartley, *Rise of Massive Resistance,* 78.

12. Greensboro has changed the name of South Elm Street, the main downtown street where the Woolworth's still sits, to "February 1st Street" in honor of the date when the students posed a challenge that none of the city fathers at the time would have found worthy of commemoration. See Dent, *Southern Journey,* 9.

13. On Greensboro, see Chafe, *Civilities and Civil Rights,* passim. See also Franklin McCain, interview, in Raines, *My Soul Is Rested,* 75–82.

14. On Baker, see Ransby, *Ella Baker,* passim.

15. Cluster, *They Should Have Served that Cup of Coffee,* 2.

16. "The Student Protest Movement, Winter 1960," report published by the Southern Regional Council, Apr. 1, 1960, 1, Cox Collection, Box X #45, Special Collections, Mitchell Memorial Library, Mississippi State University.

17. *Greensboro Daily News,* Feb. 15, 1960.

18. Chafe, *Civilities and Civil Rights,* 5.

19. Woodward, *Strange Career,* 67; Palmore, "Not-So-Strange Career," 1792–93.

20. *Asheville Citizen,* May 8, 1961.

21. Copy of Arrest Warrant and Statement in case of *State v. Charles Hauser,* Leon Ransom papers, box 1, folder 18.

22. "School Closing Project," CORE Papers, series 5, box 20, folder 10. See also Barnes, *Journey from Jim Crow,* 143–44.

23. Chafe, *Civilities and Civil Rights,* 5.

24. Margaret Price, "Toward a Solution of the Sit-In Controversy," Southern Regional Council Special Report, May 31, 1960, 5, Cox Collection, Box X #45.

25. McCain, interview, in Raines, *My Soul Is Rested,* 82.

26. Peck, *Freedom Ride,* 117; Peck, "Freedom Ride," 2.

27. *Charlotte Observer,* May 5, 1961.

28. *Charlotte Observer,* May 5, 1961.

29. Farmer, interview, in Raines, *My Soul Is Rested,* 111.

30. Perkins, "My 291 Days with CORE," 14.

31. Peck, *Freedom Ride,* 117; Peck, "Freedom Ride."

32. *Charlotte Observer,* May 8, 1961.

33. Frances Bergman to "CORE Friends," May 9, 1961; Peck, *Freedom Ride,* 117; Peck, "Freedom Ride." In the week prior to the Freedom Ride's passage through the Triangle Region, the UNC Law School announced that Julius LeVonne had been named editor-in-chief of the *North Carolina Law Review,* the highest honor a law student could receive. LeVonne was the first black student to be so honored.

34. Peck, *Freedom Ride,* 117; Peck, "Freedom Ride."

35. Quoted in *Baltimore Afro-American,* May 9, 1961.

36. Peck, *Freedom Ride,* 117–18.

37. For the best recent interpretation of the NAACP, see Berg, *Ticket to Freedom;* Jonas, *Freedom's Sword.*

38. Internecine battles continued among the groups. Thurgood Marshall's speech in Raleigh caused an unintended contretemps between the NAACP and CORE when the May 25 issue of *Jet* reported that Marshall had "rapped the sponsoring group [of the Freedom Rides] for not defending in court its members" arrested during protests: "CORE officials considered the attack 'a low blow' and an example of how the NAACP attempts to embarrass other groups in the civil rights field." CORE and the NAACP had in fact arranged for legal counsel, but Freedom Riders had also pledged to remain in jail until their trials. In any case, Marshall was incensed when he heard of the controversy, responding in a telegram to *Jet:* "I did speak in Raleigh, North Carolina Sunday, May seventh but did not mention Freedom Riders, Core, or anything in relation to either. . . . Your staff could have checked this with me before publication, especially in view of innuendo in statement. Unfairness of statement more evidenced by fact that your staff obviously did check with CORE. Would appreciate correction by you" (Thurgood Marshall to John Johnson, Johnson Publications, telegram, May 19, 1961, NAACP Papers, group III, box A 136, Library of Congress).

39. Frances Bergman to "CORE Friends," May 9, 1961.

40. Price, "Toward a Solution of the Sit-In Controversy," 5–6; "Student Protest Movement, Winter 1960," xv.

41. Perkins, "My 291 Days with CORE," 14.

42. Price, "Toward a Solution of the Sit-In Controversy," 9; "Student Protest Movement, Winter 1960," xv.

43. Peck, *Freedom Ride,* 118.

44. Douglas, *Reading, Writing, and Race,* 4–5. Douglas invokes Chafe's idea of "civility" as the approach many North Carolinians took toward race relations. Chafe makes brief mention of the aims of Charlotte's civic elite in *Civilities and Civil Rights,* 144.

45. Douglas, *Reading, Writing and Race,* 89.

46. Goldfield and Brownell, *Urban America,* 350–51.

47. Price, "Toward a Solution of the Sit-In Controversy," 9.

48. Southern Regional Council, "The Student Protest Movement," xix.

49. "School Closing Project."

50. "School Closing Project."

51. "School Closing Project."

52. *Charlotte Observer,* May 10, 1961.

53. On that same day doctors in the Progressive Plutocracy cast a vote for Dr. Jim Crow. The North Carolina Medical Society decided not to offer full membership to Negro physicians, instead relegating black doctors to "scientific memberships," a distinction that ascribed second-class citizenship on the state's African American doctors (*Charlotte Observer,* May 9, 1961).

54. Peck, *Freedom Ride,* 17; Niven, *Politics of Injustice,* 45.

55. *Baltimore Afro-American,* May 13, 1961.

56. Peck, *Freedom Ride,* 118; Peck, "Freedom Ride."

57. *Charlotte Observer,* May 9, 1961.

58. Perkins, "My 291 Days with CORE," 14.

59. *Baltimore Afro-American,* May 9, 1961. From the Charlotte arrest onward, Moses Newson's Freedom Ride reports in the *Afro,* as it was called, became frequent, several articles often appearing in a single issue.

60. Frances Bergman to "CORE Friends," May 9, 1961.

61. *Charlotte Observer,* May 9, 1961.

62. Peck, *Freedom Ride,* 118; Peck, "Freedom Ride," 2.

63. *Baltimore Afro-American,* May 9, 1961.

64. Perkins, "My 291 Days with CORE," 14.

65. Perkins, "My 291 Days with CORE," 14 n.13.

66. Perkins, "My 291 Days with CORE," 5, 14 n.13.

67. Farmer, *Lay Bare the Heart,* 199.

68. Frances Bergman to "CORE Friends," May 9, 1961.

69. Key, *Southern Politics in State and Nation,* 130.

70. Key, *Southern Politics in State and Nation,* 131.

71. See Grantham, *Democratic South,* 88; Bartley, *Rise of Massive Resistance,* 19.

72. Robert Sherrill has a fascinating chapter, "An Interlude: God and Bob Jones University," in his book *Gothic Politics in the Deep South* (216–34). Long before it became part of the cultural lexicon in the 2000 election, Bob Jones University served as a rallying place for fundamentalist conservatism in South Carolina.

73. Bartley, *Rise of Massive Resistance,* 45. Gressette's papers are in the Modern Political Collections, South Caroliniana Library.

74. Bartley, *Rise of Massive Resistance,* 131.

75. *Race Relations Law Reporter* 1 (Feb. 1956): 241, quoted in Bartley, *Rise of Massive Resistance,* 76–77.

76. Bartley, *Rise of Massive Resistance,* 77.

77. See Bryant Simon, "Race Reactions." Simon reveals that there was a window of opportunity in the 1930s when black and white workers began to mobilize politically across racial lines, but the onset of war coupled with racial demagoguery brought the politics of racism back to the fore. Simon's essay thus follows in the spirit and historiographical lineage of not one but two of C. Vann Woodward's traditions—first, that the South never had to follow an inexorable path of racism and Jim Crow (a point that Woodward most famously made in *Origins of the New South* and *Strange Career of Jim Crow*); and second, that uneasy alliances among poor and working-class whites and blacks often failed as a consequence of racial demagoguery (a point that Woodward made in his biography of Tom Watson). Appropriately, Woodward wrote the introduction for *Jumpin' Jim Crow,* and the editors dedicated the collection to him. This was Woodward's last scholarly publication, and it came out after his 1999 death.

78. On the Dixiecrat revolt, see esp. Frederickson, *Dixiecrat Revolt;* Frederickson, "'As a Man I Am Interested in State's Rights.'" See also Sherrill's chapter "Strom Thurmond: 1948 and All That," in *Gothic Politics in the Deep South* (235–54).

79. McMillen, *Citizens' Council,* 73. McMillen's observations on South Carolina are relatively brief but quite astute in explaining South Carolina's culture of resistance.

80. See, e.g., Tyson, "Dynamite and the 'Silent South.'"

81. McMillen, *Citizens' Council,* 73–80, passim.

82. Lau, *Democracy Rising,* provides the most comprehensive overview of the struggle for black equality in South Carolina.

83. Frederickson, "'As a Man I Am Interested in State's Rights,'" 264.

84. See Lau, *Democracy Rising;* "Student Protest Movement, Winter 1960," xix–xxv.

85. Woodward, *Strange Career,* 67.

86. Quoted in Silberman, *Crisis in Black and White,* 24.

87. S. Kennedy, *Jim Crow Guide,* 178.

88. See NAACP Papers, group III, box A107, "General Office File: Discrimination—Airports" folder, and box A111, "General Office File: Discrimination, Transportation, General, 1960–1962" folder. These folders contain a number of complaints about segregation and mistreatment in South Carolina and across the South, including at the Charleston and Greenville airports and on buses in Charleston, Summerville, and Spartanburg.

89. See James T. McCain Papers, Clippings File, "1956–1957, Clippings SC: Re: Transportation," South Caroliniana Library.

90. *Charleston News and Courier,* Aug. 2, 1957; *State,* Aug. 2, 1957.

91. Greenville Interdenominational Alliance and Greenville CORE, mailing, Nov. 12, 1959, and CORE, press release, Nov. 23, 1959, both in James T. McCain Papers, box 1.

92. On Rock Hill, see W. P. Moore, "Tell Them We in the South Are Dissatisfied."

93. For a firsthand account of the Rock Hill protests and jail-ins, see Thomas Gaither, "Jailed-In," CORE pamphlet, South Caroliniana Library. See also Shinault-Small, "WBEMC, 1960–2005."

94. Friendship was South Carolina's oldest junior college, having been established in 1891.

95. "Excerpts from Ted Poston's (*New York Post*) Interview with Rock Hill Students," CORE mailing, Segregation and Integration, Miscellaneous Collection, access #131, folder 3, Special Collections at Mitchell Memorial Library, Mississippi State University.

96. Gaither, "Jailed-In."

97. "Excerpts from Ted Poston's . . . Interview."

98. Gaither, "Jailed-In."

99. Quoted in Gaither, "Jailed-In," and in "Excerpts from Ted Poston's . . . Interview." Gaines's story would also provide the foundation for a CORE fundraising letter from Harry Belafonte. See Belafonte letter, William D. Workman Jr. papers, box 33, Modern Political Collections, South Caroliniana Library.

100. Gaither, "Jailed-In."

101. See McCain obituary, *State,* June 6, 2003.

102. See Lau, *Democracy Rising,* 217.

103. As evidence of this, see McCain's appointment calendars, James T. McCain Papers, box 1.

104. Ransby, *Ella Baker,* 264.

105. Quoted in Carson, *In Struggle,* 32.

106. Carson, *In Struggle,* 32. Blumberg (*Civil Rights*) and Meier and Rudwick (*CORE*) also argue that the Rock Hill sit-ins, though aborted, were a defining moment, providing a model and example for the student struggle.

107. Bartley, *New South,* 306.

108. J. Lewis, *Walking with the Wind,* 142.

109. Text of speech, and Frank Porter Graham letter, Apr. 12, 1961, both Frank Porter Graham Papers, 1819, subseries 1.2, box 61, "1961: Negroes and Race Relations: Winthrop Speech" folder.

110. Harry Golden to Frank Porter Graham, Apr. 5, 1961, Harry Golden, "What's the Matter with South Carolina?" *Crusader,* Apr. 7, 1961, various letters to Graham, all in Frank Porter Graham Papers.

111. J. Lewis, *Walking with the Wind,* 142.

112. Branch, *Parting the Waters,* 414–15. The administration's sense that it was caught in a conundrum on civil rights is illustrated in an internal White House memo that Louis Martin sent to Ted Sorenson when the Freedom Riders were in South Carolina. Martin does not espouse a position for the president to take, but rather paints a picture of the tenuous position in which the

Kennedys found themselves. He reveals that the black vote would be especially crucial in the North, and his concluding words remind Sorenson of how "the sharp edge of Negro resentment over racial discrimination can cut like a knife inside the ghetto." See Louis Martin to Ted Sorenson, memorandum, May 10, 1961, Robert F. Kennedy Papers, box 66, "White House: Memoranda, 4.1961–6/1961" folder.

113. Quoted in Branch, *Parting the Waters,* 415. A few years later, Wilkins recalled that just a couple of months before the Freedom Ride, in March 1961, the president worked to desegregate lodging facilities in South Carolina for the Civil War Centennial Commission's celebration in Charleston (Roy Wilkins, Oral History, Aug. 13, 1964, JFK Library).

114. *Rock Hill* (SC) *Evening Herald,* May 5, 1961 (first quotation), May 8, 1961 (second quotation). The *Charlotte Observer* had also announced the arrival of the group in Charlotte, and in a small article on May 5 the newspaper covered plans for the group's mass meeting in Rock Hill.

115. Quoted in *New Orleans Times-Picayune,* Apr. 7, 2001.

116. Peck, *Freedom Ride,* 118–19; Peck, "Freedom Ride."

117. J. Lewis, *Walking with the Wind,* 142. James Farmer asserts that the young tough said, "Get to the other side, boy, where the niggers go" (*Lay Bare the Heart,* 199). Suffice it to say that reconstructing dialogue in the midst of heated events is imprecise at best, even with the conflicting testimony of participants.

118. J. Lewis, *Walking with the Wind,* 142; Farmer, *Lay Bare the Heart,* 199.

119. Quoted in Farmer, *Lay Bare the Heart,* 199.

120. J. Lewis, *Walking with the Wind,* 142.

121. Quoted in *Baltimore Afro-American,* May 13, 1961.

122. J. Lewis, *Walking with the Wind,* 142. Farmer's account of the officer's words differs slightly, albeit inconsequentially.

123. Quoted in *New Orleans Times-Picayune,* Apr. 7, 2001.

124. J. Lewis, *Walking with the Wind,* 143.

125. Quoted in *Rock Hill Evening Herald,* May 10, 1961.

126. Branch, *Parting the Waters,* 416.

127. J. Lewis, *Walking with the Wind,* 143.

128. Peck, *Freedom Ride,* 118–19; Peck, "Freedom Ride," 2.

129. *Rock Hill Evening Herald,* May 10, 1961.

130. Quoted in *Rock Hill Evening Herald,* May 10, 1961.

131. *Charlotte Observer,* May 10, 1961.

132. Farmer, *Lay Bare the Heart,* 199–200.

133. *Baltimore Afro-American,* May 13, 1961.

134. *Charlotte Observer,* May 11, 1961.

135. He had hoped to work in what is now Tanzania. See Lewis's recollection in Hampton and Fayer, *Voices of Freedom,* 77.

136. J. Lewis, *Walking with the Wind,* 143–44; Branch, *Parting the Waters,* 416.

137. J. Lewis, *Walking with the Wind,* 144; Branch, *Parting the Waters,* 416 (quotation).

138. Peck, *Freedom Ride,* 121; Peck, "Freedom Ride," 2. In the article Peck describes Winnsboro as being "as ultra-segregationist as Alabama."

139. *Baltimore Afro-American,* May 13, 1961.

140. Peck, *Freedom Ride,* 121; Peck, "Freedom Ride," 2.

141. *Baltimore Afro-American,* May 13, 1961.

142. *Charlotte Observer,* May 11, 1961.

143. *Baltimore Afro-American,* May 13, 1961; *Charlotte Observer,* May 12, 1961.

144. Peck, *Freedom Ride,* 121–22; Peck, "Freedom Ride," 2.

145. Quoted in *New Orleans Times-Picayune,* Apr. 7, 2001. Thomas mistakenly conflates the incident in Rock Hill and the incident in Winnsboro. Nonetheless, there is no reason to doubt the basic contours of his recollections, which jibe with the writings and memories of Jim Peck.

146. Quoted in Halberstam, *Children,* 257. Halberstam too places the incident in Rock Hill. I use Halberstam only as a source for quotations from participants whom he interviewed.

147. Quoted in *New Orleans Times-Picayune,* Apr. 7, 2001.

148. Halberstam, *Children,* 257.

149. Quoted in *Baltimore Afro-American,* May 13, 1961.

150. Quoted in *New Orleans Times-Picayune,* Apr. 7, 2001.

151. Peck, *Freedom Ride,* 123.

6. "Blazing Hell"

1. Key, *Southern Politics in State and Nation,* 106–29, passim (quotation on 107).

2. Bartley, *Rise of Massive Resistance,* 54.

3. Bartley, *Rise of Massive Resistance,* 54–55.

4. "Race Relations in the South—1961," *A Tuskegee Institute Report,* Jan. 31, 1962, 12, Payne Papers, William Stanley Hoole Special Collections Library.

5. Bartley, *Rise of Massive Resistance,* 68.

6. Bartley, *Rise of Massive Resistance,* 69.

7. McMillen, *Citizens' Council,* 80.

8. McMillen, *Citizens' Council,* 80–91, passim.

9. DuBois, "Georgia." See also MacLean, *Behind the Mask of Chivalry,* xiv. MacLean's book focuses on the Klan in Clarke County, home of Athens and the University of Georgia. See also Chalmers, *Hooded Americanism.*

10. In the post–World War II period, an Atlanta-based organization, The Columbians, Inc., emerged as a white supremacist group that used terror and violence against blacks, Jews, and others. See Weisenburger, "Columbians, Inc."

11. "Lynchings by States and Race 1882–1959," compiled by the Depart-

ment of Records and Research, Tuskegee Institute, Nov. 1959, Payne Papers, box 3. Lynchings had declined substantially by the 1950s, but this did not make the power of terror under the cover of night any less real for black Southerners.

12. See Tuck, *Beyond Atlanta;* Brooks, "Winning the Peace"; Brooks, *Defining the Peace.*

13. "An Appeal for Human Rights," in Carson et al., *Eyes on the Prize Civil Rights Reader,* 117–18.

14. See Tuck, *Beyond Atlanta,* 111–12.

15. "The Student Protest Movement: A Recapitulation," Sept. 29, 1961, Southern Regional Council Special Report #21, Payne Papers. See also Tuck, *Beyond Atlanta.*

16. "Student Protest Movement, Winter 1960."

17. "Race Relations in the South—1961."

18. Price, "Toward a Solution of the Sit-In Controversy."

19. "Race Relations in the South—1961," 9. See also Tuck, *Beyond Atlanta.*

20. Price, "Toward a Solution of the Sit-In Controversy."

21. On the integration of the University of Georgia, see Pratt, *We Shall Not Be Moved;* Trillin, *Education in Georgia.*

22. For the best comprehensive treatment of Georgia's confrontation with civil rights, see Tuck, *Beyond Atlanta.*

23. Quoted in Meier and Rudwick, "Boycott Movement against Jim Crow Streetcars," 756.

24. Meier and Rudwick, "Boycott Movement against Jim Crow Streetcars," 756–75; Roback, "Political Economy of Segregation," 899–908, passim.

25. Meier and Rudwick, "Boycott Movement against Jim Crow Streetcars," 758–59, 760–65, 767, 774, 775, passim.

26. Gordon Carey to James Farmer, May 9, 1961, CORE Papers, series 5, box 20, folder 10.

27. Perkins, "My 291 Days with CORE," 15; Laue, *Direct Action and Desegregation,* 100.

28. Peck, *Freedom Ride,* 123; Peck, "Freedom Ride."

29. Farmer, *Lay Bare the Heart,* 200.

30. Peck, *Freedom Ride,* 123; Peck, "Freedom Ride."

31. Peck, *Freedom Ride,* 123.

32. *Boman v. Birmingham Transit Co.,* 292 F.2d. 4. See also Barnes, *Journey from Jim Crow,* 189; Laue, *Direct Action and Desegregation,* 100.

33. For the best exploration of the literal and metaphoric intersection of black and white in Atlanta, see Pomerantz, *Where Peachtree Meets Sweet Auburn.*

34. For a fascinating and insightful look at Atlanta, see Stanley Crouch's essay "Atlanta Reconstructed," collected in *Notes of a Hanging Judge,* 65–80.

35. For a case study of Atlanta's sit-in movement, see Herschelle S. Challenor's speech at the U.S. Embassy in Kinshasa, Republic of Congo, Jan. 2000,

"Martin Luther King and the Civil Rights Movement in the US: A Second Look," 8–12, passim, http://www.africanamericans.com/MartinLutherKingJr. htm (transcript in author's possession). Challenor was cochair of the Student Sit-In Movement in Atlanta in 1960 and 1961 and is now a professor at Clark Atlanta University.

36. Challenor, "Martin Luther King," 8–12, passim.

37. Carey to Farmer, May 9, 1961; Ed King to Gordon Carey, May 9, 1961, CORE Papers, series 5, box 20, folder 10.

38. At Union Station, e.g., train passengers could enter the white waiting room to buy a newspaper, but at Terminal Station they could not enter the white waiting room at all. See S. Kennedy, *Jim Crow Guide,* 184.

39. Peck, *Freedom Ride,* 123–24.

40. Carson, *In Struggle,* 33.

41. Peck, "Freedom Ride," 3; Peck, *Freedom Ride,* 124.

42. Perkins, "My 291 Days with CORE," 15 (ellipses and emphasis in original).

43. Branch, *Parting the Waters,* 416–17; J. Lewis *Walking with the Wind,* 144. Lewis had not yet rejoined the group by this point in the trip.

44. Farmer, *Lay Bare the Heart,* 200. Stephen Oates has asserted that King told his staff that "CORE started the Freedom Ride and should get the credit. We will play a supportive role," and that SCLC bought the group's tickets for Alabama. However, given the extensive planning for the trip, and the lack of evidence for King or SCLC's having purchased tickets for the group, this seems dubious. See Oates, *Let The Trumpet Sound,* 168.

45. On the KKK scouting the Ride, see Blumberg, *Civil Rights,* 82; Halberstam, *Children,* 258.

46. Quoted in Branch, *Parting the Waters,* 417. See also J. Lewis, *Walking with the Wind,* 144.

47. James Farmer, Oral History, Apr. 25, 1979, JFK Library.

48. Farmer, *Lay Bare the Heart,* 200.

49. Quoted in Farmer, *Lay Bare the Heart,* 201.

50. Farmer, *Lay Bare the Heart,* 201.

51. Quoted in Viorst, *Fire in the Streets,* 144. See also Farmer, Oral History, Apr. 25, 1979; Branch, *Parting the Waters,* 417; Farmer, *Lay Bare the Heart,* 201.

52. Farmer, *Lay Bare the Heart,* 201.

53. Branch, *Parting the Waters,* 417.

54. Peck, *Freedom Ride,* 124.

55. Clark, *Schoolhouse Door,* xi.

56. On Alabama and the Civil Rights Movement generally, see Gaillard, *Cradle of Freedom;* Thornton, *Dividing Lines.*

57. The best and fullest treatment on Scottsboro remains D. Carter, *Scottsboro.* On Communism in Alabama in the 1930s, see Kelley, *Hammer and Hoe.*

58. Key, *Southern Politics in State and Nation*, 36.

59. For variations on the Wallace quotation, see D. Carter, *Politics of Rage*, 96; Frady, *Wallace*, 127; Sherrill, *Gothic Politics in the Deep South*, 267. In a footnote Carter explores the debate over the various versions of this quotation that have become part of the Wallace legend over the years and whether or not it was actually spoken. Whether the quote is apocryphal or not, however, Wallace certainly turned race-baiting politics into an art form in Alabama and nationally in the years to come. He may not have spoken the words, but his actions down the road showed that he meant them.

60. Bartley, *Rise of Massive Resistance*, 131.

61. On massive resistance generally, see also G. Lewis, *Massive Resistance*.

62. "Lynchings by States and Race 1882–1959."

63. On the Alabama's Citizens' Council movement, see McMillen, *Citizens' Council*, 41–58, passim.

64. McMillen, *Citizens' Council*, 55.

65. McMillen, *Citizens' Council*, 58.

66. Peters, *Southern Temper*, 206–10, passim.

67. "Student Protest Movement: A Recapitulation," 4; "Student Protest Movement, Winter 1960," xiv-xv.

68. On the movement in Tuskegee, see Norrell, *Reaping the Whirlwind*. The literature on Birmingham is vast and at times seems overwhelming. A substantial sampling of the most important works on that city's hostility to racial justice will follow in the pages to come. For another important local study, related to Lowndes County, see Eagles, *Outside Agitator*.

69. "Freedom Ride," Southern Regional Council Report, May 1961, Payne Papers.

70. Quoted in Bartley, *New South*, 306.

71. Quoted in *Time*, June 2, 1961, 14.

72. *Montgomery Advertiser-Journal*, May 14, 1961.

73. Quoted in *Time*, June 2, 1961, 14.

74. Palmore, "Not-So-Strange Career," 1795–96. See also Roback, "Political Economy of Segregation," 913–14.

75. For a history of the Civil Rights Movement in Anniston that reveals how well the city was able to overcome its Freedom Ride legacy, see Noble, *Beyond the Burning Bus*.

76. Clark, *Schoolhouse Door*, 146.

77. Clabaugh, "Reporting the Rage," 44.

78. "Document #9 on Human Rights in Alabama," John F. Kennedy Papers, White House Central Files, box 362, "HU2/ST1—1961" folder, JFK Library.

79. News release, Jan. 4, 1961, NAACP Papers, group III, box A111, General Office File: "Discrimination, Transportation, General, 1960–1962."

80. Fred Gray to Robert Carter, Jan. 11, 1961, NAACP Papers, group III,

box A111, General Office File: "Discrimination, Transportation, General, 1960–1962."

81. "Document #9 on Human Rights in Alabama."

82. Jim Peck, interview, in Hampton and Fayer, *Voices of Freedom*, 78.

83. Quoted in *New Orleans Times-Picayune*, Apr. 7, 2001.

84. Halberstam, *Children*, 260.

85. *Baltimore Afro-American*, May 20, 1961.

86. Quoted in *Baltimore Afro-American*, May 27, 1961. Newson went on to write: "I have no idea what Cpl. Cowling or Cpl. Sims feel about integration. But they are men who believe in the law and in fulfilling their duty. As long as I live I will never forget the showdown look on Cpl. Cowling's face after he brought his baggage aboard the bus and started strapping on his pistol while gazing out over the angry mob. Alabama may not want to do it, but someone should pay tribute to these law officers." On Newson and the Freedom Rides, see also Roberts and Klibanoff, *Race Beat*, esp. 242–45.

87. See Roy Franklin Robinson, FBI testimony, May 19, 1961, Freedom Rider Files (FR Files hereafter), Birmingham Public Library, #111.6.1.

88. See, e.g., the picture in the *Jackson Daily News*, May 15, 1961. See also Alabama state investigator Harry Sims's reinterview testimony to FBI, May 24, 1961, FR Files, #111.6.1; SAC to FBI Director, May 17, 20, 1961, FR Files, #111.2.1.1.13.

89. Quoted in *New York Post*, May 18, 1961; see also Wexler, *Eyewitness History*, 129.

90. For Jones's account, see his FBI testimony, May 17, 1961, FR Files, #111.6.1.

91. *Baltimore Afro-American*, May 20, 1961. The FBI later identified the car's driver as Jerry Zenith Willingham. See SAC to FBI Director, May 17, 1961.

92. Thomas, interview, in Raines, *My Soul Is Rested*, 113.

93. *New Orleans Times-Picayune*, Apr. 7, 2001.

94. Quoted in *Birmingham Post-Herald*, May 15, 1961.

95. Thomas, interview in Raines, *My Soul Is Rested*, 113. For Thomas's account of events a few days after the fact, see also Thomas, testimony to FBI, May 15, 1961, FR Files, #111.6.1.

96. Quoted in W. C. Wade, *Fiery Cross*, 310.

97. Calvin Thrash, testimony to FBI, May 21, 1961, FR Files, #111.6.1. Mr. Thrash was not a Freedom Rider, but one of several regular bus passengers caught up in the frenzy.

98. SAC to FBI Director, May 17, 1961, May 18, 1961, FR Files, #111.2.2, May 25, 1961, FR Files, #111.2.7; memorandum, n.d., FR Files, #111.2.3. Llewallyn, Roberts, and Eason were among several KKK members responsible for the brunt of the destruction. In addition to the voluminous FBI files, see also Thornton, *Dividing Lines*, 246. The Anniston attacks were not even supposed to happen

as they did: the main attack was to take place at the next stop, in Birmingham. Kenneth Adams, Exalted Cyclops of the Dixie Klan in Anniston, was the mastermind behind the events in Anniston. See, e.g., FBI memorandum, Sept. 19, 1961, FR Files, #111.3.12.

99. Quoted in *Birmingham Post-Herald,* May 15, 1961.

100. Mr. K. V. Forbus, FBI testimony, Oct. 28, 1961, Mrs. K. V. Forbus, FBI testimony, Oct. 28, 1961, both FR Files, #111.4.5; Genevieve Hughes, FBI testimony, May 19, 1961, FR Files, #111.6.1. The agents make note of the fact that even five days later, Hughes still showed the effects of smoke inhalation.

101. Perkins, "My 291 Days with CORE," 15.

102. On Postiglione, see Roberts and Klibanoff, *Race Beat,* 245.

103. Farmer, *Lay Bare the Heart,* 203; J. Lewis, *Walking with the Wind,* 146.

104. Noble, *Beyond the Burning Bus,* 33.

105. Quoted in *New Orleans Times-Picayune,* Apr. 7, 2001.

106. Farmer, *Lay Bare the Heart,* 202; J. Lewis, *Walking with the Wind,* 145.

107. *Baltimore Afro-American,* May 27, 1961.

108. *Baltimore Afro-American,* May 20, 1961.

109. *New Orleans Times-Picayune,* Apr. 7, 2001. See also Thomas, interview, in Raines, *My Soul Is Rested,* 114; Peck, *Freedom Ride,* 125.

110. Quoted in McWhorter, *Carry Me Home,* 203. See also J. Lewis, *Walking with the Wind,* 145; *Baltimore Afro-American,* May 20, 1961. Governor Patterson always insisted that he and Director of Public Safety Floyd Mann had sent the plainclothes officers to join the Greyhound in Atlanta and accompany it through Alabama. See Raines, *My Soul Is Rested,* 114 (note).

111. Perkins quoted in UPI news story, Swarthmore Peace Collection, DG 13, series E, box 21, "Resource Material—Press Clippings—Freedom Rides" folder.

112. UPI put out a photo showing Cowling guiding passengers to safety as a highway patrolman helped to keep the angry mob away. See *New York Times,* May 15, 1961.

113. *Baltimore Afro-American,* May 20, 1961.

114. *Baltimore Afro-American,* May 27, 1961.

115. SAC to FBI Director, May 14, 1961, FR Files, #111.2.1.1.12.

116. Thomas, interview, in Raines, *My Soul Is Rested,* 115.

117. Alabama State Investigator Harry Sims, reinterview testimony to FBI, May 24, 1961, FR Files, #111.6.1.

118. Quoted in Walter Bergman, "Alabama Story."

119. Charles Person, FBI testimony, May 17, 1961, FR Files, #111.2.4.

120. Quoted in W. C. Wade, *Fiery Cross,* 310.

121. Peck, *Freedom Ride,* 127; Peck, "Freedom Ride," 3; McWhorter, *Carry Me Home,* 204. The extent of Bergman's injuries was first discovered after he went to a Detroit hospital in Sept. 1961 for acute appendicitis. See SAC to FBI Director, Sept. 18, 1961, FR Files, #111.3.12.

122. Walter Bergman, "Alabama Story." See also Walter Bergman, FBI testimony, May 17, 1961, FR Files, #111.2.4.

123. Quoted in Branch, *Parting the Waters,* 419.

124. Quoted in Peck, *Freedom Ride,* 127.

125. Farmer, *Lay Bare the Heart,* 202. See also Frances Bergman, FBI testimony, May 17, 1961, FR Files, #111.2.4.

126. Person, FBI testimony, May 17, 1961.

127. See Herman Harris, FBI testimony, May 18, 1961, Ivor Moore, FBI testimony, May 17, 1961, and Isaac Reynolds, FBI testimony, May 18, 1961, all FR Files, #111.2.4.

128. Quoted in Walter Bergman, "Alabama Story."

129. Herblock's (Herb Block) syndicated political cartoons could be seen across the country. He was the editorial cartoonist for the *Washington Post,* and this particular cartoon appeared across the country, including in the South. See, e.g., *Asheville Citizen,* May 20, 1961.

130. Peck, *Freedom Ride,* 127; Peck, "Freedom Ride," 3.

131. Branch, *Parting the Waters,* 420.

132. Walter Bergman, "Alabama Story."

7. The Magic City

1. The literature on Birmingham during the segregation and civil rights eras is extensive. Some of the most important and popular recent works on civil rights are devoted to the city and its crises. Perhaps no city in the South has inspired as much writing about its troubled history. Informing this section of this chapter in particular are Eskew, *But for Birmingham;* Eskew, "Freedom Ride Riot"; Thornton, *Dividing Lines,* 141–379; Kelley, *Race Rebels,* chap. 3: "Congested Terrain: Resistance on Public Transportation," and chap. 4: "Birmingham's Untouchables: The Black Poor in the Age of Civil Rights"; Manis, *Fire You Can't Put Out;* T. Davis, *Weary Feet,* 20–132; See also Harrison Salisbury's article "Fear and Hatred Grip Birmingham," *New York Times,* Apr. 12, 1960. Finally, see McWhorter, *Carry Me Home.* While heavily detailed and written from the perspective of a Birmingham native and respected journalist, McWhorter's Pulitzer Prize–winning book is also flawed. For articles detailing its shortcomings, see S. J. Bass, "Chariots Swinging Down Low"; Derek Catsam, "'Bombingham' Revisited," Nov. 2002, http://www.h-net.org/reviews/showrev.cgi?path=249601040241446 (transcript in author's possession).

2. Leighton, "Birmingham, Alabama." See also Eskew, *But for Birmingham,* 11.

3. On Vulcan, see T. Davis, *Weary Feet,* 53; Salisbury, "Fear and Hatred"; McWhorter, *Carry Me Home,* 31–33.

4. Quoted in Cash, *Mind of the South,* vii.

5. *New York Times,* Apr. 12, 1960.

6. The best portraits of Connor emerge throughout Eskew, *But for Birmingham;* Manis, *Fire You Can't Put Out;* and McWhorter, *Carry Me Home.*

7. See Kelley, *Race Rebels,* 55–100, passim.

8. For the best and most comprehensive treatment of Shuttlesworth, see Manis, *Fire You Can't Put Out.* Although a biographer is supposed to find heightened importance in his subject, Manis is probably accurate when he claims, "Put very bluntly, without Fred Shuttlesworth the 1963 Birmingham protests could not have happened, and without those demonstrations Congress would have ended racial segregation in public accommodations later than it did" (ix).

9. Price, "Toward a Solution of the Sit-In Controversy," 2.

10. Carey to Farmer, May 9, 1961.

11. Manis, *Fire You Can't Put Out,* 263.

12. Eskew, *But for Birmingham,* 156–57; McWhorter, *Carry Me Home,* 201.

13. James Peck, "A Freedom Rider's Story: Incident in Alabama," *New York Post,* May 16, 1961.

14. *New York Times,* Apr. 12, 1960, reprinted in Library of America, *Reporting Civil Rights: Part One,* 447–52.

15. Peck, "Freedom Rider's Story."

16. Estimates vary widely as to how many members of the Klan greeting party and their associates met that day.

17. Peck, *Freedom Ride,* 128.

18. Peck, "Freedom Rider's Story."

19. Perkins, "My 291 Days with CORE," 15.

20. James Peck, FBI testimony, May 18, 1961, FR Files, #111.2.4.

21. Walter Bergman, "Alabama Story," 8.

22. Peck, "Freedom Rider's Story."

23. Branch, *Parting the Waters,* 421.

24. Walter Bergman, "Alabama Story," 8.

25. See Roberts and Klibanoff, *Race Beat,* 246–52.

26. McWhorter, *Carry Me Home,* 199.

27. *New York Times,* May 15, 1961.

28. Olson, *Freedom's Daughters,* 183.

29. Quoted in McWhorter, *Carry Me Home,* 206.

30. McWhorter, *Carry Me Home,* 206–7.

31. See *Birmingham Post-Herald,* May 15, 1961. Captions of the famous photograph often misidentified the victim as Peck.

32. *Birmingham News,* May 15, 1961. See also Clabaugh, "Reporting the Rage," 45. Clabaugh's *Southern Historian* article is the only extensive account of the press coverage of the Freedom Rides.

33. *Birmingham News,* May 15, 1961.

34. *Birmingham News*, May 15, 1961. On the attack on Lake, also see *Birmingham Post-Herald*, May 15, 1961.

35. Branch, *Parting the Waters*, 421–22.

36. Frances Bergman, FBI testimony, May 17, 1961.

37. FBI Report of Special Agent Francis W. Norwood, June 15, 1961, FR Files, #111.2.12. See also Rowe, *My Undercover Years with the Ku Klux Klan*, 42. Not surprisingly, much of Rowe's report is not especially reliable, and I only use his reports where they confirm what is already known or where he provides his own insight into matters.

38. Peck, FBI testimony, May 18, 1961.

39. Frances Bergman, FBI testimony, May 17, 1961.

40. J. Lewis, *Walking with the Wind*, 146.

41. See Anderson-Bricker, "Making a Movement," chap. 8.

42. Walter Bergman, "Alabama Story," 8.

43. Peck, *Freedom Ride*, 128–29.

44. Walter Bergman, "Alabama Story," 8.

45. Quoted in McWhorter, *Carry Me Home*, 209.

46. Peck, *Freedom Ride*, 129.

47. Quoted in *Montgomery Advertiser*, May 15, 1961. See also Manis, *Fire You Can't Put Out*, 266–67.

48. Peck, "Freedom Rider's Story."

49. Quoted in McWhorter, *Carry Me Home*, 211.

50. Peck, *Freedom Ride*, 129.

51. Quoted in Manis, *Fire You Can't Put Out*, 267.

52. McWhorter, *Carry Me Home*, 212.

53. Peck, *Freedom Ride*, 130.

54. McWhorter, *Carry Me Home*, 209.

55. J. Lewis, *Walking with the Wind*, 146.

56. Quoted in W. C. Wade, *Fiery Cross*, 311.

57. See FBI memorandum, May 15, 1961, FR Files, #111.2.1.1.12.

58. Birmingham Police Department Surveillance Files, File #1125.5.18(b), Birmingham Public Library.

59. *Birmingham News*, May 15, 1961.

60. *Baltimore Afro-American*, May 27, 1961.

61. George Huddleston, speech, May 15, 1961, *Congressional Record*, May 1961, quoted in Wexler, *Eyewitness History*, 130.

62. Quoted in "Freedom Ride," May 1961. Also quoted in *Birmingham News*, May 16, 1961.

63. *Birmingham News*, May 15, 1961.

64. *Birmingham News*, May 16, 1961.

65. *Washington Post*, May 20, 1961.

66. *Washington Post*, May 20, 1961. On the internal workings of the news-

papers in Birmingham regarding the Freedom Rides, see McWhorter, *Carry Me Home,* 212, 213–15; Eskew, *But for Birmingham,* 160; Manis, *Fire You Can't Put Out,* 267–68; Roberts and Klibanoff, *Race Beat,* 248–49.

67. Quoted in Barnett Papers, ANP press release, box 96, folder 5/61, Chicago Historical Society.

68. All quoted in *Baltimore Afro-American,* May 27, 1961.

69. Barry M. Cohen to James Morgan, May 15, 1961, James W. Morgan Papers, File #266.24.26, Birmingham Public Library.

70. W. T. Duer to James Morgan, May 15, 1961, James W. Morgan Papers, File #266.24.26.

71. Sarah Veronis to James Morgan, May 15, 1961, James W. Morgan Papers, File #266.24.26.

72. "Californian Forever" to James Morgan, May 15, 1961, James W. Morgan Papers, File #266.24.26.

73. J. A. Reeves to James Morgan, May 26, 1962, James W. Morgan Papers, File #266.24.26.

74. James W. Morgan Papers, File #266.24.26.

75. *Miami Herald,* May 16, 1961.

76. Quoted in Barnett Papers, ANP press release, box 96, folder 5/61.

77. *Washington Post,* May 16, 1961.

78. Edward Fields, a rabid anti-Semite, was one of the leaders of the National States Rights Party. Field had provided Howard Smith with the call tipping him off to the bus station mauling.

79. Quoted in Ashmore, *Hearts and Minds,* 326.

80. See FBI SAC Report, May 12, 1961, FR Files, #111.1.9, May 18, 1961, FR Files, #111.2.2.

81. G. Lewis, *Massive Resistance,* 140.

82. Rostow, "Freedom Riders and the Future," 18.

83. *Memphis Press-Scimitar,* May 31, 1961.

84. Civil Case #1718, U.S. District Court, Middle District of Alabama, Montgomery Division, 70A811, box 70 at B/15/06/63, National Archives, Southeast Region.

85. See Rowe, *My Undercover Years with the Ku Klux Klan,* passim. Gary May's recent book *The Informant* offers the best and most comprehensive treatment of Rowe that readers are likely to get. See also Raines, *My Soul Is Rested,* 115–16; J. Lewis, *Walking with the Wind,* 147. Evidence of Rowe's FBI informant status can be found in the FR Files at the Birmingham Public Library, including #111.2.10, 111.3.2, 111.1.9, 111.1.1.1.3, 111.1.1.1.1, 111.1.1.1.5, 111.1.1.1.6, 111.2.1.1.11.

86. McWhorter, *Carry Me Home,* 198.

87. Schlesinger, *Robert Kennedy and His Times,* 317.

88. Wofford, *Of Kennedys and Kings,* 152. Wofford relates that it was only

in 1980, when the *New York Times* acquired a confidential 1979 Justice Department report on Gary Thomas Rowe's complete role, that Burke Marshall learned of Hoover's advance knowledge of the attack. According to Wofford, "Marshall was stunned and is sure that he and the Attorney General would have taken prompt action." The Justice Department understated the situation in 1979: "In hindsight, it is indeed unfortunate that the bureau did not take additional action to prevent violence, such as notifying the Attorney General and the United States Marshals Service, who might have been able to do something" (152 [note]). According to Thomas Reeves, of the five black agents among some fifty-five hundred agents in 1961, three worked as servants (*Question of Character*, 339).

89. See McWhorter, *Carry Me Home*, 212–13.

90. Rowe, *My Undercover Years with the Ku Klux Klan*, 38, 39. Rowe provides the details of the plan on pp. 38–42. See also May's treatment in *The Informant*, 26–49.

91. McWhorter, *Carry Me Home*, 201–2.

92. Although Rowe's account is useful in providing background for the Klan's role, its ties to the local power structure, and some of the planning, his depiction of the attack itself is virtually useless, as what is not entirely invented exists primarily to either vindicate his actions or to brag.

93. *Baltimore Afro-American*, May 27, 1961.

94. Olson, *Freedom's Daughters*, 183.

95. Quoted in S. J. Bass, *Blessed Are the Peacemakers*, 37.

96. J. Lewis, *Walking with the Wind*, 147.

97. For a rigorous critique of the political wisdom of this thought process, see Niven, *Politics of Injustice*, passim, esp. 172–91. The most thorough recent treatment of Kennedy's civil rights policy is Bryant, *Bystander*, whose Freedom Ride coverage can be found in chap. 16 (261–82). For a more contemporary perspective, see Bickel, "Civil Rights."

98. Clark, *Schoolhouse Door*, 146.

99. Quoted in the *Charlotte Observer*, May 10, 1961.

100. Goodwin, *Remembering America*, 311.

101. For a concise treatment of the changing conceptions of federalism and civil rights, see Derthick, "Crossing Thresholds."

102. White, *Making of the President*, 173.

103. Sorenson, *Kennedy*, 478.

104. Indeed, the FBI drew up several memoranda regarding the Freedom Rides in Apr. and May 1961. See FBI, memoranda, Apr. 24, 1961, FR Files, #111.1.8, May 9, 1961, FR Files, #111.1.9, and May 13, 1961, FR Files, #111.1.6.

105. Marshall, interview, Feb. 27, 1970.

106. Seigenthaler, interview, July 10, 1968.

107. A May 4, 1961, FBI memorandum reveals that Booker had also spoken with C. D. DeLoach of the FBI (FR Files, #111.1.9).

108. See Ricky Shuttlesworth, interview, in E. Levine, *Freedom's Children,* 72–73.

109. Quoted in Manis, *Fire You Can't Put Out,* 264.

110. Peck, *Freedom Ride,* 130.

111. Perkins, "My 291 Days with CORE," 16.

112. Peck, "Freedom Rider's Story."

113. Quoted in *Baltimore Afro-American,* May 27, 1961.

114. Quoted in Manis, *Fire You Can't Put Out,* 268.

115. *New York Times,* May 16, 1961.

116. Quoted in *New York Times,* May 16, 1961.

117. Quoted in *New York Times,* May 16, 1961.

118. Quoted in Manis, *Fire You Can't Put Out,* 268.

119. Robert Kennedy and the Justice Department went to work almost immediately to try to get local and state "authorities to act and afford protection" for the Riders on their intended passage from Birmingham to Montgomery on the afternoon of May 15, but no "definite commitments" had "been received from the local authorities in Alabama and Mississippi" (C. A. Evans, FBI memorandum, May 15, 1961, FR Files, #111.2.1.1.11).

120. Wofford, *Of Kennedys and Kings,* 152. See also John Kennedy statement, John F. Kennedy Papers, box 96, "Civil Rights, Alabama, 5/1/61–5/12/63" folder.

121. Simeon S. Booker, Oral History, Apr. 24, 1967, JFK Library.

122. Branch, *Parting the Waters,* 426; Burke Marshall, Oral History, May 29, 1964, JFK Library.

123. Navasky, *Kennedy Justice,* 21.

124. Quoted in E. Thomas, *Robert Kennedy,* 129.

125. Quoted in *New York Times,* May 16, 1961.

126. "Untold Story of the 'Freedom Riders,'" 77.

127. "Untold Story of the 'Freedom Riders,'" 77.

128. "Untold Story of the 'Freedom Riders,'" 77–78.

129. Peck, *Freedom Ride,* 131.

130. Manis, *Fire You Can't Put Out,* 268; McWhorter, *Carry Me Home,* 217.

131. Perkins, "My 291 Days with CORE," 16.

132. Branch, *Parting the Waters,* 427–28.

133. Quoted in *Baltimore Afro-American,* May 27, 1961. See also Reynolds, FBI testimony, May 18, 1961.

134. See FBI memoranda, May 16, 1961, FR Files, #111.2.1.1.12, and May 15, 1961, FR Files, #111.2.1.1.11.

135. That someone turned out to be Hubert Page, one of the local KKK higher-ups (McWhorter, *Carry Me Home,* 217).

136. Peck, *Freedom Ride,* 131.

137. *Baltimore Afro-American,* May 27, 1961.

138. Peck, *Freedom Ride,* 132.

139. John Seigenthaler, Oral History, Feb. 22, 1966, JFK Library.

140. Seigenthaler, interview, July 10, 1968.

141. McWhorter, *Carry Me Home*, 217–18.

142. Quoted in Eskew, *But for Birmingham*, 159; Manis, *Fire You Can't Put Out*, 270.

143. Quoted in Manis, *Fire You Can't Put Out*, 270.

144. Quoted in Eskew, *But for Birmingham*, 159.

145. Quoted in Eskew, *But for Birmingham*, 160–61.

146. Quoted in Manis, *Fire You Can't Put Out*, 270.

147. UPI Story, May 16, 1961, Cox Collection, #45, box 1-A, folder 1, "Alabama."

148. FBI memorandum, May 16, 1961, FR Files, #111.2.1.1.12.

149. Seigenthaler, interview, July 10, 1968. See also Seigenthaler, Oral History, Feb. 22, 1966.

150. Booker, Oral History, Apr. 24, 1967.

151. FBI memorandum, May 16, 1961, FR Files, #111.2.1.1.12.

152. Seigenthaler, interview, July 10, 1968.

153. Seigenthaler, interview, July 10, 1968; Seigenthaler, Oral History, Feb. 22, 1966.

154. Quoted in Schlesinger, *Robert Kennedy and His Times*, 317.

155. Walter Bergman, "Alabama Story," 8.

156. Quoted in R. Reeves, *President Kennedy*, 124.

157. *Washington Post*, May 17, 1961.

158. FBI memorandum, FR Files, #111.3.1. See also the Birmingham Police Department's interviews with Melvin Dobe, May 17, 1961, Jessie Oliver Faggard, May 16, 1961, and Jessie Thomas Faggard, May 17, 1961, all Birmingham Police Department Surveillance Files, File #1125.5.18.

159. FBI memorandum, Nov. 29, 1961, FR Files, #111.4.12. See also FBI memorandum, May 16, 1961, FR Files, #111.2.1.1.12.

160. McWhorter, *Carry Me Home*, 219–20.

161. McWhorter, *Carry Me Home*, 247.

162. Quoted in *Baltimore Afro-American*, May 27, 1961.

163. Quoted in Barnett Papers, ANP press release, box 96, folder 5/61. On the Civil Rights Movement in New Orleans, see Rogers, *Righteous Lives*.

164. The crowd number comes from FBI estimates. Many more people were forced to listen from outside as the church was full (FBI memorandum, May 18, 1961, FR Files, #111.2.2).

165. Person was connected with the New Zion Baptist Church, and he had received phone calls in which the callers used "vile language" and threatened to "drop a pineapple on the church and blow them up" (FBI memorandum, May 18, 1961).

166. Quoted in *Baltimore Afro-American*, May 27, 1961.

167. *Baltimore Afro-American*, May 27, 1961.

168. *Baltimore Afro-American,* May 27, 1961.

169. Walter Bergman, "Appraisal of Freedom Ride."

170. Quoted in *New York Post,* May 16, 1961.

171. Peck, "Freedom Rider's Story."

172. Alfred Hassler to Jim Peck, May 25, 1961, Swarthmore Peace Collection, DG 13, series E, box 19.

173. *Baltimore Afro-American,* May 27, 1961. Protests occurred concurrently in Cincinnati, Oberlin, Yellow Springs, and Columbus, Ohio; Mount Carroll and Urbana-Champaign, Illinois; Boston; Berkeley and Los Angeles; Nashville; St. Louis; Madison, Wisconsin; Lawrence, Kansas; South Bend, Indiana; Minneapolis; Augusta, Georgia; Rochester, New York; Washington, D.C.; Philadelphia; Boulder, Colorado; Lynchburg, Virginia; Ann Arbor and Detroit, Michigan; Corbin, Kentucky; New Brunswick, New Jersey; Austin, Texas; Chapel Hill, North Carolina; and Albuquerque, New Mexico.

174. Jim Peck to Al Hassler, May 27, 1961, Swarthmore Peace Collection, DG 13, series E, box 19.

175. Peck, interview, Feb. 19, 1970.

8. "I'm Riding the Front Seat to Montgomery This Time"

1. Branch, *Parting the Waters,* 424.

2. J. Lewis, *Walking with the Wind,* 145.

3. J. Lewis, *Walking with the Wind,* 148.

4. Lucretia Collins, "The Freedom Ride," SNCC Papers, subgroup A, series 8, box 55, folder 228, "Freedom Rides," Martin Luther King Center. This is an extended transcript of an interview Collins did with movement leader James Forman about the Rides.

5. Nash, interview, in Hampton and Fayer, *Voices of Freedom,* 82. Nash has said this a number of times, variously, over the years. I have heard her say it at two Freedom Riders reunions, and she expanded on it in a conversation we had in Apr. 2001.

6. J. Lewis, *Walking with the Wind,* 148.

7. Farmer, Oral History, Apr. 25, 1979.

8. Farmer, *Lay Bare the Heart,* 203.

9. Farmer, Oral History, Apr. 25, 1979.

10. J. Lewis, *Walking with the Wind,* 149.

11. Quoted in Olson, *Freedom's Daughters,* 185. See also Robnett, *How Long?* 104.

12. Nash had been runner-up in Chicago's Miss America preliminaries.

13. Manis, *Fire You Can't Put Out,* 271.

14. Quoted in Branch, *Parting the Waters,* 431.

15. J. Lewis, *Walking with the Wind,* 149.

16. Quoted in Robnett, *How Long?* 104.

17. Branch, *Parting the Waters*, 430–31.

18. See Nash, interview, in Hampton and Fayer, *Voices of Freedom*, 82.

19. Ransby, *Ella Baker*, 265–67.

20. Branch, *Parting the Waters*, 431.

21. Farmer, *Lay Bare the Heart*, 204.

22. Seigenthaler, interview, July 10, 1968. See also Seigenthaler, Oral History, Feb. 22, 1966; Marshall, Oral History, May 29, 1964.

23. Seigenthaler, interview, July 10, 1968; Seigenthaler, Oral History, Feb. 22, 1966.

24. Collins, "Freedom Ride."

25. Branch, *Parting the Waters*, 431.

26. See Birmingham police officers' interviews with Brooks (May 17, 1961) and Zwerg (May 18, 1961), both Birmingham Police Department Surveillance Files, File #1125.5.18, and Zwerg and Zwerg Freedom Rider Surveillance File #1125.5.19.

27. Quoted in J. Lewis, *Walking with the Wind*, 151. See also Lewis, interview with Jack Bass and Walter De Vries, Nov. 20, 1973, Southern Oral History Program, #4007: A-73 (Lewis), Southern Historical Collection.

28. Collins, "Freedom Ride"; J. Lewis, *Walking with the Wind*, 151.

29. J. Lewis, *Walking with the Wind*, 151.

30. J. Lewis, *Walking with the Wind*, 151–52.

31. Collins, "Freedom Ride."

32. J. Lewis, *Walking with the Wind*, 152.

33. J. Lewis, *Walking with the Wind*, 152.

34. "Hallelujah, I'm a Travelin'," 33.

35. J. Lewis, *Walking with the Wind*, 152.

36. Quoted in J. Lewis, *Walking with the Wind*, 152.

37. Ed King to "Fellow Sit-In Leaders," May 18, 1961, CORE Papers, series 5, box 62, folder 5.

38. Branch, *Parting the Waters*, 432.

39. King to "Fellow Sit-In Leaders," May 18, 1961.

40. J. Lewis, *Walking with the Wind*, 153.

41. King to "Fellow Sit-In Leaders," May 18, 1961.

42. Lewis, interview, in Raines, *My Soul Is Rested*, 118.

43. J. Lewis, *Walking with the Wind*, 153.

44. Much of Route 31 is now Interstate 65.

45. Collins, "Freedom Ride."

46. Quoted in J. Lewis, *Walking with the Wind*, 153.

47. Collins, "Freedom Ride."

48. Cluster, *They Should Have Served That Cup of Coffee*, 5.

49. J. Lewis, *Walking with the Wind*, 154.

50. J. Lewis, *Walking with the Wind,* 154.

51. J. Lewis, *Walking with the Wind,* 155; Collins, "Freedom Ride."

52. J. Lewis, *Walking with the Wind,* 155.

53. *New York Herald Tribune,* May 21, 1961; *Jackson Daily News,* May 22, 1961; J. Lewis, *Walking with the Wind,* 156.

54. Collins, "Freedom Ride."

55. Mann, interview, in Hampton and Fayer, *Voices of Freedom,* 84.

56. John Patterson, Oral History, May 26, 1967, JFK Library.

57. See Gaillard, *Cradle of Freedom,* 96–97.

58. Seigenthaler, interview, July 10, 1968; Seigenthaler, Oral History, Feb. 22, 1966.

59. Seigenthaler, interview, July 10, 1968; Seigenthaler, Oral History, Feb. 22, 1966.

60. Patterson denied that he ever intended to avoid Kennedy, asserting instead that Kennedy never understood the difficult political position in which the Freedom Ride crisis had put him. Thus, he simply thought things had gotten so bad that "I just couldn't talk to them any more" (Patterson, Oral History, May 26, 1967). See also Drew Pearson's syndicated column in the wake of the Montgomery incidents (*Mobile Press Register,* May 24, 1961), "Segregation" subject file, Alabama Department of Archives and History. For an indication of the Kennedy administration's frustration level with Patterson, see Robert Kennedy's statement to John Patterson, Robert F. Kennedy papers, Attorney General's General Correspondence, Folder—Civil Rights, Alabama, May 1961: Statements, Draft Pages, box 10.

61. Seigenthaler, interview, July 10, 1968; Seigenthaler, Oral History, Feb. 22, 1966.

62. Seigenthaler, interview, July 10, 1968; Seigenthaler, Oral History, Feb. 22, 1966.

63. Quoted in Seigenthaler, interview, July 10, 1968.

64. Seigenthaler, interview, in Hampton and Fayer, *Voices of Freedom,* 85.

65. Seigenthaler, interview, in Hampton and Fayer, *Voices of Freedom,* 84–85.

66. Mann, interview, in Hampton and Fayer, *Voices of Freedom,* 84.

67. Quoted in Seigenthaler, interview, in Hampton and Fayer, *Voices of Freedom,* 86.

68. Quoted in Seigenthaler, interview, in Hampton and Fayer, *Voices of Freedom,* 86.

69. Seigenthaler, interview, July 10, 1968; Seigenthaler, Oral History, Feb. 22, 1966.

70. Memorandum of May 20 phone call with Patterson, Robert F. Kennedy Papers, Attorney General's General Correspondence, Civil Rights in Alabama, May 15–20, 1961, box 10.

71. Nicholas Katzenbach, Oral History, Nov. 16, 1964, JFK Library. For more on White's involvement, see Marshall, Oral History, May 29, 1964.

72. Seigenthaler, interview, July 10, 1968; Seigenthaler, Oral History, Feb. 22, 1966.

73. *Montgomery Advertiser, New Orleans Times-Picayune, Mobile Register,* May 20, 1961. See also the file on Shuttlesworth, Birmingham Police Department Surveillance Files, File #1125.5.19. See also FR Files, #111.2.9. Farmer appealed the decision, which was upheld, the ninety days converted to three months hard labor. See FBI memorandum, Nov. 9, 1961, FR Files, #111.4.9; *Birmingham News,* Nov. 8, 1961.

74. Seigenthaler, interview, July 10, 1968; Seigenthaler, Oral History, Feb. 22, 1966.

75. Cluster, *They Should Have Served That Cup of Coffee,* 5.

76. *New York Herald Tribune,* May 21, 1961, quoted in J. Lewis, *Walking with the Wind,* 157.

9. "We've Come Too Far to Turn Back"

1. J. Lewis, *Walking with the Wind,* 157.

2. Mann, quoted in "Will the Circle Be Unbroken?" transcript, episode 10, http://www.unbrokencircle.org (transcript in author's possession).

3. Virginia Foster Durr to Burke Marshall, May 15, 1961, in Sullivan, *Freedom Writer,* 249.

4. Seigenthaler, interview, July 10, 1968; Seigenthaler, Oral History, Feb. 22, 1966.

5. Undated, untitled document, based on a report by newspaper correspondent H. W. Laird, Subject Files, Civil Rights, SG 6948, folders 37–41, Alabama Department of Archives and History.

6. Quoted in Cluster, *They Should Have Served That Cup of Coffee,* 6–7. Zwerg's parents, on the other hand, were not entirely pleased with their son's activism, and his mother even went so far as to write Robert Kennedy to try to get his help, arguing that while she supported "the humanitarian goals of any effort toward racial justice," she feared that "a group of highly idealistic and zealous students might easily be duped into subversive attitudes" (Mary Zwerg to Robert Kennedy, May 20, 1961, Robert F. Kennedy Papers, Attorney General—General Correspondence, May 15–20, 1961, box 10).

7. J. Lewis, *Walking with the Wind,* 158.

8. Collins, "Freedom Ride."

9. Quoted in *Nashville Banner,* May 22, 1961.

10. *New York Herald Tribune,* May 21, 1961.

11. Quoted in Zinn, *SNCC,* 47.

12. For a good contemporary treatment of Montgomery, see Wakefield, "Eye of the Storm."

13. Lewis, interview, Nov. 20, 1973.

14. Lewis, interview, in Raines, *My Soul Is Rested,* 120.

15. Leonard, interview, in Hampton and Fayer, *Voices of Freedom,* 87.

16. J. Lewis, *Walking with the Wind,* 158.

17. Quoted in *New York Herald Tribune,* May 21, 1961.

18. Stuart Loory of the *New York Herald Tribune* wrote in his May 21, 1961, article that the group "was attacked by a mob of 100 at first. But the mob rapidly grew into the thousands." While the latter figure seems high, the crowd surely grew to number in the hundreds.

19. J. Lewis, *Walking with the Wind,* 158.

20. Quoted in J. Lewis, *Walking with the Wind,* 158.

21. Lewis, interview, in Morrison and Morrison, *From Camelot to Kent State,* 29.

22. The *Montgomery Advertiser-Journal* would refer to the man as a "cigar-chomping troublemaker" who "whipped" the "crowd into a frenzy" (May 21, 1961). See also Collins, "Freedom Ride."

23. J. Lewis, *Walking with the Wind,* 158.

24. *Washington Star,* May 20, 1961.

25. See also Roberts and Klibanoff, *Race Beat,* 252–53.

26. Quoted in *New York Herald Tribune,* May 21, 1961.

27. Leonard, interview, in Hampton and Fayer, *Voices of Freedom,* 87.

28. Quoted in *New York Herald Tribune,* May 21, 1961. See also *Baltimore Afro-American,* May 27, 1961.

29. *Montgomery Advertiser-Journal,* May 21, 1961.

30. Leonard, interview, in Hampton and Fayer, *Voices of Freedom,* 87.

31. Quoted in Zinn, *SNCC,* 48.

32. Quoted in Frank, *Routledge Historical Atlas of the American South,* 119.

33. *New York Herald Tribune,* May 21, 1961.

34. Quoted in Wakefield, "Eye of the Storm."

35. Seay, quoted in "Will the Circle Be Unbroken?" transcript, episode 10.

36. Quoted in *Montgomery Advertiser,* May 21, 1961. See also the file on Barbee, Birmingham Police Department Surveillance Files, File #1125.5.19(b).

37. Quoted in *New York Herald Tribune,* May 21, 1961.

38. See Collins, "Freedom Ride."

39. Seigenthaler, interview, July 10, 1968; Seigenthaler, Oral History, Feb. 22, 1966.

40. Seigenthaler, interview, July 10, 1968; Seigenthaler, Oral History, Feb. 22, 1966.

41. Seigenthaler, interview, July 10, 1968; Seigenthaler, Oral History, Feb. 22, 1966.

42. Seigenthaler, interview, July 10, 1968; Seigenthaler, Oral History, Feb. 22, 1966.

43. *Montgomery Advertiser,* May 23, 1961.

44. Quoted in *Montgomery Advertiser,* May 22, 1961. See also the May 23, 1961, edition.

45. Quoted in *Nashville Banner,* May 22, 1961.

46. Quoted in Cluster, *They Should Have Served That Cup of Coffee,* 4–5.

47. J. Lewis, *Walking with the Wind,* 159.

48. Lewis, interview, in Morrison and Morrison, *From Camelot to Kent State,* 29.

49. Mann, interview, in Hampton and Fayer, *Voices of Freedom,* 89.

50. Mann, quoted in "Will the Circle Be Unbroken?" transcript, episode 10.

51. Joseph Lacey, interview in Levine, *Freedom's Children,* 73.

52. Lewis, interview, Nov. 20, 1973.

53. Patterson, Oral History, May 26, 1967.

54. On Sullivan and the Montgomery situation, see Wakefield, "Eye of the Storm." See also "Montgomery: The Big Stick," in "Racial Violence and Law Enforcement," Southern Regional Council Report, n.d., Eugene Theophilus Connor Papers, 1951, 1957–63, file #268.9.16, Birmingham Public Library.

55. *Montgomery Advertiser,* May 21, 1961; Thornton, *Dividing Lines,* 121.

56. Quoted in *New York Herald Tribune,* May 21, 1961.

57. *New York Herald Tribune,* May 21, 1961.

58. Thornton, *Dividing Lines,* 121

59. J. Lewis, *Walking with the Wind,* 160.

60. Quoted in *New York Herald Tribune,* May 21, 1961.

61. Quoted in *New York Herald Tribune,* May 21, 1961.

62. Quoted in *New York Herald Tribune,* May 21, 1961.

63. J. Lewis, *Walking with the Wind,* 160.

64. Quoted in *New York Herald Tribune,* May 21, 1961.

65. J. Lewis, *Walking with the Wind,* 161.

66. Seigenthaler, interview, July 10, 1968; Seigenthaler, Oral History, Feb. 22, 1966.

67. "Will the Circle Be Unbroken?" transcript, episode 10.

68. Seigenthaler, interview, July 10, 1968; Seigenthaler, Oral History, Feb. 22, 1966.

69. Seigenthaler, interview, July 10, 1968; Seigenthaler, Oral History, Feb. 22, 1966.

70. Quoted in *New York Herald Tribune,* May 21, 1961.

71. Seigenthaler, interview, July 10, 1968; Seigenthaler, Oral History, Feb. 22, 1966.

72. Quoted in *New York Herald Tribune,* May 21, 1961.

73. Quoted in *New York Herald Tribune,* May 21, 1961.

74. All letters in James W. Morgan Papers, Files #266.24.26 and 266.24.27.

75. All letters in "Central Office Files: Hate Materials, 1961," NAACP Papers, group III, box A151.

76. "Prevent Future Incidents of Mob Action, Bloodshed," 50 Members of Montgomery Ministerial Association, *New South* 16, no. 9 (1961): 13.

77. United Presbyterian Church USA to President Kennedy, June 1, 1961, White House Central Files, Folder HU2/CO 1, Box 365, JFK Library.

78. *Birmingham News,* May 22, 1961.

79. "To Our Fellow Citizens," *Montgomery Advertiser,* May 22, 1961.

80. On the Kennedy administration, particularly the Justice Department response, see Robert F. Kennedy, Oral History, Feb. 29–Mar. 1, 1964, JFK Library. During many of the civil rights portions of the RFK interviews, Burke Marshall was also present and answering questions.

81. Memorandum of conversation with Diane Nash, May 20, 1961, Robert F. Kennedy Papers, Attorney General's General Correspondence, Civil Rights in Alabama, May 1961, Memoranda, box 10.

82. Quoted in *New York Times,* May 21, 1961.

83. Robert F. Kennedy's statement to Patterson.

84. Robert F. Kennedy's statement to UPI, May 21, 1961, Robert F. Kennedy Papers, Attorney General's General Correspondence, Civil Rights in Alabama, May 1961 Statements, Draft Pages, box 10.

85. *Montgomery Advertiser,* May 21, 1961.

86. For a Kennedy administration perspective on the case, see Marshall, Oral History, May 29, 1964. On Klan involvement, see Cook, *Segregationists,* 132–33.

87. *United States v. U.S. Klans et al.,* U.S. District Court, Middle District of Alabama, Montgomery Division, 70A811, box 70 at B/15/06/63, National Archives and Records Administration Southeast Region.

88. *United States v. U.S. Klans.*

89. President John Kennedy, public statement, May 20, 1961, in *The Public Papers of the Presidents of the United States,* quoted in Wexler, *Eyewitness History,* 132.

90. Quoted in *New York Times,* May 23, 1961.

91. Quoted in *Montgomery Advertiser,* May 21, 1961.

92. Quoted in *New York Herald Tribune,* May 23, 1961.

93. Seigenthaler, interview, July 10, 1968; Seigenthaler, Oral History, Feb. 22, 1966.

94. J. Lewis, *Walking with the Wind,* 162.

95. "Memorandum for the Deputy Attorney General," Folder: Civil Rights, Alabama, May 1961, Statements (Draft Pages), and Kennedy to Byron White, May 21, 1961, Folder: Civil Rights, Alabama, May 21, 1961, both in Robert F. Kennedy Papers, Attorney General's General Correspondence, box 10.

96. "Memorandum for the Deputy Attorney General," May 1961. Jim Folsom, the former governor of Alabama, called the attorney general on the morning of May 22. "Had a little trouble down here, did you?" Folsom asked Kennedy. "You

have plenty of precedent on sending the marshals down here. Andrew Jackson declared martial law at the Battle of New Orleans . . . you have ample precedent for sending them down here. If I had been governor, it would not have happened. Just keep those marshals down here as long as there's trouble" (memorandum, May 22, 1961, Robert F. Kennedy Papers, Attorney General's General Correspondence, Civil Rights, Alabama, box 10).

97. Robert F. Kennedy, memorandum of phone call with Assistant Chief Brown, Robert F. Kennedy Papers, Attorney General's General Correspondence, Civil Rights, Alabama, May 21, 1961, box 10.

98. J. Lewis, *Walking with the Wind*, 162.

99. J. Lewis, *Walking with the Wind*, 162.

100. Murray Kempton, "Tear Gas and Hymns," *New York Post*, May 22, 1961, reprinted in Library of America, *Reporting Civil Rights: Part One*, 580.

101. Seigenthaler, interview, July 10, 1968; Seigenthaler, Oral History, Feb. 22, 1966.

102. Quoted in "Untold Story of the 'Freedom Riders,'" 79. See also Marshall, Oral History, May 29, 1964.

103. Robert F. Kennedy, Oral History, Feb. 29–Mar. 1, 1964.

104. Quoted in Farmer, *Lay Bare the Heart*, 204.

105. Farmer, Oral History, Apr. 25, 1979; Farmer, *Lay Bare the Heart*, 205.

106. Quoted in Kempton, "Tear Gas and Hymns," 582.

107. Kempton, "Tear Gas and Hymns."

108. King quoted in "Will the Circle Be Unbroken?" transcript, episode 10.

109. Farmer, interview, in Raines, *My Soul Is Rested*, 123.

110. J. Lewis, *Walking with the Wind*, 163.

111. "Statement Delivered at a Rally to Support the Freedom Riders," May 21, 1961, Martin Luther King Papers Project, Stanford University, Unpublished Speeches, http://www.stanford.edu/group/King/speeches/unpub (transcript in author's possession).

112. "Statement Delivered at a Rally."

113. Mann, interview, in Hampton and Fayer, *Voices of Freedom*, 92.

114. Mann, quoted in "Will the Circle Be Unbroken?" transcript, episode 10.

115. J. Lewis, *Walking with the Wind*, 163.

116. RFK to Floyd Mann, telegram, Robert F. Kennedy Papers, Attorney General's General Correspondence, Folder: Civil Rights, Alabama, May 21, 1961, box 10.

117. Kempton, "Tear Gas and Hymns." On the proclamation of martial law, see also *Montgomery Advertiser*, May 22, 1961, which published the governor's text in full on page 1.

118. Collins, "Freedom Ride."

119. On the phone negotiations, see Marshall, Oral History, May 29, 1964. According to the telephone log of the attorney general's office, King called RFK at

10:17 pm, and RFK called and spoke with King, Shuttlesworth, and Jim McShane at 1:10 A.M. and to King again at 1:30 A.M. See "Telephone Calls," Robert F. Kennedy Papers, Attorney General's General Correspondence, Folder: Civil Rights, Alabama, May 23–25, 1961, box 10.

120. Quoted in Farmer, *Lay Bare the Heart,* 206.

121. Joseph Lacey, quoted in "Will the Circle Be Unbroken?" transcript, episode 10.

122. Patton, quoted in "Will the Circle Be Unbroken?" transcript, episode 10.

123. Gilmore, quoted in "Will the Circle Be Unbroken?" transcript, episode 10.

124. J. Lewis, *Walking with the Wind,* 163.

125. Patton, quoted in "Will the Circle Be Unbroken?" transcript, episode 10.

126. J. Lewis, *Walking with the Wind,* 165.

127. On the first injunction and the KKK, see *Montgomery Advertiser,* May 22, 1961.

128. Marshal, Oral History, May 29, 1964.

129. J. Mills Thornton has written of Judge Johnson, "It is difficult to overstate how important for the future of Montgomery was the presence of Frank Johnson" (*Dividing Lines,* 132).

130. Perkins, "My 291 Days with CORE," 16.

131. Quoted in J. Lewis, *Walking with the Wind,* 166; Farmer, Oral History, Apr. 25, 1979; Farmer, *Lay Bare the Heart,* 207.

132. Farmer, Oral History, Apr. 25, 1979.

133. Farmer, Oral History, Apr. 25, 1979; Farmer, *Lay Bare the Heart,* 207.

134. J. Lewis, *Walking with the Wind,* 167.

10. Mississippi

1. Key, *Southern Politics in Race and Nation,* 229.

2. Woodward, *Origins of the New South,* 151.

3. McMillen, *Citizens' Council,* 15–40, passim (Patterson quotation on 16–17). See also H. Carter, "Citadel of the Citizens' Council"; W. F. Minor, "The Citizens' Councils—An Incredible Decade of Defiance," W. F. Minor Papers, box 2, folder 80, "Minor: Citizens' Councils," Special Collections, Mitchell Memorial Library.

4. For a recent book on the Sovereignty Commission, see Katagiri, *Mississippi State Sovereignty Commission.* For an article showing the manifestations of the commission, see Butler, "Mississippi State Sovereignty Commission and Beach Integration." The Sovereignty Commission had very little to do with the Freedom Riders, perhaps because the majority were from out of state and the apparatus of the commission was such that it was mainly reactive during the Freedom Rides crisis. Nonetheless, the Sovereignty Commission Papers in Jackson contain a stack of documents, mostly information on the Riders who were ar-

rested in the summer of 1961, and a perfunctory clippings file. See State Sovereignty Commission Files, Freedom Riders, Mississippi Department of Archives and History.

5. Bartley, *Rise of Massive Resistance,* 180–81.

6. *New York Times,* Mar. 31, 1961. For articles revealing how the Citizens' Councils had lost favor among some white Mississippians in early 1961, see an editorial in Hodding Carter's *Greenville Delta Democrat Times,* May 18, 1961, and a report by Claude Sitton in the Mar. 30, 1961, *New York Times.* Some were also beginning to question the means and motives of the Sovereignty Commission. See, e.g., the editorial in the *Jackson State Times,* Mar. 16, 1961. Hodding Carter sent the Kennedys a telegram after the Montgomery events, asking them "to station United States Marshals and if necessary military units in every sizeable bus station in the South with authority to retaliate in kind against any goon Kluxer or other yellow bellied trash who are violating our nation's laws and common decency." Carter believed that 90 percent of the South's editors would be behind him—an assertion that probably entails more wishful thinking than reality. See Hodding Carter to Robert F. Kennedy, May 20, 1961, Robert F. Kennedy Papers, Attorney General's General Correspondence, Folder: AR AB, May 15–20, 1961, box 10.

7. Quoted in Cobb, *Most Southern Place on Earth,* 228.

8. Silver, *Mississippi.*

9. On Mississippi's various coach laws and the legal responses to them in the late nineteenth and early twentieth centuries, see Palmore, "Not-So-Strange Career," 1782–93, 1801–4, passim.

10. *Keys v. Carolina Coach Co.,* 64 MCC 769 (1955).

11. *Jackson Daily News,* Dec. 20, 1955.

12. *Jackson Daily News,* Jan. 9, 1956.

13. *Jackson Daily News,* Jan. 10, 1956.

14. *Jackson Daily News,* Jan. 12, 1956.

15. *Jackson Daily News,* Apr. 25, 1956.

16. *Memphis Commercial Appeal,* Oct. 5, 1957.

17. "Monthly Report: 'Registration and Voting,' 'Fund-raising,' and 'Memberships,'" NAACP, Mississippi State Office, Apr. 11, 1958, in Evers-Williams and Marable, *Autobiography of Medgar Evers,* 94–96. See also Dittmer, *Local People,* 79.

18. *Jackson Daily News,* May 22, 1961.

19. Quoted in *Memphis Commercial Appeal,* May 23, 1961.

20. Quoted in *Jackson Daily News,* May 22, 1961.

21. Quoted in *Memphis Commercial Appeal,* May 23, 1961.

22. Quoted in *Memphis Commercial Appeal,* May 23, 1961.

23. McDonald, "Freedom Rider Speaks His Mind."

24. Marshall, Oral History, May 29, 1964. See also Marshall's comments in

Robert F. Kennedy, Oral History, Feb. 29–Mar. 1, 1964 (Marshall sat in on the RFK interview, interjecting his own views and corrections).

25. Robert F. Kennedy, Oral History, Feb. 29–Mar. 1, 1964.

26. All quoted in *Memphis Commercial Appeal,* May 24, 1961.

27. Quoted in J. Lewis, *Walking with the Wind,* 167–68.

28. The Freedom Rides would prove to be a formative experience for White, civil rights and belief in a strong national government becoming hallmarks of his judicial career. See *New York Times,* July 1, 2001.

29. Quoted in *Memphis Commercial Appeal,* May 24, 1961.

30. Marshall and Patterson, transcript of telephone conversation, May 22, 1961, Robert F. Kennedy Papers, Attorney General's Correspondence, "CR in Alabama," May 22, 1961, box 10.

31. RFK and Barnett, transcript of telephone conversation, May 23, 1961, Robert F. Kennedy Papers, Attorney General's Correspondence, "CR in Alabama," May 23–25, 1961, box 10.

32. *Jackson Daily News,* May 23, 1961.

33. *Jackson Daily News,* May 24, 1961.

34. *Jackson Clarion-Ledger,* May 24, 1961; *Citizens' Council,* June 1961, Citizens' Council Collection, folder 16, Special Collections at the Mitchell Memorial Library.

35. *Jackson Daily News,* May 24, 1961.

36. *Jackson Daily News,* May 24, 1961.

37. J. Lewis, *Walking with the Wind,* 167.

38. Branch, *Parting the Waters,* 470; J. Lewis, *Walking with the Wind,* 168.

39. On the Tougaloo sit-ins, see Ed King Collection, esp. the Clipping File, Tougaloo College Archives. See also Meredith, *Three Years in Mississippi,* 91–98.

40. *New York Times,* Mar. 30, 1961.

41. *Baltimore Afro-American,* June 3, 1961.

42. *Baltimore Afro-American,* June 3, 1961.

43. Robert F. Kennedy, draft statement, May 24, 1961, and Ross Barnett to Robert F. Kennedy, telegram, May 23, 1961, both Robert F. Kennedy Papers, Attorney General's General Correspondence, "CR in Alabama, May 1961, Statements" and "May 23–25, 1961" (respectively), box 10.

44. Quoted in *Time,* June 2, 1961.

45. *Memphis Commercial Appeal,* May 25, 1961.

46. Farmer, *Lay Bare the Heart,* 2.

47. Quoted in *Time,* June 2, 1961.

48. *Baltimore Afro-American,* June 3, 1961.

49. Marshall, Oral History, May 29, 1964. See also *Baltimore Afro-American,* June 3, 1961.

50. *Baltimore, Afro-American,* June 3, 1961. See also Telephone Memo, May 24, 1961, Robert F. Kennedy Papers, "CR in Alabama, May 23–25, 1961," box 10.

51. Quoted in Dittmer, *Local People,* 90.

52. *New York Times,* May 25, 1961.

53. *Baltimore Afro-American,* June 3, 1961.

54. *Time,* June 2, 1961.

55. *Jackson Daily News,* May 25, 1961.

56. *Jackson Daily News,* May 24, 1961.

57. *Jackson Daily News,* May 24, 1961.

58. *Baltimore Afro-American,* June 3, 1961.

59. Quoted in *Time,* June 2, 1961.

60. *Jackson Daily News,* May 24, 1961.

61. Meredith, *Three Years in Mississippi,* 98. Meredith's application for admission to Ole Miss would be the topic of a scathing editorial in the May 31, 1961, *Meridian Star.*

62. Farmer, *Lay Bare the Heart,* 3; Farmer, interview, in Raines, *My Soul Is Rested,* 124; J. Lewis, *Walking with the Wind,* 168.

63. Telephone Memo, May 24, 1961.

64. Farmer, interview, in Hampton and Fayer, *Voices of Freedom,* 93.

65. Farmer, *Lay Bare the Heart,* 3–5.

66. The Mississippi National Guard troops were commanded by Sonny Montgomery. Montgomery and Lewis would serve in Congress together thirty years later (J. Lewis, *Walking with the Wind,* 169).

67. Frank Holloway, *New South,* July–Aug. 1961.

68. Farmer, interview, in Hampton and Fayer, *Voices of Freedom,* 92–93.

69. J. Lewis, *Walking with the Wind,* 169.

70. J. Lewis, *Walking with the Wind,* 169; Farmer, *Lay Bare the Heart,* 5; Farmer, interview, in Hampton and Fayer, *Voices of Freedom,* 93; "Hallelujah, I'm a Travelin'," 33.

71. Farmer, interview, in Hampton and Fayer, *Voices of Freedom,* 94.

72. Farmer, Oral History, Apr. 25, 1979.

73. Farmer, *Lay Bare the Heart,* 1.

74. Holloway, *New South,* July–Aug. 1961.

75. J. Lewis, *Walking with the Wind,* 169.

76. Farmer, *Lay Bare the Heart,* 6.

77. *Memphis Commercial Appeal,* May 25, 1961.

78. Ross Barnett, interview with Neil McMillen, Mississippi Oral History Program of the University of Southern Mississippi, vol. 26, 1975.

79. *New Orleans Times-Picayune,* June 11, 1961. Both Barnett and Thompson were affiliated with the Citizens' Councils. See *Jackson Daily News,* May 31, 1961; *Citizens' Council,* June 1961.

80. See *Jackson Daily News* and *New York Times,* May 25, 1961.

81. *Memphis Commercial Appeal,* May 25, 1961.

82. *Memphis Commercial Appeal,* May 25, 1961; *Jackson Daily News,* May 25, 1961.

83. Quoted in Schlesinger, *Robert Kennedy and His Times,* 322. On Kennedy's relationship with Eastland, see also Niven, *Politics of Injustice,* 103–5.

84. Quoted in Stern, *Calculating Visions,* 60.

85. Quoted in Schlesinger, *Robert Kennedy and His Times,* 322.

86. Robert F. Kennedy, Oral History, Feb. 29–Mar. 1, 1964.

87. Quoted in Dittmer, *Local People,* 94.

88. *Jackson Daily News,* May 24, 1961.

89. *Memphis Commercial Appeal,* May 25, 1961.

90. Quoted in Schlesinger, *Robert Kennedy and His Times,* 321.

91. Dittmer, *Local People,* 94. This is the argument at the heart of Niven, *Politics of Injustice.*

92. Meier and Rudwick, *CORE,* 139.

93. Quoted in Powledge, *Free At Last?* 278.

94. *Baltimore Afro-American,* June 3, 1961.

95. Quoted in Wofford, *Of Kennedys and Kings,* 155; Schlesinger, *Robert Kennedy and His Times,* 322; Branch, *Parting the Waters,* 475.

96. Quoted in Wofford, *Of Kennedys and Kings,* 155–56; Branch, *Parting the Waters,* 476.

97. Quoted in Wofford, *Of Kennedys and Kings,* 156.

98. *Memphis Commercial Appeal,* May 25, 1961.

99. Quoted in Stern, *Calculating Visions,* 60.

100. "Freedom Ride," May 1961.

101. Quoted in Dittmer, *Local People,* 94.

102. *Jackson Daily News,* May 25, 1961.

103. *Jackson Daily News,* May 25, 1961.

104. *McComb Enterprise-Journal,* May 25, 1961.

105. *Jackson Clarion Ledger,* May 25, 1961.

106. *Vicksburg Sunday Post,* May 28, 1961.

107. *Clarksdale Press Register,* May 25, 1961.

108. "Copy of Remarks by David Brinkley, May 24, 1961," CORE Papers, series 5, box 31, folder 9.

109. "Copy of Remarks by David Brinkley, May 24, 1961."

110. *Baltimore Afro-American,* June 3, 1961.

111. Marvin Rich to NBC, Marvin Rich to Newton Minnow, Marvin Rich to *New York Times,* all May 24, 1961, CORE Papers, series 5, box 31, folder 9.

112. Julian Goodman to Marvin Rich, May 26, 1961, CORE Papers, series 5, box 31, folder 9. The FCC used Peck's appearance as a pretext to deny CORE's complaint. See Ben F. Waple to Marvin Rich, July 10, 1961, CORE Papers, series 5, box 26, folder 8.

113. NAACP, press release, May 26, 1961, John F. Kennedy Presidential Papers, White House Staff Files, Harris C. Wofford Jr. File, folder 2, box 14.

114. Marvin Rich to *New York Times,* May 26, 1961, CORE Papers, series 5, box 31, folder 9.

115. Marvin Rich to *New York Times,* May 26, 1961.

116. *Baltimore Afro-American,* June 3, 1961.

11. Jailed In

1. *Baltimore Afro-American,* June 3, 1961.

2. Quoted in Goldstein, *Williams Sloane Coffin Jr.,* 113–14.

3. Goldstein, *Williams Sloane Coffin Jr.,* 116.

4. Quoted in Goldstein, *Williams Sloane Coffin Jr.,* 116–17.

5. Quoted in Schlesinger, *Robert Kennedy and His Times,* 321. Variation quoted in Wofford, *Of Kennedys and Kings,* 156.

6. Quoted in Wofford, *Of Kennedys and Kings,* 156.

7. Marshall, Oral History, May 29, 1964.

8. See Goldstein, *William Sloane Coffin Jr.,* 115.

9. Quoted in *Time,* June 2, 1961.

10. Quoted in *Memphis Commercial-Appeal,* May 27, 1961. See also Goldstein, *William Sloane Coffin, Jr.,* 119.

11. "Freedom Ride," May 1961.

12. Perkins, "My 291 Days with CORE," 16.

13. See Goldstein, *William Sloane Coffin Jr.,* 122.

14. *Clarion-Ledger,* May 26, 1961. On the role of communism and civil rights more generally, see Woods, *Black Struggle, Red Scare;* G. Lewis, *White South and the Red Menace.*

15. Farmer, interview, in Raines, *My Soul Is Rested,* 126.

16. Farmer, Oral History, Apr. 25, 1979.

17. *Memphis Commercial-Appeal,* May 27, 1961.

18. *Memphis Commercial-Appeal,* May 27, 1961. See also Leonard, interview, in Hampton and Fayer, *Voices of Freedom,* 94; J. Lewis, *Walking with the Wind,* 170.

19. SCLC, press release, May 24, 1961, NAACP Papers, group III, box A136, General Office File: Freedom Ride, 1961–1962; SCLC, Report of May 26, 1961, Meeting, CORE Papers, series 5, box 26, folder 1, "SCLC."

20. Robert Kennedy, Voice of America address, May 25, 1961, Robert F. Kennedy Papers, "CR in Alabama, May 23–25, 1961," box 10.

21. *Jackson Daily News,* May 25, 1961.

22. *Jackson Daily News,* May 25, 1961.

23. *Memphis Commercial Appeal,* May 26, 1961.

24. *Clarion Ledger* and *Jackson Daily News,* May 28, 1961.

25. Quoted in *Jackson Daily News,* June 23, 1961. See also Katagiri, *Mississippi State Sovereignty Commission,* 97.

26. *Jackson Daily News,* May 28, 1961; *Memphis Commercial-Appeal,* May 28, 1961. See also Collins, "Freedom Ride."

27. *Memphis Commercial-Appeal,* May 29, 1961.

28. See "Freedom Ride: Notes from the Memory of David Fankhauser," Feb. 12, 1995, Feb. 19, 1998, Oct. 20, 1998, Dec. 4, 1998, http://biology.clc.uc.edu/Fankhauser/Society/freedom_rides/Freedom_Ride_DBF.htm (transcript in author's possession). See also Fankhauser File, Birmingham Police Surveillance Files, 1947–1980, File #1125.5.19(b).

29. "Freedom Ride: Notes from the Memory of David Fankhauser."

30. *Memphis Commercial Appeal,* May 29, 1961.

31. *Memphis Commercial Appeal,* May 31, 1961. That same day's *Jackson Daily News* ran another two-column, full-page, scathing editorial about the Freedom Riders, counterpoising Mississippi with the urban North.

32. Farmer, interview, in Raines, *My Soul Is Rested,* 126.

33. The announced hunger strikes took place among an undisclosed number of inmates in both the city and the county jails (*Jackson Daily News,* June 1, 1961).

34. J. Lewis, *Walking with the Wind,* 169–70.

35. Farmer, *Lay Bare the Heart,* 11.

36. Farmer, interview, Sept. 28, 1968.

37. Quoted in Peck, *Freedom Ride,* 143.

38. Quoted in Dittmer, *Local People,* 90.

39. Farmer, *Lay Bare the Heart,* 8.

40. "Freedom Ride: Notes from the Memory of David Fankhauser."

41. J. Lewis, *Walking with the Wind,* 169.

42. Holloway, *New South,* July–Aug. 1961.

43. Quoted in Farmer, *Lay Bare the Heart,* 9.

44. Quoted in Farmer, *Lay Bare the Heart,* 9.

45. Quoted in Farmer, *Lay Bare the Heart,* 9.

46. Elizabeth Wyckoff to Gordon Carey, June 15, 1961, in "Mississippi Letters," CORE Papers, series 5, box 62, folder 3.

47. Quoted in Farmer, *Lay Bare the Heart,* 10.

48. Quoted in Farmer, interview, in Raines, *My Soul Is Rested,* 126–27.

49. Holloway, *New South,* July–Aug. 1961.

50. See Holloway, *New South,* July–Aug. 1961.

51. *Memphis Commercial-Appeal,* May 30, 1961.

52. *Memphis Commercial Appeal,* June 3, 1961.

53. See Dittmer, *Local People,* 96. For an example of a letter from a Freedom Rider biding his time in the city jail before being shipped to Parchman, see Gordon Harris's letters to his family, June 26, June 30, 1961, in "Mississippi Letters," CORE Papers, series 5, box 62, folder 3.

54. Farmer, *Lay Bare the Heart*, 7. The administration did keep close tabs on events in Mississippi jails throughout the summer. Though there was no administration intervention, the president's Civil Rights Subcabinet Group met several times throughout the summer of 1961. See Notes from Civil Rights Subcabinet group meetings, June–July 1961, John F. Kennedy Presidential Papers, White House Staff Files, Harris C. Wofford Jr. File, folder 2, box 14.

55. See, e.g., Gordon Carey, telegram, May 29, 1961, CORE Papers, series 5, box 62, folder 12.

56. See, e.g., NAACP Papers, group III, box A136, General Office File: Freedom Rides, 1961–1962.

57. Lewis Everline and Abraham Bassford to Al Hassler/FOR, June 1, 1961, Swarthmore Peace Collection, DG 13, series E, box 19.

58. See, e.g., SRC letters, in Marion A. Wright Papers, series 1, folder 142, "SRC—June-Aug. 1961," Southern Historical Collection.

59. Arsenault, in his invaluable appendix to *Freedom Riders,* places the total number of Freedom Riders (excluding the Journey of Reconciliation) at 436 (533–87).

60. Quoted in Dittmer, *Local People,* 95.

61. *Jackson Daily News,* May 28, 1961. On the role of Ward and the *Jackson Daily News* generally, see Davies and Smith, "Jimmy Ward and the *Jackson Daily News.*"

62. John Patterson to John F. Kennedy, June 3, 1961, in memorandum to RFK, Robert F. Kennedy Papers, Attorney General's General Correspondence, "CR in Alabama, Jan.–June 1961," box 9.

63. Oshinsky, *"Worse Than Slavery."*

64. J. Lewis, *Walking with the Wind,* 171. See also Holloway, *New South,* July–Aug. 1961.

65. J. Lewis, *Walking with the Wind,* 171. See also Roberts and Klibanoff, *Race Beat,* 254.

66. William Mahoney, quoted in Peck, *Freedom Ride,* 147–48.

67. J. Lewis, *Walking with the Wind,* 171.

68. Farmer, interview, in Raines, *My Soul Is Rested,* 127.

69. Quoted in J. Lewis, *Walking with the Wind,* 172; Farmer, *Lay Bare the Heart,* 23.

70. *Jackson State Times,* June 24, 1961.

71. Zinn, *SNCC,* 54.

72. See Schultz, *Going South,* 36–41, passim. Among these women were Silver, Helene Wilson, Teri Perlman, Joan Trumpauer, Jane Rossett, Betsy Wychoff (who had arrived first among this group and whose arrests occurred between June 4 and June 23), Del Greenblatt, Winona Beamer, Lee Berman, Claire O'Connor, Kathy Pleune, Jo Adler, Kay Kittle, Elizabeth Slade Hirschfield, and Pauline Knight. This is not an exhaustive list but rather reflects those named in Silver's own diaries as recounted in Schultz.

73. Schultz, *Going South*, 41 (first quotation); *Jackson State Times*, June 24, 1961 (second quotation).

74. Quoted in *Jackson State Times*, June 24, 1961.

75. Quoted in Schultz, *Going South*, 41.

76. *Jackson State Times*, June 24, 1961.

77. "Freedom Ride: Notes from the Memory of David Fankhauser."

78. J. Lewis, *Walking with the Wind*, 173.

79. See Carmichael, *Ready for Revolution*, 178–215.

80. Leonard, interview, in Hampton and Fayer, *Voices of Freedom*, 95–96. See also Williams, *Eyes on the Prize;* Carmichael, *Ready for Revolution*, 205–6.

81. See, e.g., Fred Clark, Oral History, Mississippi Oral History Program of the University of Southern Mississippi; Carmichael, *Ready for Revolution*, 206.

82. "Freedom Ride: Notes from the Memory of David Fankhauser."

83. Schultz, *Going South*, 42.

84. Quoted in Zinn, *SNCC*, 55.

85. Ransby, *Ella Baker*, 292. If fomenting women's leadership roles was one of Baker's goals, she achieved it, for as Ransby points out, Smith would go on five years later to become the first woman to serve as SNCC's executive secretary, succeeding James Forman.

86. Farmer, Oral History, Apr. 25, 1979.

87. Farmer, Oral History, Apr. 25, 1979.

88. Quoted in Peck, *Freedom Ride*, 150.

89. Memo on Price Chatham, June 21, 1961, Burke Marshall Papers, Chronological File June 1961, box 1; Rhys Chatham to President Kennedy, June 21, 1961, and Wofford to Rhys Chatham, June 30, 1961, both Harris Wofford papers, alphabetical file, "Freedom Rides," box 3.

90. Farmer, interview, in Raines, *My Soul Is Rested*, 127.

91. "Freedom Ride: Notes from the Memory of David Fankhauser."

92. J. Lewis, *Walking with the Wind*, 172.

93. "Chronology of Events Involving Freedom Rides," NAACP papers, group III, box A136, General Office File: "Freedom Rides 1961–1961."

94. "Freedom Ride: Notes from the Memory of David Fankhauser."

95. Unknown male Freedom Rider to CORE, n.d., "Mississippi Letters," CORE Papers, series 5, box 62, folder 3.

96. "Freedom Ride: Notes from the Memory of David Fankhauser."

97. C. T. Vivian, interview, in Hampton and Fayer, *Voices of Freedom*, 96.

12. Conclusion

1. Erskine, "Polls: Demonstrations and Race Riots," 656.

2. See Carl Rachlin to Marvin Rich, memorandum, Aug. 16, 1961, CORE Papers, series 5, box 20, folder 9.

3. ICC Ruling MC-C-3358. See also James Farmer, CORE Memo, Sept. 25, 1961, CORE Papers, series 1, box 2, folder 8.

4. Farmer, interview, Sept. 28, 1968.

5. Branch, *Parting the Waters*, 478.

6. "Names and Trial Dates of Southern Freedom Riders," July 1961, CORE Papers, series 5, box 62, folder 2.

7. See, e.g., Harold Andrews to Gordon Carey, June 6, 1961, CORE Papers, series 5, box 62, folder 2. Andrews had hoped to go on the initial Freedom Ride, but he was in the process of getting a federal job and could not go. But as he wrote Carey, "Once you are in this integration fight, it is hard to get out of it." He went down to Montgomery and was one of the many Riders who joined in Montgomery, rode to Jackson, and faced arrest.

8. CORE Memo, July 27, 1961, CORE Papers, series 5, box 21, folder 2.

9. Farmer, interview, Sept. 28, 1968.

10. See, e.g., "How Freedom Riders Hurt Mississippi," *Jet*, Aug. 17, 1961, 14–21.

11. On the Inc. Fund, see Farmer, interview, in Raines, *My Soul Is Rested*, 28–29.

12. Allan Knight Chalmers, "Committee of 100" fund-raising letter, Nov. 6, 1961, Swarthmore Peace Collection, DG 13, series E, box 19.

13. "Jailed Freedom Riders Need Your Support," *Berkeley Review*, June 22, 1961, Swarthmore Peace Collection, DG 13, series E, box 19.

14. *Memphis Commercial Appeal*, Aug. 14, 1961.

15. L. C. Bates, Little Rock Field Secretary, NAACP Memorandum, Subject: "Stranded Freedom Rider," NAACP Papers, group III, box A136, General Office File: "Freedom Rides, 1961–1962."

16. *Jackson Daily News*, June 27, 1961. Mize would continue to be a thorn in the side of the movement and of the Kennedys, who had hoped that the legal system would make federal action unnecessary, particularly as the Meredith saga played itself out through 1961 and especially 1962.

17. Quoted in *Memphis Commercial Appeal*, Feb. 18, 1964.

18. Quoted in *Memphis Commercial Appeal*, Feb. 18, 1964.

19. "Freedom Ride, May 1961," May 30, 1961. See also Arsenault, *Freedom Riders*, 276–77.

20. Quoted in J. Lewis, *Walking with the Wind*, 174.

21. Certainly by the 1950s there had already been a massive transformation in demographics in the United States as a result of the Great Migration of blacks from the South to the North. This migration resulted from two interrelated forces: the economic opportunities offered in the North as the result of the industrialization of World Wars I and II and the desire to escape from Jim Crow. On the economic pull, see esp. G. Wright, *Old South, New South*. On the larger migration, see Lemann, *Promised Land*.

22. *Jackson Daily News,* Sept. 28, 1955.

23. Quoted in *Jackson Daily News,* Sept. 28, 1955.

24. *Jackson Daily News,* Nov. 17, 1955.

25. "Keep the Dark Tide Moving North," Citizens' Council Publication, n.d., Citizens' Council Collection, access #331, folder 5.

26. Association of Citizens' Councils, "Community Plan to Counteract Agitators," n.d., Cox Collection, #45, box 1-b, folder 72.

27. "Segregation and Integration," Citizens' Council pamphlet, n.d., Miscellaneous Collection, folder 1, Special Collections at the Mitchell Memorial Library.

28. *Citizens' Council,* Jan. 1959, Cox Collection, box 1-b, folder 58.

29. For a marvelous history of "Back to Africa" movements and other black connections with Africa, see J. T. Campbell, *Middle Passages.*

30. "Segregation and Integration," Citizens' Council pamphlet, n.d., Miscellaneous Collection, folder 1, Special Collections, Mitchell Memorial Library.

31. It is worth noting that by the early to mid-1960s, a new "Back to Africa" movement had begun, with white supremacists and black organizations such as Chicago's "Peace Movement of Ethiopia" both advocating African repatriation and migration. See, e.g., *Richmond Times-Dispatch,* Sept. 19, 1965; *Columbia* (SC) *State,* Sept. 21, 1965; Peace Movement of Ethiopia Mailing, Phi Alpha Theta Civil Rights Collection, box 1, F-8, access #85-75, Special Collections, Mitchell Memorial Library.

32. *Citizens' Council,* Jan. 1959, Cox Collection.

33. On the Reverse Freedom Ride generally, see Webb, "'Cheap Trafficking in Human Misery.'"

34. Citizens' Council Broadside, n.d., Citizens' Council Collection, access #331, folder 13.

35. "Freedom Rides-North Society," Membership Card, Citizens' Council Collection, access #331, folder 13.

36. *Jackson Daily News,* May 5, 1962.

37. *Jackson Daily News,* May 5, May 6, 1962.

38. *Jackson Daily News,* May 20, 1962.

39. *Jackson Daily News,* May 5, 1962.

40. *Jackson Daily News,* May 31, 1962.

41. *Memphis Commercial Appeal,* May 21, 1962. For an examination of the state of affairs in Northern cities, see Theoharis and Woodward, *Freedom North.*

42. *Memphis Press-Scimitar,* June 1, 1962.

43. *Memphis Press-Scimitar,* June 1, 1962.

44. *Jackson Daily News,* May 19, 1961.

45. *U.S. News and World Report,* May 7, 1962, 54–56.

46. *Jackson Daily News,* May 25, 1963.

47. George Gallup, *Gallup Poll,* American Institute of Public Opinion, in *Memphis Commercial Appeal,* May 25, 1962.

48. Gallup, *Gallup Poll.*

49. *Jackson Daily News,* May 27, 1962.

50. *Jackson Daily News,* May 27, 1962.

51. *Jackson Daily News,* May 27, 1962.

52. *Jackson Daily News,* May 27, 1962.

53. *Jackson Daily News,* May 27, 1962.

54. *Jackson Daily News,* June 14, 1962.

55. Gallup, *Gallup Poll.*

56. On the state of segregation in public accommodations in Maryland, see Maryland Commission on Interracial Problems, *Newsletter* 1, no. 1 (1961), and "Annual Report of the Commission on Interracial Problems and Relations to the Governor and General Assembly of Maryland," Baltimore, Jan. 1962, both Payne Papers, box 1.

57. Carmichael, *Ready for Revolution,* 163. For Carmichael's perspective on the Route 40 campaign, see 163–65.

58. *Washington News,* Oct. 20, 1961; *Baltimore Sun,* Oct. 20, 1961; *Washington Post and Times Herald,* Oct. 21, 1961; *Washington Star,* Oct. 20, 1961; *Wilmington Journal,* Oct. 21, 1961; *Baltimore News-Post,* Oct. 21, 1961. See also Juanita Jackson Mitchell to Archie D. Williams, Oct. 27, 1961, CORE Papers, series 5, box 68, folder 1. On the linkages among the State Department, the Cold War, African diplomats, the Civil Rights Movement, and the Route 40 Freedom Ride, see Romano, "No Diplomatic Immunity."

59. CORE, memo to U.S. Department of Justice and Interstate Commerce Commission, Nov. 7, 1961, CORE Papers, series 5, box 68, folder 1.

60. Gordon Carey, memo to CORE Groups, Officers and Advisory Committee, Nov. 1, 1961, CORE Papers, series 5, box 68, folder 1.

61. CORE, memo to U.S. Department of Justice and Interstate Commerce Commission, Nov. 7, 1961.

62. *Winona Times,* June 20, 1963.

63. Gordon Carey to CORE Chapters, (Southern) Students, and Southern Colleges, Feb. 19, 1962, CORE Papers, series 5, box 68, folder 1.

64. CORE, press release, Nov. 8, 1961, CORE Papers, series 5, box 68, folder 1.

65. Transcript of Editorial #95, WFBR Radio, CORE Papers, series 5, box 68, folder 1.

66. Dispatcher Sheets for Route 40 program, CORE Papers, series 5, box 68, folder 2.

67. Gordon Carey, memo to CORE Chapters and Advisory Committee, Nov. 15, 1961, CORE Papers, series 5, box 68, folder 1. See also *Hilltop* (Howard University), Nov. 10, 1961. On the proposed law, see "Annual Report of the Commission on Interracial Problems and Relations."

68. Joan C. Browning, "Shiloh Witness," in Curry et al., *Deep in Our Hearts,* 66.

69. Lee W. Formwalt, "A Short History of the Southwest Georgia Civil

Rights Movement," supplement to the *Albany Herald* celebrating the opening of the Southwest Georgia Civil Rights Museum, Nov. 15, 1998, http://members. surfsouth.com/~mtzion/history.htm (transcript in author's possession). See also Zinn, *SNCC,* 124–23, 145, passim.

70. Browning, "Shiloh Witness," 68–72.

71. Dick Bruner, introduction to film treatment for "Freedom Rides," Nov. 1961, CORE Papers, series 1, box 2, folder 8.

72. Marvin Rich Memo, "Freedom Ride Film," Nov. 28, 1961, CORE Papers, series 1, box 2, folder 8. It is worth pointing out that McDonald's role in the Freedom Rides seems to be a point of some contention, as he was apparently something of a disruptive force during much of the trip. He was one of at least two who seems to have caused the others some difficulties, though there is little in the direct record to detail what problems may have emerged on the buses.

73. Farmer, interview, Sept. 28, 1968.

74. *Binghamton Press,* Dec. 9, 1962.

75. *Charleston Post,* Dec. 11, 1962; *Columbia State,* Dec. 8, 1962.

76. *Bennington Banner,* Dec. 8, 1962.

77. Farmer, interview, Sept. 28, 1968.

78. Farmer, interview, Sept. 28, 1968.

79. *Washington Post,* Sept. 7, 2002.

80. See Ann Curthoys, "The Freedom Ride—Its Significance Today," public lecture, National Museum of Australia, Sept. 4, 2002 (copy obtained from Curthoys in author's possession). See also "1965 Freedom Rides," in Horton, *Encyclopaedia of Aboriginal Australia.*

81. "1965 Freedom Rides."

82. John Pilger, "Charles Perkins—An Obituary," http://www.johnpilger. com/page.asp?partid=166 (transcript in author's possession).

83. In addition to the Pilger obituary, see also the obituary at http://www. eniar.org/news/perkins.html (transcript in author's possession).

84. "Time Frame—Characters," http://www.abc.net.au/time/chars/char5.htm (transcript in author's possession).

85. See http://www.peacebus.com (transcript in author's possession).

86. See "Subject File: Freedom Rides," Mississippi Department of Archives and History.

87. I attended the reunions in Washington and New Orleans and helped to provide historical documents for the event in Jackson.

88. S. Ralph Harlow, "Paul Revere and the Freedom Riders," NAACP Papers, group III, box A136, General Office File: "Freedom Rides, 1961–1962."

89. Quoted in Schlesinger, *Robert Kennedy and His Times,* 323.

90. James Farmer, "The Non-Violent Revolution," *Workmen's Circle Call,* Nov. 1961, 4.

91. Brinkley, "Veterans of a Domestic War."

92. For an example of how many in Anniston worked to overcome the legacy of the Freedom Rides, see Noble, *Beyond the Burning Bus.*

93. Hank Thomas, remarks at 2001 Tulane University Cambridge Conference, "Freedom Struggles in the Atlantic World," Apr. 7, 2001.

94. Quoted in *New Orleans Times-Picayune,* Apr. 7 2001. Thomas made a similar comment that day at the Tulane conference.

Bibliography

Archives

Alabama Department of Archives and History, Montgomery
Amistad Research Center, Tulane University
Archives and Special Collections at the University of Mississippi
Birmingham Public Library
Buncombe County (NC) Law Library
Chicago Historical Society
Fairfax (VA) County Public Libraries
Fisk University Special Collections
Howard University's Moorland-Spingarn Research Center
John F. Kennedy Presidential Library, Boston
Library of Congress
Martin Luther King Jr. Center
Marymount University
Mississippi Department of Archives and History in Jackson
National Archives, College Park (MD) and the Southeastern Division, East Point (GA)
Richland County (SC) Public Library
Rock Hill (SC) Public Library
South Caroliniana Library. University of South Carolina
Southern Historical Collection. University of North Carolina, Chapel Hill
Special Collections at the Mitchell Memorial Library. Mississippi State University
Special Collections Library at the University of Tennessee-Knoxville
State Historical Society of Wisconsin
Swarthmore College Peace Collection
Tougaloo College
University of Southern Mississippi Special Collections
Virginia Historical Society
William Stanley Hoole Special Collections Library. University of Alabama

Oral Histories

The Freedom Riders have conducted dozens of interviews over the years. Although I have corresponded with several of them and spoken with many, I did not conduct formal interviews. I have found that the abundance of oral histories

381

already in existence provided clearer answers for my questions, with the benefit of closer proximity in time to the events that they describe. I consulted and extensively used the oral histories in the archives at the University of Southern Mississippi, Howard University, the University of North Carolina, the Library of Congress, the State Historical Society of Wisconsin, the Mississippi Department of Archives and History, and the John F. Kennedy Library, in addition to the extensive published oral histories listed in the bibliography.

Published Collections of Primary Sources and Oral Histories

Birnbaum, Jonathan, and Clarence Taylor, eds. *Civil Rights since 1787: A Reader on the Black Struggle.* New York: New York University Press, 2000.

Blaustein, Albert P., and Robert L. Zangrando, eds. *Civil Rights and the Black American: A Documentary History.* New York: Simon and Schuster, 1970.

Carson, Clayborne, et al., eds. *The Eyes on the Prize Civil Rights Reader.* New York: Viking, 1991.

Cluster, Dick, ed. *They Should Have Served That Cup of Coffee: 7 Radicals Remember the 60's.* Boston: South End Press, 1979.

Collier-Thomas, Bettye, and V. P. Franklin. *My Soul Is a Witness: A Chronology of the Civil Rights Era, 1954–1965.* New York: Henry Holt, 1999.

Davies, Arthur P., J. Saunders Redding, and Joyce Ann Joyce, eds. *The New Cavalcade: African American Writing from 1760 to the Present.* 2 vols. Washington, DC: Howard University Press, 1991.

Frank, Andrew K., ed. *The Routledge Historical Atlas of the American South.* New York: Routledge, 1999.

Grant, Joanne, ed. *Black Protest: History, Documents and Analyses, 1619 to the Present.* New York: Fawcett Premiere, 1968.

Hampton, Henry, and Steve Fayer, eds. *Voices of Freedom: An Oral History of the Civil Rights Movement from the 1950s through the 1980s.* New York: Bantam, 1991.

Levine, Ellen, ed. *Freedom's Children: Young Civil Rights Activists Tell Their Own Stories.* New York: Puffin, 1993.

Library of America. *Reporting Civil Rights: Part One: American Journalism 1941–1963.* New York: Library of America, 2003.

———. *Reporting Civil Rights: Part Two: American Journalism, 1963–1973.* New York: Library of America, 2003.

Meier, August, and Elliott Rudwick. *Black Protest in the Sixties.* Chicago: Quadrangle Books, 1970.

Mullane, Deirdre, ed. *Crossing the Danger Water: Three Hundred Years of African American Writing.* New York: Anchor Books, 1993.

Raines, Howell, ed. *My Soul Is Rested: The Story of the Civil Rights Movement in the Deep South.* New York: Penguin, 1983.

Sepinuck, Stephen L., and Mary Pat Treuthart, eds. *The Conscience of the Court: Selected Opinions of Justice William J. Brennan Jr. on Freedom and Equality.* Carbondale: Southern Illinois University Press, 1999.

Wexler, Sanford, ed. *An Eyewitness History of the Civil Rights Movement.* New York: Checkmark Books, 1999.

Wilson, Sondra Kathryn, ed. *The Crisis Reader: Stories, Poetry and Essays from the NAACP's* Crisis *Magazine.* New York: Modern Library, 1999.

Wish, Harvey, ed. *The Negro since Emancipation.* Englewood Cliffs, NJ: Prentice-Hall, 1964.

Books

Abraham, Henry J. *Freedom and the Court: Civil Rights and Liberties in the United States.* New York: Oxford University Press, 1982.

Agnew, Jean-Christophe. *A Companion to Post-1945 America.* Oxford: Blackwell, 2002.

Anderson, Jervis. *Bayard Rustin: Troubles I've Seen, a Biography.* New York: Harper Collins, 1997.

Anderson, Terry. *The Movement and the Sixties: Protest in America from Greensboro to Wounded Knee.* New York: Oxford University Press, 1996.

Arsenault, Raymond. *Freedom Riders: 1961 and the Struggle for Racial Justice.* New York: Oxford University Press, 2006.

Ashmore, Harry. *Hearts and Minds: A Personal Chronicle of Race in America.* Cabin John, MD: Seven Locks Press, 1988.

Ayers, Edward L. *The Promise of the New South: Life after Reconstruction.* New York: Oxford University Press, 1992.

Badger, Anthony J. *New Deal/New South: An Anthony J. Badger Reader.* Fayetteville: University of Arkansas Press, 2007.

Baldwin, Lewis V., et al., eds. *The Legacy of Martin Luther King, Jr.: The Boundaries of Law, Politics and Religion.* Notre Dame, IN: University of Notre Dame Press, 2002.

Ball, Howard. *A Defiant Life: Thurgood Marshall and the Persistence of Racism in America.* New York: Crown Publishers, 1998.

Balogh, Brian, ed. *Integrating the Sixties.* University Park: Pennsylvania State University Press, 1996.

Barnes, Catherine. *Journey from Jim Crow: The Desegregation of Southern Transit.* New York: Columbia University Press, 1983.

Barrett, Russell H. *Integration at Ole Miss.* Chicago: Quadrangle Books, 1965.

Barron, Milton L., ed. *Minorities in a Changing World.* New York: Alfred A. Knopf, 1967.

Bartley, Numan. *The New South, 1945–1980.* Baton Rouge: Louisiana State University Press, 1995.

———. *The Rise of Massive Resistance: Race and Politics in the South during the 1950s.* Baton Rouge: Louisiana State University Press, 1997.

Bass, Jack. *Taming the Storm: The Life and Times of Judge Frank M. Johnson Jr. and the South's Fight over Civil Rights.* New York: Anchor Books, 1993.

Bass, S. Jonathan. *Blessed Are the Peacemakers: Martin Luther King, Jr., Eight White Religious Leaders, and the "Letter from Birmingham Jail."* Baton Rouge: Louisiana State University Press, 2001.

Belknap, Michael R. *Federal Law and Southern Order: Racial Violence and Constitutional Conflict in the Post-Brown South.* Athens: University of Georgia Press, 1995.

Bell, Inge Powell. *CORE and the Strategy of Nonviolence.* New York: Random House, 1968.

Bennett, David H. *The Party of Fear: The American Far Right from Nativism to the Militia Movement.* New York: Vintage Books, 1995.

Berg, Manfred. *"The Ticket to Freedom": The NAACP and the Struggle for Black Political Integration.* Gainesville: University Press of Florida, 2005.

Berman, William C. *The Politics of Civil Rights in the Truman Administration.* Columbus: Ohio State University Press, 1970.

Bernstein, Irving. *Promises Kept: John F. Kennedy's New Frontier.* New York: Oxford University Press, 1991.

Bethel, Leonard L. *Africana: An Introduction and Study.* Dubuque, IA: Kendall/Hunt Publishing Company, 1999.

Blumberg, Rhoda Lois. *Civil Rights: The 1960s Freedom Struggle.* New York: Twayne Publishers, 1995.

Boles, John B. *A Companion to the American South.* Malden, MA: Blackwell Publishers, 2002.

Boles, John B., and Evelyn Thomas Nolen, eds. *Interpreting Southern History: Historiographical Essays in Honor of Sanford W. Higginbotham.* Baton Rouge: Louisiana State University Press, 1987.

Booker, Simeon. *Black Man's America.* Englewood Cliffs, NJ: Prentice-Hall, 1964.

Borstelmann, Thomas. *The Cold War and the Color Line: American Race Relations in the Global Arena.* Cambridge: Harvard University Press, 2001.

Boyd, Herb, ed. *Autobiography of a People: Three Centuries of African American History Told by Those Who Lived It.* New York: Anchor Books, 2000.

Boyle, Sarah Patton. *The Desegregated Heart: A Virginian's Stand in a Time of Transition.* Charlottesville: University Press of Virginia, 2001.

Branch, Taylor. *Parting the Waters: America in the King Years, 1954–1963.* New York: Simon and Schuster, 1988.

———. *Pillar of Fire: America in the King Years, 1963–1965.* New York: Simon and Schuster, 1998.

Brauer, Carl M. *John F. Kennedy and the Second Reconstruction.* New York: Columbia University Press, 1977.

Brinkley, Douglas. *Rosa Parks.* New York: Viking, 2000.

Brooks, Jennifer. *Defining the Peace: World War II Veterans, Race, and the Remaking of Southern Political Tradition.* Chapel Hill: University of North Carolina Press, 2004.

Bryant, Nick. *The Bystander: John F. Kennedy and the Struggle for Black Equality.* New York: Basic Books, 2006.

Burner, David. *Making Peace with the 1960s.* Princeton: Princeton University Press, 1996.

Burner, David, and Thomas R. West. *The Torch Is Passed: The Kennedy Brothers and American Liberalism.* New York: Brandywine, 1984.

Burner, Eric R. *And Gently He Shall Lead Them: Robert Parris Moses and Civil Rights in Mississippi.* New York: New York University Press, 1994.

Cagin, Seth, and Philip Dray. *We Are Not Afraid: The Story of Goodman, Schwerner, and Chaney and the Civil Rights Campaign for Mississippi.* New York: Bantam Books, 1988.

Carmines, Edward G., and James A. Stimson. *Issue Evolution: Race and the Transformation of American Politics.* Princeton: Princeton University Press, 1989.

Caro, Robert A. *The Years of Lyndon Johnson: Master of the Senate.* New York: Alfred A. Knopf, 2002.

Campbell, Clarice T. *Civil Rights Chronicle: Letters from the South.* Jackson: University Press of Mississippi, 1997.

Campbell, James T. *Middle Passages: African American Journeys to Africa, 1787–2005.* New York: Penguin, 2006.

Carmichael, Stokely. *Ready for Revolution: The Life and Struggles of Stokely Carmichael (Kwame Ture).* New York: Scribner, 2003.

Carson, Clayborne, ed. *The Autobiography of Martin Luther King Jr.* New York: Warner Books, 1998.

———. *In Struggle: SNCC and the Black Awakening of the 1960s.* Cambridge: Harvard University Press, 1995.

Carter, Dan. *The Politics of Rage: George Wallace, the Origins of the New Conservatism, and the Transformation of American Politics.* New York: Simon and Schuster, 1995.

———. *Scottsboro: A Tragedy of the American South.* Baton Rouge: Louisiana State University Press, 1979.

Cash, W. J. *The Mind of the South.* New York: Vintage Books, 1991.

Chafe, William. *Civilities and Civil Rights: Greensboro, North Carolina and the Black Struggle for Freedom.* New York: Oxford University Press, 1982.

Chalmers, David M. *Hooded Americanism: The History of the Ku Klux Klan.* New York: New Viewpoints, 1976.

Chappell, David. *Inside Agitators: White Southerners in the Civil Rights Movement.* Baltimore: Johns Hopkins University Press, 1996.

Chastman, Gary Miles, ed. *In the Spirit of Martin: The Living Legacy of Dr. Martin Luther King, Jr.* Atlanta: Tinwood Books, 2002.

Chestnut, J. L., Jr., and Julia Cass. *Black in Selma: The Uncommon Life of J. L. Chestnut Jr.* New York: Anchor Books, 1991.

Clark, E. Culpepper. *The Schoolhouse Door: Segregation's Last Stand at the University of Alabama.* New York: Oxford University Press, 1995.

Clayton, Bruce, and John Salmond. *Debating Southern History: Ideas and Action in the Twentieth Century.* Lanham, MD: Rowman and Littlefield, 1995.

Clendinen, Dudley, ed. *The Prevailing South: Life and Politics in a Changing Culture.* Atlanta: Longstreet Press, 1993.

Cobb, James C. *The Most Southern Place on Earth: The Mississippi Delta and the Roots of Regional Identity.* New York: Oxford University Press, 1992.

Cohodas, Nadine. *The Band Played Dixie: Race and the Liberal Conscience at Ole Miss.* New York: Free Press, 1997.

Cook, James Graham. *The Segregationists.* New York: Appleton-Century-Crofts, 1962.

Couto, Richard A. *Ain't Gonna Let Nobody Turn Me Round: The Pursuit of Racial Justice in the Rural South.* Philadelphia: Temple University Press, 1991.

Crouch, Stanley. *Notes of a Hanging Judge: Essays and Reviews, 1979–1989.* New York: Oxford University Press, 1990.

Curry, Constance, et al. *Deep in Our Hearts: Nine White Women in the Freedom Movement.* Athens: University of Georgia Press, 2000.

Curthoys, Ann. *Freedom Ride: A Freedom Rider Remembers.* Sydney: Allen and Unwin, 2002.

Dailey, Jane, Glenda Elizabeth Gilmore, and Bryant Simon, eds. *Jumpin' Jim Crow: Southern Politics from Civil War to Civil Rights.* Princeton: Princeton University Press, 2000.

Dallek, Robert. *An Unfinished Life: John F. Kennedy, 1917–1963.* Boston: Little, Brown and Company, 2003.

Davidson, Osha Gray. *The Best of Enemies: Race and Redemption in the New South.* New York: Scribner, 1996.

Davies, David R., ed. *The Press and Race: Mississippi Journalists Confront the Movement.* Jackson: University Press of Mississippi, 2001.

Davis, Jack E., ed. *The Civil Rights Movement.* Malden, MA: Blackwell Publishers, 2001.

Davis, Michael D., and Hunter R. Clark. *Thurgood Marshall: Warrior at the Bar, Rebel on the Bench.* New York: Citadel Press, 1994.

Davis, Townsend. *Weary Feet, Rested Souls: A Guided History of the Civil Rights Movement.* New York: W. W. Norton, 1998.

D'Emilio, John. *Lost Prophet: The Life and Times of Bayard Rustin.* Chicago: University of Chicago Press, 2003.

Dent, Tom. *Southern Journey: A Return to the Civil Rights Movement.* New York: William Morrow and Co., 1997.

Dittmer, John. *Local People: The Struggle for Civil Rights in Mississippi.* Urbana: University of Illinois Press, 1995.

Douglas, Davison M. *Reading Writing and Race: The Desegregation of the Charlotte Schools.* Chapel Hill: University of North Carolina Press, 1995.

Doyle, William. *An American Insurrection: James Meredith and the Battle of Oxford, Mississippi, 1962.* New York: Anchor, 2001.

Dudziak, Mary L. *Cold War Civil Rights: Race and the Image of American Democracy.* Princeton: Princeton University Press, 2000.

Dulany, W. Marvin, ed. *Born to Serve: A History of the Woman's Baptist Educational and Missionary Convention of South Carolina.* Charleston: Publishing Associates, 2006.

Dyson, Eric Michael. *I May Not Get There with You: The True Martin Luther King, Jr.* New York: Touchstone, 2000.

Eagles, Charles W., ed. *Is There a Southern Political Tradition?* Jackson: University Press of Mississippi, 1996.

———. *Outside Agitator: Jon Daniels and the Civil Rights Movement in Alabama.* Chapel Hill: University of North Carolina Press, 1993.

Edwards, Harry. *Black Students.* New York: Free Press, 1970.

Egerton, John. *Speak Now against the Day: The Generation before the Civil Rights Movement in the South.* Chapel Hill: University of North Carolina Press, 1994.

Ely, James W., Jr. *The Crisis of Conservative Virginia: The Byrd Organization and the Politics of Massive Resistance.* Knoxville: University of Tennessee Press, 1976.

Eskew, Glenn. *But for Birmingham: The Local and National Movements in the Civil Rights Struggle.* Chapel Hill: University of North Carolina Press, 1997.

Etheridge, Eric. *Breach of Peace: Portraits of the 1961 Mississippi Freedom Riders.* New York: Atlas, 2008.

Eubanks, W. Ralph. *Ever Is a Long Time: A Journey into Mississippi's Dark Past.* New York: Basic Books, 2003.

Evans, Sara. *Personal Politics: The Roots of Women's Liberation in the Civil Rights Movement and the New Left.* New York: Vintage, 1980.

Evers-Williams, Myrlie, and Manning Marable, eds. *The Autobiography of Medgar Evers: A Hero's Life and Legacy through His Writings, Letters, and Speeches.* New York: Basic Books, 2005.

Fairclough, Adam. *Better Day Coming: Blacks and Equality, 1890–2000.* New York: Viking, 2001.

———. *Race and Democracy: The Civil Rights Struggle in Louisiana, 1915–1972.* Athens: University of Georgia Press, 1995.

———. *To Redeem the Soul of America: The Southern Christian Leadership Conference and Martin Luther King, Jr.* Athens: University of Georgia Press, 1987.

Farmer, James. *Lay Bare the Heart: An Autobiography of the Civil Rights Movement.* New York: Plume/Penguin, 1986.

Feldman, Glenn, ed. *Before Brown: Civil Rights and White Backlash in the Modern South.* Tuscaloosa: University of Alabama Press, 2004.

———. *Politics, Society, and the Klan in Alabama 1915–1949.* Tuscaloosa: University of Alabama Press, 1999.

———. *Reading Southern History: Essays on Interpreters and Interpretations.* Tuscaloosa: University of Alabama Press, 2001.

Findlay, James F., Jr. *Church People in the Struggle: The National Council of Churches and the Black Freedom Movement, 1950–1970.* New York: Oxford University Press, 1993.

Frady, Marshall. *Wallace.* New York: Meridian Books, 1970.

Franklin, John Hope. *Race and History: Selected Essays 1938–1988.* Baton Rouge: Louisiana State University Press, 1989.

Frazier, E. Franklin. *Black Bourgeoisie.* New York: Collier Books, 1968.

Frederickson, Kari. *The Dixiecrat Revolt and the End of the Solid South, 1932–1968.* Chapel Hill: University of North Carolina Press, 2001.

Freidel, Frank. *FDR and the South.* Baton Rouge: Louisiana State University Press, 1965.

Friedland, Michael B. *Lift Up Your Voice Like a Trumpet: White Clergy and the Civil Rights and Antiwar Movements, 1954–1973.* Chapel Hill: University of North Carolina Press, 1998.

Gaillard, Frye. *Cradle of Freedom: Alabama and the Movement That Changed America.* Tuscaloosa: University of Alabama Press, 2004.

Gaines, Kevin K. *African Americans in Ghana: Black Expatriates and the Civil Rights Era.* Chapel Hill: University of North Carolina Press, 2006.

Gardner, Michael R. *Harry Truman and Civil Rights: Moral Courage and Political Risks.* Carbondale: Southern Illinois University Press, 2002.

Garrow, David J. *Bearing the Cross: Martin Luther King, Jr. and the Southern Christian Leadership Conference.* New York: Vintage, 1988.

———. *The F.B.I. and Martin Luther King, Jr.* New York: Penguin, 1984.

Gaston, Paul M. *The New South Creed: A Study in Southern Mythmaking.* Montgomery: New South Books, 2002.

Gates, Robbins L. *The Making of Massive Resistance: Virginia's Politics of Public School Desegregation, 1954–1956.* Chapel Hill: University of North Carolina Press, 1964.

Gerstle, Gary. *American Crucible: Race and Nation in the Twentieth Century.* Princeton: Princeton University Press, 2001.

Gilje, Paul A. *Rioting in America.* Bloomington: Indiana University Press, 1996.

Gitlin, Todd. *The Sixties: Years of Hope, Days of Rage.* New York: Bantam Books, 1989.

Golden, Harry. *Only in America.* Cleveland: World Publishing Company, 1958.

Goldfield, David. *Black, White, and Southern: Race Relations and Southern Culture 1940 to the Present.* Baton Rouge: Louisiana State University Press, 1990.

Goldfield, David, and Blaine Brownell. *Urban America: A History.* 2nd ed. Boston: Houghton Mifflin, 1990.

Goldstein, Warren. *William Sloane Coffin Jr.: A Holy Impatience.* New Haven: Yale University Press, 2004.

Goodwin, Richard N. *Remembering America: A Voice from the Sixties.* Boston: Little, Brown and Company, 1988.

Graham, Hugh Davis, ed. *Civil Rights in the United States.* University Park: Pennsylvania State University Press, 1994.

Grantham, Dewey. *The Democratic South.* Athens: University of Georgia Press, 1963.

———. *The South in Modern America: A Region at Odds.* New York: Harper Perennial, 1994.

Gray, Fred. *Bus Ride to Justice: The Life and Works of Fred Gray.* Montgomery: New South Books, 2002.

Green, McLaughlin Constance. *The Secret City: A History of Race Relations in the Nation's Capital.* Princeton: Princeton University Press, 1967.

Greenberg, Jack. *Crusaders in the Courts: How a Dedicated Band of Warriors Fought for a Civil Rights Revolution.* New York: Basic Books, 1994.

Griffin, Larry J., and Don H. Doyle. *The South as an American Problem.* Athens: University of Georgia Press, 1995.

Guthman, Edwin O., and Jeffrey Shulman. *Robert Kennedy in His Own Words.* New York: Bantam Press, 1988.

Halberstam, David. *The Children.* New York: Random House, 1998.

Hale, Grace Elizabeth. *Making Whiteness: The Culture of Segregation in the South, 1890–1940.* New York: Vintage, 1998.

Hendrickson, Paul. *Sons of Mississippi.* New York: Alfred A. Knopf, 2003.

Higham, John, ed. *Civil Rights and Social Wrongs: Black White Relations since World War II.* University Park: Pennsylvania State University Press, 1997.

Horton, David, ed. *The Encyclopaedia of Aboriginal Australia.* Canberra: Aboriginal Studies Press for the Australian Institute of Aboriginal and Torres Strait Islander Studies, 1994.

Jacoway, Elizabeth, et al., eds. *The Adaptable South: Essays in Honor of George Brown Tindall.* Baton Rouge: Louisiana State University Press, 1991.

Jonas, Gilbert. *Freedom's Sword: The NAACP and the Struggle against Racism in America.* New York: Routledge, 2007.

Jones, Jacqueline. *American Work: Four Centuries of Black and White Labor.* New York: W. W. Norton, 1998.

———. *The Dispossessed: America's Underclass from the Civil War to the Present.* New York: Basic Books, 1992.

Kantrowitz, Stephen. *Ben Tillman and the Reconstruction of White Supremacy.* Chapel Hill: University of North Carolina Press, 2000.

Kapur, Sudarshan. *Raising Up a Prophet: The African-American Encounter with Gandhi.* Boston: Beacon Press, 1992.

Katagiri, Yasuhiro. *The Mississippi State Sovereignty Commission: Civil Rights and States' Rights.* Jackson: University Press of Mississippi, 2001.

Kelley, Robin D. G. *Hammer and Hoe: Alabama Communists during the Great Depression.* Chapel Hill: University of North Carolina Press, 1990.

———. *Race Rebels: Culture, Politics, and the Black Working Class.* New York: Free Press, 1996.

Kennedy, Randall. *Race, Crime, and the Law.* New York: Pantheon Books, 1997.

Kennedy, Stetson. *Jim Crow Guide: The Way It Was.* Boca Raton: Florida Atlantic University Press, 1990.

Key, V. O. *Southern Politics in State and Nation.* Knoxville: University of Tennessee Press, 1996.

King, Martin Luther, Jr. *Stride toward Freedom: The Montgomery Story.* San Francisco: Harper and Row, 1958.

———. *Where Do We Go from Here: Chaos or Community?* Boston: Beacon Press, 1967.

Klarman, Michael J. *From Jim Crow to Civil Rights: The Supreme Court and the Struggle for Racial Equality.* Oxford: Oxford University Press, 2004.

Kluger, Richard. *Simple Justice.* New York: Alfred A. Knopf, 1976.

Lassiter, Matthew D., and Andrew B. Lewis, eds. *The Moderates' Dilemma: Massive Resistance to School Desegregation in Virginia.* Charlottesville: University Press of Virginia, 1998.

Lau, Peter F. *Democracy Rising: South Carolina and the Fight for Black Equality since 1865.* Lexington: University Press of Kentucky, 2006.

Laue, James H. *Direct Action and Desegregation, 1960–1962: Toward a Theory of the Rationalization of Protest.* Brooklyn: Carlson Publishing, 1989.

Lawson, Steven F. *Black Ballots: Voting Rights in the South, 1944–1969.* Lanham, MD: Lexington Books, 1999.

———. *Civil Rights Crossroads: Nation, Community, and the Black Freedom Struggle.* Lexington: University Press of Kentucky, 2003.

———. *Running for Freedom: Civil Rights and Black Politics in America since 1941.* New York: McGraw Hill, 1991.

Lawson, Steven, and Charles Payne. *Debating the Civil Rights Movement, 1945–1968.* Lanham, MD: Rowman and Littlefield, 1998.

Lemann, Nicholas. *The Promised Land: The Great Black Migration and How It Changed America.* New York: Alfred A. Knopf, 1991.

Leonard, Joseph T. *Theology and Race Relations.* Milwaukee: Bruce Publishing Company, 1963.

Levine, Daniel. *Bayard Rustin and the Civil Rights Movement.* New Brunswick: Rutgers University Press, 2000.

Lewis, David L. *King: A Biography.* Urbana: University of Illinois Press, 1978.

Lewis, George. *Massive Resistance: The White Response to the Civil Rights Movement.* London: Hodder Headline, 2006.

————. *The White South and the Red Menace: Segregationists, Anticommunism, and Massive Resistance, 1945–1965.* Gainesville: University Press of Florida, 2004.

Lewis, John. *Walking with the Wind: A Memoir of the Movement.* New York: Simon and Schuster, 1998.

Lincoln, C. Eric, ed. *Martin Luther King, Jr.: A Profile.* New York: Hill and Wang, 1984.

Litwack, Leon. *Trouble in Mind: Black Southerners in the Age of Jim Crow.* New York: Alfred A. Knopf, 1998.

Lofgren, Charles A. *The Plessy Case: A Legal-Historical Interpretation.* Oxford: Oxford University Press, 1987.

Long, John D. *South of Main: A History of the Water Street Community of Salem, Virginia.* Charlottesville: Virginia Foundation for the Humanities, 2000.

Long, Michael G. *Against Us, but for Us: Martin Luther King, Jr., and the State.* Macon, GA: Mercer University Press, 2002.

Lovett, Bobby L. *The Civil Rights Movement in Tennessee: A Narrative History.* Knoxville: University of Tennessee Press, 2005.

MacLean, Nancy. *Behind the Mask of Chivalry: The Making of the Second Ku Klux Klan.* New York: Oxford University Press, 1994.

Madison, James H. *A Lynching in the Heartland: Race and Memory in America.* New York: Palgrave MacMillan, 2001.

Manis, Andrew M. *A Fire You Can't Put Out: The Civil Rights Life of Birmingham's Reverend Fred Shuttlesworth.* Tuscaloosa: University of Alabama Press, 1999.

Mann, Robert. *The Walls of Jericho: Lyndon Johnson, Hubert Humphrey, Richard Russell, and the Struggle for Civil Rights.* New York: Harcourt, Brace and Co., 1996.

Marable, Manning. *Race, Reform, and Rebellion: The Second Reconstruction in Black America, 1945–1990.* Jackson: University Press of Mississippi, 1991.

Margolick, David. *Beyond Glory: Joe Louis vs. Max Schmelling, and a World on the Brink.* New York: Vintage, 2006.

Martin, Waldo E. *Brown v. Board of Education: A Brief History with Documents.* Boston: Bedford/St. Martins, 1998.

Matusow, Allen. *The Unraveling of America: A History of Liberalism in the 1960s.* New York: Harper and Row, 1984.

May, Gary. *The Informant: The FBI, the Ku Klux Klan, and the Murder of Viola Liuzzo.* New Haven: Yale University Press, 2005.

McCoy, Donald R., and Richard T. Ruetten. *Quest and Response: Minority Rights and the Truman Administration.* Lawrence: University Press of Kansas, 1973.

McGill, Ralph. *The South and the Southerner.* Boston: Little, Brown and Co., 1963.

McLauren, Melton. *Separate Pasts: Growing Up White in the Segregated South.* Athens: University of Georgia Press, 1987.

McMillen, Neil. *The Citizens' Council: Organized Resistance to the Second Reconstruction, 1954–1964.* Urbana: University of Illinois Press, 1994.

———. *Dark Journey: Black Mississippians in the Age of Jim Crow.* Urbana: University of Illinois Press, 1990.

———, ed. *Remaking Dixie: The Impact of World War II on the American South.* Jackson: University Press of Mississippi, 1997.

McWhorter, Diane. *Carry Me Home: Birmingham, Alabama: The Climactic Battle of the Civil Rights Revolution.* New York: Simon and Schuster, 2001.

Meier, August, and Elliott Rudwick. *Along the Color Line: Explorations in the Black Experience.* Urbana: University of Illinois Press, 1976.

———. *CORE: A Study in the Civil Rights Movement, 1942–1968.* New York: Oxford University Press, 1973.

Meredith, James. *Three Years in Mississippi.* Bloomington: Indiana University Press, 1966.

Meriwether, James. *Proudly We Can Be Africans: Black Americans and Africa, 1935–1961.* Chapel Hill: University of North Carolina Press, 2002.

Miller, Loren. *The Petitioners: The Story of the Supreme Court of the United States and the Negro.* Cleveland: Meridien Books, 1967.

Moody, Anne. *Coming of Age in Mississippi.* New York: Laurel, 1968.

Moore, Leonard J. *Citizen Klansmen: The Ku Klux Klan in Indiana, 1921–1928.* Chapel Hill: University of North Carolina Press, 1991.

Morris, Aldon D. *The Origins of the Civil Rights Movement: Black Communities Organizing for Change.* New York: Free Press, 1986.

Morris, Willie. *The Ghosts of Medgar Evers: A Tale of Race, Murder, Mississippi, and Hollywood.* New York: Random House, 1998.

Morrison, Joan, and Robert K. Morrison. *From Camelot to Kent State: The Sixties Experience in the Words of Those Who Lived It.* New York: Oxford University Press, 2001.

Motley, Constance Baker. *Equal Justice under Law: An Autobiography.* New York: Farrar, Straus and Giroux, 1998.

Murray, Pauli. *Song in a Weary Throat: An American Pilgrimage.* New York: Harper and Row, 1987.

Muse, Benjamin. *Virginia's Massive Resistance.* Bloomington: Indiana University Press, 1961.

Myers, Martha A. *Race, Labor and Punishment in the New South.* Columbus: Ohio State University Press, 1998.

Myrdal, Gunnar. *An American Dilemma: The Negro Problem and Modern Democracy.* New York: Harper and Row, 1962.

Navasky, Victor S. *Kennedy Justice*. New York: Atheneum, 1971.

Netherton, Nan, et al. *Fairfax County, Virginia: A History*. Fairfax: Fairfax County Board of Supervisors, 1978.

Niven, David. *The Politics of Injustice: The Kennedys, the Freedom Rides, and the Electoral Consequences of a Moral Compromise*. Knoxville: University of Tennessee Press, 2003.

Noble, Phil. *Beyond the Burning Bus: The Civil Rights Revolution in a Southern Town*. Montgomery: New South Books, 2003.

Norrell, Robert J. *Reaping the Whirlwind: The Civil Rights Movement in Tuskegee*. New York: Vintage, 1986.

Nossiter, Adam. *Of Long Memory: Mississippi and the Assassination of Medgar Evers*. Reading, MA: Addison-Wesley, 1994.

Oates, Stephen. *Let the Trumpet Sound: The Life of Martin Luther King, Jr.* New York: Mentor, 1982.

O'Brien, Gail Williams. *The Color of the Law: Race, Violence, and Justice in the Post–World War II South*. Chapel Hill: University of North Carolina Press, 1999.

Olson, Lynne. *Freedom's Daughters: The Unsung Heroines of the Civil Rights Movement from 1830 to 1970*. New York: Touchstone, 2001.

Oshinsky, David M. *"Worse Than Slavery": Parchman Farm and the Ordeal of Jim Crow Justice*. New York: Free Press, 1996.

Patterson, James T. *Brown v. Board of Education: A Civil Rights Milestone and Its Troubled Legacy*. New York: Oxford University Press, 2001.

Payne, Charles. *I've Got the Light of Freedom: The Organizing Tradition and the Mississippi Freedom Struggle*. Berkeley: University of California Press, 1995.

Peck, James. *Freedom Ride*. New York: Simon and Schuster, 1962.

Peters, William. *The Southern Temper*. Garden City, NJ: Doubleday, 1959.

Plummer, Brenda Gayle. *Rising Wind: Black Americans and U.S. Foreign Affairs, 1935–1960*. Chapel Hill: University of North Carolina Press, 1996.

————, ed. *Window on Freedom: Race, Civil Rights, and Foreign Affairs 1945–1988*. Chapel Hill: University of North Carolina Press, 2003.

Polenberg, Richard. *One Nation Divisible: Class, Race, and Ethnicity in the United States since 1938*. New York: Viking, 1991.

Pomerantz, Gary M. *Where Peachtree Meets Sweet Auburn: The Saga of Two Families and the Making of Atlanta*. New York: Scribner, 1996.

Powe, Lucas A. *The Warren Court and American Politics*. Cambridge, MA: Belknap, 2000.

Powledge, Fred. *Free At Last? The Civil Rights Movement and the People Who Made It*. Boston: Little, Brown and Co., 1991.

Pratt, Robert A. *The Color of Their Skin: Education and Race in Richmond, Virginia, 1954–1989*. Charlottesville: University Press of Virginia, 1992.

————. *We Shall Not Be Moved: The Integration of the University of Georgia.* Athens: University of Georgia Press, 2002.

Randolph, Lewis A., and Gayle T. Tate. *Rights for a Season: The Politics of Race, Class, and Gender in Richmond, Virginia.* Knoxville: University of Tennessee Press, 2003.

Ransby, Barbara. *Ella Baker and the Black Freedom Movement: A Radical Democratic Vision.* Chapel Hill: University of North Carolina Press, 2003.

Reed, Merl E. *Seedtime for the Modern Civil Rights Movement: The President's Committee on Fair Employment Practice, 1941–1946.* Baton Rouge: Louisiana State University Press, 1991.

Reeves, Richard. *President Kennedy: Profile of Power.* New York: Touchstone, 1993.

Reeves, Thomas. *A Question of Character: A Life of John F. Kennedy.* Rocklin, CA: Prima Publishing, 1992.

Rise, Eric W. *The Martinsville Seven: Race, Rape and Capital Punishment.* Charlottesville: University Press of Virginia, 1998.

Roberts, Gene, and Hank Klibanoff. *The Race Beat: The Press, the Civil Rights Struggle, and the Awakening of a Nation.* New York: Vintage, 2007.

Robnett, Belinda. *How Long? How Long? African-American Women in the Struggle for Civil Rights.* New York: Oxford University Press, 1997.

Rogers, Kim Lacy. *Righteous Lives: Narratives of the New Orleans Civil Rights Movement.* New York: New York University Press, 1993.

Rowan, Carl T. *Dream Makers, Dream Breakers: The World of Justice Thurgood Marshall.* Boston: Little, Brown, & Company, 1993.

Rowe, Gary Thomas, Jr. *My Undercover Years with the Ku Klux Klan.* New York: Bantam, 1976.

Rustin, Bayard. *Down the Line: The Collected Writings of Bayard Rustin.* Chicago: Quadrangle, 1971.

————. *Strategies for Freedom: The Changing Patterns of Black Protest.* New York: Columbia University Press, 1976.

Salmond, John A. *"My Mind Set on Freedom": A History of the Civil Rights Movement, 1954–1968.* Chicago: Ivan R. Dee, 1997.

Savage, Barbara Diane. *Broadcasting Freedom: Radio, War, and the Politics of Race, 1938–1948.* Chapel Hill: University of North Carolina Press, 1999.

Schlesinger, Arthur M., Jr. *Robert Kennedy and His Times.* New York: Ballantine Books, 1978.

————. *A Thousand Days: John F. Kennedy in the White House.* New York: Fawcett Premiere, 1965.

Schneider, Mark Robert. *"We Return Fighting": The Civil Rights Movement in the Jazz Age.* Boston: Northeastern University Press, 2002.

Schultz, Debra L. *Going South: Jewish Women in the Civil Rights Movement.* New York: New York University Press, 2002.

Sellers, Cleveland. *The River of No Return: The Autobiography of a Black Militant and the Life and Death of SNCC*. Jackson: University Press of Mississippi, 1990.

Shapiro, Herbert. *White Violence and Black Response: From Reconstruction to Montgomery*. Amherst: University of Massachusetts Press, 1988.

Shattuck, Gardiner H., Jr. *Episcopalians and Race: Civil War to Civil Rights*. Lexington: University Press of Kentucky, 2000.

Sherrill, Robert. *Gothic Politics in the Deep South: Stars of the New Confederacy*. New York: Grossman Publishers, 1968.

Shipler, David K. *A Country of Strangers: Blacks and Whites in America*. New York: Alfred A. Knopf, 1997.

Shull, Steven A. *American Civil Rights Policy from Truman to Clinton: The Role of Presidential Leadership*. Armonk, NY: M. E. Sharpe, 1999.

Silberman, Charles E. *Crisis in Black and White*. New York: Random House, 1964.

Silver, James W. *Mississippi: The Closed Society*. New York: Harcourt, Brace and World, 1966.

Simpkins, Francis Butler. *The South Old and New: A History, 1820–1947*. New York: Alfred A. Knopf, 1948.

Sitkoff, Harvard. *A New Deal for Blacks: The Emergence of Civil Rights as a National Issue: The Depression Decade*. New York: Oxford University Press, 1981.

———. *The Struggle for Black Equality, 1954–1980*. New York: Hill and Wang, 1981.

Skates, John Ray. *Mississippi: A Bicentennial History*. New York: W. W. Norton, 1979.

Smith, J. Douglas. *Managing White Supremacy: Race, Politics, and Citizenship in Jim Crow Virginia*. Chapel Hill: University of North Carolina Press, 2002.

Sorenson, Theodore. *Kennedy*. New York: Harper and Row, 1965.

Stanton, Mary. *Freedom Walk: Mississippi or Bust*. Jackson: University Press of Mississippi, 2003.

Stern, Mark. *Calculating Visions: Kennedy, Johnson and Civil Rights*. New Brunswick, NJ: Rutgers University Press, 1992.

Sullivan, Patricia. *Days of Hope: Race and Democracy in the New Deal Era*. Chapel Hill: University of North Carolina Press, 1996.

———. *Freedom Writer: Virginia Foster Durr, Letters from the Civil Rights Years*. New York: Routledge, 2003.

Tate, Gayle, and Lewis Randolph, eds. *Dimensions of Black Conservatism in the United States: Made in America*. New York: Palgrave, 2002.

Taylor, William Banks. *Down on Parchman Farm: The Great Prison in the Mississippi Delta*. Columbus: Ohio State University Press, 1999.

Theoharis, Jeanne F., and Komozi Woodard, eds. *Freedom North: Black Freedom Struggles outside the South, 1940–1980*. New York: Palgrave-Macmillan, 2003.

————. *Groundwork: Local Black Freedom Movements in America.* New York: New York University Press, 2005.

Thernstrom, Stephen, and Abigail Thernstrom. *America in Black and White: One Nation, Indivisible.* New York: Simon and Schuster, 1997.

Thomas, Brook, ed. *Plessy v. Ferguson: A Brief History with Documents.* Boston: Bedford, 1997.

Thomas, Evan. *Robert Kennedy: His Life.* New York: Simon and Schuster, 2000.

Thornton, J. Mills. *Dividing Lines: Municipal Politics and the Struggle for Civil Rights in Montgomery, Birmingham, and Selma.* Tuscaloosa: University of Alabama Press, 2002.

Trillin, Calvin. *An Education in Georgia: Charlayne Hunter, Hamilton Holmes, and the Integration of the University of Georgia.* Athens: University of Georgia Press, 1991.

Tuck, Stephen G. N. *Beyond Atlanta: The Struggle for Racial Equality in Georgia, 1940–1980.* Athens: University of Georgia Press, 2001.

Tushnet, Mark V. *Making Civil Rights Law: Thurgood Marshall and the Supreme Court, 1936–1961.* New York: Oxford University Press, 1994.

————. *Making Constitutional Law: Thurgood Marshall and the Supreme Court, 1961–1991.* New York: Oxford University Press, 1997.

————. *The NAACP's Legal Strategy against Segregated Education, 1925–1950.* Chapel Hill: University of North Carolina Press, 1987.

Tyson, Timothy B. *Radio Free Dixie: Robert F. Williams and the Roots of Black Power.* Chapel Hill: University of North Carolina Press, 1999.

Viorst, Milton. *Fire in the Streets: America in the 1960s.* New York: Touchstone, 1979.

Vollers, Maryanne. *Ghosts of Mississippi: The Murder of Medgar Evers, the Trials of Byron De La Beckwith, and the Haunting of the New South.* Boston: Little, Brown and Co. 1995.

Von Eschen, Penny. *Race against Empire: Black Americans and Anticolonialism, 1937–1957.* Ithaca: Cornell University Press, 1997.

Wade, Richard C. *Slavery in the Cities: The South, 1820–1860.* London: Oxford University Press, 1964.

Wade, Wyn Craig. *The Fiery Cross: The Ku Klux Klan in America.* New York: Oxford University Press, 1987.

Wallenstein, Peter. *Blue Laws and Black Codes: Conflict, Courts and Social Change in Twentieth Century Virginia.* Charlottesville: University of Virginia Press, 2004.

Watson, Mary Ann. *The Expanding Vista: American Television in the Kennedy Years.* Durham: Duke University Press, 1994.

Watters, Pat. *Down to Now: Reflections on the Southern Civil Rights Movement.* Athens: University of Georgia Press, 1993.

Whalen, Charles, and Barbara Whalen. *The Longest Debate: A Legislative History of the Civil Rights Act.* New York: Mentor, 1985.

White, Theodore. *The Making of the President, 1964: A Narrative History of American Politics in Action.* New York: Atheneum, 1965.

Whitfield, Stephen J. *A Death in the Delta: The Story of Emmett Till.* Baltimore: Johns Hopkins University Press, 1988.

Wilkins, Roy. *Standing Fast: The Autobiography of Roy Wilkins.* New York: Viking Press, 1982.

Williams, Juan. *Eyes on the Prize: America's Civil Rights Years, 1954–1965.* New York: Penguin, 1988.

———. *My Soul Looks Back in Wonder: Voices of the Civil Rights Experience.* New York: AARP/Sterling Publishing, 2004.

Williamson, Joel, ed. *The Origins of Segregation.* Boston: D. C. Heath and Company, 1968.

———. *A Rage for Order: Black-White Relations in the American South since Emancipation.* New York: Oxford University Press, 1986.

Wofford, Harris. *Of Kennedys and Kings: Making Sense of the Sixties.* New York: Farrar, Straus, Giroux, 1980.

Wolpert, Stanley. *Gandhi's Passion: The Life and Legacy of Mahatma Gandhi.* New York: Oxford University Press, 2001.

Woods, Jeff. *Black Struggle, Red Scare: Segregation and Anti-Communism in the South, 1948–1968.* Baton Rouge: Louisiana State University Press, 2004.

Woodward, C. Vann. *The Burden of Southern History.* New York: Vintage, 1960.

———. *Origins of the New South 1877–1913.* Baton Rouge: Louisiana State University Press, 1951.

———. *The Strange Career of Jim Crow: A Commemorative Edition.* New York: Oxford University Press, 2002.

Wright, Gavin. *Old South, New South: Revolutions in the Southern Economy since the Civil War.* New York: Basic Books, 1986.

Wright, Richard. *Black Boy (American Hunger): A Record of Childhood and Youth.* New York: Harper Perennial, 1993.

———. *Native Son.* New York: Harper Perennial, 1993.

Wynes, Charles E. *Race Relations in Virginia, 1870–1902.* Charlottesville: University of Virginia Press, 1961.

Young, Andrew. *An Easy Burden: The Civil Rights Movement and the Transformation of America.* New York: Harper Collins, 1996.

Zinn, Howard. *SNCC: The New Abolitionists.* Boston: Beacon Press, 1965.

Articles

Arsenault, Ray. "'You Don't Have to Ride Jim Crow': CORE and the 1947 Journey of Reconciliation." In *Before Brown: Civil Rights and White Backlash in the Modern South,* ed. Glenn Feldman, 21–67. Tuscaloosa: University of Alabama Press, 2004.

Bass, S. Jonathan. "Chariots Swinging Down Low: Questions of Reliability, Credibility, and Originality in a Popular Book on Birmingham." *Alabama Review* 46, no. 3 (2003): 194–99.

Berg, Manfred. "Black Civil Rights and Liberal Anticommunism: The NAACP in the Early Cold War." *Journal of American History* 94, no. 1 (2007): 75–96.

Bergman, Walter. "The Alabama Story: A Freedom Rider's Story: 'Then They Began Beating Us.'" *New America*, June 2, 1961, 1, 8.

Bickel, Alexander M. "Civil Rights: The Kennedy Record." *New Republic*, December 15, 1962, 11–16.

Brinkley, Douglas. "Veterans of a Domestic War." *New York Times Magazine*, January 2, 2000, 44.

Brooks, Jennifer. "Winning the Peace: Georgia Veterans and the Struggle to Define the Political Legacy of World War II." *Journal of Southern History* 66, no. 3 (2000): 563–604.

Brown, Flora Bryant. "NAACP Sponsored Sit-Ins by Howard University Students in Washington, DC, 1943–1944." *Journal of Negro History* 85, no. 4 (2000): 274–86.

Butler, J. Michael. "The Mississippi State Sovereignty Commission and Beach Integration, 1959–1963: A Cotton-Patch Gestapo?" *Journal of Southern History* 68, no. 1 (2002): 107–48.

Carter, Hodding, III. "Citadel of the Citizens' Council." *New York Times Magazine*, November 12, 1961, 23, 125–27.

Catsam, Derek. "Into the Maw of Dixie: The Freedom Rides, the Civil Rights Movement, and the Politics of Race in South Carolina." *Proceedings of the South Carolina Historical Association 2005*, 1–20.

———. "James Peck." In *American National Biography*, gen. ed. Mark Carnes, 433–44. Print supplement #2. New York: Oxford University Press, 2005.

———. "New Negro Alliance." In *Organizing for Change*, ed. Nina Mjagkij, 514–15. New York: Garland, 2001.

Chafe, William H. "The Gods Bring Threads to Webs Begun." *Journal of American History* 86, no. 4 (2000): 1531–51.

Clabaugh, Jason Paul. "Reporting the Rage: An Analysis of Newspaper Coverage of the Freedom Rides of May, 1961." *Southern Historian* 14 (Spring 1993): 41–57.

Cook, Robert. "(Un)Furl That Banner: The Response of White Southerners to the Civil War Centennial of 1961–1965." *Journal of Southern History* 67, no. 4 (2002): 879–912.

Crofts, Daniel W. "The Warner-Foraker Amendment to the Hepburn Bill: Friend or Foe of Jim Crow?" *Journal of Southern History* 39, no. 3 (1973): 341–58.

Davies, David R., and Judy Smith, "Jimmy Ward and the *Jackson Daily News*." In *The Press and Race: Mississippi Journalists Confront the Movement*, ed. David R. Davies, 84–109. Jackson: University Press of Mississippi, 2001.

Derthick, Martha. "Crossing Thresholds: Federalism in the 1960s." In *Integrat-*

ing the Sixties, ed. Brian Balogh, 64–80. University Park: Pennsylvania State University Press, 1996.

DuBois, W. E. Burghardt. "Georgia: Invisible Empire State." *Nation,* January 21, 1925.

Dudziak, Mary L. "Birmingham, Addis Ababa, and the Image of America." In Plummer, *Window on Freedom,* 163–99.

Dunbar, Leslie W. "The Annealing of the South." *Virginia Quarterly Review* 37, no. 4 (1961): 495–507. Reprinted as a pamphlet by the Southern Regional Council. University of Tennessee Special Collections, Civil Rights Collection, Southern Regional Council Literature, box 5.

Eagles, Charles W. "Toward New Histories of the Civil Rights Era." *Journal of Southern History* 66, no. 4 (2000): 815–48.

Eddy, Mrs. George A. "Alexandria Council Seeks Improved Race Relations." *New South,* June 1961, 6.

Elliott, Mark. "Race, Color Blindness, and the Democratic Public: Albion W. Tourgée's Radical Principles in *Plessy v. Ferguson.*" *Journal of Southern History* 67, no. 2 (2001): 287–330.

Erskine, Hazel. "The Polls: Demonstrations and Race Riots." *Public Opinion Quarterly* 31 (1967–68): 655–77.

Eskew, Glenn T. "The Freedom Ride Riot and Political Reform in Birmingham, 1961–1963." *Alabama Review* 49, no. 3 (1996): 181–220.

Estes-Hicks, Onita. "The Way We Were: Precious Memories of the Black Segregated South." *African American Review* 27, no. 1, special issue, *Black South Issue,* part 1 of 2 (1993): 9–18.

Frederickson, Kari. "'As a Man I Am Interested in State's Rights': Gender, Race and the Family in the Dixiecrat Party, 1948–1950." In Dailey et al., *Jumpin' Jim Crow,* 260–74.

"Freedom Rider: A Virginia Town Honors Irene Morgan Kirkaldy, Who Kicked Jim Crow Off a Greyhound Bus in 1944." *People Weekly,* August 28, 2000, 104.

Gaines, Kevin. "The Historiography of the Struggle for Black Equality since 1945." In *A Companion to Post-1945 America,* ed. Jean-Christophe Agnew, 211–34. Oxford: Blackwell, 2006.

Gyant, LaVerne. "Passing the Torch: African American Women in the Civil Rights Movement." *Journal of Black Studies* 26, no. 5, special issue, *The Voices of African American Women in the Civil Rights Movement* (1996): 629–47.

Hall, Jacquelyn Dowd. "The Long Civil Rights Movement and the Political Uses of the Past." *Journal of American History* 91, no. 4 (2005): 1233–63.

"'Hallelujah, I'm a Travelin'.'" *Southern Exposure* 9, no. 1 (1981): 33.

Hart, John. "Kennedy, Congress and Civil Rights." *Journal of American Studies* 13, no. 2 (1979): 165–78.

Hershman, James H., Jr. "Massive Resistance Meets Its Match: The Emergence of a Pro–Public School Majority." In Lassiter and Lewis, *Moderates' Dilemma,* 104–33.

"The Higher Education of James Farmer." *Journal of Negro History* 18 (1997–98): 79.

Horne, Gerald. "The Civil Rights Congress." In *Civil Rights since 1787: A Reader on the Black Struggle,* ed. Jonathan Birnbaum and Clarence Taylor, 321–23. New York: New York University Press, 2000.

Horowitz, David Allen. "White Southerners' Alienation and Civil Rights: The Response to Corporate Liberalism, 1956–1965." *Journal of Southern History* 54, no. 2 (1988): 173–200.

Jacobson, Cordell. "Desegregation Rulings and Public Attitude Changes: White Resistance or Resignation?" *American Journal of Sociology* 84, no. 3 (1978): 698–705.

Kelley, Robin D.G. "'We Are Not What We Seem': Rethinking Black Working Class Opposition in the Jim Crow South." *Journal of American History* 80, no. 1 (1993): 75–112.

Kesey, Ken. "The Merry Pranksters Meet Jim Crow." *Rolling Stone,* July 6–20, 2000, 92, 157.

Klarman, Michael J. "How *Brown* Changed Race Relations: The Backlash Thesis." *Journal of American History* 81, no. 1 (1994): 81–118.

Krenn, Michael. "The Unwelcome Mat: African Diplomats in Washington during the Cold War Years." In Plummer, *Window on Freedom,* 163–80.

Lauter, Paul. "Versions of Nashville, Visions of American Studies: Presidential Address to the American Studies Association, October 27, 1994." *American Quarterly* 47, no. 2 (1995): 185–203.

Lawson, Jim. "On Nonviolence." *Southern Exposure* 9, no. 1 (1981): 31.

Lawson, Steven F. "'I Got It from the *New York Times*': Lyndon Johnson and the Kennedy Civil Rights Program." *Journal of Negro History* 67, no. 2 (1982): 159–73.

Lechner, Ira M. "Massive Resistance: Virginia's Great Leap Backward." *Virginia Quarterly Review* 74, no. 8 (1998): 631–40.

Leighton, George R. "Birmingham, Alabama: The City of Perpetual Promise." *Harper's Magazine,* August 1937, 225–42.

Lichtman, Allan. "The Federal Assault against Voting Discrimination in the Deep South, 1957–1967." *Journal of Negro History* 54, no. 4 (1969): 346–67.

Long, Herman H. "Racial Desegregation in Railroad and Bus Transportation." *Journal of Negro Education* 23, no. 3, special issue, *Next Steps in Racial Education* (1954): 214–21.

McAdam, Doug. "The Biographical Consequences of Activism." *American Sociological Review* 54 (October 1989): 744–60.

McDonald, Jimmy. "A Freedom Rider Speaks His Mind." In *Freedomways Reader: Prophets in Their Own Country,* ed. Esther Cooper Jackson, 59–64. Boulder, CO: Westview, 2000.

Meier, August, and Elliott Rudwick. "The Boycott Movement against Jim Crow Cars Streetcars in the South, 1900–1906." *Journal of American History* 55, no. 4 (1969): 756–75.

————. "Negro Boycotts of Segregated Streetcars in Virginia, 1904–1907." *Virginia Magazine of History and Biography* 81, no. 4 (1973): 479–87.

Mueller, John. "Trends in Political Tolerance." *Public Opinion Quarterly* 52 (1998): 1–25.

Murphy, John M. "Domesticating Dissent: The Kennedys and the Freedom Rides." *Communication Monographs* 59, no. 1 (1992): 61–78.

Osborn, William S. "Curtains for Jim Crow: Law, Race and the Texas Railroads." *Southwestern Historical Quarterly* 105, no. 3 (2002): 393–427.

Pacifico, Michele F. "'Don't Buy Where You Can't Work': The New Negro Alliance of Washington." *Washington History* (Spring–Summer 1994): 66–88.

Palmore, Joseph R. "The Not-So-Strange Career of Interstate Jim Crow: Race, Transportation, and the Dormant Commerce Clause, 1878–1946." *Virginia Law Review* 83, no. 8 (1997): 1773–1817.

Peck, James. "Not So Deep Are the Roots." *Crisis,* September 1947, 273–74, 282–83.

Pleasants, Julian. "Frank Graham and the Politics of the New South." In *The Adaptable South: Essays in Honor of George Brown Tindall,* ed. Elizabeth Jacoway et al., 176–211. Baton Rouge: Louisiana State University Press, 1991.

Pratt, Robert A. "New Directions in Virginia's Civil Rights Historiography." *Virginia Magazine of History and Biography* 104, no. 1 (1996): 149–56.

Purcell, Trevor. "Putting the Race Back in History: History and Discourse in Studies of Diaspora Blacks." *Transforming Anthropology* 10, no. 2 (2001): 30–35.

Randolph, A. Philip. "Why Should We March." *Survey Graphic* 31 (November 1942): 488–89. Reprinted in *The Negro since Emancipation,* ed. Harvey Wish, 158–62. Englewood Cliffs, NJ: Prentice-Hall, 1964.

Randolph, Lewis A. "The Civil Rights Movement in Richmond, 1940–1977: Race, Class, and Gender in the Structuring of Protest Activity." *Proteus* 15, no. 1 (1998): 63–71.

Rise, Eric W. "Race, Rape, and Radicalism: The Case of the Martinsville Seven, 1949–1951." *Journal of Southern History* 58, no. 3 (1992): 461–90.

Roback, Jennifer. "The Political Economy of Segregation: The Case of Segregated Streetcars." *Journal of Economic History* 46, no. 4 (1986): 893–917.

Robnett, Belinda. "African-American Women in the Civil Rights Movement, 1954–1965: Gender, Leadership, and Micromobilization." *American Journal of Sociology* 101, no. 6 (1996): 1661–93.

Romano, Renee. "No Diplomatic Immunity: African Diplomats, the State Department, and Civil Rights, 1961–1964." *Journal of American History* 87, no. 2 (2000): 546–79.

Rostow, Eugene V. "The Freedom Riders and the Future." *Reporter,* June 22, 1961, 18–21.

Sherman, Richard. "'The Last Stand': The Fight for Racial Integrity in Virginia in the 1920s." *Journal of Southern History* 54, no. 1 (1988): 69–92.

Shinault-Small, Muima A. "The WBEMC, 1960–2005: Marching Onward, Looking Upward, and Creating a Legacy along the Way." In *Born to Serve: A History of the Baptist Educational and Missionary Convention of South Carolina,* ed. W. Marvin Dulaney, 75–77. Charleston: Publishing Associates, 2006.

Simon, Bryant. "Race Reactions: African American Organizing, Liberalism, and White Working-Class Politics in Postwar South Carolina." In Dailey et al., *Jumpin' Jim Crow,* 239–59.

Singer, Joseph William. "No Right to Exclude: Public Accommodations and Private Property." *Northwestern University Law Review* 90, no. 4 (1996): 1283–1497.

Smith, J. Douglas. "The Campaign for Racial Purity and the Erosion of Paternalism in Virginia, 1922–1930: 'Nominally White, Biologically Mixed, and Legally Negro.'" *Journal of Southern History* 68, no. 1 (2002): 65–106.

———. "'When Reason Collides with Prejudice': Armistead Lloyd Boothe and the Politics of Moderation." In Lassiter and Lewis, *Moderates' Dilemma,* 822–50.

Smith, Tom W. "Liberal and Conservative Trends in the United States since World War II." *Public Opinion Quarterly* 54 (1990): 479–507.

Smith, Tom, and Glenn Dempsey. "The Polls: Ethnic Social Distance and Prejudice." *Public Opinion Quarterly* 47 (1983): 584–600.

Stern, Mark. "John F. Kennedy and Civil Rights: From Congress to the Presidency." *Presidential Studies Quarterly* 19, no. 4 (1989): 797–824.

———. "Presidential Strategies and Civil Rights: Eisenhower, the Early Years, 1952–1954." *Presidential Studies Quarterly* 10, no. 4 (1989): 769–96.

Sweeney, James R. "A New Day in the Old Dominion: The 1964 Presidential Election." *Virginia Magazine of History and Biography* 102, no. 3 (1994): 307–48.

———. "Whispers in the Golden Silence: Harry F. Byrd, John F. Kennedy, and Virginia Democrats in the 1960 Presidential Election." *Virginia Magazine of History and Biography* 99, no. 1 (1991): 3–44.

Thomas, Clarence. "The Virtue of Defeat: *Plessy v. Ferguson* in Retrospect." *Supreme Court Historical Society Journal* 2 (1997): 15–24.

"Three Questions of Law." *Time,* June 2, 1961.

Tyson, Timothy B. "Dynamite and the 'Silent South': A Story from the Second Reconstruction in South Carolina." In Dailey et al., *Jumpin' Jim Crow,* 275–97.

———. "Robert F. Williams, 'Black Power' and the Roots of the African American Freedom Struggle." *Journal of American History* 85, no. 2 (1998): 540–70.

"Untold Story of the 'Freedom Riders.'" *U.S. News and World Report,* October 23, 1961, 76–79.

Wakefield, Dan. "Eye of the Storm." *Nation,* May 7, 1960, 395–405.

Webb, Clive. "'A Cheap Trafficking in Human Misery': The Reverse Freedom Rides of 1962." *Journal of American Studies* 38, no. 2 (2004): 249–72.

Weisenburger, Steven. "The Columbians, Inc.: A Chapter of Racial Hatred from the Post–World War II South." *Journal of Southern History* 69, no. 4 (2003): 823–60.

Web Site

Southern Regional Council. Transcripts for "Will the Circle Be Unbroken?" Twenty-six-episode radio series on the Civil Rights Movement, http://www .unbrokencircle.com. Transcript in the author's possession.

Dissertations, Theses, and Unpublished Papers

Anderson-Bricker, Kristin. "Making a Movement: The Meaning of Community in the Congress of Racial Equality, 1958–1968." Ph.D. diss., Syracuse University, 1997.

Catsam, Derek. "'A Brave and Wonderful Thing': The Freedom Rides and the Integration of Interstate Transport, 1941–1965." Ph.D. diss., Ohio University, 2003.

Hershman, James Howard, Jr. "A Rumbling in the Museum: The Opponents of Virginia's Massive Resistance." Ph.D. diss., University of Virginia, 1973.

Moore, William Pendleton. "'Tell Them We in the South Are Dissatisfied': Politics of Race and Civil Rights Activism in Rock Hill." Master's thesis, University of South Carolina, 2002.

Taylor, Susan Antoinette. "The Nashville Sit-In Movement, 1960." Master's thesis, Fisk University, 1972.

Woods, Jeff. "Maroon Scare: Integration and Anticommunism in the South, 1954–1968." Ph.D. diss., Ohio University, 2000.

Documentaries and Videos

"Ain't Scared of Your Jails." *Eyes on the Prize: America's Civil Rights Years,* episode 3. Boston: Blackside, 1986.

The Anniston Bus Bombing: The Fire That Helped Ignite the Flame of Freedom. Anniston: Action Video, n.d.

You Don't Have to Ride Jim Crow! Produced by Robin Washington. Durham: New Hampshire Public Television, 1995, 2007.

Index